EFFECTS OF DIRECTED ENERGY WEAPONS

EFFECTS OF DIRECTED ENERGY WEAPONS

Philip E. Nielsen

Library of Congress Cataloging-in-Publication Data

Nielsen, Philip E., 1944–
    Effects of Directed Energy Weapons
    /Philip E. Nielsen.
            p.   cm.
    Includes bibliographical references and index.

    1. United States.   Air Force—Aviation—History.   2. Air Power—
United States.
    3. United States—Armed Forces—Management—History.
    I. Title
    VG93.B36   1994
    359.9′4′ 0973—dc20   94–1937
                                                                                CIP

Contents

Tables

List of Symbols

I have tried to keep common symbols consistent throughout the text. Unfortunately, there aren't enough letters to go around, and some symbols are so common in the literature that custom has been retained even though it results in multiple usage. Context is usually adequate to sort out any ambiquity , and terms which are limited to specific sections are identified in the table below.

Many symbols are used with subscripts to identify specific values, such as T_i for initial temeprature. These are identified as they are used, and will typically have have consistent meaning only in a specific treatment or argument.

The "units " mentioned in the tabel below are typical ones used in the text. They'll let you know the dimensions associated with a specific quantity, but are by no means exclusive. Energy, for example, may be expressed in Joules or electron volts (see Appendix A).

Symbol	Meaning	Units	Comments
A	Activation energy	eV	Chapter 3
A	Area	cm^2	
a	Acceleration	cm/sec^2	=dv/dt
a	Particle radius	cm, μm	
a	Speed of Sound	cm/sec	=3×10^4 cm/sec (Chap 3,5)
B	Brightness	W/sr	Chapter 3,4
B	Brightness	Amp/m^2 sr	Chapter 5
B	Magnetic Field	Gauss	Chapter 5
b	Impact parameter	cm	Chapter 5
C	Heat Capacity	J/gm °K	
C	Stiffness	Nt/m^2,J/m^3	Relates stress to strain (Chapters 2,3)
Cd	Drag Coefficient	Dimensionless	Chapter 2
C$_N$	Refractive Index structure factor	m$^{-1/3}$	Chapter 3
c	Speed of light	m/sec	= 3×10^8 m/sec
D,d	Diameter	cm	
D	Thermal Diffusivity	cm^2/sec	= k/Cp
D	Relative Depth	dimensionless	See Figure 5–31

dQ/dx	Gradient of Q	Q/cm^2	The slope of a curve of any quantity Q vs distance
d^2Q/dx^2	2nd Derivative of Q	Q/cm^2	The slope of a curve of dQ/dx vs distance
dQ/dt	Rate of change of Q	Q/sec	The slope of a curve of any quantity Q vs time
E	Energy	Joules, eV	
E	Electric Field	Volts/m	Chapter 5
e	base of natural logarithms		≈ 2.72
e	electron charge	Columb	$= 1.6 \times 10^{-19}$ Coul
e	Strain	demensionless	Chapters 2, 3
e*	Stain at Failure	dimensionless	Strain corresponding to P*
F	Fluence	J/cm^2	Energy density on a surface
F	Force	Newtons	
f	focal length	km	
f	fractional ionization	dimensionless	
G	Gravitational Constant	$Nt\ m^2/kg^2$	$= 6.67 \times 10^{-11}\ Nt\ m^2/kg^2$
g	Acceleration of Gravity	m/sec^2	$= 9.8\ m/sec^2$
g	gain (stimualted scattering)	cm/W	Chapter 3
h	altitude	km	= height above earths surface
h_o	atmospheric scale ht	km	= 7km
h	Target Thickness	cm	Chapter 2
h	Planck's Constant	Joule sec	Relates photon energy to frequncy of light $= 6.63 \times 10^{-34}$ J sec
I	Current	Amperes	Chapter 5
I	Impulse	Nt sec	$= \int F\ dt$
I*	Specific Impulse	dyn sec/J	Efficiency of momentum transfer with lasers (Chap 3)
Isp	Specific Impulse	sec	Rocket impulse/weight of fuel used (Chap 2)
I	Ionization Potential	eV	Chapters 3, 4, 5

j	Current Density	Amp/m^2	Chapter 5
K	Kinetic Energy	Joules	Some authors use T. Kinetic energy is used most in Chapters 2 and 5
K	Attenuation coeffficent	km^{-1}	Used in Chapters 3 and 4
k	Thermal Conductivity	W/cm °K	in u = −k dT/dx
k	Boltzmann's Constant	J/°K	converts temperature to energy = 1.38 x 10^{-23}J/^{0}K
L,l	length	cm	
Lm	Heat of Fusion	J/gm	
Lv	Heat of Vaporization		
M,m	mass	grams, kg	
N, n	number density	cm^{-3}	
Nt	Thermal Distortion factor	dimensionless	Chapter 3
n	index of refraction	dimensionless	Chapters 3, 4
P	Pressure	Nt/cm^2, J/cm^3	
P	Stress	Nt/cm^2, J/cm^3	Chapters 2, 3 (stress is the equivalent of pressure in a Solid)
P*	Modulus of Rupture	Nt/cm^2,J/cm^3	Stress at which a solid fails Chapters 2, 3
p	Momentum	gm cm/sec	= mv
Q	intensity	W/cm^2	Reradiation from a plasma Chapter 3
Q	Impact parameter ratio	dimensionless	Chapter 5
q	electric charge	Coulombs	Chapter 5
R,r	radius	cm	used for radial distances
R	reflectivity	dimensionless	fraction of light reflected Chapters 3, 4
Re	earth radius	km	≈ 6370 km
Re*	effective earth radius	km	Chapter 4
Ri	ionization rate	sec^{-1}	
r$_c$	cyclotron radius	cm	Chapter 5
r$_0$	coherence length	cm	Chapter 3
S	Intensity of Radiation	W/cm^2	

t	time	seconds	
t_p	pulse width	seconds	
t_d	magnetic diffusion time	seconds	Chapter 5
T	Wave Period	seconds	Chapter 3
T	Perpendicular Energy	Joules	$= \gamma m <v_\perp^2>/2$, Chapter 5
T	Temperature	°K, °C	
T_m	Melting Point		
T_v	Vaporization Point		
$T_\perp$	Perpendicular T		Measures random motion perpendicular to beam direction
u	Energy Flow Rate	W/cm²	From Thermal Conduction: $u = -k \, dT/dx$
u	LSD or LSC velocity	cm/sec	Chapter 3
V, v	Velocity	cm/sec	
$V_\perp$	perpendicular V	cm/sec	velocity perpendicular to beam motion (Chapter 5)
W	Work	Joules	
w	beam radius	cm	
Z, z	range	km	
Z_r	Rayleigh Range	km	

Greek Symbols

Symbol	Meaning	Units	Comments
α (alpha)		km	Constant in equation of central motion (Chapter 2)
α	Absortivity	dimensionless	fraction of incident radiation absorbed (Chapters 3,4)
β (beta)	velocity ratio	dimensionless	$= v/c$, Chapter 5
γ (Gamma)	specific heat ratio	dimensionless	Chapter 3
γ	Relativistic factor	dimensionless	$= 1/(1 - v^2/c^2)^{1/2}$, Chapter 5
Δ (Delta)	"change in"	various	ΔT = change in T, etc.
δ (delta)	skin depth	cm	Chapters 3, 4
ϵ (epsilon)	orbital eccentricity	dimensionless	Chapter 2
ϵ	electron energy	eV, Joules	Chapters 3,4
ϵ_0	permittivity of free space	farad/m	$= 8.85 \times 10^{-12}$ fd/m
θ (theta)	beam divergence	radians	
θ	angle	radians	
λ (lambda)	Wavelength	cm, μm	Chapters 3, 4
ν (nu)	Frequency	sec^{-1}	
ν_0	Collision Frequency	sec^{-1}	Chapters 3,4
ρ (rho)	mass density	gm/cm^3	Chapter 5
ρ	charge density	Coul/cm^3	Chapter 5
Σ (sigma)	Conductivity	mho/m	σ is a more common notation
σ (sigma)	Stefan-Boltzmann Constant	W/cm^2 °K^4	Relates radiation from a Black Body to its Temperature $= 5.67 \times 10^{-12}$ W/cm^2 °K^4
σ	cross section	cm^2	
τ (tau)	orbital period	hours	Chapter 2
ϕ (phi)	elevation angle	radians	
ω (omega)	Radian Frequency	sec^{-1}	$= 2\pi\nu$

List of Figures

Acknowledgments

Philip L. Taylor first taught me the importance of insight as opposed to mathematical elegance in dealing with physical phenomena, and Greg Canavan showed me the power of zero order analysis in sorting through a problem to see the factors that were driving the solution and its behavior. While teaching physics at the Air Force Institute of Technology, I benefited from discussions with numerous colleagues, most notably Michael Stamm and George Nickel, who helped me to clarify my ideas and offered numerous examples. Later, while engaged in operations research analysis at the Air Force Studies and Analyses Agency, Thomas Hopkins joined me in many hours of thought-provoking discussion and was also kind enough to read and comment upon the initial manuscript for this book.

The concept for the book developed while I was at the National Defense University (NDU) during 1987–1988. Fred Kiley of NDU Press and LtGen Bradley Hosmer, who was then NDU president, encouraged its development and publication. Since then, NDU Press has been saddled with what is arguably the most complex book that they have ever published. I am grateful to successive administrations at the press for putting up with the equations and graphics and for keeping the project alive during times of tight budgets and other priorities. Special credit should go to George Maerz, who has been associated with the project from its inception, and to Jeffrey Smotherman, who worked hard to bring it to closure, and finally succeeded.

Finally, I should acknowledge my wife, Mary Jane, and children, Aaron, June, and David. They had the patience to put up with me when I was researching and writing the text, and the faith to put up with my optimism that the project would one day come to a successful conclusion.

Preface

This book is on the effects of directed energy weapons. That is, how they propagate to and interact with targets. Propagation and target interaction are the key elements in an analysis of a weapon's utility to accomplish a given mission. For example, the effectiveness of a nuclear missile is determined by the yield of its warhead and the accuracy of its guidance, and the effectiveness of a rifle is determined by the type of round fired, the range to the target, and the skill of the soldier who fires it. Directed energy weapons are no different. But while there are books and manuals that deal with the issues affecting the utility of nuclear missiles and rifles, there is no comparable source of information for directed energy weapons. I have tried to fill that void with this book.

Weapons are devices which deliver sufficient energy to targets to damage them. Weapon design involves a dialog between weapon designers, and military planners. Designers create means of projecting energy, and planners have targets that they would like to destroy. Effective design requires a knowledge of the targets and the circumstances of their engagement, and effective planning requires a knowledge of the weapons and their characteristics. But in new and emerging areas of weaponry, designers and planners often don't speak the same language. As a result, designers can operate in ignorance of operational realities, and planners can assume that anything involving new technology will meet all their needs. This book should also serve as an introduction to the language of directed energy weapons for military planners and other non-technical persons who need to understand what the engineers and scientists involved in their development are talking about.

Chapter 1 outlines basic philosophies and ideas that are used throughout the book. The other chapters are each devoted to a specific type of directed energy weapon, and are reasonably self-contained. Therefore, a reader interested primarily in one weapon type will find it sufficient to read Chapter 1 together with the chapter of interest. In some cases, duplication is avoided by developing topics in great detail in one chapter, and presenting them again in a summary form in other chapters. The reader is referred to the detailed discussion for any elaboration that may be required.

I have assumed no technical background other than that associated with an introductory college-level physics course. Some knowledge of algebra and trigonometry is assumed. A knowledge of calculus would be helpful but is not required. Equations are provided so that those with sufficient interest and motivation can extend the results in the text. Numerous graphs and examples will enable casual readers to skim over any material which seems too mathematical.

Weaponry is not a precise science. Propagation paths and target details are never known precisely. You wouldn't want to go hunting for bear with a rifle whose bullet was precisely designed to just penetrate the skin of an average bear, only to come up against a bear that had just put on weight for the winter! You'd probably prefer a rifle designed to work against the biggest conceivable bears. The same is true of directed energy weapons. Too much precision in effects calculations is unwarranted, and a certain amount of conservatism is required in defining operational parameters. Therefore, I have kept arguments physical and intuitive at the expense of mathematical rigor. All formulas and expressions should be considered correct to "zero order"—good enough to produce answers within an order of magnitude of the "correct" result. No attempt has been made to incorporate the latest and most accurate experimental data, as these are under continual revision. Rather, the material presented here is designed to enable you to place theories and results in the proper context. Extensive notes and references are provided for those who'd care to go into any topic in greater depth.

EFFECTS OF DIRECTED ENERGY WEAPONS

1: Basic Principles

Overall Theme

This book deals with the effects of directed energy weapons, treating such diverse types of weaponry as lasers, particle beams, microwaves, and even bullets. In order to understand these weapons and their effects, it is necessary first to develop a common framework for their analysis. [It is a thesis of this book that all weapons may be understood as devices which deposit energy in targets, and that the energy which must be deposited to achieve a given level of damage is relatively insensitive to the type of weapon employed.] Nuclear weapons may be characterized in terms of megatons, bullets in terms of muzzle velocity, and particle beams in terms of amperes of current, but when this jargon is reduced to common units for energy absorbed by a target, similar levels of damage are achieved at similar levels of energy deposited.

Of course, energy cannot be deposited in a target unless it's first delivered there. Therefore, an important element in understanding weapons is a knowledge of how they deliver (or "propagate") their energy. Some loss of energy is invariably associated with this propagation, whether it's the atmospheric drag on a bullet or the absorption of microwaves by raindrops. A weapon must therefore produce more energy than needed to damage a target, since some of its energy will be lost in propagation. As a result, weapon design depends upon two factors. First, the anticipated target, which determines the energy required for damage. And second, the anticipated scenario (range, engagement time, etc.) which determines how much energy must be produced to insure that an adequate amount is delivered in the time available. This chapter is devoted to developing this theme, introducing concepts and tools which will be used throughout the remainder of the book.

A Word About Units

Since our goal is to reduce the jargon associated with different types of weaponry to common units, the choice for these common units is obviously of interest. For the most part, we'll use metric units, where length is in meters, mass in kilograms, and time in seconds. In these units, energy is expressed as *Joules*.[1] A Joule is approximately the energy required to lift a quart of milk a distance of three feet, or 1/50000 (2×10^{-5}) of the energy it takes to brew a cup of coffee.[2] Scientists and engineers frequently prefer to express quantities in units which depart from the standard, since units that result in numerical values of order 1–10 are easier to talk about. For example, it's easier to say (and remember) that the ionization potential of hydrogen is 13.6 electron volts than to say that it's 2.2×10^{-18} Joules. Since published literature on directed energy weapons is full of such specialized units and terminology, we'll follow convention and depart from standard units when others are more appropriate to the subject at hand. However, we'll always try to bring things back to a common denominator when summaries and comparisons are made. Appendix A is a summary of units which are common in the field of directed energy weapons, along with the relationships among them.

Developing Damage Criteria

If we are to determine how much energy a weapon must produce to damage a target, we need to know two things—how much energy it takes to damage a target, and what fraction if the energy generated will be lost in propagating to it. These will be developed in detail for different weapon types in subsequent chapters. For the moment, we'll consider some of the fundamental issues which affect damage and propagation independent of weapon type.

The Energy Required for Damage

In order to be quantitative about the amount of energy necessary for damage, we must first define what we mean by damage. For a military system, this could be anything from an upset in a target's computer, preventing it from operating, to total vaporization. These two extremes are usually referred to as "soft" and "hard" damage, respectively. Clearly, soft damage is much more sensitive to specific details of the system under attack than hard damage. Without knowing the details of a computer, its circuits, and the hardness of its chips, we won't know if it's been upset until we see it in operation, whereas vaporizing it produces immediate feedback on the effectiveness of an attack. On the other hand, vaporizing a target will require more energy than degrading its performance. We'll concentrate in this book on hard or catastrophic damage for two reasons: it avoids target-specific details which are often classified, and it provides a useful first cut at separating weapon parameters which will almost certainly result in damage from those for which the likelihood of damage is questionable, or for which more detailed analysis is required.

As a simple example of the kind of energies necessary to achieve damage, let's first consider what it takes to vaporize an ice cube.[3] If we have taken this ice cube from a freezer, its temperature is below the temperature at which it will melt. We must first supply enough energy to raise its temperature to the melting point. Clearly the amount of energy required to do so will be proportional to both the necessary temperature rise and the amount of ice in the cube. The mathematical expression for this relationship is $E = mC(T_m-T_i)$, where E is the energy required (Joules), m the mass of the ice cube (grams), T_i its initial temperature (degrees Celsius or Kelvin), T_m the melting temperature, and C a constant of proportionality known as the heat capacity (J/gm $^\circ$C). For water, C is approximately 4.2 Joules per gram per degree, so that if the ice cube has a mass of 50 grams and is initially at a temperature of -10 $^\circ$C, 2100 Joules of energy will be required to raise it to the melting point at 0°C.

Having raised the ice cube to the melting point, we must melt it. The amount of energy required to convert one gram of solid to one gram of liquid at the melting point is known as the heat of fusion, symbolized by L_m. For water, this is about 334 Joules per gram, so that 16,700 additional Joules of energy would be required to melt our ice cube once we had invested the 2100 Joules necessary to raise it to the melting point.

At this point, our ice cube is a puddle of water at 0°C. Some might consider this damage enough. If, however, we insist on vaporizing it, we must raise it to the boiling point by supplying an additional amount of energy $E = mC (T_v-T_m) = 21,000$ Joules, where T_v is the vaporization temperature (100°C), and we must convert the molten water at T_v to vapor at the same temperature by supplying the heat of vaporization, L_v. The heat of vaporization is about 2440 Joules per gram for water, so that an investment of 122,000 additional Joules is required to finally do away with our 50 gram puddle of water. The total energy required from beginning to end to vaporize the 50 gram ice cube is thus 2,100 + 16,700 + 21,000 + 122,000 = 161,800 Joules. It is interesting to note that the heat of vaporization accounts for about 75% of the energy required. This should not be surprising—a lot of energy is needed to separate the bonds which hold the molecules of a solid or liquid together and disperse them as vapor. Figure 1–1 is a plot of how the temperature of the ice cube varies as energy is deposited, along with its physical state at various points along the way. If the energy is deposited at a constant rate or power (Watts = Joules/second), the bottom scale is also proportional to time.[4] Clearly, the vast majority of time and energy are taken up in vaporizing the molten cube.

Having considered the simple example of melting and vaporizing an ice cube, let's turn our attention to materials of more interest from a military standpoint. Table 1–1 summarizes the heat capacities, heats of fusion, and vaporization for some common materials.[5] An examination of Table 1–1 reveals some interesting facts. First, it's clear that there isn't a great deal of variation from one material to another. Within a column, the entries are (roughly) within a factor of two or three of one another. This is fortunate, and means that we'll be able to make order of mag-

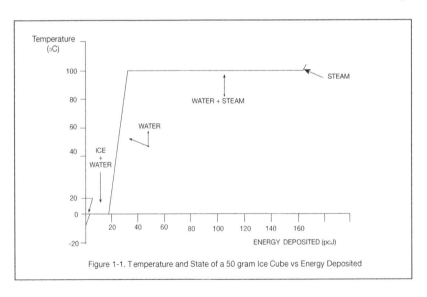

Figure 1-1. Temperature and State of a 50 gram Ice Cube vs Energy Deposited

4

nitude damage estimates without our results being sensitive to the type and construction of target under attack. Second, as in the ice example, the energy required by the heat of vaporization represents the greatest portion of the energy budget in vaporizing a target. Third, it appears from this table that about 10,000 Joules will be sufficient energy to vaporize a gram of almost anything. Given that most solid materials have a density on the order of 1–10 grams per cubic centimeter, this is equivalent to saying that 10,000 Joules is sufficient energy to vaporize about a cubic centimeter of anything.

It's interesting to note that 10,000 Joules is close to the energy delivered by a wide range of weapons. A few examples will serve to illustrate this point. A typical rifle round has a mass of about 10 grams, and is fired with a muzzle velocity of about 1000 m/sec.[6] This corresponds to a kinetic energy ($mv^2/2$) of 5,000 Joules. In its March 1979 issue, *Scientific American* has an article on ancient Roman siege catapults, and reports that a typical catapult could throw a stone weighing 20 kilograms over a range of 200 meters.[7] A calculation of the kinetic energy required for so massive a stone to travel so far results in an estimate of 40,000 Joules. Finally, a more recent issue of *Scientific American* (January, 1985) has a report on medieval crossbows, and reports that a typical bow could launch an 85 gram bolt over a range of 275 meters.[8] The energy required to do this is approximately 13,000 Joules.

MATERIAL	DENSITY (gm/cm³)	MELTING POINT, T_m (°C)	VAPORIZATION POINT, T_v (°C)	HEAT CAPACITY (J/gm°C)	HEAT OF FUSION (J/gm)	HEAT OF VAPORIZATION (J/gm)
ALUMINUM	2.7	660	2500	0.9	400	11000
COPPER	8.96	1100	2600	0.38	210	4700
MAGNESIUM	1.74	650	1100	1.0	370	5300
IRON	7.9	1500	3000	0.46	250	6300
TITANIUM	4.5	1700	3700	0.52	320	8800

Table 1-1. Thermal Properties of Common Metals

Is Energy Alone Sufficient for Damage?

Table 1–1 and the examples above might suggest that something on the order of 10,000 Joules could be a good "all purpose damage criterion," useful as a measure of the amount of energy a weapon must deliver to damage a target. But there are two observations which suggest that there is more to weaponry than the mere generation of energy. First, consider the detonation of a nuclear weapon. A bomb releases lots of energy: one kiloton of yield corresponds to about 4×10^{12} (4,000,000,000,000) Joules.[9] This far exceeds a 10,000 Joule damage criterion, yet at a distance of less than a mile from a one kiloton detonation a concrete structure would be undamaged.[10] Over the same range an artillery shell with only 10,000 Joules of energy could easily destroy such a structure. Second, consider the sun. In a 24 hour period, it deposits about 5,000 Joules of energy over every square centimeter of the earth's surface[11], yet we see no evidence of cars melting in parking lots, people being fried (except voluntarily, on beaches!), or houses bursting into flame. Clearly, something more than energy is required for damage. The energy must also be delivered over a small region and in a short time to the target. In other words, energy is not the only factor important in establishing damage criteria. Also important are the density of energy on the target (Joules per square centimeter, often called "fluence"), and the rate of energy delivery, or power (Joules/second, or Watts).[12] Let's consider the physical basis for these results.

Energy Density Effects. Figure 1–2 contrasts a kiloton nuclear detonation and an artillery shell, both of which are used to attack a structure at a range of one mile. The vast majority of the energy released by the bomb does not intersect the target and is "wasted" from the standpoint of damaging it. By contrast, the artillery shell is a "directed energy" weapon, delivering all its energy right to the target in question. To be more quantitative, if we spread the energy in the bomb over the surface of a sphere at a range of one mile, we find that the energy density is only about 13 Joules per square centimeter, far less than the energy density of about 10,000 Joules per square centimeter which the artillery round applies at the point of penetration.

Once the effect of area is understood, it is easy to show that nuclear weapon effects are consistent with the energy delivery associated with bullets, siege catapults, and crossbows. Reinforced concrete buildings suffered severe damage at ranges of about 0.1 mile from the point of detonation of the weapons employed against Hiroshima and Nagasaki.[13] Since these weapons had yields of about 20 kT, they released about 8×10^{13} joules of energy. At a range z of 0.1 mile (= 1.6×10^4 cm), the energy density would have been about 8×10^{13} J$/4\pi z^2$, or 2.5×10^4 J$/$cm^2 Therefore, when the spreading of the blast energy is accounted for, a result consistent with other weapon types emerges.

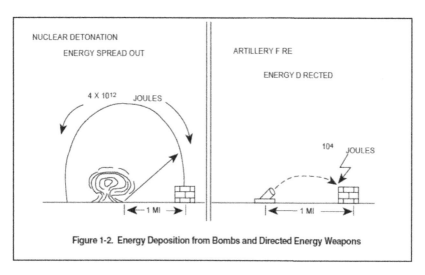

Figure 1-2. Energy Deposition from Bombs and Directed Energy Weapons

Energy Delivery Rate Effects. Next, consider the observation that if energy is delivered over too long a period, it is not effective in damaging targets. This is because if energy isn't delivered in a short time, the target can shed energy as rapidly as it's deposited, and so won't heat up to the point of sustaining damage. Cars in a parking lot heat up in the sun until they become so hot that thay radiate energy away as rapidly as it's being deposited. After that, their temperature remains constant. People on the beach perspire and cool by evaporation. Only if energy is delivered more rapidly than the target can handle it will damage ensue. There are three main mechanisms by which energy can be carried away from a target: conduction, convection, and radiation.

7

Conduction or, more properly, thermal conduction, is the process by which energy flows from hot regions to cold as a result of hot, agitated molecules bumping into and exciting, or heating, their neighbors. In this way the hot molecules lose energy and the cold molecules gain energy until a uniform temperature is reached throughout. This process is well known through everyday experience. The handle of a spoon in a coffee cup becomes hot as energy flows from the hot portion of the spoon, in the cup, to the cold portion, along the handle. Physicists speak of this as a flow of energy "downhill" along a "temperature gradient," as illustrated in Figure 1–3.

The term temperature gradient is just a fancy expression for the slope of the curve of temperature vs distance illustrated in Figure 1–3. The steeper this slope, the faster energy will flow. Physically, what's happening is that the energy and temperature are trying to smooth out and come to equilibrium. Energy flows until the temperature is the same everywhere, the temperature curve is flat, and the temperature gradient goes to zero. The mathematical expression which captures this relationship is:

$$u = -k \, (dT/dx)$$

where u is the rate of flow of energy across a surface (Joules per square centimeter per second, or (Watts/cm^2), dT/dx the slope of the temperature curve (degrees per centimeter), and k a constant of proportionality known as the thermal conductivity. The minus sign in this expression reflects the fact that if the slope is negative (temperature decreasing in the positive direction) the energy flow will be in the positive direction, and vice versa. The thermal conductivity, k, can vary greatly from one material to another. Copper, which conducts energy well, has a k of about 4.2 J/ sec cm deg, while air, a thermal insulator, has a k of about 0.00042 J/sec cm deg—three orders of magnitude less.

As a result of the energy flow u that results from thermal conductivity, the temperature T in different regions of the target will change. In some regions, T will increase, and in others, T will decrease. Figure 1–4 illustrates how a knowledge of u throughout a target can be used to calculate the rate of change of temperature within it.

Shown in the figure is a thin region within a target having a cross section A and a thickness dx. There is some flow of energy

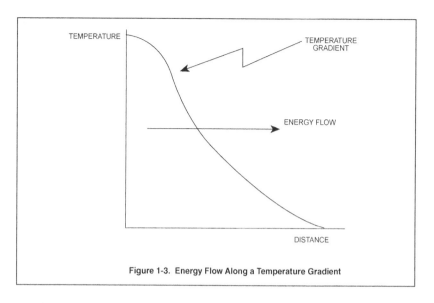

Figure 1-3. Energy Flow Along a Temperature Gradient

(Joules per square centimeter per second) into the region, denote U_{in}, and some flow out of the region, denoted U_{out}. If these two quantities are not equal, then the amount of energy within this region will increase or decrease, and the temperature within it will rise or fall. In the example of Figure 1–4, the flow out is less than the flow in, with the result that the temperature within the region illustrated will increase. What is the rate at which the temperature will change? It is a straightforward exercise to use the heat capacity (C) of the target material to relate the change of energy within the region shown in Figure 1–4 to a change in temperature, and to use the thermal conduction equation $U = -k\, dT/dx$ to relate the difference in energy flow into and out of the region $(U_{in}-U_{out})$, to a change in the temperature gradient, dT/dx, across the region. This results in what is known as the thermal diffusion equation:

$$dT/dt = (k/C\rho)(d^2T/dx^2).$$

In this expression, k is the thermal conductivity, C the heat capacity, and ρ the density of the target material (gm/cm^3). Physically, this equation makes a lot of sense. It tells us that the temperature will change in a region if the temperature gradient changes across that region, so that energy does not merely flow through it, but increases or decreases within it. The quantity

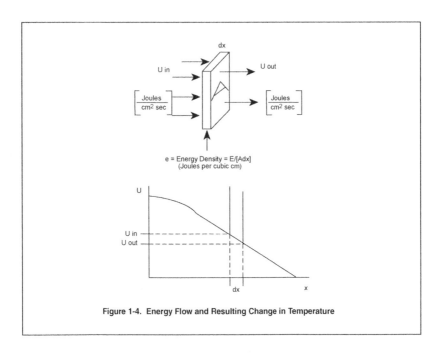

Figure 1-4. Energy Flow and Resulting Change in Temperature

d^2T/dx^2 is the slope of a curve of dT/dx as a function of x, just as dT/dx is the slope of a curve of T as a function of x. The quantity $(k/C\rho)$ is known as the thermal diffusivity, and is frequently denoted D. Interestingly enough, D does not vary much from one material to another, and is typically on the order of 1–10 square centimeters per second. This is because materials of low density (ρ), such as air, also tend to have a low thermal conductivity (k), and vice versa, so that the ratio is similar over a variety of materials.

Mathematically, the thermal diffusion equation is a second order differential equation, and cannot be solved without the aid of a computer except in a few special cases. Those special cases have been studied extensively, however, because of the importance of this equation in engineering problems where understanding heat flow and the resulting changes in temperature is necessary.[14] One such case which is of interest from the standpoint of understanding weapon effects is illustrated in Figure 1–5.

Figure 1–5 shows how the temperature on the interior of a solid varies with time if the surface is maintained at a constant temperature, T. As you can see on the left hand side of the figure, and as you might expect, the heated region propagates into the target, which ultimately would all be heated to the temperature T. On the right hand side, the distance into the target to which the heat has propagated has been plotted as a function of time. This distance obeys a rather simple law: $x \approx \sqrt{Dt}$, where the symbol $\approx$ means "approximately equal to." A similar relationship applies in almost every problem of heat flow: temperature moves to fill in up to its equilibrium value at a rate which varies as the square root of time. This result is frequently of use in developing criteria for target damage from different weapon concepts, and will be used extensively in subsequent chapters.

Physically, thermal conduction arises because temperature is related to the random motion of molecules. It is a microscopic process. As molecules become hotter, they "wiggle" more, bump into their neighbors, and agitate them as well. In this way, the hotter molecules cool down by giving up energy, the cooler molecules warm up by gaining energy, and the whole assembly moves towards a constant, equilibrium temperature. By contrast, *convection* is a process in which heat is carried away through the macroscopic motion of molecules. A common example is the wind from a fan. The macroscopic flow of air induced by a fan can carry hot air away from an attic, for example, and lower its temperature much more efficiently than thermal conduction. In the study of

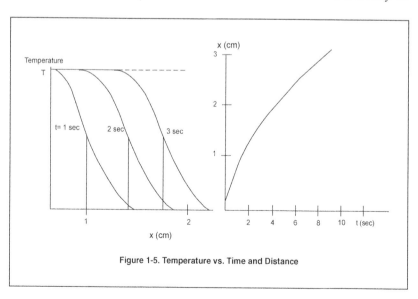

Figure 1-5. Temperature vs. Time and Distance

weapon effects, convection is an important source of energy loss in a number of situations. Many targets, such as airplanes, are moving rapidly through the air. There is a motion-induced wind across the surface of these targets which can be an important factor in establishing their damage threshold from weapons such as lasers which deposit energy primarily on a target's surface (see Chapter 3). In other cases, since hot air is lighter than cold air and tends to rise, the process of heating a region can itself set air into motion, affecting the threshold and extent of damage.

Mathematically, the change of temperature due to convection can be handled as illustrated in Figure 1–6. Shown in this figure is a region of space in which the temperature is varying with distance with a temperature gradient, dT/dx. Wind of velocity V comes along and time dt blows this temperature profile downstream to the point indicated by the dotted line. As a result, the temperature at some point $\times$ drops in time dt from T to T–V (dT/dx) dt. Thus, the rate of change of T in time at point $\times$ is dT/dt = –V dT/dx. This expression for the effect of wind on the temperature at a point clearly makes sense—if the wind velocity V is stronger, the temperature drops more rapidly, and if the temperature is the same everywhere, so that the temperature gradient dT/dx is zero, then the wind serves only to replace hot air with more hot air, and the temperature does not drop.

For a target to lose energy by thermal conduction or convection, it must be immersed in the atmosphere, water, or some other

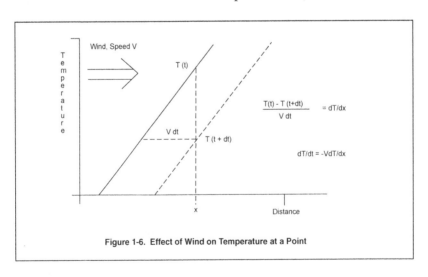

Figure 1-6. Effect of Wind on Temperature at a Point

medium to supply the necessary molecules to carry the energy away. Yet even targets in the vacuum of outer space can lose energy through *radiation*. As the molecules and atoms in a target heat up, some of the energy that their temperature represents resides in internal degrees of freedom. That is, the molecules are not only moving randomly in space, but are also vibrating, rotating, and in other ways incorporating energy into their internal structure. It is a well established fact that molecules can give up internal energy of this sort by emitting electromagnetic radiation. Electromagnetic radiation is discussed in detail in the introduction to Chapter 3, since it is crucial to an understanding of lasers and their interaction with matter, but we're all familiar with certain types of radiation, such as light, radio waves, and microwaves.

As a target becomes hot, the molecules within it begin to give up some of their energy as radiation. In some cases, this radiation is visible as light, such as the radiation from the hot filament in a light bulb, or from a red hot piece of iron in a forge. In other cases, the radiation may be of a type which we can't see with our eyes, such as the infrared radiation emitted by warm objects and detectable only with special equipment. But all of this radiation is a source of energy loss, limiting the rise in a target's temperature as energy is deposited within it.

The mathematical details of how much radiation a given target will emit at a given temperature can be quite complex,[15] but one special case which can be treated in detail is the radiation from a "black body." A black body is a mathematically ideal surface which would absorb all the radiation incident upon it, and therefore would in equilibrium radiate away more energy than any other object. The total intensity of radiation, S (Watts/cm^2) emerging from the surface of a black body at temperature T is $S = \sigma T^4$, where $\sigma = 5.67 \times 10^{-12}$ Watts/cm^2 K^4, and is known as the Stefan-Boltzmann constant.[16]

Figure 1–7 is a plot of the radiation from a black body as a function of temperature. The important point to note is the strong dependence on temperature. Since radiation is proportional to the fourth power of T, it does not become important until fairly high temperatures are reached. Moreover since any real object will radiate to a lesser extent than the ideal black body, Figure 1–7 is an upper bound to the potential for energy loss through radiation from a target.

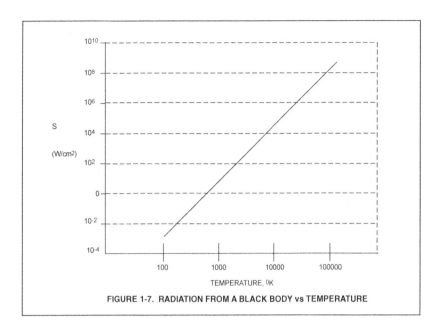

FIGURE 1-7. RADIATION FROM A BLACK BODY vs TEMPERATURE

Implications

In looking at what it takes to damage targets, we've seen that damaging targets depends not only on delivering energy, but also on concentrating the energy in both space and time. In space, we need to deliver something like 10,000 Joules per square centimeter of target surface, either at a single point, as with a bullet, or over the whole surface, as with a nuclear weapon. In time, this energy must be delivered more rapidly than the target can get rid of it through such energy loss mechanisms as thermal conduction, convection, and radiation. Our task in subsequent chapters will be to look at how each weapon type deposits energy in a target, and then to consider energy deposition and loss rates to determine criteria for damaging the target. The fluence (Joules/cm^2) or intensity (Watts/cm^2) necessary to damage a target will typically vary with the time or pulse width that the weapon engages the target, and will have the form shown in Figure 1-8. For extremely short times, energy is deposited into the target so rapidly that there is no way for radiation, conduction, or other energy loss mechanisms to carry it away. For short pulse widths (less than t_1 in the figure), the fluence necessary to damage the target is a constant, and the intensity necessary to damage

14

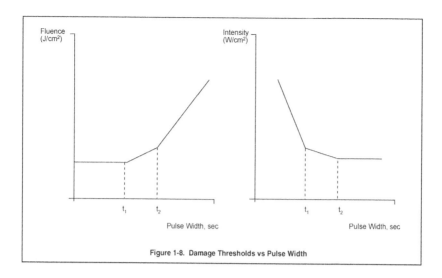

Figure 1-8. Damage Thresholds vs Pulse Width

it decreases linearly with pulse width. At longer interaction times, such as between t_1 and t_2 in the figure, some of the energy deposited is carried away before it can contribute to damage, and so the fluence to achieve damage begins to rise with pulse width. Finally, beyond some long pulse width such as t_2 in the figure, energy is deposited too slowly to do any damage unless some minimum intensity is exceeded, and the energy threshold is proportional to pulse width.

Scaling

An important task which will face us as we develop damage threshold curves like those shown in Figure 1-8 will be to determine how the curves shift or "scale" as important parameters of the problem are varied. For example, thermal conduction may be an important factor in establishing the intensity level at which a target will damage. Knowing how the damage threshold depends on (or scales with) this parameter, we can immediately determine the threshold for targets of different materials if we know the threshold for one. This is particularly useful when the mathematics of deriving damage thresholds is so complex that simplifying assumptions must be made. As a result of these assumptions, we may not have confidence in the magnitude of the damage threshold derived, yet feel that the scaling is well established through our analysis. In this case, experimental data can

15

be taken in the laboratory and used as a starting point for scaling to situations where the powers, ranges, or target parameters are quite different from those in the lab. Of course, doing this with confidence requires a good understanding of how things scale and where transitions occur from one type of scaling to another.

"All-Purpose" Damage Criteria

It is beyond the scope of this book to develop damage criteria for each type of directed energy weapon against all targets of potential interest. There are too many such targets, and the details of their design and construction are in most cases not well enough known to permit detailed analysis. Therefore, it would be useful to have some generic criteria that could be applied to a first approximation in developing the weapon parameters which are likely to achieve damage.

We have made a start along these lines by restricting our attention to such "hard" damage mechanisms as target melting or vaporization. As we saw in Table 1–1, the energy required to vaporize a cubic centimeter of most materials is about 10^4 Joules, and indeed, most weapons damage targets when they are capable of delivering a fluence of about 10^4 J/cm^2 to them on time scales

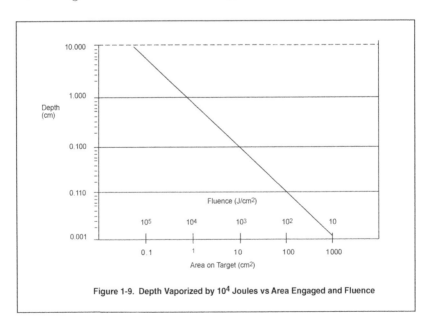

Figure 1-9. Depth Vaporized by 10^4 Joules vs Area Engaged and Fluence

too short for the energy to be rejected. The reason for this is suggested by Figure 1–9, which shows the depth to which 10^4 Joules can vaporize a target as a function of the area over which this energy is spread. As you can see from the figure, 10^4 Joules is only capable of vaporizing a significant depth of target when the area over which it is spread is such that the fluence is on the order of $10^4 \, J/cm^2$. At significantly lower fluences, the depth vaporized would not be sufficient even to penetrate the skin of most targets.

The fact that so many weapons place energies on the order of $10^4 \, J/cm^2$ on target, together with Figure 1–9, suggest that we can take $10^4 \, J/cm^2$ as an all-purpose damage criterion, and assert that making a hole in a target to a depth of about 1 centimeter is sufficient to damage almost anything. Is there a rational basis for such a conclusion, and what are the limitations to keep in mind while applying it?

First of all, it is important to recognize that in saying that a weapon must be able to vaporize to a depth on one centimeter into a target, we are being very conservative. Most targets are less than a centimeter thick, if we count only the thickness of solid matter that must be penetrated to prevent the target from functioning. The outer surface of an automobile, for example, is sheet metal whose thickness is far less than a centimeter. If a weapon were to penetrate that surface near the gas tank, it would then propagate through several centimeters of air with little opposition before encountering the surface of the tank, which is itself less than a centimeter in thickness. Thus, an automobile might be damaged through rupture of its gasoline tank at fluences much less than $10^4 \, J/cm^2$. On the other hand, if the weapon were to penetrate the hood and encounter the engine block, it could encounter considerably more mass, and the fluence necessary for damage would be correspondingly greater.

Additionally, the mechanism of target damage need not be vaporization of a hole clear through it. A bullet, for example, penetrates by pushing material aside, rupturing the bonds that hold the target together along a few lines, rather than throughout the volume that it passes. Intuitively, it should take less energy to move material aside than to vaporize it entirely. A laser might vaporize a thin layer of the target's surface with such rapidity that the vapor, in blowing off, exerts a reaction force on the target that deforms or buckles it. In short, we need to consider the specific mechanisms by which each weapon type interacts with matter, and take these into account in establishing the fluence or intensity requirements for damage. Thus, the interaction with matter of the weapons considered in this book is a significant topic in subsequent chapters.

We have seen that there are two ways in which an all-purpose damage criterion might need to be modified to reflect the energy requirements in a realistic scenario—the effective thickness of the target, in terms of the mass which must be penetrated, may be greater or less than a nominal one centimeter, and the mechanism by which penetration occurs may be different from pure vaporization. The second issue is a matter of physics, and will be treated in detail for each weapon type. The first issue is a function of the target to be attacked, and can be dealt with here only in the most general of terms.

One way of capturing the relative thickness of material a weapon would encounter in attacking a target is to look at the "average thickness" of the target. This number is obtained by finding the thickness of a plate having the same mass and surface area as the target. In effect, the target's innards are plastered against its walls to give a feel for how much mass would be encountered on a random path through it. Figure 1–10 shows the average thickness of some typical targets, based on rough available data on mass and surface area.[17]

From Figure 1–10, you can see that in satellites and aircraft, where weight is at a premium, there is relatively little mass for a weapon to encounter. Tanks, on the other hand, have thick layers of protective armor, and an ICBM is literally filled with solid propellant. This creates the intuitive picture that the threshold for damaging a satellite will be less than that for damaging an ICBM or tank. Published estimates of the energy needed to damage targets suggest that fluences on the order of 10^4 J/cm^2 are required to damage thick targets, whose thickness is on the order of a centimeter or greater. Therefore, a possible zero-order approach to establishing damage criteria would be to use that value for thick targets, and degrade it for thinner targets in proportion to the effective thickness. This would suggest, for example, that the fluence necessary to damage a satellite would be on the order of 100 J/cm^2, a value which is also consistent with published estimates.[18]

Will the tank and ICBM be equally difficult to damage? Probably not, since damaging the tank requires penetrating its thick armor, while damaging the ICBM does not require penetrating all its solid fuel. You only need to penetrate its relatively thin skin, and gases will vent through the hole, altering the rocket thrust so that a successful flight is not possible. Thus, even measures of average hardness such as the effective thickness shown in Figure 1–10 need to be tempered with some feeling for the construction of the target and the mechanisms by which it may be damaged.

In subsequent chapters, we will generally use 10^4 J/cm^2 as a nominal damage threshold for hard targets engaged by weapons on short time scales. This will be done primarily as a means of establishing the general parameters within which weapon propagation and interaction should be studied. This threshold should not, of course, be taken as a definitive number, since the thickness of target penetration and the mechanism of interaction could be different from those which this criterion implies. Wherever possible, results will be provided in such a way that you can supply whatever damage criterion you feel appropriate, adjusting weapon performance parameters appropriately. And when the mechanisms of target interaction are considered, their implications from the standpoint of damage criteria will be discussed in detail.

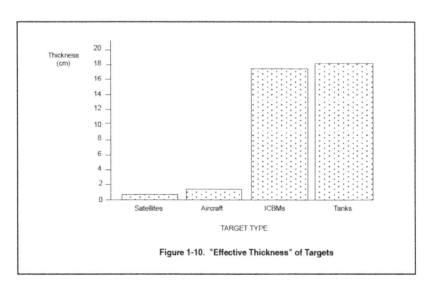

Figure 1-10. "Effective Thickness" of Targets

Energy Spread and Loss in Propagation

At the beginning of this chapter, we indicated that there are two essential elements necessary to understand the interaction of weapons with targets: the energy which must be deposited within the target if it is to be damaged, and the losses which will be sustained as energy propagates from the weapon to the target. Knowing these two things, it's possible to design an effective weapon which will produce sufficient energy in a short enough time that damage criteria can be met even after propagation losses are accounted for. In general, there are two types of energy loss in propagation: the spreading of energy such that some of it does not interact with the target, and the wasting of energy in interactions with a physical medium, such as the atmosphere, through which it passes on the way to the target. The first type of loss will occur whether the weapon and target are located on earth or in the vacuum of space, while the second will occur primarily when either the weapon or the target lies within the atmosphere.[19] Let's consider each type of loss in turn.

Energy Spread

In discussing damage criteria, two contrasting weapon types were discussed: directed energy weapons, in which all the energy transmitted is brought to bear on the target, and bombs, in which the energy is spread out indiscriminately over an ever expanding sphere. All real weapons fall between these extremes, since even lasers and other weapons which have been characterized as being "directed energy" have some inherent spread associated with their propagation.[20] This may be due to physical reasons which cannot be overcome, such as the diffraction of light as it emerges from a laser, or due to practical or engineering limitations, such as the spread of bullets on a target which occurs even when a skilled marksman aims consistently at a single point. The concepts of *divergence* and *jitter* are used to describe these effects, and are illustrated in Figure 1–11. In the upper half of the figure, laser light emerges from a device and, after propagating a distance z to its target, has spread to a beam size R. This spreading, which is known as "beam divergence," may be characterized in terms of the angle, θ, which the beam envelope makes. The beam size R and the range z are related through the simple geometrical relationship R=zθ.

In the lower half of the figure, a beam of particles or bullets is being fired, and due to a lack of shot-to-shot reproducibility the shot group occupies a size R at range z. The angular spread θ, resulting from this jitter in the aiming and firing mechanism is related to the range, z, and diameter of the shot pattern, R, through the same geometrical relationship.

Under realistic circumstances, both divergence and jitter can contribute to the energy spread from a weapon. For example, a laser beam will have some divergence related to the wavelength of the light, and some jitter resulting from the accuracy of its pointing and tracking mechanism. In either case, this spread in energy means that the weapon in question may have to put out much more energy than the nominal 10,000 Joules in order to insure that 10,000 Joules are actually brought to bear on a small area of the target. As we have seen, a bomb is an extreme example of this phenomenon. The bottom line is that there is no perfect directed energy weapon, and an adequate description of any weapon must include some measure of its departure from

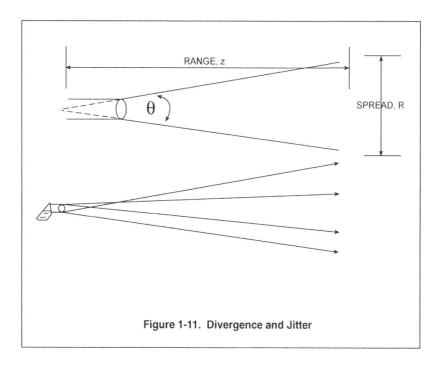

Figure 1-11. Divergence and Jitter

perfection. Considerable time and effort will be devoted in subsequent chapters to the mechanisms which cause energy from each weapon type to spread on its way to the target, and how this divergence is affected by parameters which are under the control of the weapon designer, such as energy, pulse width, and initial beam radius.

Energy Losses

Not all the energy emitted by a weapon will make it to the target. Some will inevitably be lost through energy losses to the atmosphere. Table 1–2 provides a summary of some of the loss mechanisms which can affect the weapon types considered in this book.

As you can see from Table 1–2, there are numerous mechanisms by which energy can be lost from weapons propagating in the atmosphere. Indeed, these mechanisms can feed on themselves to increase energy losses. For example, the heating of the air through which a laser beam passes can modify the atmospheric density within the beam channel in such a way as to increase the divergence of the beam. Such "nonlinear" effects are often a feature of the propagation of energy that is sufficiently intense to damage targets. As a result, the subject of propagation in the atmosphere occupies a larger volume of text than any other subject in this book. That's not to say that this is the most important topic in the book. Indeed, the difficulties associated with atmospheric propagation have caused interest in many weapon types to shift to applications that can be accomplished in the vacuum of space.

Chapter Summary

The study of weapon effects is in essence a study of energy—how it propagates to, interacts with, and is redistributed within a target. The goal of this study is to determine under what conditions sufficient energy will accumulate within a target to damage it. In order to achieve damage, energy must be concentrated both in space and time. The following fundamental ideas will find application throughout the remainder of this book.

1. The necessary concentration of energy in space (fluence) for a hard target kill is on the order of 10,000 Joules per square centimeter. This fluence will serve as an upper bound for our

Weapon Type	Energy Loss Mechanisms
Kinetic Energy (bullets, rockets)	Atmospheric Drag
Lasers	Absorption by molecules Scattering by molecules Absorption by aerosols (small particles) Scattering by aerosols
Microwaves	Absorption by molecules Scattering by molecules Absorption by water droplets Scattering by water droplets
Particle Beams	Energy losses to electrons Scattering from nucleii Scattering from electrons Radiation

Table 1-2. Energy Losses in Propagation

analyses, since many targets of interest may be damaged at lower fluences (see Figure 1–10).

2. For 10,000 Joules per square centimeter to achieve damage, it must be concentrated in time so that it cannot flow and be redistributed within the target. Energy deposition is manifested in a temperature rise which is proportional to the mass and heat capacity of the region over which the energy is absorbed. The redistribution and loss of energy occurs through three primary mechanisms: thermal conduction, convection, and radiation. When the time scale for weapon-target interaction is such that these mechanisms can come into play, the fluence necessary for damage will begin to rise. Eventually, a point will be reached where the damage threshold is more properly characterized as an intensity dependent threshold ($Watts/cm^2$) than a fluence dependent threshold (J/cm^2) The main task of each subsequent chapter will be to determine what these thresholds are and where in interaction time the transition between them occurs (see Figure 1–8).

3. Directed energy weapons are those for which the energy is directed at the target. However, no weapon fully meets this ideal. All are characterized by some level of beam divergence, which spreads the energy out as it propagates, and jitter, in

which multiple shots do not follow exactly the same path. Divergence and jitter are characterized in terms of an angle, θ which relates beam spread, R, to range to target, Z, through the mathematical relationship $R = Z\theta$.

4. In the atmosphere, various energy loss mechanisms (absorption, scatter, etc), will cause some fraction of the energy directed at a target to be lost in propagation to it. This must be accounted for in developing weapon design criteria. A weapon must be capable of giving up the energy that will be lost in propagating over the anticipated range to target and still place sufficient fluence or intensity on the target to damage it.

Where We're Going

Each chapter to follow is devoted to a specific type of directed energy weapon, and is organized into the following main sections.

• An introduction, in which the fundamentals of each weapon type are developed.

• A discussion of propagation in a vacuum. Here the factors responsible for the divergence associated with each weapon type are discussed in detail, and used to develop criteria for placing a damaging level of fluence on target in the absence of atmospheric effects.

• A section on propagation in the atmosphere, where energy loss mechanisms and their implications from the standpoint of a weapon's design and its ability to deliver damaging fluence within the atmosphere are discussed.

• A section on interaction with targets. The specific mechanisms by which each weapon type deposits energy in targets are discussed, and the resulting advantages and disadvantages of that weapon type are highlighted. The implications of weapon specific target interaction mechanisms from the standpoint of damage criteria will be addressed.

• Notes and references. These are presented as a guide to more detailed literature for those interested in examining any topic in greater depth.

Each chapter is self-contained, and may be read without reference to any other. In some cases, however, topics which are developed in great detail in one chapter are presented in a more cursory form in others, with reference to the chapter containing a more detailed treatment for those who find this less than satisfying.

Notes and References

1. The "Joule" as a unit of energy derives its name from James P. Joule (1818–1889), whose experiments on heat and work established the equivalence between them, and led to the law of conservation of energy.

2. The estimate of the energy it takes to brew a cup of coffee assumes that it is a 6 oz cup, and that the water must be raised about 80C in temperature.

3. Heating, melting, and vaporization are discussed in any text on thermodynamics, such as Chapter 11 of Mark W. Zemansky, *Heat and Thermodynamics* (New York: McGraw-Hill, 1957). In general, all thermodynamic quantities such as heat capacity, heat of fusion, and heat of vaporization are functions of temperature and pressure.

4. The "Watt" as a unit of power derives its name from James Watt (1736–1819), the inventor of the steam engine.

5. The data in Table 1–1 were taken from "Physical Constants of Inorganic Compounds" in Robert C. Weast (ed.), *Handbook of Chemistry and Physics,* 45th ed. (Cleveland, OH: Chemical Rubber Co., 1964), and from Tables 22.06 and 22.07 in Herbert L. Anderson (ed.), *Physics Vade Mecum* (New York: American Institute of Physics, 1981). Similar data for other materials are available in almost any physics or engineering handbook.

6. See C. J. Marchant-Smith and P. R. Halsam, *Small Arms and Cannons* (Oxford: Brassey's Publishers, 1982).

7. Werner Soedel and Vernard Foley, "Ancient Catapults," *Scientific American* 240, 150 (March, 1979).

8. Vernard Foley, George Palmer, and Werner Soedel, "The Crossbow," *Scientific American* 252, 104 (January, 1985)

9. More precisely, the nuclear equivalent of one kiloton of TNT is by definition 10^{12} calories, or 4.184×10^{12} Joules. See Table D, section 1.02, *Physics Vade Mecum* (note 5).

10. Chapter V, Samuel Glasstone and Philip J. Dolan, *The Effects of Nuclear Weapons,* 3rd ed. (Washington, DC: US Government Printing Office, 1977). This book is an excellent reference on all things having to do with nuclear weapon effects.

11. The intensity of radiation from the sun, or solar constant, is 0.134 W/cm². The actual intensity received at any point on the earth will vary with the time of year and latitude, because in reaching any given point solar radiation must propagate through different thicknesses of atmosphere and will strike at different angles.

12. The units relating to the strength and density of energy striking a surface are perhaps less standard than any others, since different conventions have evolved in different branches of physics. We will use "fluence" for J/cm², and "intensity" for W/cm². Be aware that others may use these terms differently, and it's good practice to check the units associated with such terms to be sure of their meaning.

13. See Figures 5.20, 5.22, and 5.23 of Glasstone and Dolan (note 10).

14. The standard reference is H. Carslaw and J. C. Jaeger, *Conduction of Heat in Solids*, 2nd ed. (Oxford: Clarendon Press, 1959). A less theoretical approach, with an emphasis on graphical solutions to problems arising in chemical engineering, can be found in Aksel L. Lydersen, *Fluid Flow and Heat Transfer* (New York: Wiley-Interscience, 1979).

15. A good treatment of thermal radiation can be found in Section II of Ya. B. Zel'dovich and Yu. P. Raizer, *Physics of Shock Waves and High-Temperature Hydrodynamic Phenomena,* vol I (New York: Academic Press, 1966).

16. See Equation 2.16 in Zel'dovich and Raizer (note 15).

17. The effective thicknesses shown in Figure 1–10 are averages of calculations for specific weapons made with data available from a variety of sources. There is, of course, considerable uncertainty involved in estimating a target's surface area from its published dimensions, especially for something like a satellite or tank. Satellite data are from Reginald Turnill, ed. *Jane's Spaceflight Directory* 3rd ed. (London: Jane's Publishing, 1987). Aircraft data are from William Green and Gordon Swanborough, *Observers Directory of Military Aircraft,* (New York: Arco Publishing, 1982), and from Norman Polmar, *The Ships and Aircraft of the U.S. Fleet,* 12th ed. (Annapolis, MD Naval Institute Press, 1981). ICBM data are from Bernard Blake (ed) *Janes Weapon Systems*, 1987–88 (New York: Jane's Publishing, 1987). Tank data are from *United States Army Weapon Systems, 1987*, Department of the Army, 1987.

18. Estimates of damage thresholds for ICBMs and satellites can be found in the "Report to the APS of the Study Group on Science and Technology of Directed Energy Weapons," *Reviews of Modern Physics 59*, Part II (July, 1987). See Section 3.1.2 and Chapter 6.

19. Some type of energy loss through interaction with a physical medium could occur even in space. For example, a weapon may need to propagate through the exhaust plume of a rocket, or the target may even eject or be covered by some type of absorbing, protective material as a countermeasure against attack.

20. Interestingly enough, there have recently been suggestions that the radiation from a nuclear weapon could be focused, making it more of a directed energy weapon. See Theodore B. Taylor, "Third Generation Nuclear Weapons," *Scientific American* 256, p. 30 (April, 1987).

2: KINETIC ENERGY WEAPONS

The word *kinetic* comes from the Greek verb *to move*, and kinetic energy weapons are those for which it is the energy of a moving projectile, such as a bullet or rocket, which damages the target. Kinetic energy weapons are the oldest form of directed energy weapon, spears and catapult stones being early examples of weapons in this category. In some classification schemes, the term *directed energy weapon* is reserved for modern, high technology devices such as lasers or particle beams, and kinetic energy weapons are kept in a class by themselves. Nevertheless, they properly fit the definition which we have adopted for directed energy weapon—their energy is aimed or directed at a target, and intercepts a small fraction of the target's surface area. Including them in this book is appropriate from the standpoint of completeness, and serves as a useful point of departure for the more esoteric discussions in later chapters. The general approach taken in this chapter is also the same as that we will use throughout. We'll first discuss some of the fundamental concepts needed to understand kinetic energy weapons, then their propagation or travel towards a target, and finally their interaction with a target and the mechanisms by which the target is damaged.

Fundamentals of Kinetic Energy Weapons

Kinetic energy is the energy which an object has by virtue of its motion.[1] Mathematically, the kinetic energy of an object having a mass M and velocity v is $K = Mv^2/2$. This definition makes sense on physical grounds. We'd expect that at the same velocity (say 55 mph) a more massive object (such as a semi truck) would have more energy, and be more likely to damage an object it encountered, than a less massive object (such as a motorcycle). Similarly, if two objects have the same mass, we'd expect the one moving at the greater velocity to have more energy.

An important principle of physics is that energy is a conserved quantity. That is, the energy of an object can't increase unless it gains this energy from some outside source. An object is given kinetic energy when outside forces act on it, doing work and accelerating it. An object loses kinetic energy when it, in turn, exerts forces and does work on a second object. The energy lost can appear as kinetic energy in the second object, such as when one billiard ball strikes another. It can also appear as random energy (heat), or disrupt the second object's structure, such as when a bullet pierces a target.

Mathematically, the kinetic energy gained or lost when an object is accelerated can be found from Newton's law: $F = Ma$, where F is the force acting on the object, M is its mass, and a is the acceleration (rate of change of velocity, dv/dt) which the object experiences. From Newton's law, you can see that a greater force will accelerate an object more rapidly, and that more massive objects are more resistant to acceleration than lighter ones. In metric (MKS) units, mass is expressed in kilograms, acceleration in m/sec^2, and force in Newtons.[2]

It is important to recognize that force, velocity, and acceleration are all what is known as vector quantities—those which require both a magnitude and a direction to be completely specified.[3] For example, a bullet which is moving at 1,000 m/sec toward us is quite different from one which is moving at 1,000 m/sec away from us. Therefore, to specify the velocity of an object we need to provide both its speed and the direction in which it is moving. Similarly, the force applied to a object might be in the same direction as its velocity, in which case the object will be accelerated, or it might be in a direction opposite to its velocity, in which case it will be decelerated. The force on an object might even be in a direction which is unrelated to its velocity. For example, gravity exerts a force on all objects which accelerates them towards the center of the earth, regardless of their direction of motion.

The forces which act on an object are independent of one another, and the object's motion is simply the sum of the motions which each force acting alone would have produced. For example, a bullet fired from a gun feels both the force of gravity, which makes it move downward, and a drag force from the resistance of the air through which it propagates, which slows its velocity in the forward direction. The study of how the projectile from a kinetic energy weapon propagates is simply an analysis of the forces which act on it and their resultant effect on the projectile's motion. Figure 2–1 illustrates how forces affect the motion of an object.

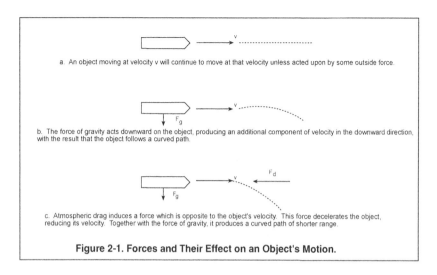

a. An object moving at velocity v will continue to move at that velocity unless acted upon by some outside force.

b. The force of gravity acts downward on the object, producing an additional component of velocity in the downward direction, with the result that the object follows a curved path.

c. Atmospheric drag induces a force which is opposite to the object's velocity. This force decelerates the object, reducing its velocity. Together with the force of gravity, it produces a curved path of shorter range.

Figure 2-1. Forces and Their Effect on an Object's Motion.

When a projectile encounters a target, interest shifts from the forces felt by the projectile to those felt by the target. The two are related, of course. The forces which the projectile exerts on the target, possibly damaging it, are mirror images of the forces which the target exerts on the projectile, slowing it down and probably damaging it as well. Two principles are of value in evaluating the interaction between a kinetic energy weapon and its target. One is conservation of energy, which says that any energy lost from the projectile must be given to the target. Therefore, if a projectile enters a target with one velocity and emerges from the other side with a lower velocity, the energy transferred to the target is the difference between the kinetic energies on entry and exit. A second principle is conservation of momentum. The momentum of an object is the product of its mass and velocity, Mv. Conservation of momentum requires that the total momentum of the projectile and target be the same before and after they interact. Therefore, if a target is initially at rest and is struck by a projectile whose momentum is Mv_o, the target's momentum and that of the projectile after the interaction will sum to Mv_o. In applying the principle of conservation of momentum, it must be remembered that the velocities are all vector quantities, so that their direction, as well as their magnitude, must be taken into account.

When two bodies such as a projectile and target interact, conservation of energy and momentum are useful in evaluating the energy and velocity of each following the interaction. They are not, however, generally sufficient to predict the damage done to the target. This is because damage is usually some internal disruption of the target, rather than a change in such gross features as velocity or energy.[4] Physical damage of a target is usually determined by the pressure the target feels, the area over which this pressure is applied, and the time for which the pressure applied. *Pressure* is the force a target feels, divided by the area over which that force is applied.

Pressure is a useful concept because the response of a target to an applied force depends upon the area over which that force is applied. For example, if a hammer strikes a wooden table, it will probably only dent the wood. But if the hammer strikes a nail, and the nail in turn strikes the table with the same force, the smaller area represented by the nail will result in a greater pressure, and the nail will probably penetrate the table's surface.

The total force felt by a target is the pressure applied multiplied by the area over which it is applied. A target's response will depend on total force as well. A man may lean against a structure, applying a certain pressure to it with his palm, and do no damage. Yet the wind may apply the same pressure over the whole structure, and the total force could be sufficient to topple it.[5]

Finally, the time over which a force is applied is important in determining a target's response. Squeezing an object with a sufficiently high pressure will gradually alter its shape, with the amount of deviation being proportional to the length of time the squeeze is applied. The product of force times the time over which the force is applied is known as *impulse*.[6] The momentum and energy of a kinetic energy weapon, together with the resulting force, pressure, and impulse transmitted to a target, are the key parameters which enter into any discussion of target damage. Table 2–1 is a summary of these parameters and the relationships among them.

Of course, the specific damage to be anticipated in a given situation depends not only on the parameters of the projectile, but also on the nature of the target. How structures respond to forces applied to them, and the criteria for their damage, is an engineering subject known as *strength of materials*. It's well beyond the scope of this book to go into this subject in any detail. For purposes of understanding the effects of kinetic energy weapons, it will be sufficient to deal with general principles and generic results.

Parameter	Symbol	Units	Definition	Comments
Kinetic Energy	K	Joules (J)	$Mv^2/2$	M, v = Projectile mass, velocity
Momentum	p	kg m/sec	Mv	K and p are conserved when particles collide
Force	F	Newtons (Nt)	$M\,dv/dt$	also $F = dp/dt$
Pressure	P	Nt/m^2	Force / Area	Force / Area = Energy / Volume J/m^3 Nt/m^2
Impulse	I	Nt sec	Force X Time	

Table 2-1. Parameters Affecting Target Response and Damage

33

Propagation in a Vacuum

Any weapon must reach a target before it can damage it, and propagation can alter the physical parameters with which the weapon engages the target. For example, atmospheric drag will slow a bullet, so that it will be less effective at a given range. Additionally, the environment through which weapon propagates can affect its motion, and must be compensated for in aiming the weapon. For example, a strong wind will deflect a bullet. Therefore, understanding the constraints which propagation places on a weapon is the first step in examining its utility for a given application. Two cases are of interest—propagation in a vacuum, which characterizes kinetic energy weapons employed in space, and propagation in the atmosphere, which characterizes their employment on earth. Of course, there are cases in which the propagation of a weapon takes it through both environments, such as when a ballistic missile launches and reenters through the atmosphere, yet spends a substantial portion of its propagation path in the vacuum of space. Situations like this are easily treated by analyzing each phase of the weapon's flight in turn. We'll first consider propagation in a vacuum.

Two types of force affect the propagation of a kinetic energy weapon in the vacuum of space—internal forces resulting from any rocket motor which the weapon may have, and external forces resulting from the environment through which it propagates. In a vacuum, the only significant external force is that of gravity. We'll first consider the propagation of a projectile which has no propulsion of its own, and whose motion is determined only by gravity and the initial conditions given it by the weapon launcher. We'll then consider necessary modifications for a projectile with on-board propulsion.

Motion Under the Influence of Gravity

The effects of gravity on the motion of an object are described by the *law of universal gravitation*.[7] This law says that there is an attractive force between any two bodies, whose magnitude is proportional to the product of their masses, and inversely proportional to the square of the distance between them. Mathematically, this is expressed as $F = GMm/r^2$, where M and m are the masses of the two bodies, r is the distance separating them, and G is a constant (= 6.67×10^{-11} nt m^2/kg^2) known logically enough as the gravitational constant. The gravitational force is a relatively weak one, even though it's responsible for such useful features as our being held to the surface of the earth, and not drifting off into space. For example, two bowling balls, each having a mass of about 4.5 kg and separated by a distance of 1 meter, are attracted to each other with a force of only 1.4×10^{-9} nt (3×10^{-10} lb). It is only because of the very large mass of the earth (6×10^{24} kg) that the bowling balls are held to the earth with the much more substantial force of 44 nt (10 lb).

As the example of the bowling balls makes clear, gravitational forces are important when a kinetic energy weapon interacts with massive astrophysical objects such as the sun, earth, or moon. They are not important and need not be considered when objects of ordinary size interact with one another. Therefore, a kinetic energy weapon will not home in on its target through attractive gravitational forces, but will be affected in its flight to the target by a gravitational pull towards the earth. This effect which must be accounted for in aiming the weapon.

When dealing with the propagation of directed energy weapons in a vacuum, we're of course considering applications in outer space. The atmosphere gradually decreases in density with altitude, and becomes negligible at altitudes on the order of 100–200km.[8] Therefore, propagation in a vacuum is of interest for "strategic" applications, where the target and the weapon are in outer space, and the distance between them can be very large. A geosynchronous satellite, for example, orbits at an altitude of 40,000 km. The study of how objects move in space near the earth is known as *orbital mechanics*, since the first practical application was found in predicting the motion of artificial earth satellites.

It is straightforward to determine the path of a body of mass m moving under the influence of the gravitational force from a much larger body of mass M, such as the earth.[9] All paths are of the form $\alpha/r = 1 + \epsilon \cos\theta$ where α and ϵ are constants, r is the distance of the body from the center of the earth, and θ is the angle which locates the body along its path, as illustrated in Figure 2–2.

The parameter ϵ is known as the *eccentricity* of the body's path. Some of these paths are very familiar. For example, if $\epsilon = 0$, then r is a constant α independent of θ and the path or trajectory is simply a circular orbit with the earth at its center. If ε lies between 0 and 1, the trajectory is an ellipse, with the center of the earth at one focus. If ε = 1, the trajectory is a parabola, and if ε is greater than one, it is a hyperbola. Some of these trajectories are shown in Figure 2–3.

The elliptical and circular trajectories shown on the left hand side of the Figure 2–3 are those of satellites orbiting the earth. Parabolic or hyperbolic trajectories are those of bodies which have sufficient energy to escape the gravitational pull of the earth. It is also possible for the trajectory of an object in space to intersect the surface of the earth, such as that shown on the right hand side of the figure, which is characteristic of an intercontinental ballistic missile (ICBM).

With kinetic energy weapons, the object is to make the weapon intersect the target at some point on its trajectory. In this case, interest lies in determining how the angle θ shown in Figure 2–2 varies with time, since θ determines the position of an object on its

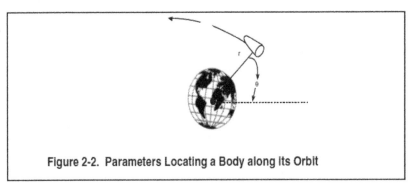

Figure 2-2. Parameters Locating a Body along its Orbit

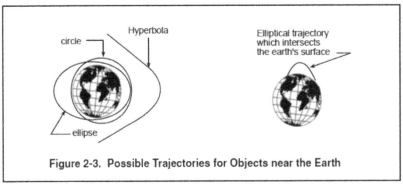

Figure 2-3. Possible Trajectories for Objects near the Earth

path. To locate the trajectory in space, we also need to know how that trajectory is oriented with respect to the earth. It requires six different parameters to completely specify an object's trajectory and the location of the object on that trajectory.[10] The specific data which serve to locate a body on its trajectory around the earth are known as *orbital elements* or *ephemeris data*. These are cataloged for satellites which are in constant orbit around the earth, and must be rapidly calculated for objects like ICBMs or kinetic energy weapons, whose trajectory may be a partial orbit of short duration. Attacking an object in space with a kinetic energy weapon involves predicting the motion of the object, and then firing the weapon with orbital elements that will result in its intersecting the target object at some time in the future.

Let's be more quantitative for the simple case of an object in a circular orbit around the earth, illustrated in Figure 2–4. From the law of gravitation, there is an attractive force between the object in orbit and the earth, having a magnitude $F = GmM/r^2$ where M is the mass of the earth, m the mass of the satellite, and r the distance from the satellite to the center of the earth. The altitude h of the satellite is less than r by an amount equal to the radius of the earth, since the distance r which enters into the law of gravitation is that between the centers of the objects concerned.[11] The velocity v of the satellite is parallel to the surface of the earth, and therefore perpendicular to F, as illustrated in the

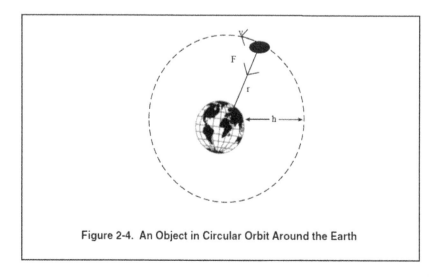

Figure 2-4. An Object in Circular Orbit Around the Earth

figure. This force accelerates the satellite in a downward direction, with the result that it follows a circular path, continually "falling" towards the center of the earth. The situation is entirely analogous to swinging a rock on a string—the rock would like to fly off in a direction away from the swinger, but the string is continually pulling it back, as gravity does in the case of the satellite. The acceleration felt by an object constrained to move in a circular path of radius r at a constant velocity v is v^2/r, so that Newton's law, $F = ma$, becomes $GmM/r^2 = mv^2/r$ in this case.[12] This expression is easily solved for the velocity which an object must have to orbit the earth at a radius r: $v = (GM/r)^{1/2}$. Interestingly, this velocity is independent of the satellite's mass—all objects orbiting at a given radius will have the same velocity, regardless of how big they are. This is because the gravitational force on an object is proportional to its mass. As it becomes more massive and resistant to acceleration, the gravitational force increases proportionally to compensate. The time τ that it takes the satellite to go around the earth once is called the *period* of the orbit, and is just the circumference of the circular path divided by the satellite's velocity:

$$\tau = 2\,\pi r/v = 2\pi r^{3/2}/(GM)^{1/2}.$$

Figures 2–5 and 2–6 are plots of the orbital velocity, v, and period, τ, as a function of altitude (h). From these figures, you can see that as an object's orbit gets further from the earth, its velocity slows down and the time it takes to go around goes up. A case of particular interest is a geosynchronous satellite. At an altitude of about 42,000 km, such a satellite has a period of 24 hours, the same as the rotational period of the earth. In an equatorial orbit, it would appear from the surface of the earth to remain fixed over a single point. Communication satellites have orbital altitudes in this range. The space shuttle and many other satellites operate at much lower altitudes, on the order of 200km. This region is known as "low earth orbit."

You can see from Figure 2–5 that the velocities of objects in orbit around the earth are on the order of several thousand meters per second. Speeds like this are greater than the muzzle velocities from typical infantry weapons, which are on the order of 1,000 m/sec. Therefore, a kinetic energy weapon in space probably has more than enough kinetic energy to damage a target. The trick is

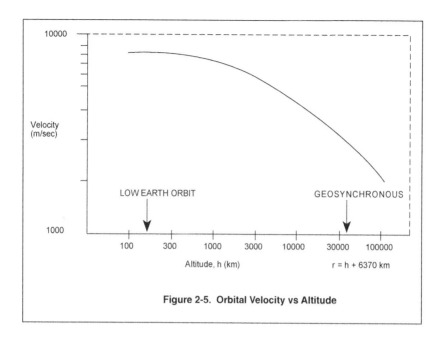

Figure 2-5. Orbital Velocity vs Altitude

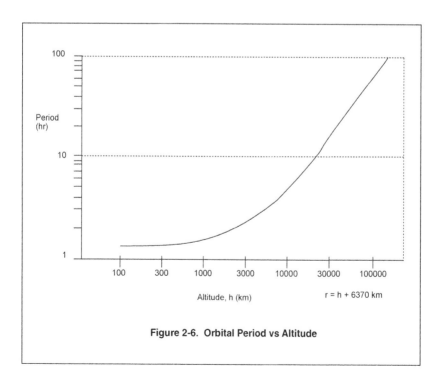

Figure 2-6. Orbital Period vs Altitude

to arrange the trajectory of the weapon so that it intersects the trajectory of the target object.

If the launcher for a kinetic energy weapon is in a given orbit, and a round is to be launched to intersect a target in another orbit, the kinetic energy round must be given an impulse to launch it on a new orbit that will intersect the target's orbit at a place and time when the target is there. You will recall (see Table 2–1) that impulse is simply the force applied to an object multiplied by the time that force is applied. When a kinetic energy round is launched, the force is generally quite high, and the time of application quite short, so that the round may be considered to have been given an instantaneous kick in some direction. Mathematically, the impulse given to an object is equal to the change in its momentum Δp, and since momentum is $p = mv$, this is equivalent to some change in velocity, Δv. Therefore, it is traditional among those who deal in orbital mechanics and orbital transfer to speak of how much "Δv" a launcher or rocket has as a means of specifying its potential to intersect other objects in a timely manner. A large Δv implies a potential for more maneuvering, and the ability to encounter a targeted object more rapidly. Figure 2–7 is suggestive of how Δv affects the ability to engage targets.

Shown in Figure 2–7 is a kinetic energy weapon following some trajectory in space, as indicated by the center line. At some time, an impulse can be delivered to this weapon, changing its velocity v by an amount Δv. Now Δv can be applied in the same direction as v, in which case the velocity of the weapon increases and it moves up to a higher orbit, or it can be in the opposite direction, dropping it down into a lower orbit, or it can be in any direction in between, as indicated by the sphere of possible directions in which Δv may be applied. For each choice of direction for Δv, the round will arrive somewhere different at some later time t_1. The

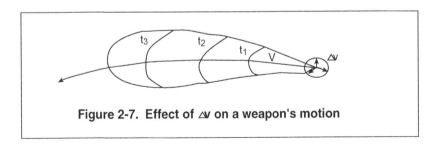

Figure 2-7. Effect of Δv on a weapon's motion

surface labeled t_1 locates those points which the round might reach at t_1 given an appropriate choice in the application of Δv. At some later time t_2, the round has the potential to reach points within the surface labeled t_2 and so on.

Clearly, the reach of the weapon within a given time span depends on the amount of Δv which its launcher can provide to it. Therefore, there is considerable interest in developing rocket fuels which have a high *specific impulse*, or ratio of impulse to weight of propellant employed. If a small weight of propellant can burn to yield a large impulse, there is a high specific impulse, and a very efficient weapon. For space-borne systems, keeping the specific impulse high is especially important, since the cost of launching things into orbit places a premium on weight reduction. Mathematically, specific impulse is defined as $I_{sp} = Ft/mg$, where Ft is the impulse (Force $\times$ time) given to the round, m the mass of propellant employed to deliver the impulse, and g is a constant (= 9.8 m/sec²) which converts mass to weight.[13] Most rocket fuels have an I_{sp} on the order of 200–400 sec. The advantages of advanced technology fuels are usually expressed in terms of their potential for achieving higher I_{sp}.

Figure 2–6 makes it clear that even though objects in orbit around the earth have considerable speed, the large distances involved mean that considerable time, on the order of several hours, can be required for them to traverse the distance from one point to another. Therefore, increasing the reach of a weapon by increasing the impulse it can provide to its rounds is not sufficient to insure that targets can be engaged in a timely manner. The weapon may well be on the other side of the earth at the time a target emerges. Thus, multiple weapons must be deployed in space to insure that one is in place near the point where a target is expected to appear at the time that it does. The arrangement of weapons and the orbits they're deployed in is known as a *constellation*. Establishing the constellation of kinetic energy weapons for a given scenario involves tradeoffs among the altitude of the orbit, the impulse which can be given to the weapon rounds, and timelines available for target engagement. It is beyond the scope of this book to discuss these issues, but the literature is full of lively discussion on constellation sizing.[14]

The Motion of Powered Weapons

In the previous section, we assumed that a kinetic energy weapon moved towards its target only under the influence of gravity and an initial impulse from a launcher. It is also possible for the weapon to have on board an engine and control devices to steer it towards its target. Such an engine could be used throughout the weapon's flight, or could be reserved for fine tuning the trajectory as the weapon neared its target, making the initial calculation of orbital parameters for the weapon less difficult. Kinetic energy weapons which have some measure of on-board terminal guidance to their target have been referred to as "smart rocks." [15]

An object in powered flight feels two forces: that of gravity and that from its engine. In this case, Newton's law, F=ma, becomes $GmM/r^2 + F_r = dp/dt$, where the first term is that of gravity and F_r is the additional force from the engine. The acceleration term, ma, must be expressed in terms of the rate of change of momentum, $dp/dt = d(mv)/dt$, since the mass of the object is not fixed, but decreases with time as fuel is expended.

The solution to Newton's law when a rocket motor adds significantly to the acceleration of gravity is scenario-dependent, and a general solution cannot be presented. However, it is easy to show that a substantial amount of fuel is required for an on-board engine to add to the forces experienced by a weapon throughout its flight. The specific impulse of an engine is the ratio of the total impulse delivered to an object divided by the weight of fuel expended: $I_{sp} = F_r t/mg$. Therefore, the force contributed to the weapon by its motor is $F_r = mg\, I_{sp}/t$. This force will be comparable to the gravitational force if $F_r \approx Gm_t M/r^2$, where m_t is the total mass of the weapon, to distinguish it from the mass of the fuel, m. Therefore, if F_r is to rival gravity as an influence on the weapon's motion, $mg\, I_{sp}/t \approx Gm_t M/r^2$. This expression can be solved for the ratio of fuel mass to total vehicle mass: $m/m_t = (R_e/r)^2\, t/I_{sp}$.[16]

What does the expression $m/m_t = (R_e/r)^2\, t/I_{sp}$ tell us? The radius of the earth is about 6400 km, and satellites orbit at altitudes from about 100–20,000 km above this. Therefore, the factor $(R_e/r)^2$ is somewhere between 0.1 and 1. This means that the ratio of fuel to total mass will approach unity if the duration of powered flight is between one and ten times I_{sp}. Since I_{sp} is on the order of 200–400 seconds (3–7 minutes), you can see that unless a substantial fraction of the weapon's mass is devoted to fuel, the amount of time a kinetic energy weapon can engage in powered flight is limited compared to orbital time scales (see Figure 2–6). This means that weapons with on-board propulsion would generally use it in two phases—an initial phase, to aquire the orbital parameters necessary to approach the target; and a final phase, to "fine-tune" the trajectory to strike the target. Therefore, even the flight of powered weapons is described over most of their path as the flight of weapons given an initial impulse toward their target.

Summary: Propagation in a Vacuum

1. Two forces affect the motion a body in space—the gravitational attraction of the earth, and any propulsive force. The propulsive force can be either an impulse from a launcher or a reaction force from an on-board rocket.

2. Gravitational forces are very strong because of the large mass of the earth. Therefore, bodies in motion under the influence of the earth's gravitational field have substantial velocities ($\approx$5000 m/sec), and sufficient kinetic energy to meet damage criteria. This means that the weapon launcher or on-board propulsion are designed more to bring about the intersection of the weapon and the target than to impart sufficient kinetic energy for damage.

3. Because of the large distances involved in space, flight times from one point to another can be very long. Therefore, large numbers of orbiting weapon launchers are required to insure the timely interception of targets. Requirements can be reduced as propulsion systems are developed with a capacity to impart a greater velocity change (Δv) to weapons on launch.

Implications

Kinetic energy weapons could be among the first weapons employed in space because of their proven technology. Their disadvantages lie in long flight times from weapon to target, the need for accurate target trajectory data to insure interception, and the number of deployed launchers needed to insure timely target engagement. These disadvantages have spurred interest in such high technology directed energy weapons as lasers and particle beams, which project energy at or near the speed of light, and have the potential to defend a greater volume of space.

Propagation in the Atmosphere

Gravitational Forces

Just as in space, kinetic energy weapons within the atmosphere are subject to the force of gravity. However, the fact that we are now within the atmosphere and near the surface of the earth enables certain simplifying assumptions to be made. For all practical purposes, the earth's atmosphere extends to an altitude no greater than about 100 km. At this altitude, atmospheric density is only about 10^{-7} of its value at sea level, and can have very little effect on the flight of a projectile, at least in the near term. Since the radius of the earth is about 6,400 km, you can see that the extent of the atmosphere is but a small perturbation, about 1.5%, to the radius of the earth. This means that the force of gravity, $F = GmM/r^2$, does not vary significantly for projectiles whose flight is limited to altitudes within the earth's atmosphere. Therefore, it is adequate for most calculations to assume that the product GM/r^2 is a constant, roughly equal to GM/R_e^2, for projectiles in the atmosphere. This constant is known as the acceleration of gravity, and is commonly denoted by the symbol g. Within the atmosphere, then, the force of gravity is towards the earth's surface, and its magnitude is given by the simpler relationship $F = mg$. The value of g is about 9.8 m/sec^2 in MKS units.[17]

Additionally, the ranges of kinetic energy weapons within the atmosphere are much less than the radius or circumference of the earth. Artillery rounds, for example, might have ranges of 30 km or so, and the employment of rifle rounds is limited to the user's visual range or less. Over distances this short, the curvature of the earth is not an important factor. Figure 2–8 illustrates that in propagating a distance z along a horizontal path, the earth's surface drops by a distance $d = R_e - (R_e^2 - z^2)^{1/2}$. Over a 100 km range, this distance is less than a kilometer. Therefore, the drop-off d can usually be neglected for an atmospheric projectile.

For the propagation of kinetic energy weapons in the atmosphere, then, it can be assumed to a first approximation that the force of gravity is a constant, and the curvature of the earth may be neglected. This second approximation is equivalent to assuming that the earth is flat, although of course terrain features, such as mountains or trees, could well interfere with the propagation of a kinetic energy projectile. This set of assumptions has been used for many years in *ballistics*, the study of projectile motion in the at-

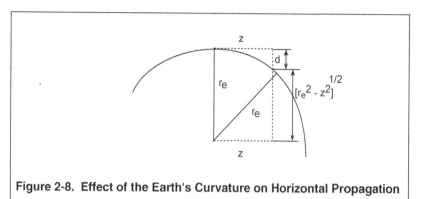

Figure 2-8. Effect of the Earth's Curvature on Horizontal Propagation

mosphere.[18] Let's first consider the motion of a projectile under these assumptions alone, neglecting any further atmospheric effects such as wind or drag.

For a projectile in motion under the constant force of gravity, Newton's law (F = ma) becomes simply mg = ma, or g = a. In other words, the projectile is accelerated towards the surface of the earth at a constant rate, g, which is independent of its mass. This says that light objects should fall as fast as heavy objects. Experience tells us that this is not so: the reason for this discrepancy is drag, or the friction between objects in motion and the air through which they pass. The refinement which drag makes to the equations of motion will be discussed next. For the moment, we'll focus on the effect of gravity alone.

The solution to Newton's law for the motion of a projectile under the influence of gravity is best understood by breaking its motion into two parts—in the downrange direction, denoted by z, and up or down in altitude, denoted by h. There is a corresponding velocity downrange, v_z, and of rising or falling, v_h. These are illustrated in Figure 2–9.

As you can see from Figure 2–9, at some point in time the projectile has propagated a distance z downstream, and is at an altitude h above the surface of the earth. The projectile's velocity, v, may be broken up into two components: v_z, the rate at which z is increasing, and v_h, the rate at which h is increasing or decreasing. When v_h is positive, the projectile is rising, and when it's negative, the projectile is falling.

The solutions to Newton's law for v_h, v_z, h, and z when a projectile is acted upon by the force of gravity are as follows:

$$v_h = v_{oh} - gt$$
$$v_z = v_{oz}$$
$$h = v_{oh}t - gt^2/2$$
$$z = v_{oz}t$$

In these equations v_{oh} and v_{oz} are the projectile's initial velocities in the h and z directions, respectively. Since gravity acts only to pull the projectile towards the surface of the earth, it does not affect v_z, and the projectile moves downrange at a constant velocity, with z growing linearly in time. On the other hand, v_h is steadily decreasing in time, due to the force of gravity, and eventually becomes negative, so that the projectile falls. The range of the projectile can be found by solving the expression for h for the time t_o at which h = 0 and the projectile strikes the earth. This time can then be inserted into the equation for z to see how far downrange, z_r, the projectile will have gone when it strikes the earth. The result of this procedure is that $t_o = 2 v_{oh}/g$, and $z_r = 2 v_{oh} v_{oz}/g$.

The initial velocity components (v_{oh}, v_{oz}) given to the projectile are crucial in determining its range—the greater they are, the further the particle will go. From a practical standpoint, v_{oh} and v_{oz}

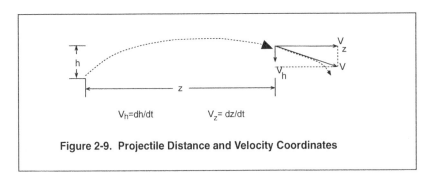

Figure 2-9. Projectile Distance and Velocity Coordinates

are not independent. The device which launches the projectile will give it some total velocity, such as the muzzle velocity of a bullet emerging from a rifle. This velocity is then apportioned between v_{oh} and v_{oz} by setting the elevation angle of the launcher. As shown in Figure 2–10, a given elevation angle ϕ produces velocity components $v_{oh} = v \sin\phi$ and $v_{oz} = v \cos \phi$. In the extreme case where $\phi = 90°$, the projectile goes straight up and comes back down at the point of launch: when $\phi = 0°$, the projectile strikes the ground almost immediately, and similarly has no range. The maximum range is achieved when $\phi = 45°$, and $v_{oh} = v_{oz} = 0.707\ v$. Figure 2–11 is a plot of range as a function of elevation angle.

In summary, if gravity alone were to act on a projectile fired near the surface of the earth, its range would be determined solely by the velocity imparted to it and by the elevation angle with which it was launched. The shape and mass of the projectile do not enter into the analysis, and do not affect its propagtion.

Drag Forces

Many of the results from the previous section make sense—our everyday experience tells us that if we throw a stone faster it will

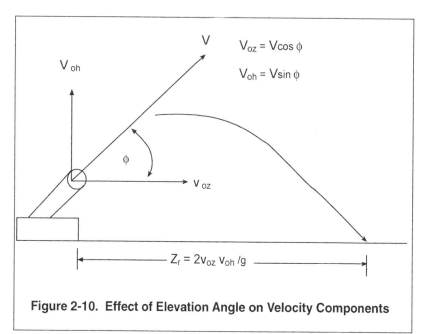

Figure 2-10. Effect of Elevation Angle on Velocity Components

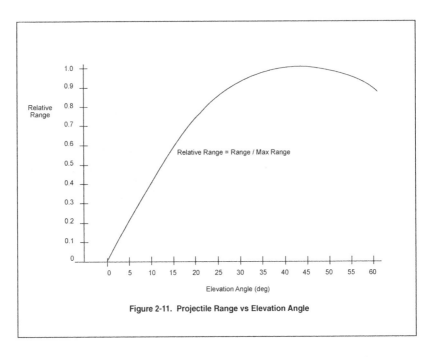

Figure 2-11. Projectile Range vs Elevation Angle

go farther, and that if it is thrown with some elevation between 0° and 90°, it will go farther than it will at either of these extremes. Other results are at odds with our experience. A massive rock will propagate farther than a light styrofoam ball of the same shape, and an aerodynamically shaped projectile will go farther than poorly shaped one of the same mass. Clearly, propagation in the atmosphere means more than propagation under gravity with assumptions appropriate to being near the surface of the earth. As a projectile moves through the atmosphere, it must push aside the air through which it passes. This results in a force on the projectile which is known as *drag*. Drag acts in a direction opposite to that of the projectile's motion, as shown in Figure 2–12.

Unlike gravity, which always pulls towards the surface of the earth, drag opposes the projectile's motion through the air, and is directed opposite to its velocity. Therefore, drag forces have a component both downrange and in altitude. When a progectile is rising, drag slows its ascent. When it is falling, drag slows its rate of fall. And in the downrange direction, drag lowers a projectile's velocity and reduces its range.

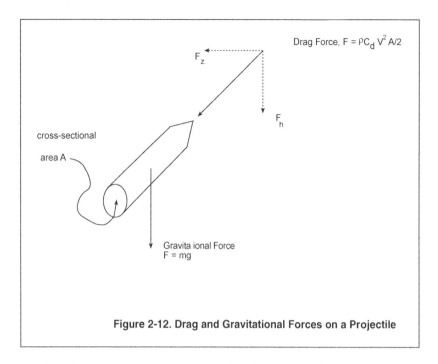

Figure 2-12. Drag and Gravitational Forces on a Projectile

What factors affect the magnitude of the drag force? The cross-sectional area A that the projectile presents to the air through which it passes will be important. The greater this area, the more air must be pushed aside as the projectile propagates, and the greater the drag. This principle is employed in parachutes, which open to a large cross-sectional area, increasing drag and slowing the descent of a falling body. The density of the atmosphere, ρ, will also be important. The lower ρ becomes, the less air must be pushed aside, and the lower drag should be. This effect is taken advantage of by long distance aircraft, which prefer to operate at high altitudes, where the density of the air and drag are less, improving fuel efficiency.

The speed of the projectile will be important, since one which is moving rapidly will encounter more air in a given amount of time. Finally, the shape of the projectile will be important. One which is streamlined can slip through the air with less drag than one which presents a flat surface on its forward edge. All of these common-sense features are embodied in the expression for the drag force: $F_d = C_d A \rho v^2 / 2$. In this expression, A is the area of the projectile as viewed end-on, ρ is the density of the air through which it travels, and v is its velocity. The combination of parameters $\rho v^2/2$ has a simple physical interpretation as the average kinetic energy density represented by the air molecules which are, from the projectile's point of view, rushing forward to meet it. Physically, this kinetic energy density is the pressure which a flat plate would feel if it were rushing through the air with velocity v. When multiplied by the cross-sectional area A, the total drag force felt by such a flat plate results. The *drag coefficient*, C_d, is a measure of how much better a given projectile is than a flat plate from the standpoint of its shape reducing drag.

In the presence of atmospheric drag, Newton's Law (F = ma) leads to the following equations which need to be solved for the velocity and position of the projectile, both downrange and in altitude:

$$m \, dv_h/dt = -mg - C_d \, A \, \rho \, v \, v_h/2$$

$$m \, dv_z/dt = -C_d \, A \, \rho \, v \, v_z/2$$

In these coupled equations, v is the projectile's total velocity, $(v_z^2 + v_h^2)^{1/2}$. There is no general solution to these equations, since they depend on parameters which vary with the environment (ρ), the shape of the projectile (C_d, A), its mass, and flight profile. Nevertheless, a few general conclusions are immediately apparent. Most importantly, the mass of the projectile is now a big player in its trajectory. Dividing the equations of motion through by m, you can see that the magnitude of the drag term relative to the gravitational term depends upon $C_d \, A/m$, and can be reduced if m can be increased while the other factors are held constant. For projectiles of a similar shape and material, A and m will rise in proportion to one another—an increase in mass will be accompanied by a corresponding increase in size and cross-sectional area. The only way to reduce the ratio of A to m is to go to materials of high density, where a large amount of mass occupies a relatively small volume. This is one reason why high density materials, such as lead or depleted uranium, are favored for kinetic energy projectiles.

Other than reducing the ratio of A to m through the use of high density materials, the only way to reduce the effect of drag is to lower the drag coefficient, C_d. The drag coefficient is a function both of the shape of the projectile and its velocity. Some of the factors which affect C_d are illustrated in Figure 2–13.[19] The lines in the figure indicate what happens to the air as the projectile passes through it. First of all, the air which is ahead of the projectile must be pushed aside. In a sense, the projectile acts like a piston as it rushes through the air. This compresses the air directly ahead of the projectile, and the work expended in doing so is reflected in drag. A longer, sharper tip will reduce the amount of drag which results from compression of the air ahead of the projectile.

After a projectile has pushed the air aside, it must pass through it. There will be a contribution to drag from the friction of the air which passes along the surface of the projectile. The contribution of this "skin friction" to drag will be greater as the surface area of the projectile increases, and is therefore of less importance for things like rifle or artillery rounds, than for larger objects such as rockets.

Finally, after a projectile has passed through a given region of space, the air must return to fill in the hole left by its passage. This results in a region of turbulence behind the projectile. In this region, the air does not flow smoothly, but collapses back in a series of eddies, just as a ship leaves a turbulent wake behind in the water. Just as with ships, this *base drag* can be reduced by shaping the trailing edge of the projectile, so that it doesn't end as abruptly as the one illustrated in Figure 2–13.

The expression for the drag force, $F_d = C_d \, A \, \rho v^2 / 2$, appears to suggest that C_d is independent of the projectile's velocity, v. This

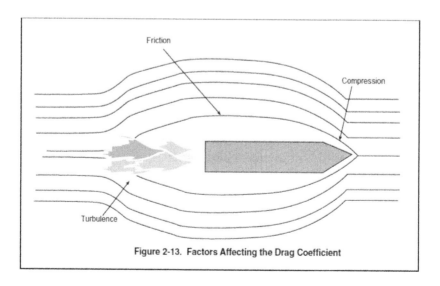

Figure 2-13. Factors Affecting the Drag Coefficient

is only a rough approximation over a narrow range of velocities. The drag coefficient is a function of velocity, and becomes much greater as a projectile's velocity exceeds the speed of sound. This is because the speed of sound is the velocity with which pressure disturbances can propagate through the atmosphere. The compression of the air ahead of the projectile creates such pressure disturbances. If the projectile is supersonic, these disturbances cannot relieve themselves by moving out ahead of it, but must pass to the side. This results in the generation of strong shock waves, along with an increase in the drag coefficient, when a projectile exceeds the speed of sound. Most modern projectiles do, in fact, exceed the speed of sound (about 0.3 km/sec). The sharp crack of a rifle bullet is the "sonic boom" which results from the shock waves generated by its passage. The energy carried by these shock waves is reflected in a loss, through drag, from the kinetic energy of the bullet. Figure 2–14 is a plot of the drag coefficient as a function of velocity for two different shapes of projectile. You can see the increase in C_d which accompanies passage through the speed of sound, as well as the effect of different shapes in changing the amount of drag, particularly at supersonic speeds.[20]

Because drag and its effect on propagation depends on a projectile's mass, shape, and velocity, the form a kinetic energy projectile takes will depend upon its projected mission. A shape which is optimal for propagation over a given range may not be optimal for acceleration in the projectile launcher, and a shape which is optimal for acceleration or propagation may not be optimal from the standpoint of delivering kinetic energy to a target. For example, the ball shaped projectile shown in Figure 2–14 has a lower drag coefficient at supersonic velocities than the bullet shaped projectile, yet cannon balls have long been abandoned as kinetic energy weapons, since the bullet shape seals better within the barrel of a gun, and is more effectively accelerated by a given amount of propellant. We'll have more to say about these tradeoffs later in the chapter. For the moment, it's sufficient to note that drag can have a significant effect on the propagation of a projectile in the atmosphere.

Newton's laws for the motion of a projectile under the influence of both gravity and atmospheric drag may be solved quantitatively through numerical integration on a computer. From a qualitative standpoint, drag has the effect of reducing both the maximum altitude and the range achieved by a projectile. Figure 2–15 is a plot of

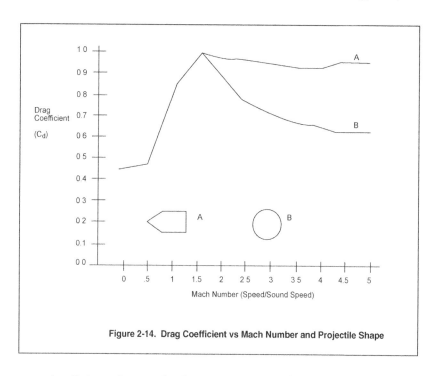

Figure 2-14. Drag Coefficient vs Mach Number and Projectile Shape

a projectile's trajectory both in vacuum and in air under the assumption of two different drag coefficients, and Table 2–2 contrasts the maximum range for two types of kinetic energy projectile in air with what their range would be if there were no atmospheric drag.

Other Forces

To this point we have looked at the roles that gravity and drag play in the propagation of a kinetic energy projectile in the atmosphere. While these are the forces that determine the gross features of a projectile's trajectory, there are other forces as well. One of the most important of these is the force resulting from any cross-wind, or air motion perpendicular to the projectile's path.

Drag results from the pressure exerted by the wind which results from the relative motion between the projectile and the air. Any naturally occurring wind will also exert a pressure on a projectile. Since the natural wind is not necessarily parallel to a projectile's path, there will be a force tending to deflect it from its aimpoint. This force will be less than that of drag, since typical wind velocities are much less than the velocities with which kinetic energy

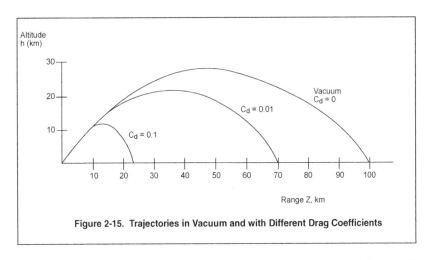

Figure 2-15. Trajectories in Vacuum and with Different Drag Coefficients

Type of Projectile	Max Range in Air	Max Range in Vacuum
300 mm Morter	11 km	16 km
7 62mm Rifle	4 km	70 km

Table 2-2. Effect of Drag on Projectile Range [21]

weapons propagate. Nevertheless, it does not take too great a deviation from the desired path for a kinetic energy round to miss its target. Consider, for example, the mortar round listed in Table 2–1. It has a muzzle velocity on the order of 400 m/sec, and drag in the forward direction shortens its range by about 5 km. Suppose there is a cross wind of about 10 km/hr (6.2 mi/hr or 3 m/sec).

Since this wind speed is about 0.008 of the wind speed resulting from forward motion, an initial guess at the sideways deflection would be about 0.008 × 5 km, or 40 meters (about 120 ft). deflection of this magnitude could easily cause the mortar to miss its target, and would have to be accounted for in directing the weapon's fire. Of course, a precise prediction of the deflection would have to account for the fact that the cross section of the round as viewed from the side is greater than that viewed from the front, the wind velocity may vary from point to point along the projectile's trajectory, and the effective "drag coefficient" at velocities characteristic of natural winds will be different from that at typical muzzle velocities. Therefore, from a practical standpoint, wind forces require that aiming be done on a "shoot-look-shoot" basis, with rounds initially fired according to theory, and adjustments then made based on impact point observations.

Additional forces result from the rotation of the earth. Newton's law (F = ma) assumes that the forces and accelerations are measured against a set of fixed coordinates, not moving in space. Yet the earth is spinning from west to east, and a projectile launched to the east has a greater velocity than one launched to the west. The motion of the earth adds an effective force to the equations of motion for a projectile which varies with the latitude of the launcher, as well as the bearing along which projectile is fired. Weapons whose sights have been adjusted for operation in the northern hemisphere will miss their targets in the southern hemisphere, simply because some of these rotational forces differ in sign above and below the equator.[22]

Instabilities

To this point, we have treated the propagation of a projectile as though it were a single point in space of mass m, accelerated according to Newton's law by various forces. However, a real projectile has a finite shape. The interaction of this shape with the air can cause it to become unstable, tumbling so that drag is much increased and propagation prevented. How this can happen is illustrated in Figure 2–16. The single point on a projectile which follows the trajectory predicted by Newton's law is known as the center of mass. Suppose the projectile is not pointed directly along the trajectory, but has some angle relative to it, as illustrated in the figure.

Since the projectile is moving in the air, there is an effective wind on it. As shown in the top part of the figure, this wind causes a pressure on the projectile. In the average, this pressure results in drag. Looking more closely, you can see that if the projectile has some angle relative to its direction of propagation, pressure above the center of mass will tend to flip the projectile over, while pressure below the center of mass will tend to straighten it out. An instability will occur if the pressure above the center of mass exceeds the pressure below the center of mass, and the projectile flips over.

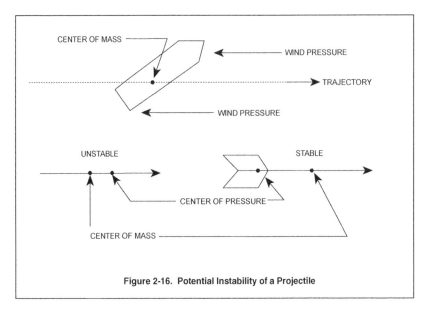

Figure 2-16. Potential Instability of a Projectile

In tumbling, aerodynamic stream-lining is lost, drag increases by orders of magnitude, and useful propagation ceases.

In more technical terms, the average point at which wind pressure appears to be applied is known as the center of pressure, and if the center of pressure is ahead of the center of mass the projectile will be unstable, while if it is behind the center of mass it will be stable.[23] The bottom portion of the figure illustrates two projectiles. The first is unstable, since the broad head on the projectile represents a large area over which pressure can be applied ahead of the center of mass. The second is stable, since a larger, counterbalancing area has been added to the rear of the projectile. This is why arrows have feathers on their trailing edge.

In some cases "feathers," in the form of fins, are still employed for stability on projectiles such as rockets or bombs. For gun launched projectiles, this approach is not practical since fins would prevent the seal between the projectile and gun barrel which is necessary for the detonating charge to accelerate the round. Early guns used balls as projectiles, since they are absolutely stable, with their center of pressure and center of mass at the same point regardless of orientation. In the search for greater range, however, a better seal within the barrel is required, and this demands that the rear of the projectile be flat. Reduction of drag demands that the front be pointed. In consequence, most of the mass in a modern projectile is toward its rear, and it is very easy for the center of mass to lie behind the center of pressure, causing an instability. This problem has been overcome by spinning the projectile, which imparts gyroscopic forces that counter the tendency to tumble, just as a spinning top resists the efforts of gravity to tumble over on its side.

Gyroscopic stabilization is not without penalty, however. Some of the energy which would otherwise go into the kinetic energy of the projectile must be invested in rotational energy, and the projectile shape which is best stabilized in this way may not be desirable from the standpoint of other propagation parameters. For example, short, fat tops are easier to stabilize than long, skinny ones. Yet a short, fat projectile would have a large cross sectional area and a large drag force. Accordingly, the design of kinetic energy rounds results from tradeoffs among competing factors which affect range, stability, and even, as we'll see later, target interaction.

Summary: Propagation in the Atmosphere

1. Gravity and drag are the main forces which affect the propagation of a projectile in the atmosphere. Because propagation in the atmosphere means that a projectile is near the earth's surface, gravitational forces may normally be considered constant and directed downward at a flat earth. Drag opposes the forward motion of a projectile, and is proportional to its area as viewed from the front, the density of the air, and the square of its velocity.

2. In the absence of drag, a projectile will have its maximum range when launched at an elevation of 45°. Drag reduces both the range and altitude achieved by a projectile launched at a given elevation angle.

3. The constant of proportionality between the drag on a flat plate and that on a given projectile is known as the drag coefficient. It measures how well streamlining has reduced the pressure of the air on the front of the projectile. The drag coefficient is generally greater for projectiles moving at supersonic speeds.

4. Other factors which affect propagation in the atmosphere include winds, which blow a projectile off course, and the rotation

of the earth, which imparts latitude and azimuth dependent forces to it.

5. Projectiles will be unstable, and tumble in flight, if their center of pressure lies ahead of their center of gravity. The design of a projectile for atmospheric use must include stability-enhancing features, such as tail fins or spinning. These features may detract from other desirable attributes for the projectile.

Implications

The propagation of kinetic energy weapons in the atmosphere is much more complex than in a vacuum, where the rules of the game are well known and can be accounted for ahead of time in sending a projectile to its target. Propagation in the atmosphere is upset by random factors, such as wind, which can't be accounted for ahead of time. The shape of a projectile intended for atmospheric use may not be ideal from the standpoint of target interaction, and energy may be "wasted" to insure propagation through spinning the projectile or overcoming drag.

These general features will be seen throughout this book. Propagation in a vacuum for kinetic energy weapons, lasers, microwaves, and particle beams proceeds by well defined and understood physical laws. In the atmosphere, additional effects come into play which make putting energy on a target much more difficult. It is unfortunate that we and most of the targets we'd care to engage exist within the atmosphere. Only in recent years has the technology existed to place objects in space, making the question of propagation in a vacuum of more than academic interest.

Interaction with Targets

Important Parameters

After its propagation either through space or the atmosphere, a kinetic energy projectile will (hopefully) strike its target. At this point, we hope that a significant amount of the projectile's kinetic energy will be transferred to the target, damaging it. What are some of the factors which will affect the probability of exceeding the threshold for damage?

Pressure and Impulse. Pressure is the force applied per unit area as the projectile strikes the target, and impulse is the integral of force over time (roughly speaking, the force applied multiplied by the time for which it is applied). High pressure and high impulse will be more effective in damaging targets than low pressures or impulses. How much pressure and impulse a round delivers to a target will depend upon its kinetic energy, shape, and the material of which it is made. For example, a very skinny or sharply pointed projectile will apply high pressures to the the point of impact, since its forces will be concentrated over a very small area. A projectile made of a soft, deformable material such as lead may deliver a greater impulse than a very rigid one, which could strike and bounce off the target in a short period of time.

Angle of Attack. A glancing blow will be less effective than one which is head-on. Therefore, the angle with which the projectile strikes the target is important in determining the response of both projectile and target. As Figure 2–17 illustrates, a projectile may ricochet and have little effect at a high angle of attack, yet penetrate the target and cause severe damage at a low angle of attack.

Target Material and Shape. The material and shape of a projectile will affect the pressure and impulse it delivers; the material and shape of a target will affect its response. Some materials are softer than others, and targets can be protected by covering them with a material (armor) that is very hard and resistant to damage. Table 2–3, for example, shows the amount of kinetic energy re-

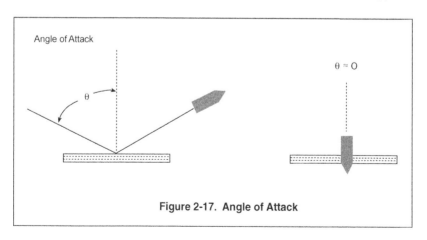

Figure 2-17. Angle of Attack

Target Type	Energy for Penetration (Joules)
Unprotected Man	80
23 cm Timber	200
Very light armor	770
0.5 cm concrete	1500
1.2 cm brick	3000

Table 2.3. Kinetic Energy Required for 7.62 mm Projectiles to Penetrate Targets [24]

quired for a given projectile (a standard 7.62 mm NATO rifle round) to penetrate different materials of varying thickness.

Proper shaping of a target can affect the angle of attack with which a round is likely to strike. Thus, armored objects are made very smooth and rounded, increasing the probability of a large angle of attack. There is little chance of a round striking head-on to a flat surface if the target is properly shaped.

What is Damage?

Recognizing that various parameters will affect damage, how can we determine the optimal combination of these parameters to achieve a given level of damage? First of all, we need to recognize that a wide variety of effects are possible when a projectile strikes a target, all of which might be adequate for damage. Some of these possible effects are illustrated in Figure 2–18.

A projectile may simply tear the target material, pushing it aside and penetrating the surface, as illustrated on the left hand side of the figure, or, it may shatter the target material so that both projectile and target fragments emerge from the rear surface, as illustrated in the center. It's even possible that while the projectile may not penetrate the target, shock waves will propagate through the target and throw flakes of material off of the back surface, as illustrated on the right hand side of the figure. This is known as spallation, and can damage a target even in cases where its surface is not penetrated.

From a military standpoint, all three of the outcomes illustrated in Figure 2–18 may be equally effective in damaging or

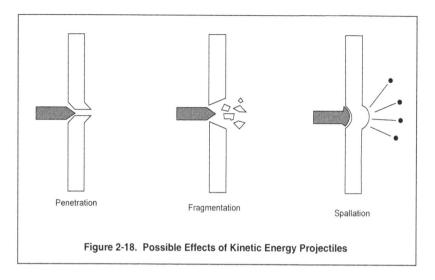

Penetration

Fragmentation

Spallation

Figure 2-18. Possible Effects of Kinetic Energy Projectiles

negating a target. Yet the criteria for achieving them might be quite different, and scale differently with the shape, energy, and other parameters of the projectile. Thus, damage criteria can be more of an art than a science. There is more than one way to achieve a given end. As a result, there is a danger that in optimizing a projectile for a specific type of damage, a solution may be found which is not optimal when other damage mechanisms are considered. In addition, the entire range of issues related to projectile acceleration, propagation, and target destruction must be considered in weapon design.

Figure 2–18 shows just a small sample of the wide range of phenomena that can occur when a projectile strikes a target. Typically, what will happen depends upon the kinetic energy of the projectile, the material and shape it has, and the material and thickness of the target. Predicting what will happen is a complex problem in predicting the response of a solid to a time varying pressure and impulse. Since exact predictions of damage are highly dependent on the type of target and what it's made of, the most we can attempt to do in this book is look at some of the general principles and orders of magnitude involved.

General Principles

The solid material which a projectile strikes differs from the atmosphere in having an internal structure and resistance to any change in the configuration of its atoms or molecules. In a gas, molecules are free to wander about at will, and have no significant interaction with one another. In a solid, on the other hand, molecules are so close that they are bound to one another. The forces which bind them can be thought of simplistically as represented by the springs shown in Figure 2–19.These springs have some equilibrium length, as well as some inherent stiffness, or resistance to stretching or squeezing. As a result, a solid resists either compression, an attempt to squeeze it into a smaller volume, or tension, an attempt to stretch it out. In general, the length of the springs and their stiffness may be different in different directions, so that the response of a material may depend on how forces are oriented relative to the arrangement of atoms within it. Forces applied to a solid are referred to as *stress*. Under stress, the springs in a solid will be compressed or stretched, and its volume will change slightly. The change in volume of a solid under stress is known as *strain*.

If stresses are sufficiently low, the strain is proportional to the stress, just as the length of a spring is proportional to the force applied to it. Under these conditions, the response of the material is said to be *elastic*. However, if the stresses become too great, the material can become permanently deformed, just as a spring which is stretched beyond its *elastic limit* will be permanently deformed. When this happens, strain is no longer proportional to stress, the response of the material is said to be *plastic*. Finally,

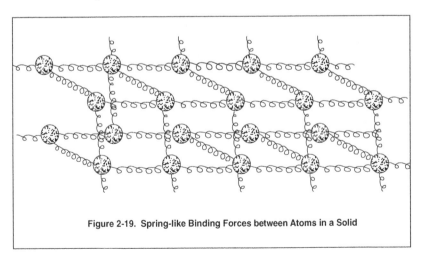

Figure 2-19. Spring-like Binding Forces between Atoms in a Solid

if extreme stresses are applied to a solid, the springs or bonds between the atoms can actually be broken, and the atoms will be free to move around at will under the influence of these forces, just as a gas would. At this point, the response of a solid is no different from that of a gas.

Dimensionally, the stress in a solid is the force applied per unit area at a point, and has the same dimensions as pressure. Strain is the fractional change in volume, $\Delta V/V$, resulting from a given stress, and is dimensionless. Mathematically, the relationship between stress and strain is of the form $P = Ce$, where P is the applied stress, e is the strain, and C is a constant of proportionality known as the *stiffness coefficient*, which has the dimensions of a pressure. It is important to note that while the pressure in a gas can only be positive, the stress in a solid can be either negative (compression) or positive (tension).[25]

Since $P = Ce$, the fractional change in dimension induced by a given stress on a solid will be small as long as P << C. The fractional change will be large, with the likelihood that the elastic limit will be exceeded, when P becomes comparable to C. If P is much greater than C, the strength of the bonds holding the atoms together in a solid are almost irrelevant, and the solid will respond as a gas. Therefore, the first step in analyzing the response of a target to a kinetic energy projectile is to compare the stresses or pressures anticipated when the projectile strikes the target with the stiffness coefficients that characterize the target material. Table 2–4 provides stiffness coefficients for some common metals at room temperature. The data in the table reflect

Material	Stiffness Coefficients, C_{11} (at 300°K) ($\times 10^{11}$ Nt/m^2 or J/n^3)
Tungsten	5.233
Copper	1.684
Aluminum	1.068
Lead	0.495

Table 2.4. Stiffness Coefficients of Common Metals [26]

63

what we already know from experience—that lead is a relatively soft material, easy to deform, for example, with the stresses that might be applied by a hammer. And tungsten, a stiff, brittle material, finds much of its application in the high temperature, aerospace environment.

In contrast with the stiffness coefficients in Table 2–4, atmospheric pressure is only about 10^5 Nt/m^2. Therefore, pressures in excess of about 10^6 atmospheres are required to make a solid respond like a gas to the impact of a projectile. How much pressure is expected from the impact of a projectile? You may recall that the drag pressure felt by a projectile traveling through an atmosphere of density ρ is on the order af $\rho v^2/2$—the kinetic energy density of the air rushing to meet the projectile. In a similar manner, if a target sees a projectile of density ρ_o and velocity V rushing at it, we'd expect it to feel a pressure on impact of order $\rho_o v^2/2$. This estimate of pressure on impact is shown in Figure 2–20 as a function of projectile velocity for projectiles of density 11.6 and 2.7 gm/cm^3 (lead and aluminum, respectively).

Figure 2–20 shows that pressures in excess of typical stiffness coefficients will be generated when projectile velocities exceed something on the order of 5–10,000 m/sec. For purposes of comparison, the speed of sound is about 300 m/sec, the muzzle velocities of small arms are about 1000 m/sec, and the speed of objects in low earth orbit is about 8000 m/sec. Therefore, you can see that kinetic energy weapons in space are likely to induce high pressures on targets. At these pressures, targets respond like a high-density gas, their internal binding energies being negligible, at least initially. Kinetic energy weapons in the atmosphere, on the other hand, will create stresses within targets that lead to a plastic or elastic response.

Damage in Space—Hypervelocity Impacts

Impacts of projectiles with targets at velocities well in excess of the speed of sound are known as "hypervelocity" impacts. The target's binding energies can initially be neglected, and it responds as a compressible fluid (gas). The binding energies of the projectile are comparable to those of the target, so it, too, behaves like a fluid on impact, and target and projectile material intermingle. The target's initial response is similar to the impact of a drop of water on

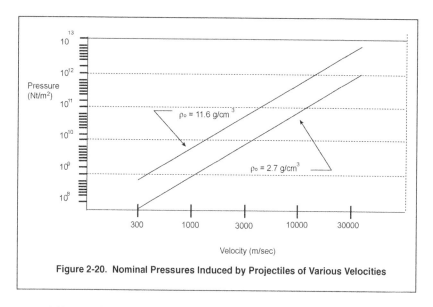

Pressure (Nt/m²)

$\rho_0 = 11.6 \text{ g/cm}^3$

$\rho_0 = 2.7 \text{ g/cm}^3$

Velocity (m/sec)

Figure 2-20. Nominal Pressures Induced by Projectiles of Various Velocities

a puddle, as shown in Figure 2–21. This figure shows the sequence of events when an aluminum sphere strikes an aluminum target at a velocity of about 7000 m/sec. The projectile is severely deformed in striking the target, and at late times the distinction between projectile and target material has disappeared.

If the projectile and target were indeed fluid and not solid, the disruption caused by the impact would go away, just as the crater formed when a stone strikes the surface of a pond fills in. However, in a solid, target material resolidifies in whatever configuration it finds itself at the time when externally applied stresses become small compared to the internal stiffness constants. In this way, the impact shown in Figure 2–21 would leave a crater in the target, whose appearance would be roughly like the last of the four shown in sequence.

Beyond the crater shown in Figure 2–21, there is a region of plastic deformation, where the density of the material might be permanently altered, and beyond that a region into which elastic waves will propagate. These waves, which are analogous to sound waves in air, can be quite intense, and if the rear surface of the target is not too far away they can cause spallation, as they reflect off the rear and head back towards the front surface. This is because at the surface of a target its strength is less than on the interior, since molecules on the surface have no molecules beyond

65

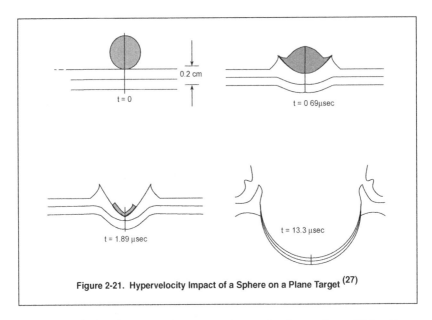

0.2 cm

t = 0

t = 0 69μsec

t = 1.89 μsec

t = 13.3 μsec

Figure 2-21. Hypervelocity Impact of a Sphere on a Plane Target [27]

them to inhibit their motion away from the boundary. This situation is somewhat analogous to a whip. A wave started at the handle of the whip can cause its tip to move supersonically, creating the characteristic crack of a "sonic boom," as it reflects at the tip and heads back towards the handle.

The depth of the crater in Figure 2–21 is a measure of the penetrating power of the spherical projectile. If the target's surface were thinner than this crater, the projectile would penetrate, and a spray of projectile and target material would fly into the target's interior. It is these secondary projectiles which would likely cause militarily significant damage, since the surface of most targets merely covers and protects important components which lie on the interior. It would be of value to have a way of predicting the requirements for a projectile to penetrate a target of a given material and thickness. For hypervelocity impacts, it's easy to develop empirical formulas to relate projectile parameters to crater depth. This is because the energies are so great, and the projectile so severely deformed, that its initial shape is not an important factor in the process. Rather, the projectile can be modeled simply as a source of momentum and energy deposited on the target's surface.[28]

How can we develop an expression to correlate projectile parameters with target damage? The procedure is analogous to that employed for nuclear weapons and other explosives. In essence, an explosion represents the release of a large amount of energy in a small amount of space. Since the energy is released in a volume which is small compared to the range of the anticipated effects, the explosion may be treated as a point source of energy. The effect of an explosion is overpressure—strong shock waves which travel out from the source of an explosion, damaging objects which they encounter. Pressure is force per unit area, or energy per unit volume. Therefore, if the shock wave from an explosion has traveled outward a distance r, the overpressure at that distance should be approximately $E/(4\pi r^3/3)$, where E is the energy released by the explosion, and $4\pi r^3/3$ is the volume of a sphere of radius r. If a given target is destroyed by an over- pressure P, this relationship can be solved for the range to which such a target could be destroyed: $r = (3E/4\pi P)^{1/3}$. This result, that the range of the effects from an explosive scales as the cube root of the energy released, is well established as a method of estimating the destructive power of nuclear weapons.[29]

In an analogous way, we might imagine that the range of some effect (such as crater size) from a projectile will scale with the kinetic energy it carries. A projectile whose characteristic size is L has a volume on the order of L^3, and a mass on the order of ρL^3, where ρ is the density of the projectile material. If the projectile has velocity V, its kinetic energy, $MV^2/2$, will be on the order of $\rho L^3 V^2/2$. Thinking that the kinetic energy (K) is the primary factor responsible for the creation of a crater of depth D (and volume on the order of D^3), it would be reasonable to suppose that $D^3=bK$, where b is an appropriate constant of proportionality. This reasoning leads to the conclusion that D^3 is proportional to $\rho L^3 V^2$, or that D/L is proportional to $\rho^{1/3} V^{2/3}$. Alternatively, if we were to believe that the primary factor responsible for a crater of depth D was not the energy of the projectile, but rather its momentum ($\approx \rho L^3 V$), we would conclude that D/L should be proportional to $\rho^{1/3} V^{1/3}$. In either case, if we believe that crater depth is determined by projectile mass times some power of its velocity, we conclude that the ratio of crater depth to projectile size, D/L, should vary as the cube root of the projectile's density multiplied by some power of its velocity.

Such a relationship has been demonstrated through "numerical experiments," in which detailed computer calculations were made of a target's response to projectiles of different density, shape, size, and velocity.[30] These showed that if the projectile kinetic energy density $\rho V^2/2$ exceeds about four times the target's stiffness constants, the ratio of crater depth to projectile size, D/L, scales as $\rho^{1/3} V^{0.58}$. The scaling with velocity is somewhat less than the 2/3 power that results from scaling with energy, and greater than the 1/3 power that results from scaling with momentum. This suggests that both energy and momentum are factors in the response of a target to the impact from a hypervelocity projectile. Figure 2–22 is an approximate plot of D/L as a function of V. The figure assumes that scaling with $V^{0.58}$ is valid, and that the projectile density is the same as that of the aluminum target. The curve in the figure may be scaled as $(\rho/\rho_t)^{1/3}$ to cases where the projectile density, ρ, differs from that of the target, ρ_t.

Figure 2–22 may be used to estimate the projectile size necessary to penetrate a target of a given thickness at a given velocity. Suppose that we need to penetrate a 1 cm target with a projectile whose velocity is 10 km/sec. From Figure 2–22, D/L is about 6 at this speed, so that the projectile size must be $L \approx D/G = 0.17$ cm. You can see from this example that even small debris in space can damage satellites at the velocities characteristic of earth orbit.

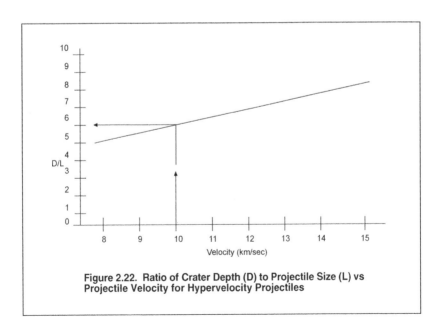

Figure 2.22. Ratio of Crater Depth (D) to Projectile Size (L) vs Projectile Velocity for Hypervelocity Projectiles

It is interesting to compare the kinetic energies of the projectiles responsible for the craters in Figure 2–22 with an all-purpose damage criterion of 10,000 Joules (see Chapter 1). Figure 2–23 is a plot of the kinetic energy required per centimeter of crater depth as a function of projectile velocity, assuming that the projectile has a characteristic size, L, of 1 centimeter. As the figure demonstrates, the "all-purpose criterion" is a pretty good guess of the energy required for a hypervelocity projectile to place a cm–radius hole in a cm–thick target.[31]

Damage in the Atmosphere—Lower Velocity Impacts

You will recall from Table 2–4 and Figure 2–20 that when the velocity of a projectile falls below about 5,000 m/sec, the pressure it exerts as it impacts a target will fall below the target's stiffness coefficients. In this velocity range, which is characteristic of projectiles fired within the atmosphere, the energy and momentum of the projectile are no longer sufficient to determine the target's response. Rather, the material, shape, and angle of attack of the projectile, along with specific details of the target's construction, become much more important in establishing the target's response. It is therefore more difficult to establish general rules and scaling relationships for target response in this case than for hypervelocity

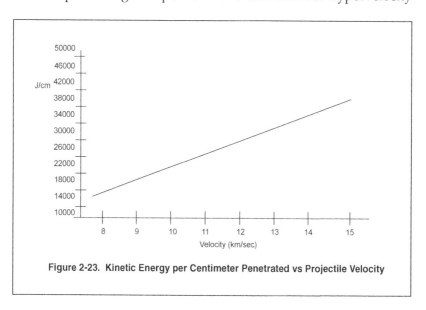

Figure 2-23. Kinetic Energy per Centimeter Penetrated vs Projectile Velocity

impacts. Figure 2–24 presents a simplified picture of some of the factors which need to be accounted for when a lower-velocity projectile strikes a target and attempts to penetrate it.

Figure 2–24 shows a plate of thickness h, supported by a structural member of diameter D. This plate is struck at its center by a projectile of diameter d and length l, which bends the plate inward a distance x. Obviously, this produces a strain P in the plate. The strain is a tensile one, which tries to pull the plate apart. The direction of this strain is along the thickness of the plate, at an angle θ to the plate's original, flat orientation. Therefore, the component of strain in the upward direction, resisting the motion of the projectile, is $P \sin \theta \approx P\, 2x/D$.[32] The total force which the projectile feels is this strain (force/area) multiplied by the area over which the tension is applied. This area is that of the cylindrical plug under the projectile, πdh. Therefore, the force on the projectile is $P(2x/D)\pi dh$.

As the projectile interacts with the plate, x and P increase. At some point, P exceeds a critical value P^* at which the plate will rupture. P^* is known as the *modulus of rupture*, and can be found tabulated for different materials in engineering handbooks.[33] The work (Joules) which the projectile expends to

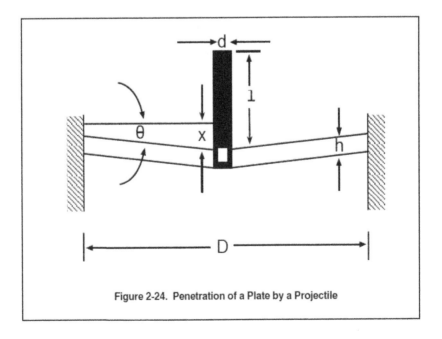

Figure 2-24. Penetration of a Plate by a Projectile

rupture the plate is the integral of force over distance[34], or roughly W = $P^*(2x_c^2/D)$ πdh, where x_c is the value of x at which the plate ruptures. This work must be done at the expense of the projectile's kinetic energy K, so that a criterion for the projectile to penetrate the plate is K=$P^*(2x_c^2/D)$πdh.

The only unknown in this expression is the distance x_c. It can be shown that $e^* \approx 2x_c^2/D^2$, where e^* is the strain which corresponds to the stress P^*.[35] Using this result, the criterion for projectile penetration becomes K=P^*e^*πdhD, where d is the diameter (caliber) of the projectile, h the thickness of the target, and D the diameter of the structural member supporting the target plate. This implies that target penetration is easier for

• Thinner projectiles, which apply a greater pressure at the point of impact. This is another reason why pointed projectiles are preferred even if not required for purposes of drag reduction in propagation.

• Thinner targets, which have less mass to penetrate.

• Rigid targets, whose structural supports are closer together. This is because a very rigid target has less room to "give" before it is penetrated.

For aluminum, P^* is about 3×10^8 Nt/m², and e^* is about 0.15.[36] Therefore, the kinetic energy K = P^*e^*πdhD necessary for a 1 cm projectile to penetrate a 1 cm thick sheet of aluminum supported at a distance of 0.1 m is about 1400 Joules. This value is consistent with the penetration energies shown in Table 2–2, suggesting that this model for target penetration is not unrealistic, and contains the essential features of damaging targets whose response is plastic.[37] It's also interesting to note that this energy and those in Table 2–2 are about an order of magnitude less than the energies necessary for penetration by hypervelocity impact (see Figure 2–23). This is because fewer bonds between the atoms in a solid have to be broken when a projectile pushes its way through than when it must effectively vaporize a whole plug of material underneath it.

Even in the simple case just considered, plate penetration depends on details of the target's construction, such as the diameter D of the plate's support. Damage criteria are obviously more difficult to develop when penetration is through plastic deformation of the material, rather than through hypervelocity impact. The fundamental reason for this is that at slower projectile velocities, stress waves can travel from the point of impact to structural members, whose rigidity affect the target's response. In a hypervelocity impact, all of the action is over before any information about that impact can be transmitted to structural members. This transmission of information occurs at the speed of sound within the material, which is proportional to the square root of the stiffness constant. Further details of plate penetration by projectiles may be found in Reference 37.

In most cases, it's not possible to know in advance such details as the exact materials a target may be made of or how it is constructed. Even if these were known, the physical parameters these materials possess and the resulting damage criteria can only be determined through detailed experiment and analysis. Therefore, it is impractical to determine in advance the exact response of a given target to a particular type of projectile of a given kinetic energy. The most we can hope to do is use theory as a guide in scaling experimental results to projectiles of different energies and targets of different thickness or structure. The validity of this process depends upon the extrapolation not being too great. In general, different formulas are required to correlate weapon effects in different parameter regimes. The subject of projectile-target interaction is known as *terminal ballistics*. There is considerable literature on this subject to enable you to correlate and extrapolate weapon effects under different circumstances.[38]

Tradeoffs

The specific design of a kinetic energy round for use in the atmosphere will inevitably involve tradeoffs. If it is accelerated in a gun barrel, it will be accelerated to a greater velocity if it has a large base for the pressure of gases in the weapon to act on, and is short, so that its total mass and inertia are not too great. As it propagates, however, a short, squat projectile will feel a lot of drag, and lose considerable energy. Drag can be reduced with a long, pointed projectile, but such a round may be unstable and require spin or fins. Finally, when striking a target, the shape which will penetrate most effectively may not be the one which would propagate best. The design of kinetic energy projectiles must therefore take into account the total mission profile.

Modern projectile design occasionally makes use of projectiles which change their configuration during the different phases of their operation, and can be more nearly optimal throughout their flight. These designs are frequently found in armor piercing rounds, which have an inherently difficult job to accomplish. An interesting example is shown in Figure 2–25.

This projectile has features designed for each portion of its flight from tube to target. Within the barrel of the gun, the sabot (a French word, which in origin means "boot") provides a seal against the wall, and a large surface area for gases to act upon. This sabot is discarded as the projectile leaves the barrel. During flight, the fins at the rear provide stabilization and the ballistic cap on the front provides a low drag coefficient. Finally, as the round encounters the target, the ballistic cap breaks away, and the penetrating cap on the interior engages the target. The shape of the penetrating cap is optimized for target effect and damage. In ways such as this a kinetic energy weapon can be designed which is near optimal throughout its flight profile. However, energy is wasted accelerating mass which does not encounter the target, and a complex design invites problems in reliability.

Summary: Target interaction

1. Unlike propagation, which follows well understood physical laws, interaction is highly scenario dependent. The effect of a projectile striking a target will depend on such weapon parame-

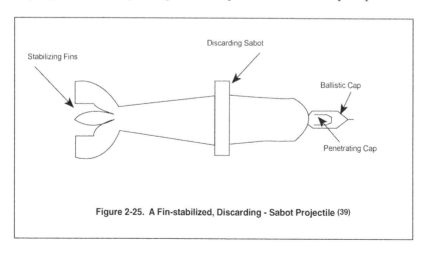

Figure 2-25. A Fin-stabilized, Discarding - Sabot Projectile (39)

ters as momentum, energy, and shape; such target parameters as material, thickness, and construction; and such scenario parameters as the angle of attack between the projectile and the target.

2. The response of a target is determined from the stress applied to it, and the resulting strain or deformation it suffers. Stress and strain are related through stiffness coefficients. When the stress is numerically much less than the stiffness coefficient, target response is elastic, with strain proportional to stress. When stress is comparable to stiffness, target response is plastic, and the target may be permanently deformed or penetrated. Finally, if stress far exceeds stiffness, a target responds as though it were a high density gas.

3. At velocities characteristic of engagements in space, projectiles produce stress far in excess of stiffness. For these hypervelocity impacts, simple scaling laws for target damage and penetration can be developed (see Figures 2–22 and 2–23). For engagements in the atmosphere, stresses are more likely to result in a plastic response. Predicting penetration under these conditions requires more detailed knowledge of projectile, target, and engagement parameters.

4. Projectile design involves tradeoffs among factors which influence acceleration, propagation, and interaction. A realistic projectile will therefore not be optimal for any one of these areas.

Implications

For engagements in space, the lack of atmospheric drag and the large velocities involved result in energies more than sufficient to cause damage. Projectile design is therefore not a critical issue in space as it is in the atmosphere. Even in the atmosphere, it is generally not advisable to optimize a weapon to defeat a specific target. In military engagements, a weapon may be employed against a variety of targets, the enemy may harden his targets, and so forth. Therefore, it is more appropriate to design a weapon to exceed estimated damage criteria throughout its useful range. What this means in practice is that our all-purpose damage criterion remains a useful estimate of the energy which a weapon must reliably place on target to achieve damage. It is interesting to note that this estimate is not too bad even for infantry weapons, which for the most part are employed against such soft targets as enemy personnel.

Chapter Summary

1. Kinetic energy weapons damage targets with their energy of motion.This energy is proportional to a projectile's mass and the square of its velocity.

2. In space, projectile motion is determined by the gravitational force of the earth, along with forces from the projectile's launcher or on board engine. Gravitational forces dominate a projectile's trajectory, and kinetic energies far exceed damage criteria. As a result, stresses in a target exceed its internal strength, and it responds like a dense gas. Details of projectile and target construction are therefore of minor importance.

3. In the atmosphere, ranges are shorter and energies less due to atmospheric drag. At these lower energies, forces internal to a target are important, and its response depends on details of construction and the engagement scenario. Projectile design for efficient propagation and interaction therefore becomes a primary concern. Optimization for propagation may conflict with optimization for target interaction, and projectile design is a compromise among competing factors.

Implications and Analogies

The finite speed of kinetic energy weapons (10 km/sec or less) means that the time to engage goes up with increasing distance, and moving targets can be engaged only if they are "led," with calculations made in advance on how to bring the weapon and target together. Therefore, considerable interest has arisen in more exotic forms of directed energy weapon, such as lasers or particle beams, in which engagement can occur at or near the speed of light. Indeed, the main focus of this book will be on these newer weapon concepts, since kinetic energy weapons have been studied for centuries and documented in many texts, both theoretical, experimental, and empirical. Nevertheless, it is worthwhile to include information on kinetic energy weapons here so that it will be apparent in later chapters that the concepts dealt with there are in essence no different than those treated here. For example, the following truths hold throughout the book:

1. Propagation in a vacuum follows well defined physical laws, which can be accounted for to insure that a weapon will place adequate energy on target. However, the long ranges associated with engagements in space place severe constraints on the energy which the weapon launcher requires to insure that lethal energies are brought to bear on the target.[40]

2. In the atmosphere, ranges are much less than in space. At the same time however, interaction with the atmosphere results in much greater energy losses. Therefore, weapon parameters (bullet shape, laser pulse width, etc) must be tailored to minimize these energy losses.

3. When the weapon encounters its target, energy must be efficiently absorbed for damage to occur. This places constraints on weapon parameters which may be at odds with those necessary for efficient propagation.

Notes and References

1. Any basic physics text will deal with the concept of kinetic energy. See, for example, Chapter 7 in David Halliday and Robert Resnick, *Physics for Students of Science* and *Engineering* (New York: John Wiley and Sons, 1962).

2. The Newton (Nt) as a unit of force is named for Sir Isaac Newton (1643–1727), whose law of acceleration, F = ma, underlies all mechanical analysis. One of the greatest physicists of all time, Newton is also remembered for the law of gravitation, for inventing calculus, and for fundamental contributions to optics. Every chapter in this book makes use of his insights and theories.

3. Vector quantities are defined by the three numbers which represent their components along three independent directions. For example, a car moving to the southeast is moving south with some speed, east with some speed, and vertically with no speed! A good discussion of vectors and the mathematics by which they are combined can be found in Chapter 2 of Halliday and Resnick (note 1).

4. Under some circumstances, deflection can be militarily adequate for "damage." For example, a missile which is diverted from its course and therefore misses its target will have been adequately damaged.

5. A man can easily exert a pressure of two pounds per square inch by pressing with his thumb on a wall. This will do no damage, but a similar pressure over whole wall will blow it in or shatter it. See Table 5.145 in Samuel Glasstone and Philip J. Dolan (eds.) *The Effects of Nuclear Weapons* (Washington, DC: U.S. Government Printing Office, 1977).

6. More precisely, impulse is the integral of force over time. See Chapter 10 in Halliday and Resnick (note 1).

7. The law of universal gravitation was developed by Newton (note 2), who in folklore, at least, was inspired by an apple falling on his head.

8. When the atmosphere becomes negligible depends to some extent on the mission under consideration. Satellites in orbit at an altitude of 200 km still feel some atmospheric drag, and, over a period of years will slow and fall to earth. For kinetic energy weapons, on the other hand, flight times are not for years, but for

hours or less, so that this effect can be neglected. A plot of atmospheric density as a function of altitude can be found in Chapter 5 (Figure 5–14).

9. Satellite motion under the influence of gravity is a special case of what is known as *central force motion*. This subject is discussed in detail in any book on mechanics, such as Jerry B. Marion, *Classical Dynamics of Particles and Systems* (New York: Academic Press, 1965). The specific results shown here may be found in Chapter 10.

10. A good discussion of how orbits are specified and the resulting paths traced over the surface of the earth may be found in Charles H. MacGregor and Lee H. Livingston (eds.), *Space Handbook*, AU–18 (Maxwell AFB, AL: Air University, 1977).

11. Strictly speaking, the distance r which appears in the law of gravitation is the distance between the centers of mass of the two objects. The center of mass is found by averaging all points within an object with the mass density at those points and their location in a coordinate system. See Marion (note 9), Chapter 3.

12. The force mv^2/r necessary to keep an object of mass m in a circular orbit at a radius r is known as a *centripetal force*. These forces are discussed in Section 6–3 of Halliday and Resnick (note 1).

13. Weight is the force which gravity exerts on an object of mass m at the surface of the earth. Since $F = GmM/r^2$, the "constant" g is GM/R_e^2, where M is the mass of the earth, and R_e its radius.

14. A good introduction to constellation sizing may be found in Appendix I of William D. Hartung, et al., *The Strategic Defense Initiative: Costs, Contractors, and Consequences* (New York: Council on Economic Priorities, 1985).

15. More recently, as increasing circuit miniaturization has permitted greater computing capability in smaller volumes, there have been proposals for "brilliant pebbles"—very small weapons which are scattered out almost like a shotgun to seek and destroy targets on their own. If these trends continue, we may some day attack objects with "genius dust!"

16. Deriving the final expression, $m/m_t = (R_e/r)^2 \, t/I_{sp}$ makes use of the definition $g = GM/R_e^2$ to eliminate g from the previous expression.

17. The constant g introduced here is the same one used in the definition of specific impulse. See note 13.

18. C. L. Farrar and D. W. Leeming, *Military Ballistics: A Basic Manual* (Oxford: Brassey's Publishers, 1983) is a good introductory text on ballistics.

19. The factors affecting drag are discussed in detail in Chapter 4 of Farrar and Leeming (note 18).

20. Figure 2–14 has been adapted from Figure 4.16 in Farrar and Leeming (note 18).

21. The data in Table 2–2 are taken from Figure 4.11 in Farrar and Leeming (note 18).

22. See Marion (note 9), Section 12.4.

23. Just as the center of mass in an object is the point arrived at by averaging positions in the object by their mass, the center of pressure is a point arrived at by averaging points on the surface with the pressure felt at those points. In effect, it is the average point at which pressure is applied to the object. Since pressure is an area phenomenon, and mass is distributed throughout an object, it should not be surprising that in general the centers of mass and pressure will be different.

24. The data in Table 2–3 were taken from Table 3.1 in C. J. Marchant-Smith and P.R. Hulsam, *Small Arms and Cannons* (Oxford: Brassey's Publishers, 1982).

25. Stressr strain, and stiffness are discussed in any text on solid state physics. See Chapter 4 of Charles Kittel, *Introduction to Solid State Physics,* 3rd ed. (New York: John Wiley and Sons, 1966).

26. The data in Table 2–4 were taken from Table 1, Chapter 4, of Kittel (note 25).

27. Figure 2–21 has been adapted from Figure 1 in J. K. Dienes and J. M. Walsh, "Theory of Impact: General Principles and the Method of Eulerian Codes," Chapter III in Ray Kinslow (ed), *High-Velocity Impact Phenomena* (New York: Academic Press, 1970).

28. The insensitivity to projectile shape in hypervelocity impacts is apparent from the rapid deformation and loss of shape which the projectile suffers, as shown in Figure 2–21.

29. See Chapter III in Glasstone and Dolan (note 5).

30. See Dienes and Walsh (note 27).

31. It would be more accurate to look at the energy expended per unit volume of crater. However, as you can see from Figure 2–21,

most of the crater's volume is reflected in its depth. The width of the crater is not substantially different from that of the projectile.

32. This approximation makes use of the fact that sin $\theta \approx$ tan θ for small θ.

33. See Section 5 in Ovid W. Eshbach (ed), *Handbook of Engineering Fundamentals* 2nd ed (New York: John Wiley and Sons, 1961), and Section 1.08 in Herbert L. Anderson (ed), *Physics Vade Mecum* (New York: American Institute of Physics, 1981).

34. See Chapter 7 in Halliday and Resnick (note 1).

35. Deriving this result makes use of the definition of e as $\Delta V/V$. The fractional change in volume can be related to the plate's change in diameter, which goes from D to $2[(D/2)^2 + x^2]^{1/2}$. For x small, this is approximately equal to $D(1 + 2x^2/D^2)$.

36. See section 6.3.5 in the "Report to the APS of the Study Group on Science and Technology of Directed Energy Weapons," *Reviews of Modern Physics* 59, Part 59 (July, 1987).

37. The approach illustrated here (and others) are discussed in G. E. Duvall, "Applications," Chapter 9 in Pei Chi Chou and Alan K. Hopkins (eds.), *Dynamic Response of Materials to Intense Impulsive Loading* (Wright-Patterson AFB, OH: A. F. Materials Laboratory, 1973).

38. A variety of expressions for the prediction and correlation of damage from lower-velocity projectiles can be found in Farrar and Leeming (note 18), as well as K.J.W. Goad and D.H.J. Halsey, *Ammunition (including Grenades and Mines)* (Oxford: Brassey's Publishers, 1982).

39. This type of projectile and other novel approaches are discussed in Farrar and Leeming (note 18), and in Goad and Halsey (note 38).

40. It may seem as though kinetic energy weapons in space violate this principle, since much of their energy is that of orbital motion. However, even this energy isn't "free," and ultimately comes from the energy in the rocket engines which placed the weapons in orbit.

3: LASERS

This chapter examines the effects of lasers—one of the first exotic directed energy weapons to capture public attention. The acronym *laser* stands for "light amplification through stimulated emission of radiation," and thus a laser is fundamentally nothing more than a device which can produce an intense, or highly energetic, beam of light. The theory of how lasers are constructed, and descriptions of the different types currently available, can be found in a wide range of texts and journal articles.[1] For purposes of this book, which deals with the effects of laser light, these details are for the most part not important.

We'll begin by looking at the fundamental principles of laser light—those features which laser light has in common with all light, and those which make it unique. With these fundamental principles in mind, we'll then look at how the energy emitted by a laser propagates to a target, both in a vacuum and within the atmosphere. Finally, we'll look at how laser energy interacts with and damages a target. Our goal will be to develop criteria which can be used to estimate how much laser energy or power would be required to damage a target at a given range, either in vacuum or in the atmosphere. Particular emphasis will be placed on how these criteria scale with such beam parameters as wavelength, pulse width, pulse energy, and so forth.

Fundamental Principles of Laser Light

Propagation

We are all familiar with light, which is a special case of what is known as *electromagnetic radiation*. Other examples of electromagnetic radiation include radio waves, x-rays, and microwaves. Electromagnetic radiation propagates through space from its source as a wave, much as a wave of water propagates through a pond from its source. The source of a water wave is obvious, such as a pebble which has been dropped into the pond, and its propagation can be easily visualized as ripples spreading out from the source. Unlike water waves, electromagnetic waves do not require a physical medium for their propagation—they can propagate even through the vacuum of space.

They can be detected when they are absorbed in an appropriate detector, such as a radio for radio waves, or the retina of the eye for light. The theory of electromagnetic radiation was first developed by James C. Maxwell in the 1860s. He recognized that a large body of seemingly diverse phenomena in electricity and magnetism could be explained and summarized in four equations, appropriately known as *Maxwell's Equations*. These equations and their implications are the subject of graduate-level physics courses, and obviously cannot be dealt with in any detail here.[2] Nevertheless, key concepts are relatively straightforward.

Waves. First, let's consider what we mean by a wave.[3] A wave is a periodic disturbance which propagates through space. It may be characterized by the amplitude of the disturbance, the periodic distance over which it repeats, and the velocity with which it propagates, as illustrated in Figure 3–1. This figure shows a wave propagating from left to right with a velocity v.

The *amplitude*, or height of the disturbance illustrated in Figure 3–1 is a measure of its strength, just as a high water wave is more likely to knock you over than a small one. The distance over

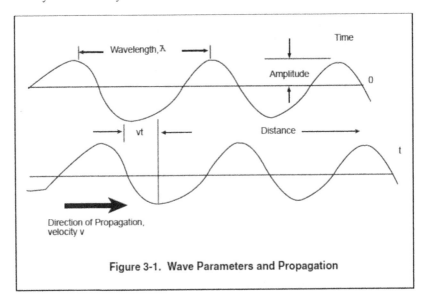

Figure 3-1. Wave Parameters and Propagation

which the disturbance repeats itself is known as the *wavelength*. Finally, the wave moves with some velocity, v, so that any feature, such as the trough shown in Figure 3–1, moves a distance vt in time t. If you are standing at a given spot and the wave is passing by, what you see will repeat in a time equal to the wavelength divided by the velocity, since over a wavelength's distance the wave repeats itself. This time in which the wave repeats is known as the *period* of the wave. The inverse of a wave's period is known as its *frequency*. By common convention, wavelength, period, and frequency are denoted by the symbols λ, T, and v, respectively. Mathematically, the relationship among these quantities is $v = v/\lambda$, or $T = \lambda/v$. The wavelength of an electromagnetic wave determines the nature of the radiation. Figure 3–2 shows the type of radiation associated with different regions of wavelength.

You can see from Figure 3–2 that electromagnetic waves span a broad range of wavelengths. The span is so great that only the logarithmic scale in the figure suffices to capture even a part of it, with wavelengths varying from the submicroscopic (X-rays and gamma rays) to the macroscopic (radio waves). Despite this diversity in wavelength, all electromagnetic radiation obeys the same physical laws. We'll briefly summarize those which are important for understanding lasers, their propagation, and their interaction with targets.

In a vacuum, all electromagnetic radiation travels at the same speed—the speed of light, commonly denoted by the symbol c.[4] Because of the general relationship between frequency and wavelength for waves, the frequency of electromagnetic radiation propagating in a vacuum is given by $v = c/\lambda$.

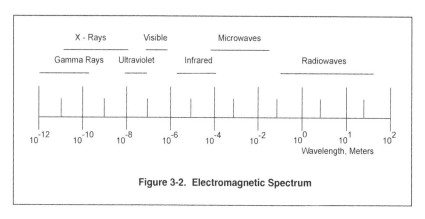

Figure 3-2. Electromagnetic Spectrum

The value of c is approximately 3×10^8 meters per second, so that the frequencies corresponding to the extremes of wavelength in Figure 3–2 are about 10^{20} cycles per second for gamma rays to about 10^6 cycles per second for radio waves. A cycle per second is known as a *Hertz*, abbreviated Hz.[5] Thus, 10^6 cycles per second is a Megahertz, a unit you may recognize from your FM radio dial.

Refraction. In a medium other than vacuum, such as air, water, or glass, electromagnetic radiation will travel at a speed less than c. The ratio of c to the speed in a particular medium is known as the *index of refraction*, and is denoted by n. In general, n will vary with wavelength and material, as illustrated in Figure 3–3.[6]

The reason the ratio between light speed in vacuum and light speed in some material is called the index of refraction is that this ratio is related to a bending which a beam of light undergoes when it travels from a medium with one index of refraction to another. This bending obeys what is known as the law of refraction, and is illustrated in Figure 3–4. The *law of refraction* states that when a ray of light passes from one material of index n_1 to another of index n_2, then the angles, θ_1 and θ_2, which the ray makes with a line perpendicular to the surface between the two materials, are related by $n_1 \sin \theta_1 = n_2 \sin \theta_2$.

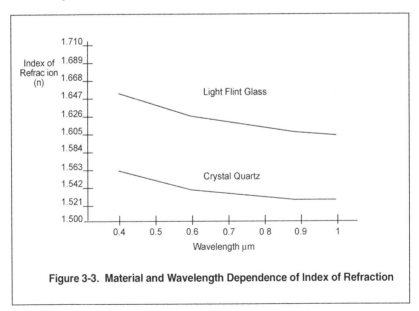

Figure 3-3. Material and Wavelength Dependence of Index of Refraction

84

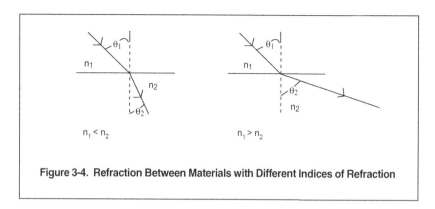

Figure 3-4. Refraction Between Materials with Different Indices of Refraction

Mathematically, the trigonometric sine function increases with the angle θ, varying from 0 when $\theta = 0$ to 1 when $\theta = 90°$. Thus, if $n_2 > n_1$, as illustrated on the left hand side of Figure 3–3, the light will be bent towards a line perpendicular to the surface, while if $n_2 < n_1$, as illustrated on the right hand side of Figure 3–3, the opposite will occur. This phenomenon is responsible for what happens when a beam of white light, containing light of all wavelengths, passes through a prism: since the index of refraction for different wavelengths is different, different wavelengths (colors) of light are bent to different degrees and separated from one another. Similarly, it is the refraction of light passing through water droplets in the air which is responsible for rainbows.

Refraction is put to good use in lenses.[7] Figure 3–5 illustrates two types of lenses: converging and diverging. It's easy to convince yourself by use of the law of refraction and Figure 3–4 that a lens which is thicker in the middle than at the edges will tend to make light rays focus to a point, while one which is thicker at the edges than the middle will make them diverge. Nearsighted persons, whose eyes focus in front of the retina, have diverging lenses in their glasses to move the focal point back, while far-sighted persons, whose eyes focus behind the retina, have their vision corrected with converging lenses. Refraction and lens theory are important to the understanding of laser propagation because, as we shall see, small density fluctuations in the atmosphere which arise due to turbulence can act as lenses and cause a light beam to be bent in random ways.

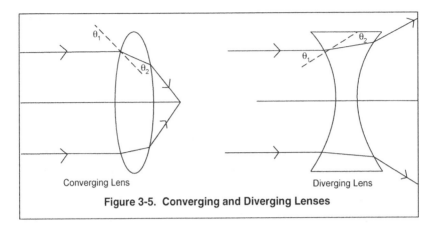

Converging Lens   Diverging Lens

Figure 3-5. Converging and Diverging Lenses

Diffraction. Another phenomenon of real importance from the standpoint of the propagation of laser light is that of *diffraction*. Diffraction refers to the spreading, or divergence, of light which emerges from an aperture of a given diameter, as shown in Figure 3–6. In this figure, a beam of light of essentially infinite beam width is passed through an aperture of diameter D. It is easily verified experimentally that the light which passes through this aperture is no longer collimated, propagating in a straight line, but rather now has some divergence angle, θ. It may be shown both theoretically and experimentally that this angle is related to D and to the wavelength, λ, of the light by the relationship $\theta \approx \lambda/D$.

The exact relationship between θ and λ/D depends on whether the aperture is square, a circle, or has some other shape (which is why we use "$\approx$" instead of "$=$"), but the expression given is approximately true in any case and will be sufficiently accurate for our purposes.[8]

You will recall from Chapter 1 that in propagating a distance z, a beam of divergence θ will expand to a width $w \approx z\theta$. Therefore, the implication of diffraction is that if you want a beam of light to travel a long range without much spreading, you must make θ small by choosing either a small wavelength or a large aperture. This is why lasers are popular as beam weapons: with wavelengths on the order of 10^{-5} cm, an aperture of modest size, such as 10 cm, will produce a divergence of only 10^{-6} radians (about $0.000006°$). By contrast, a typical radar system, with a wavelength of 10 cm, would diverge with an angle of $6°$ if beamed from a 10 centimeter aperture. This is why radar antennas must be quite large if they are

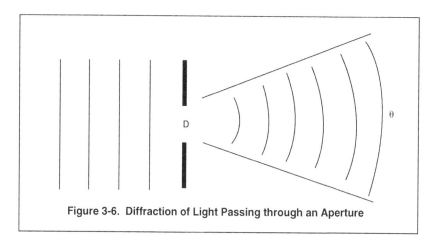

Figure 3-6. Diffraction of Light Passing through an Aperture

to beam over long distances with relatively little divergence. Chapter 4 discusses the implications of these results from the standpoint of microwaves, which have wavelengths of 1 – 10 cm.

One way of reducing the effects of diffraction to achieve a longer effective beam range without appreciable divergence is by focusing the beam as illustrated in Figure 3–7.

In Figure 3–7, a converging lens has been placed in the path of the beam. This lens, as we have seen, serves to bend the light rays inward, focusing them to a spot of radius W.[9] The width of the focal spot depends upon the focal length, f, of the lens. If f is very short, the light will be focused to a small spot, and will diverge rapidly beyond that spot. If f becomes too long, the light will diverge from the lens as though it were just an aperture.

In between these extremes, there is a focal length at which the beam will "hang together" and remain essentially collimated for the greatest distance. This focal length is known as the *Rayleigh Range*, Z_r. The beam radius at the Rayleigh Range is $W = D/3\sqrt{2}$, and the Rayleigh Range is given by $Z_r = \pi W^2/\lambda$.[10] Therefore, in practical applications, laser light can be used as a collimated beam over a distance of about twice the Rayleigh Range, or about D^2/λ, where D is the aperture from which the light emerges from the weapon, and λ the wavelength of the light. Beyond this distance, diffraction and divergence at an angle of about λ/D must be taken into account in evaluating the energy density on target.[11] Figure 3–8 shows how the Rayleigh Range varies with wavelength and aperture, and reinforces the

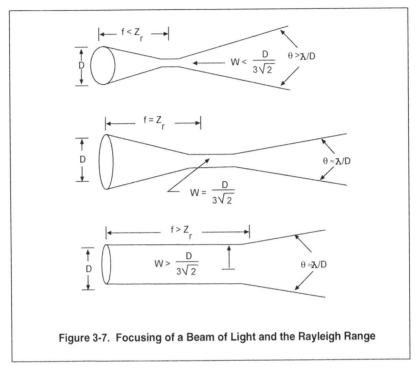

Figure 3-7. Focusing of a Beam of Light and the Rayleigh Range

idea that shorter wavelengths and larger apertures result in longer propagation distances without spreading.

Summary. To this point, we have seen that laser light is a special case of electromagnetic radiation, and is characterized by some wavelength, frequency, and a speed of c in vacuum or c/n in some other medium. When propagating from one medium to another, the light is bent according to the law of refraction, and when passing through an aperture of diameter D will spread by diffraction with a divergence angle of about λ/D. Focusing can limit diffraction spreading, but only over a range of about D^2/λ.

Laser Interaction with Matter

Having considered the fundamental features of laser propagation, we'll turn our attention to the fundamentals of laser interaction with matter—either the atmospheric gases through which the beam may propagate, or the solid targets it may engage. The interaction of electromagnetic radiation with matter was poorly under-

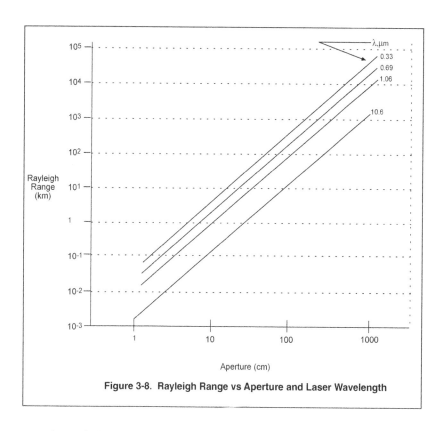

Figure 3-8. Rayleigh Range vs Aperture and Laser Wavelength

stood until the present century, when a host of experimental data and theory came together in what is now known as quantum mechanics.[12] One of the fundamental features of this theory is that light, while it *propagates* as a continuous wave, *interacts with matter* in discrete units. That is, light may be treated as a wave, subject to refraction, diffraction, and all those effects while it propagates, but when it's finally absorbed or scattered from a target, it needs to be treated as a stream of tiny little bullets.

How small are the bullets? Quantum theory tells us that light of frequency v is absorbed in units of hv, where h is a constant (Planck's constant), equal to 6.63×10^{-34} Joule seconds. This means that for red light, with a wavelength of about $0.7 \ \mu$m and a frequency of about 4×10^{14} Hz, the energy of a single bullet is h$v = 3 \times 10^{-19}$ Joules. This is a very small number—to absorb the 10,000 Joules we have taken as a zero order criterion for damage, about 3×10^{22} units (commonly called *photons*) of red light would need to be absorbed. This is why in our everyday experience the absorption of light seems continuous, just as the flow of water appears continuous—because the individual photons of light, or water molecules, though discrete, are too small to be picked up individually.

Interaction with Gases. If the discrete nature of light absorption is so small, what difference does it make? It makes a big difference, because light can only be absorbed if the energy of a photon is exactly equal to the difference between two allowed energy states in the absorbing material. This sounds complicated, but it really isn't. Just as light exists in discrete photons of energy, matter exists in discrete energy states, corresponding to different configurations of the atoms and molecules of which it is made. This is illustrated, in a rather simplistic form, in Figure 3–9. This figure shows an atom of hydrogen, which consists of a single proton being "orbited" by a single electron. Quantum mechanics tells us that only certain discrete orbits are allowed for the electron, each corresponding to a different energy.[13] The energy levels corresponding to the allowed orbits in hydrogen are shown on the right hand side of Figure 3–9.[14]

If we take the lowest energy orbit of hydrogen, or *ground state* to be the zero of energy, the next highest orbit is at 10.2 eV. (An electron volt [eV] is the energy which one electron gains in falling through a 1 volt potential—about 1.6×10^{-19} Joules.) The next highest is at 12.1 eV, and so forth. As we go up in energy, the levels get closer together, until at 13.6 eV, the *ionization potential* of hydrogen, the electron is no longer bound to the nucleus, and is free to go its own way and do its own thing.

If a photon of light encounters an atom of hydrogen, it can only be absorbed if its energy connects an occupied electronic level with an unoccupied one. Thus, if the hydrogen is in its ground state, photons of energy greater than 13.6 eV can be absorbed, since they can ionize the atom, sending its electron into one of an infinite number of free and unbound states. Photons of energy less than 13.6 eV will have much greater difficulty being absorbed. Only those of energy 10.2 eV, 12.1 eV, and so on can be absorbed as they promote an electron from the ground state to one of the higher levels. Since a photon of red light has an energy of 3×10^{-19}

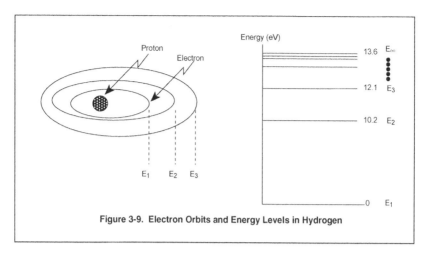

Figure 3-9. Electron Orbits and Energy Levels in Hydrogen

Joules = 1.9 eV, you can see that red light of this wavelength cannot be absorbed by hydrogen in its ground state. Hydrogen gas should be transparent to red light, and indeed it is.[15]

Laser light consists of photons in the infrared and visible light portions of the electromagnetic spectrum, with energies from about 0.1 to 3 eV. Since the ionization potentials of almost all materials lie between 10 and 20 eV, it's obvious that absorption of light in gases is generally unlikely—only photons unlucky enough to connect a few discrete energy states will be absorbed. This is in accord with everyday experience—our gaseous atmosphere is transparent to light in a broad range of wavelengths from the infrared to the ultraviolet.

As materials become more complex, their energy states become more diverse, allowing more possibilities for absorption. This is illustrated in Figure 3–10, which shows some of the energy states of molecular nitrogen (N_2).[16] You can see that there is much more structure than there is for atomic hydrogen, because the fact that two atoms have come together to form a molecule has introduced new degrees of freedom. An atom can be given energy only by exciting its electrons. A molecule can also be set to vibrating, as the atoms which make it up move back and forth against the forces which hold them together, or rotating, as they tumble around one another. As Figure 3–10 illustrates, this makes what would be single energy states for an isolated atom split into multiple energy states: for a given level of electronic excitation, there are multiple levels of vibrational excitation, and for a given degree of electronic

91

and vibrational excitation, there are multiple levels of rotational excitation. As the figure also illustrates, there is a difference in energy scale among the different type of excitations. Typically, electronic excitations are on the order of 1 – 10 eV, vibrational excitations on the order of 0.1 – 1 eV, and rotational excitations on the order of 0.01 eV.

The mixing of different molecules, as in the atmosphere, introduces more and more wavelengths at which light might be absorbed. Nevertheless, the absorption properties of gases may be adequately characterized as discrete absorption lines, separated by relatively broad regions of transmission. Figure 3–11 shows a portion of the absorption spectrum of the atmosphere, and indicates the molecules responsible for some of the absorption lines shown.

In interacting with a gas, light may not only be absorbed, but also scattered. Depending on the mechanism of scattering, it can be treated either as a macroscopic phenomenon and analyzed using wave theory, or as a microscopic phenomenon, and analyzed as an interaction between photons and atoms. For example, scattering from suspended particulate matter in the atmosphere is

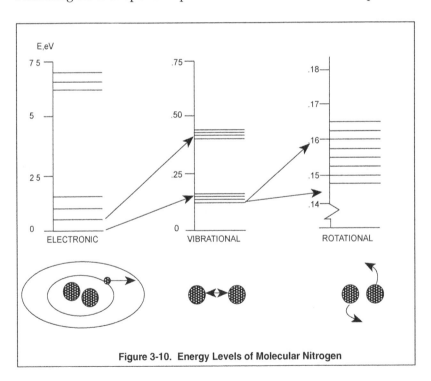

Figure 3-10. Energy Levels of Molecular Nitrogen

a macroscopic phenomenon, because the particles in question are of a size (about 10^{-4} cm) equal to or greater than the wavelength of light. On the other hand, photons may be "absorbed" and "re-emitted" by atomic and molecular species in a gas, resulting in what is effectively a scattering process by particles whose size is about 10^{-8} cm—much smaller than the wavelength of visible light. Scattering phenomena will be discussed in greater detail later in the chapter.

In summary, gases are comprised of atoms and molecules which absorb light at only certain discrete wavelengths. It would therefore be wise to choose a laser for atmospheric applications whose wavelength is not coincident with one of these absorption lines.

Interaction with Solids. How do the absorption characteristics of solids and liquids differ from those of gases? In principle, not at all, but in practice there's a big difference due to the high density of atoms which make up a solid. In essence, a solid is a macromolecule, in which about 10^{23} atoms per cubic centimeter are bound together into one huge assembly. What this means is that many, many more degrees of freedom are introduced, there are many more ways of exciting the material, and therefore there are many more wavelengths which might be absorbed. It would seem that this would make the absorption properties of solids very, very complex: but as often happens, they become so complex

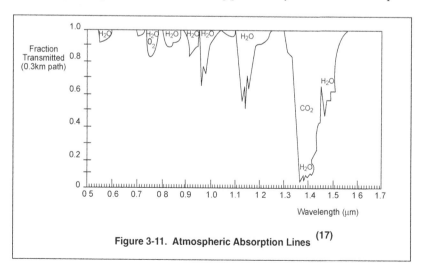

Figure 3-11. Atmospheric Absorption Lines [17]

as to be simple from a macroscopic point of view. This is analogous to the way in which the motions of the individual molecules in a gas, though chaotic and impossible to predict on an individual basis, are well described in a macroscopic sense by the equations of fluid flow. We do not need to know how each molecule is moving to know which way the wind is blowing! Figure 3–12 shows schematically what happens to the allowed energy levels as atoms of some substance are brought together to form molecules, and as molecules are brought together to form a solid.

As we have seen, the energy levels of an atom become more diverse when two or three of them are brought together into a molecule, and the individual electronic energy levels develop a lot of fine structure due to rotational and vibrational degrees of freedom. As many, many molecules are brought together to form a solid, this process continues. Eventually, the discrete energy levels become so dense as to form what are, in effect, *energy bands*: regions within which an electron may have any energy. These energy bands are separated by *energy gaps*: regions within which none of the energies are permitted to an electron. This type of structure is shown at the extreme right hand of Figure 3–12. The band of highest energies in a solid is known as the conduction band, because these energy states, as we shall see, are responsible for the conductivity of metals. The lower bands of energy states are known as the valence bands: these arise from the tightly bound, innermost electrons in the isolated atoms.[18]

What are the implications of the energy level structure for solids which is illustrated in Figure 3–12? How these energy bands are filled with electrons determines whether the solid is a metal or an insulator, and this, in turn, determines how it responds to light which is incident upon it. An *insulator* is a solid in which all the energy bands are either completely occupied with, or free of, electrons. It's easy to see why this is so: if an electric field is applied to such a solid, it tries to accelerate the electrons within it, increasing their energy. But the electrons at the top of the band can't increase in energy, since energies above them aren't allowed. Electrons just below these can't increase in energy, because the energy levels above them are filled, and so on. It's rather like a line of people, with the first person up against a brick wall: no matter how hard someone pushes at the rear of the

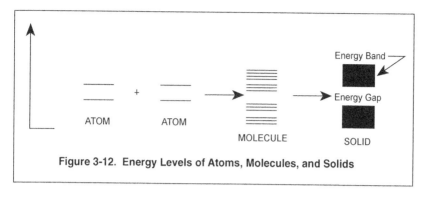

Figure 3-12. Energy Levels of Atoms, Molecules, and Solids

line, it won't go anywhere. Consequently, insulators, as their name implies, don't conduct electricity. The electrons within them simply can't flow in response to an applied electric field.

What happens to the electrons in an insulator when they encounter a photon of light? There are two possibilities. If the photon energy is less than the energy gap, the photon can't be absorbed, since it can't raise any electrons from a filled to an empty energy level. On the other hand, if the photon energy exceeds the energy gap, it can raise electrons from the valence to the conduction band, and be absorbed in the process. Thus, we anticipate that the absorption of light by insulators will be highly energy dependent, taking a great leap forward when the photon energy exceeds the energy gap. To continue the analogy introduced earlier, a line of people up against a brick wall can move forward if the first person in line is kicked over the wall! This phenomenon is well documented experimentally, as illustrated by Figure 3–13, which shows the fraction of photons transmitted through a 10^{-4} cm sample of gallium arsenide (GaAs) as a function of photon energy.

You can see from Figure 3–12 that the transmission of light by GaAs does indeed fall rapidly for photon energies above the energy gap. For all but very thin samples, GaAs is opaque to photons of energy greater than 1.521 eV, the energy gap. Table 3–1 provides the energy gaps for some common insulators, and indicates where the photons that can bridge these gaps lie in the electromagnetic spectrum.

It is easy to relate the energy gaps shown for the materials in Table 3–1 to their physical appearance. Since diamond, for example, has an energy gap which corresponds to the energy of

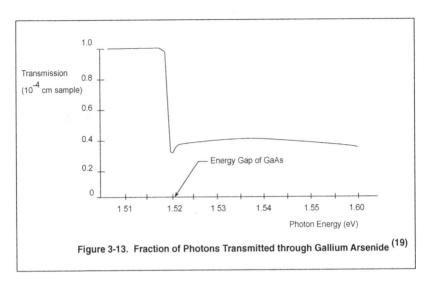

Figure 3-13. **Fraction of Photons Transmitted through Gallium Arsenide** (19)

Material	Energy Gap(eV)	Special Loca ion
Diamond	5.33	Ultraviolet
Zinc Selenide	3.6	Visible
Silicon	1.14	Infrared
Gallium Arsenide	1.521	Infrared
Lead Telluride	0.30	Infrared

Table 3-1. Some Typical Energy Gaps(20)

photons in the ultraviolet region of the electromagnetic spectrum, it should not be able to absorb photons of lesser energy, such as those in the visible region of the spectrum. The fact that diamonds appear transparent to us confirms this result. Similarly, silicon and gallium arsenide appear opaque to us—their energy gaps are less than the energy of visible photons—yet these materials are used as windows for infrared detectors, since they are transparent to photons of infrared energy.

In summary, insulators will be transparent to light whose photons have less energy than their energy gap, and opaque to light whose photons exceed the energy gap. Let's consider next the type of behavior we expect from *conductors*—materials in which the uppermost energy band is only *partially filled* with electrons.

Having a partially filled energy band greatly affects the electrical and optical properties of a material. We saw that when a band was entirely filled with electrons, an electric field couldn't accelerate any electrons, since they had nowhere to go in energy space. If, however, the band isn't full, there are states of greater energy available within the band, and an electric field can accelerate the electrons within it. This results in the flow of electricity. These materials are therefore called conductors: they conduct electricity.

We might be tempted to conclude that conductors could absorb light of any frequency, since there are energy states available for electrons to be promoted to in absorbing photons of any energy. However, this is not the case, due to the collective effect of all these electrons flowing about. You may recall from sophomore physics that "there can be no electric fields on the interior of a conductor."[21] What does this general principle mean? It means that when an electric field is applied to a conductor, the electrons within it flow so as to prevent that electric field from penetrating to the interior. This was first recognized by Michael Faraday, who proved it by sitting inside a metal box while his assistants charged up the exterior of the box to a high potential, with electric fields of such magnitude that sparks were flying all over the place. He emerged alive, thus demonstrating that the electric fields had not penetrated into the interior. Even today, the name "Faraday cage" is given to metal boxes which are used to shield electronic components from external electromagnetic fields—a typical military application is to protect electronics from external fields, including the "electromagnetic pulse" (emp) which accompanies the detonation of nuclear weapons.[22]

What does all this have to do with the absorption of light? Remember that light is a wave of electric and magnetic fields, propagating through space. If these fields can't penetrate to the interior of a conductor, how can they be absorbed? And if they can't be absorbed or propagate through, what happens to them? A clue lies in the fact that metals, which are good electrical conductors, appear shiny: they *reflect* waves of light which are incident upon them. Indeed, metallic mirrors are a common optical element in many lasers.

In the last two paragraphs we have flipped between two extremes. First, we thought that since there were energy states available for absorption in conductors, they would absorb laser light. Then, recognizing the shielding effect which flowing electrons could have, we changed our mind and thought that they would reflect laser light. The second extreme is closer to the truth, but it's still not the whole truth. There are frequencies of light which will penetrate to the interior of a conductor, and even for those frequencies which are reflected, some small portion will be absorbed. What is the physical basis for these results?

We have related the reflection of light by conductors to the flow of electrons within them. Suppose the frequency of the light is so great that its electromagnetic field changes sign more rapidly than the electrons can flow in response. In this case, the electrons do not have time to move and produce their shielding effect, and we'd expect the light to penetrate into the conductor. How great a frequency is required for this to happen? If there are n free (conducting) electrons per cubic meter in a material, then the maximum frequency at which they can respond is called the *plasma frequency*, v_p. The plasma frequency is proportional to the square root of n, and is equal to $10^{15} - 10^{16}$ Hz at the density of electrons found in typical conductors.[23] These frequencies are in the ultraviolet and X-ray portions of the electromagnetic spectrum, which is why visible light is reflected from metals, but X-rays can be used to probe them to examine the quality of welds and in other applications. A similar phenomenon occurs in the atmosphere. The density of electrons in the ionosphere is such that low frequency radio waves are reflected and can thus bounce over the horizon, enabling us to communicate overseas. Higher frequency microwaves, above the plasma frequency, will propagate through the ionosphere and can be used to communicate with spacecraft. Figure 3–14 is a plot of plasma frequency as a function of electron density, with key frequencies and densities identified.

With the concepts developed so far, we can conclude that when light encounters a conducting material, it will be mostly transmitted if its frequency exceeds the plasma frequency, and mostly reflected if its frequency is below the plasma frequency. The word "mostly" appears in the previous sentence because nothing in the world is perfect, and some small fraction of the light which is incident on a conductor will be absorbed. What is the physical basis for this absorption? Fundamentally, it arises because no conductor is perfect. There is some resistance to the flow of electrons in any material due to imperfections in its structure, the thermal vibrations resulting from its finite temperature, and so forth. What this

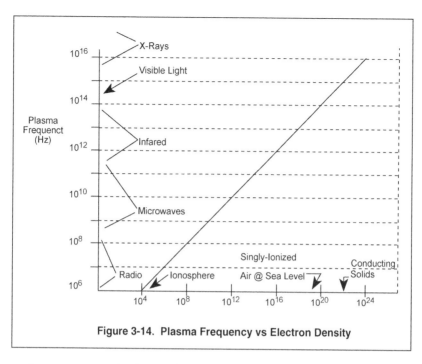

Figure 3-14. Plasma Frequency vs Electron Density

resistance means is that, while the electrons would like to flow to prevent the penetration of electromagnetic radiation, they will be retarded from doing so, with the result that light will penetrate to some degree. The depth to which light will penetrate is known as the *skin depth*, δ. It can be shown that the skin depth is inversely proportional to the square root of the product of the light frequency times a material's conductivity. Figure 3–15 is a plot of skin depth as a function of a metal's conductivity and the frequency of light incident upon it.

As you can see from the figure, the skin depth is quite small—micrometers or less—for infrared and visible wavelengths. As

	Metals	Insulators
Transmissive	Light Frequency>Plasma Frequency	Photon Energy<Energy Gap
Absorptive	Light Frequency<Plasma Frequency*	Photon Energy>Energy Gap
Reflective	Light Frequency<Plasma Frequency*	— — — — —

*Over 90% reflected, remainder absorbed

Table 3-2. Response of Metals and Insulators to Incident Light

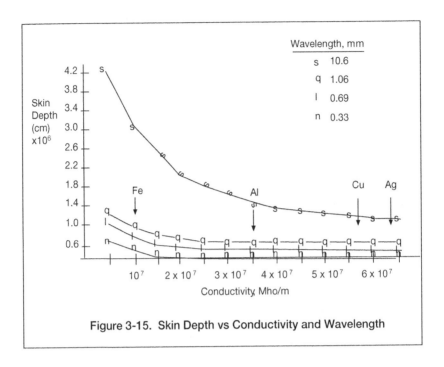

Figure 3-15. Skin Depth vs Conductivity and Wavelength

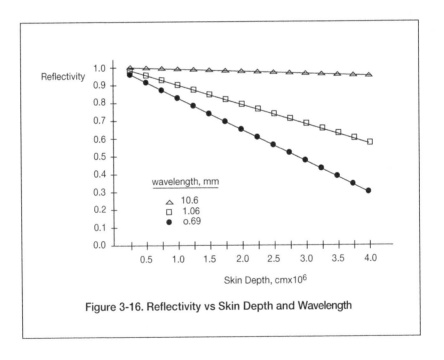

Figure 3-16. Reflectivity vs Skin Depth and Wavelength

conductivity decreases, the skin depth increases and light penetrates further into a conductor, so that a greater fraction will be absorbed.[24] The fraction of light reflected from the surface of a conducting material is given by $R = 1 - 4\pi\nu\delta/c$.

Figure 3–16 shows reflectivity as a function of skin depth and wavelength. For example, if radiation with a wavelength of 10.6μm is incident upon aluminum, which has a skin depth of about 1.6×10^{-6} cm, the reflectivity is $R = 0.98$. Thus, very little of the light incident on a metallic surface will be absorbed. This is good, if you want to use it as a mirror; and bad, if you hope to damage it with the light incident upon it.

If there's anything like a simple bottom line to the physics of light absorption in gaseous materials or solids it's this: in gases, a photon is lucky to be absorbed. Only a few, discrete frequencies will be in resonance with the gaseous absorption lines. In solids, on the other hand, a photon will be lucky to be transmitted. Its energy must lie below the energy gap of an insulator, or its frequency above the plasma frequency of a conductor. This contrast reflects our everyday experience that gases seem to be transparent, while solids are for the most part opaque.

Laser Propagation in a Vacuum

Let's now use the basic ideas developed in the previous section to investigate the propagation of laser light, first in a vacuum, and then in the atmosphere. In a vacuum, there are no gases or particles to absorb or scatter the beam, and so beam propagation involves only its spreading through diffraction. A beam of electromagnetic radiation of wavelength λ emerging from an aperture of diameter D and focused to a radius $w_0 = D/3\sqrt{2} \approx D/4$ will travel a distance roughly equal to the Rayleigh Range, $Z_r = \pi w_0^2/\lambda$, before diverging at an angle $\theta \approx \lambda/D$ (Figure 3–7). Therefore, there are two propagation limits, one in which the beam is essentially collimated, with a (roughly) constant radius w_0, and another in which it diverges, with its radius growing linearly with distance. These two regimes are sometimes called the near field and far field respectively, for the obvious reason that far field propagation occurs at a further distance from the laser source than does near field propagation.[25] In the near field, beam intensity is roughly independent of range, while in the far field, intensity will decrease as the square of the range.

Near Field Propagation

It's obvious from the expression for the Rayleigh Range that shorter wavelengths and larger apertures are favored for longer propagation as a collimated beam (see Figure 3–8). We can be more quantitative in this assessment by developing criteria for the aperture, wavelength, and power necessary to deliver a given intensity (W/cm^2) to a target at a given range without appreciable beam spreading. You will recall from Chapter 1 that damaging targets requires an energy density (fluence) on the order of 10^4 J/cm^2, delivered in a time shorter than that over which the target can redistribute or reject the energy. For longer times, the fluence necessary to damage the target increases, and ultimately it is a constant power density (intensity) that is required for damage (see Figure 1–8). In designing a laser for use as a weapon in a given scenario, the parameters which are available to play with are its power (Watts), pulse duration (pulse width, seconds), aperture, and wavelength. If it is desired to operate in the near field, some combination of these must be chosen that will allow the necessary fluence or intensity to be placed on target within the Rayleigh Range. The Rayleigh Range, $Z_r = \pi w_o^2 / \lambda$, is directly proportional to the beam area, $A = \pi w_o^2$, and the beam radius is in turn proportional to the output aperture D of the laser system. Figure 3–17 is a plot of the aperture necessary to achieve a given range in the near field for several laser wavelengths.

In looking at the Figure 3–17, it is useful to bear in mind that there are two general scenarios of interest. These are *tactical* applications, in which ranges are characteristic of those likely to be found on a battlefield (1 – 100 km), and *strategic* applications, in which ranges are characteristic of intercontinental distances or the orbital altitude of geosynchronous satellites (10^4–10^5 km). From the figure, you can see that over tactical ranges it's possible to propagate in the near field with systems whose apertures are of a reasonable size—a meter or less. Over strategic ranges, aperture sizes can approach hundreds of meters, especially for longer wavelength infrared radiation.

A laser whose output power is P (Watts) delivers an intensity S (Watts/cm^2) equal to $P/\pi w_o^2$. Since meeting damage criteria de-

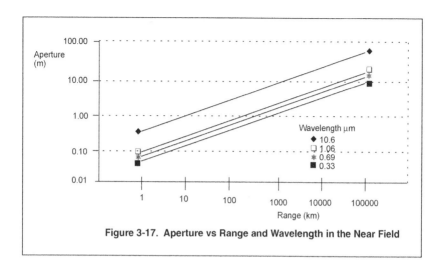

Figure 3-17. Aperture vs Range and Wavelength in the Near Field

pends upon the intensity S and the pulse duration t_p, a less power-ful laser with a small spot area might achieve damage equivalent to a more powerful laser with a larger spot size. On the other hand, the beam with the smaller area will have a smaller Rayleigh range. Figure 3–18 is a plot of the power necessary to achieve vari-ous intensities as a function of aperture size.

Figure 3–18 reinforces the idea that engaging targets in the near field is practical only at tactical ranges. Only when output aper-tures are less than a meter are power levels of 10^6 W (MW) or less sufficient to place damaging intensities on target. Figure 3–19 shows the reason for this, and also suggests why at strategic ranges it would be wiser to propagate in the far field, accepting the resulting beam divergence.

In the upper portion of Figure 3–19, a large aperture laser is seen engaging a target at a strategic range. With an aperture size of 10–100 meters, such a beam will actually be larger than many typi-cal targets, and power and energy will be wasted. In the lower portion of the figure, a smaller diameter aperture is employed. This laser will diverge, but its spot size at the target may actually be smaller than that of the large aperture laser! As a result, an en-gagement in the far field can result in a smaller, less cumbersome laser design as well as more efficient energy delivery to the target. Therefore, it's appropriate to turn our attention next to propaga-tion in the far field.

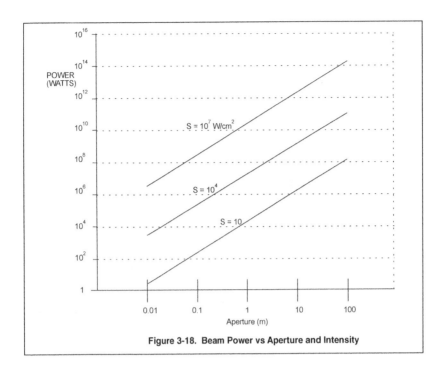

Figure 3-18. Beam Power vs Aperture and Intensity

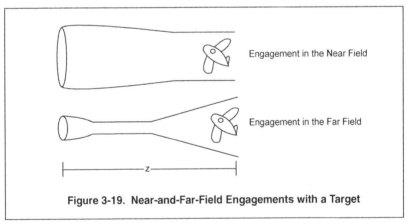

Figure 3-19. Near-and-Far-Field Engagements with a Target

Far Field Propagation

In the far field, the beam has a divergence angle $\theta \approx \lambda/D$ where D is the diameter of the final output element (lens, mirror, etc.) for the laser. Recall (Chapter 1) that divergence at an angle θ results in a beam radius $w = z\theta$ after propagation over a range Z, so that the intensity S of a laser having power P is $S = P/\pi w^2 \approx PD^2/\pi Z^2\lambda^2$. Unlike propagation in the near field, where intensity is roughly constant with the range z, in the far field it decreases as $1/Z^2$.

The decrease in intensity as $1/Z^2$ reflects the fact that in the far field the beam and its energy are spreading with distance, and the energy is no longer as "directed" as in the near field. The concept of *brightness*, illustrated in Figure 3–20, is used to quantify the extent to which a given laser beam falls between the extremes of being perfectly directed, as in the near field, and perfectly divergent, as is the detonation of a bomb.

Shown in the figure is a laser of wavelength λ with an output power P, propagating and spreading with a divergence angle $\theta \approx \lambda/D$. At some range z, the beam has a cross-sectional area $A = \pi w^2 \approx \pi z^2 \lambda^2/D^2$. If the laser's power were totally undirected, like that from a bomb, the beam would occupy a sphere of area $4\pi z^2$ at a range z. In either case the area increases as z^2, it's just the constant of proportionality that's different. The smaller that constant, the tighter the beam is, and the less it's spreading. The constant of proportionality between z^2 and the area of the beam is known as the *solid angle* that the beam occupies.[26] The unit of solid angle is called a *steradian*. The brightness of the beam illustrated in Figure 3–19 is defined to be $B = PD^2/\pi \lambda^2$, or the ratio of its power to its degree of spreading in steradians. The units of brightness, therefore, are Watts per steradian, abbreviated W/sr.

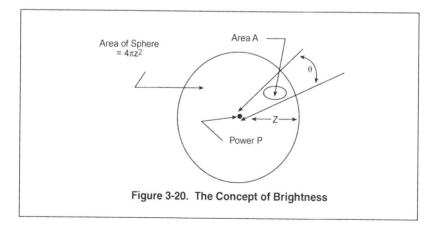

Figure 3-20. The Concept of Brightness

It is easy to see that this definition of brightness agrees with what we might think on an intuitive basis. Clearly, the brightness of a light source should be proportional to its output power—we know that a 100 Watt light bulb is brighter than a 60 Watt light bulb. Thus, the definition of B involves the power, P. Brightness should also increase as the angular cone through which the light is funneled decreases—a 60 Watt flashlight is much brighter (when it intersects our eyes) than a 60 Watt bulb, because it sends those 60 Watts in one direction, rather than in all directions. Brightness is a useful "figure of merit" for a directed energy weapon such as a laser, because it depends only on the characteristics of the laser device itself (P, D, and λ), and is independent of scenario-dependent factors such as the range, z.[27] The intensity S (W/cm^2) at a range z from a laser of brightness B is simply B/z^2. In this way, it's possible to find the range at which a laser with a given brightness can engage a target with a given intensity, as shown in Figure 3–21.

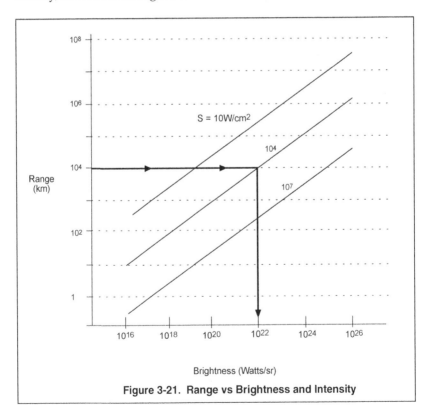

Figure 3-21. Range vs Brightness and Intensity

Figure 3–21 may be used to evaluate the tradeoffs associated with laser propagation in the far field just as Figures 3–17 and 3–18 may be used in the near field. Suppose, for example, that we wish to engage a satellite at a range of 10^4 km, and that damaging this satellite requires that an intensity of 10^4 W/cm^2 be applied to the target for a period of 0.1 second. From Figure 3–21, this requires that we have a laser with a brightness of 10^{22} W/sr. Using the definition of brightness, $B = PD^2/p\lambda^2$, this requirement can be further developed into operational parameters for the laser to engage the satellite. Suppose, for example, that we feel constrained for engineering reasons to using a 1 m (100 cm) aperture, and a wavelength of 0.7 μm (7×10^{-5} cm). Then $D^2/\pi\lambda^2 = 6.5 \times 10^{11}$, and the power of the laser must be 1.5×10^{10} W (15,000 MW). This is a pretty hefty power, and the technical challenges associated with building so powerful a device may cause us to rethink the constraints on the problem. For example, if we were to increase the aperture to 10 m, then $D^2/\pi\lambda^2$ would increase by two orders of magnitude to 6.5×10^{13}, and the necessary power would decrease by two orders of magnitude to 150 MW.

Departures from Perfect Propagation

One final point needs to be made before we can wrap up our discussion of propagation in a vacuum. To this point, we have treated our laser beam as if it were an ideal wave of electromagnetic radiation. Real lasers do not produce ideal waves for a variety of reasons, such as inhomogenieties in the active elements of the laser itself or in the lenses and mirrors which serve to couple the beam into the outside world. The result of this lack of perfection is to make a real laser beam spread more rapidly than an ideal beam. The difference between the real and the ideal is expressed as the ratio of the actual spot size to the ideal or *diffraction-limited* spot size. Thus, if you see a beam described as 1.5 times diffraction limited, you know that you can predict the spot radius by diffraction theory, multiply by 1.5, and get the actual beam radius for this particular device. For such real beams, Figures 3–17, 3–18, and 3–21 remain adequate to determine the relationships among damage criteria, wavelength, aperture, and power as long as the spot size is degraded by a factor to account for the effects of beam spreading through factors other than diffraction. Thus, for a beam which is said to be "n" times diffraction limited, the intensity at the Rayleigh Range is not $P/\pi w_0^2$, but rather $P/\pi (nw_0)^2$, and so on. Therefore, to maintain the same intensity for a beam which is "n" times diffraction limited, the power must be increased by a factor of n^2.

Another definition which is sometimes used to express the extent to which a given beam deviates from perfection is to use the ratio of the intensity of the real beam at its center to that of an ideal beam. This is called the *Strehl ratio*. If a laser beam is n times diffraction limited, the Strehl ratio is roughly $1/n^2$. An increase in the Strehl ratio or a reduction in n is often used as a measure of merit for optical systems whose purpose is to clean up a beam whose quality would otherwise be unacceptable.

Summary: Propagation in Vacuum

The following key points serve to summarize our discussion of laser propagation in a vacuum:

1. A laser will propagate as a collimated beam, with little spreading, over a distance on the order of $\pi D^2/\lambda$, where D is the diameter of the last optical element in the laser and its associated beam steering devices. Figure 3–17 shows the apertures necessary to achieve propagation without spreading as a function of range. Limiting the aperture to a modest size limits propagation to tactical ranges, on the order of 100 km or less. The power necessary to place a given intensity on target also becomes very large at long ranges, as illustrated in Figure 3–18. Figures 3–17 and 3–18 may be used together to evaluate tradeoffs in aperture, wavelength, and power in this propagation limit, which is known as the near field.

2. Over ranges greater than that for which it remains collimated, the beam radius grows with a divergence angle $\theta = \lambda/D$, so that the intensity decreases with range Z as $1/Z^2$. The constant of proportionality between the beam intensity S (W/cm^2) and $1/Z^2$ is known as the "brightness" of the beam, $B = PD^2/\pi\lambda^2$. figure 3–21 relates brightness to the range over which a given intensity may be placed on target. This propaga-

tion limit, which is appropriate for strategic applications with ranges greater than 1,000 km, is known as the far field.

3. Imperfections invariably present in real lasers cause them to spread at a rate greater than that predicted by diffraction theory. The ratio between real and ideal spot radius is known as the number of times "diffraction limited" the beam is, and the ratio of the real intensity at a given point to the ideal intensity is known as the "Strehl ratio."

Implications

As a directed energy weapon, a laser offers a lot of advantages. In tactical applications, propagation is with relatively little beam spread, so that the intensity on target is roughly independent of range. This is a useful feature, since in tactical engagements there can be considerable variation in the ranges at which targets may appear. Over strategic ranges, the beam will spread and its intensity will decline with distance, but this is somewhat compensated for by the fact that strategic scenarios are generally more stylized, with ranges and time scales for engagements predictable in advance.

In either case, there is a clear advantage from the standpoint of propagation in using as large an aperture and as small a wavelength as possible. Increasing the aperture is limited by engineering considerations—it may not be possible to construct a huge lens or mirror of sufficient quality to keep the beam close to diffraction limited, and large optical elements will have a lot of inertia, making the pointing and tracking of the beam on its target difficult. Reducing the wavelength is limited more by physical considerations—the materials and technology to develop lasers of arbitrarily short wavelength either do not exist or have yet to be discovered. And as wavelength gets shorter, photon energy increases and the atmosphere becomes increasingly opaque, as photons become able to connect energy states of the atmospheric gases and be absorbed. Therefore, it is appropriate to consider beam propagation in the atmosphere next, and consider the additional constraints this will have on beam parameters.

Laser Propagation in the Atmosphere.

In the atmosphere, beam propagation and divergence are to a first approximation the same as in a vacuum, with the added feature that interaction of the beam with atmospheric constituents causes it to lose photons. The intensity of the beam then decreases with range for two reasons: divergence increases the beam size, and atmospheric interactions reduce the energy that it carries. Having already quantified the first of these effects, we will turn our attention to the second. Photons may be lost from the beam in several ways. They may be scattered or absorbed by atmospheric gases or particulate contaminants. They may be bent from the beam by the lensing effect of density fluctuations in the atmosphere. And at high intensities, they may cause the air through which the beam passes to break down into an absorbing plasma. These and related effects will be considered in this section.

Absorption and Scattering

Earlier in this chapter we discussed the absorption and scattering of light by both gases and solids. While the atmosphere is composed primarily of gases, solids are present, too, in the form of suspended particulate matter (water droplets and dust, or *aerosols*). Both contribute their part to energy losses from a propagating laser beam. In our discussion of fundamentals, we concentrated our attention on the interaction of a single photon of light with a single molecule of gas. Our task now is to extend that analysis to the case where many photons of light encounter many molecules of gas, as well as small, suspended particles.

Molecules. When a photon encounters a molecule of gas, it may be absorbed or scattered. The probability of this happening is expressed in terms of the *cross section*, σ, for such an event to occur.[28] This concept is illustrated in Figure 3–22. Imagine that a laser beam of area A is propagating through a thickness dz of atmosphere in which there are N molecules per cubic centimeter. The total number of molecules that photons within the beam will encounter is NAdz. If each of these molecules has an effective "size" or cross section σ, the area blocked off by the molecules will be a = N σAdz. Therefore, the probability that a pho-

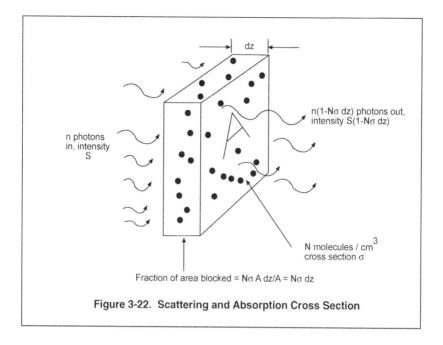

Figure 3-22. Scattering and Absorption Cross Section

ton will collide with a molecule and be lost from the beam through absorption or scattering is the ratio of the area blocked off to the total area, $a/A = N\sigma dz$. This means that if n photons enter the region shown in the figure, $nN\sigma dz$ will be lost from the beam. Since the beam intensity, S, is proportional to the number of photons n, it follows that S decreases by an amount $dS = -SN\sigma dz$ in propagating a distance dz.

The equation $dS = -SN\sigma dz$ is well known in mathematics. Its solution for the intensity $S(z)$ which a beam whose original intensity was $S(0)$ will have after propagating a distance z is $S(z) = S(0)\, e^{-N\sigma z}$. This result is known as *Bouguer's Law* or *Lambert's Law*.[29] It simply states that as light propagates through the atmosphere (or any substance, for that matter) its intensity decreases exponentially over the distance traveled. The quantity $N\sigma$ is traditionally denoted K and is called the *attenuation coefficient*. The distance over which a beam's intensity will decrease by a factor of $1/e$ (about $1/3$) is $1/K$, called the *absorption length*. The product $Kz = N\sigma Z$ is known as the *optical depth*, and is a measure of the effective thickness, from the standpoint of absorption, of the medium through which the light has traveled.

111

Figure 3–23 is a plot of S(z)/S(0), the fraction of a beam's intensity transmitted over a range z, as a function of optical depth Kz. You can see from this figure that for ranges z much greater than 1/K, large amounts of energy will be lost from the beam. Clearly, we must choose the parameters of a laser so that K is as small as possible, and the effective propagation range, 1/K, as large as possible.

Our derivation of the absorption law looked at the probability of a photon interacting with a single type of molecule, with a cross section σ. Within the atmosphere, there are many types (species) of molecules present (N_2, O_2, CO_2, etc). The probability of interaction with one is independent of the probability of interaction with another. That is, photons lost through interaction with one type of molecule may be added to those lost through interaction with another. As a result, the attenuation coefficients attributable to each type of molecule may simply be added: $K = K(N_2) + K(O_2) + K(CO_2) + \ldots \ldots$(etc). Furthermore, the attenuation coefficient due to each molecular type is in turn comprised of two parts, one for the absorption of photons by that type, and one for their scattering: $K(CO_2) = K$ (Absorption by CO_2) + K(Scattering by CO_2), and so on.

Clearly, attenuation in the atmosphere can be quite complex, with a variety of terms contributed from different molecular species, whose relative abundance and importance might change with latitude, longitude, relative humidity, and other climatic factors. Each of these terms may have a different dependence

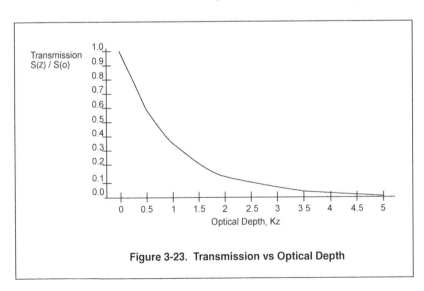

Figure 3-23. Transmission vs Optical Depth

upon laser wavelength, since a given wavelength may not be absorbed by one type of molecule, yet be strongly absorbed by another. Therefore, it should not be surprising that a considerable body of literature has developed in this area, ranging from detailed studies of the absorption by a single molecule to gross measurements of how much light penetrates the atmosphere as a function of frequency under given climactic conditions.[30] We can only scratch the surface and provide a general feeling for atmospheric absorption and scattering.

Figure 3–24 is an overview of atmospheric attenuation over a broad range of wavelengths.[31] This figure shows some of the broad windows for the propagation of laser light. However, there is considerable fine structure which the scale of this figure does not reveal. This is shown in the bottom portion of Figure 3–24, which is an expanded view of one narrow region in the upper half.

From Figure 3–24, you can see that even within what appears to be a propagation window, there may be narrow absorption bands at specific frequencies. Therefore, the choice of laser wavelength can be critical for propagation. For example, recent measurements of the output frequencies from a DF chemical laser have resulted

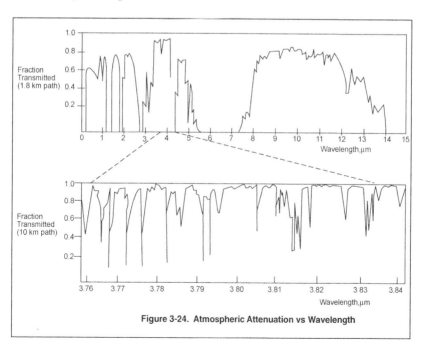

Figure 3-24. Atmospheric Attenuation vs Wavelength

in a changing one wavelength from 3.7886 to 3.7902 μm.[32] This change has been sufficient to alter the assessment of how much of this light would penetrate a 10 km path at sea level from about 90% to about 50%. This is one reason why free-electron lasers have recently received considerable interest. Unlike most lasers, whose output frequencies are fixed by the active, light- producing material in them, free-electron lasers are tunable in wavelength, offering greater flexibility in adjusting the output for efficient atmospheric propagation.

To this point, we have seen that the intensity of a laser beam will decrease with distance as $S(z) = S(0) e^{-Kz}$, where K, the attenuation coefficient, is a sum of terms representing absorption and scattering by the different species present in the atmosphere. Given K and knowing the range z required for a given application, Figure 3–23 can be used to evaluate the resulting decrease in intensity or brightness. This decrease can then be used to modify our results for propagation in a vacuum, allowing us to develop new criteria for target damage in atmospheric applications. For example, Figure 3–18 says that a laser power of 10 kW is required to deliver an intensity of 10^4 W/cm² in a collimated beam with a 3 cm aperture. If the beam is propagating in the atmosphere, and K is such that only 50% of the intensity is transmitted over the range to the target, we would need to use a 20 kW laser, so that after 50% attenuation we would have 10 kW left over to meet the intensity requirement on target. Alternatively, we might choose a laser with a different wavelength, for which the attenuation would be less.

A further complication arises in longer range strategic applications. The atmospheric parameters which determine K may change over a long range, so that K is not constant, but varies with distance. This would occur, for example, in using a ground-based laser to attack the moon. As the beam goes up through the atmosphere, K, which is proportional to the density of molecules, is steadily decreasing. Eventually, the beam leaves the atmosphere and over the greater part of its range is propagating in a vacuum. We would greatly overestimate the amount of beam attenuation by using exponential absorption with a K appropriate to the atmosphere at sea level, and a z equal to the range to the moon! In cases like this, we must modify our treatment of attenuation and allow K to be a function of z. If K is a variable, dependent upon z, the solution to our original equation, $dS/dz = -KS$, becomes $S(z) = S(0) \exp[-\int_0^z K(z)\,dz]$.

This "improved" version of the exponential attenuation law looks complicated, but its interpretation is straightforward. It says we must *integrate* K over the path length. In effect, we split the beam's path into many small segments. Over each, K is effectively constant, and exponential attenuation can be used. The total effect is then given by the sum of the optical depths over each small path segment. Doing this in any realistic case requires the use of a computer model which can keep track of how the distribution of molecules and their density varies with altitude, and can use these data to calculate an altitude dependent attenuation coefficient. There is, however, a simple model which is reasonably accurate, can be solved analytically, and gives a good feel for the effect of altitude dependence upon beam attenuation.

Within the lower atmosphere (0–120 km), density varies exponentially with altitude.[33] That is, the density of molecules $N(h)$ at altitude h is related to the density $N(0)$ at sea level by the relationship $N(h) = N(0) \exp(-h/h_o)$, where the constant h_o is about 7 km. Since K ($= \sigma N$) is also proportional to N, we can to a first approximation say that $K(h) = K(0)\exp(-h/h_o)$.[34]

Suppose that we are fire a laser into the air at some angle ϕ, as illustrated in Figure 3–25. The beam's altitude h is related to its range z and the elevation angle ϕ through the simple geometrical relationship $h = z \sin \phi$. When $\phi = 0$, $h = 0$ for any z, and when $\phi = 90°$, h and z are identical. Using this relationship between h and z, and assuming $K(h) = K(0) \exp(-h/h_o)$, we can evaluate the optical depth to any range z. The result is shown in Figure 3–26.[35]

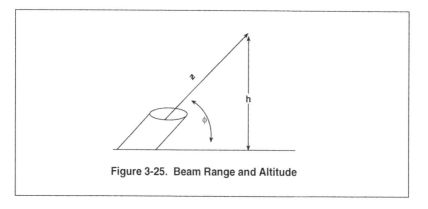

Figure 3-25. Beam Range and Altitude

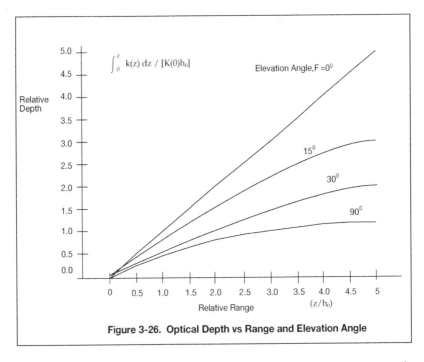

Figure 3-26. Optical Depth vs Range and Elevation Angle

Figure 3–26 is a plot of the optical depth to a range z, normalized to $K(0)h_o$, as a function of z, normalized to h_o. At $\phi = 0_o$, the beam is propagating horizontally, the atmospheric density is constant, and the optical depth increases linearly with distance, as we would expect. At $\phi = 90°$, the beam is propagating straight up, rapidly emerges from the atmosphere, and beyond that point the optical depth no longer increases. At intermediate angles, the beam has greater and greater lengths of atmosphere to propagate through before it emerges from the atmosphere, and so the optical depth approaches a limiting value later and of a higher value. For ranges less than h_o, the altitude over which atmospheric density changes significantly, the optical depth is roughly independent of elevation angle.

Figure 3–26 can be used together with our results for vacuum propagation to estimate attenuation for long range applications and its impact on laser requirements. For example, let's return to the case where we wish to attack the moon. If at sea level the attenuation coefficient at the frequency of our laser is 0.1 km^{-1}, and if we are able to shoot when the moon is directly overhead ($\phi = 90°$), then by Figure 3–26 the optical depth will be $K(o)h_o$, or 0.7.

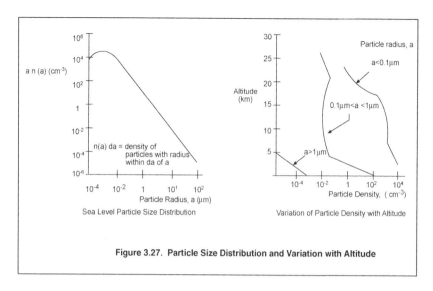

Figure 3.27. Particle Size Distribution and Variation with Altitude

We can then use Figure 3–23 to see that for this optical depth, laser intensity and brightness will be about 0.6 of what they would have been in a vacuum. Therefore, the brightness requirements necessary to place a given intensity on target, obtained from Figure 3–20, must be increased by a factor of 1/0.6, or about 1.7.

Small Particles (Aerosols). To this point, we've looked at the attenuation of a laser beam due to the gases (molecules) which comprise the majority of the atmosphere. We must next consider the effect of small solid or liquid aerosols which are invariably suspended in the atmosphere, especially near the surface. Figure 3–27, for example, shows the number density of suspended particles as a function of particle radius at sea level, along with the way in which the density of particles in different size ranges varies with altitude.[36] This figure must, of course, be considered somewhat notional, since the actual particle size distribution can vary greatly, depending on the local climate and wind conditions.[37]

A number of important things are apparent from Figure 3–27. First, particles in excess of 1μm are quite rare, and largely confined to regions near the surface of the earth. Second, the range of particle sizes is comparable to the wavelengths of lasers operating from the visible to far infrared ($0.4 - 10\mu$m). The absorption and scattering of light by solid particles becomes quite complex to analyze when the particle size is comparable to the

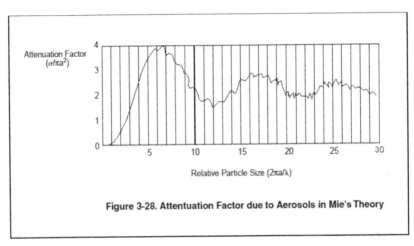

Figure 3-28. Attentuation Factor due to Aerosols in Mie's Theory

wavelength of the light. The relevant theory is known as *Mie Scattering Theory* for its developer, a German meteorologist.[38] The development of this theory is beyond the scope of this book, but its essence is summarized in Figure 3–28.

Figure 3–28 shows how the actual attenuation cross section for a dielectric aerosol (in this case water) compares to its physical size, πa^2, as a function of $2\pi a/\lambda$, where a is the aerosol radius and λ the wavelength of the light. There are various dips and bumps in the cross section, reflecting resonances between particle size and light wavelength, but for the most part σ is on the order of $2\pi a^2$, especially when a is much larger than λ. Somewhat crudely, you might think that each particle contributes twice its physical cross section to light attenuation because it can contribute to attenuation in two ways—through absorption and scattering.[39]

Curves similar to Figure 3–28 are available in the literature for a variety of different particle types, both dielectric and metallic.[40] As a general rule, they exhibit behavior similar to that shown in Figure 3–28—σ falls to zero as $2\pi a/\lambda$ goes to zero, but for $2\pi a/\lambda > 1$, σ is in the neighborhood of $2\pi a^2$. Given Figure 3–27, which suggests that the majority of aerosols are of a size less than 1μm, we can conclude that the effect of aerosols on light attenuation will be greater for visible lasers ($\lambda = 0.4 - 0.7$ μm) than for those operating in the infrared ($\lambda = 1$–10μm). The relative particle size, $2\pi a/\lambda$, is shown in Figure 3–29 as a function of wavelength and particle size. This figure may be used with Figure 3–28 to estimate the contribution of aerosols to light attenuation. However,

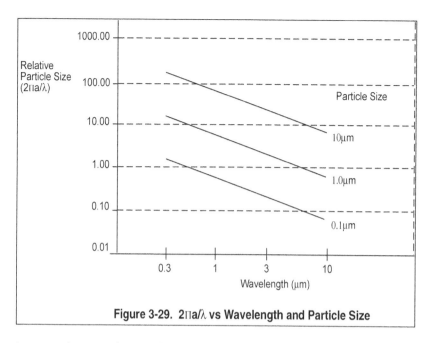

Figure 3-29. 2∏a/λ vs Wavelength and Particle Size

it must be emphasized that under realistic circumstances the density and type of aerosols can vary greatly from day to day. Thus, the operational use of lasers will require that site-specific surveys be made and that beam brightness be increased to enable meeting damage criteria under "worst case" conditions.

Just as the attenuation coefficient for a mixture of molecules may be obtained as the sum of the coefficients contributed by each molecule present, the total attenuation coefficient when aerosols are suspended in the atmosphere is the sum of contributions from the molecules and the aerosols taken separately. Molecules and aerosols can contribute to attenuation in roughly equal amounts, but for quite different reasons. The attenuation coefficient K is σN, where σ is the attenuation cross section and N the density of the attenuator. Molecules have a very small attenuation cross section $10^{-25} - 10^{-26}$ cm^2), but their density is quite large (3×10^{19}/cm^3 at sea level). By contrast, particles can have a very large cross section ($\approx 3 \times 10^{-8}$ cm^2), but their density is quite low (1/cm^3 or less).

Summary: Absorption and Scattering.

1. Beam intensity S (Watts/cm^2) decreases exponentially as a function of the distance of propagation, z: $S(z) = S(0)e^{-Kz}$. Figure

119

3–23 is a plot of this relationship. K is known as the attenuation coefficient, and Kz as the optical depth.

2. The attenuation coefficient, K, is a sum of contributions resulting from absorption and scattering by both molecular and aerosol species in the atmosphere. Figure 3–24 is representative of the wavelength dependence of K due to the molecules in the atmosphere, and Figure 3–28 of the wavelength dependence of K due to aerosols.

3. The attenuation coefficient, K, is proportional to the density N of molecules or aerosols present. When the propagation distance, z, is such that K varies over z, the optical depth is not Kz, but the integral of K over z: $\int_0^z K(z)dz$. Figure 3–26 provides an example of how the variation of atmospheric density with altitude affects optical depth as a function of range and elevation angle for a ground based laser.

4. At sea level, the contributions of molecules and aerosols to attenuation are roughly equal. However, large aerosols fall off rapidly with altitude, as indicated in Figure 3–22.

Index of Refraction Variations

Turbulence and the Coherence Length. In the previous section, we saw that the variation of atmospheric density with altitude had an effect on energy absorption and scattering. This was a very large-scale effect, occuring over distances comparable to that over which the atmospheric density varies to a significant extent (7 km). In this section, we'll turn our attention to the effect on propagation of small-scale fluctuations in atmospheric density, which result from the turbulence induced as the sun heats the atmosphere each day.

Small-scale fluctuations do not affect absorption or scattering because they tend to average out when the optical depth is computed over a long path. But they can still have a profound effect on beam propagation through the variations they cause in the index of refraction of the air. When light passes through regions of differing refractive index, as in a lens, it is bent (see Figures 3–4 and 3–5). Density fluctuations can have the effect of introducing many tiny "lenses" into the beam.

Though the index of refraction of air is close to the value of 1 which characterizes a vacuum, there is a small deviation which varies with density and wavelength as shown in Figure 3–30.[41]

As you can see from Figure 3–30, the index of refraction of air is pretty close to the value of 1 which is appropriate for a vacuum. For example, at 0.4 μm wavelength, n is 1.00028 at 15 °C, and 1.00026 at 30 °C. Nevertheless, small fluctuations of this order can have a significant effect over long propagation distances. As a simple example, suppose that light of 0.4 μm wavelength is propagating through air at a temperature of 30 °C, and enters a region where the temperature is 15 °C at an angle of 45°. The law of refraction ($n_1 \sin \theta_1 = n_2 \sin \theta_2$) can be used to find that the angle θ_2 with which the light emerges from the interface between these regions is 44.99885442°. This is very little deflection, the difference from 45°, being only 0.0011°, or about 2×10^{-5} radians. Yet over a propagation path of 100 km this would mean a beam deflection of about 2 m—more than enough to cause the beam to miss a target which it might otherwise hit. Of course, in the real world the beam will encounter regions of higher and lower temperature and will wander back and forth, and the sizes of the regions of temperature fluctuation may be smaller than the beam itself, sending different portions of the

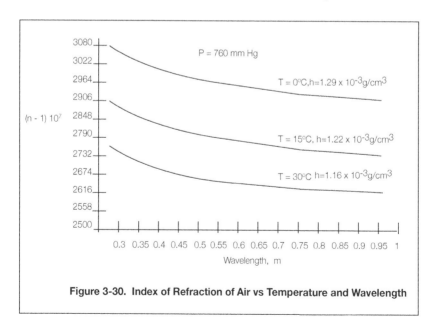

Figure 3-30. Index of Refraction of Air vs Temperature and Wavelength

121

beam front in diverse directions. The net result will be a lessening of the beam intensity on target which is difficult to predict in advance. We must see if we can quantify this effect and, if possible, compensate for it in the design of our laser beam.

In principle, it's possible to know and account for fluctuations in the index of refraction if we know how temperature and density vary along the beam path. In practice, of course, it's impossible to know these quantities everywhere within the beam path at all times—they're constantly shifting. What we need is a macroscopic parameter which can capture the effect of microscopic density fluctuations in a straightforward way. There *is* such a parameter, known as the *coherence length* and denoted r_o.[42] The physical meaning of the coherence length is illustrated in Figure 3–31.

Figure 3–31 shows a laser beam of diameter D propagating through the air. In a vacuum, the beam would diverge through diffraction at an angle $\theta \approx \lambda/D$, as indicated by the heavy outline in the figure. However, density fluctuations in the atmosphere have the effect of introducing many tiny "lenses" into the beam volume. These are suggested by the small bubbles which appear within the beam volume, and they have the effect of breaking up the unity, or coherence, of the beam front. In effect, the beam is split up into many tiny beams, each of which encounters a slightly different environment. The coherence length, r_o, may be

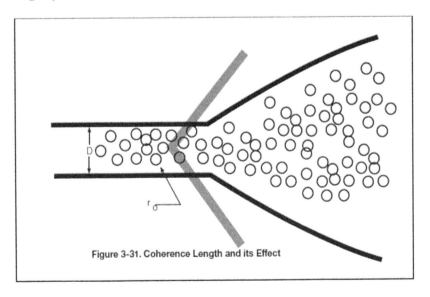

Figure 3-31. Coherence Length and its Effect

thought of as the average size of these little lenses, or as the average diameter of the small sub-beams into which the main beam is split.

If a laser beam is split into sub-beams of size r_o, we would expect its divergence to be governed by the size r_o of the sub-beams, rather that the size D of the original beam. The divergence angle of a beam of diameter D propagating through an atmosphere with coherence length r_o is shown in Figure 3–32. You can see that our supposition is correct, and when $r_o \ll D$, the divergence angle of the beam becomes not λ/D, but λ/r_o.

Figure 3–32 gives us the capability to account for the effect of atmospheric density fluctuations on beam propagation, provided we know the coherence length. A look at Figure 3–31 suggests that the coherence length will depend on a number of factors:

• The degree of turbulence along the beam path, which establishes the physical size of the little density inhomogenieties.

• The wavelength of the light, which establishes the optical depth of the inhomogenieties, since index of refraction depends on wavelength.

• The total path length from beam to target, since the further the beam travels, the more inhomogenieties of various sizes will be encountered.

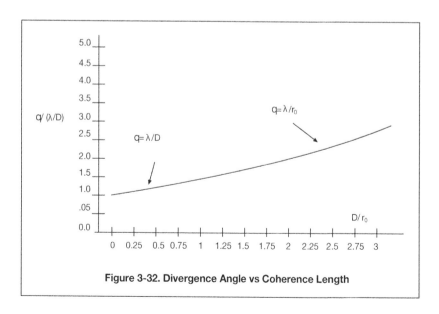

Figure 3-32. Divergence Angle vs Coherence Length

123

All of these factors do, in fact, affect r_o. A theoretical expression which takes all of them into account is

$$r_o = [0.423 \, (2\pi/\lambda)^2 \int_o^z C_N^2(z)dz]^{-3/5}.$$

In this expression, the quantity $C_N(z)$ is known as the *refractive index structure coefficient*, and characterizes the turbulence at a point z along the beam path.[43] By integrating the square of this quantity over the whole beam path, the total integrated effect of turbulence is taken into account. If C_N is known, r_o can in principle be calculated over any beam path, and the resulting effect on beam propagation accounted for. Unfortunately, this is easier said than done. Measurements of C_N have been obtained experimentally by probing the atmosphere with a laser, examining the effect of turbulence on its propagation. Typical data are shown in Figure 3–33.[44]

As you can see from the figure, turbulence is least during the hours of darkness, when there is no solar heating to introduce temperature inhomogenieties. There is usually a large rise right after sunrise, followed by a pattern of rough proportionality to solar intensity. Superimposed on this, however, are fluctuations of as much as 30–50% on time scales of less than an hour.[45] As a function of altitude, C_N decreases, since solar heating is greatest near the ground, where the greatest proportion of the solar energy is absorbed.

On the basis of data such as that shown in Figure 3–33, it has been calculated that r_o will be on the order or 5–10 cm for visible wavelength light propagating from ground to space.[46] Since the beam aperture D would probably be greater than this for propaga-

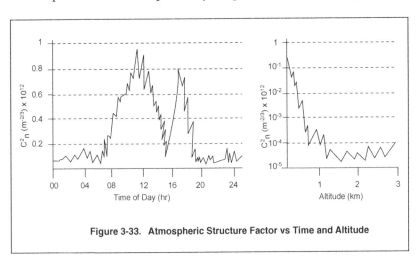

Figure 3-33. Atmospheric Structure Factor vs Time and Altitude

tion over such a long range, you can see that beam divergence is much increased by turbulence. This could make achieving damage criteria in the presence of turbulence virtually impossible. For example, we saw in Figure 3–21 that to place an intensity S of 10^4 W/cm^2 on a target at a range of 10^4 km we would need a beam of brightness 10^{22} W/sr. This requires a power of 150 MW at an aperture of 10 m. If turbulence reduces the effective aperture to 10 cm, power requirements increase by a factor of 10^4, to 1500 GW. Practically speaking, this type of fix is not possible, because it leads us into intensities where laser design becomes increasingly difficult, and more fundamentally because when intensities become too great, there are nonlinear propagation effects, such as air breakdown, which effectively prevent beam propagation. Nonlinear effects are discussed later in this section.

Figure 3–34 provides a convenient summary of our discussion, showing how brightness varies with the ratio of r_o to D. Using Figure 3–34, you can determine the effect of a given degree of turbulence, as measured by r_o, on the brightness if a given laser. To regain the original brightness, laser power must be increased appropriately. Since this will typically take us into intensities which are unacceptable for one reason or another, there has arisen considerable interest in being able to compensate in some way for the

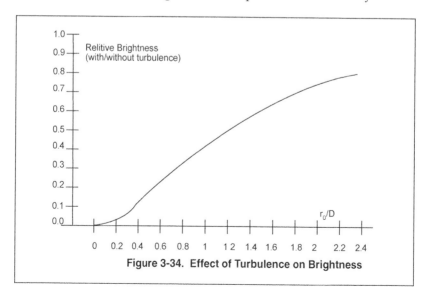

Figure 3-34. Effect of Turbulence on Brightness

effects of atmospheric turbulence on propagation. The techniques for doing so are known as *adaptive optics*.

Adaptive Optics. Adaptive optics makes use of the fact that if we know what the atmosphere is like along the beam path, it's possible to send out the beam distorted in such a way that turbulence will in fact straighten it out! This may seem far-fetched, but the general principle is straightforward, and is illustrated in   Figure 3–35. In the upper portion of the figure, a beam of light encounters a lens which might represent a cell of turbulence. This lens focuses the light, so that it diverges. In the bottom   portion of the figure, a second lens has been introduced, identical to the first, and positioned at twice the focal distance from it. This lens has the effect of presenting a diverging beam to the original lens, which then proceeds to focus it back into a parallel beam. The second lens compensates for the first, so that the net result is as though the first lens were not present. The idea behind adaptive optics is to compensate for the many little "lenses" of turbulence in a similar way. All we need to do is know what's out there and *compensate* the beam, mixing up its initial parameters in such a way that the optical path which it traverses acts to convert the mixed-up beam into the beam we'd have in the absence of that optical path.

The practical problem in carrying out this approach is knowing what's out there so we can compensate for it, since turbulence changes from moment to moment. We need a way to obtain real-time feedback on the environment, and to use that information in adjusting the beam appropriately. This is a formidable task, but not impossible, and it has been accomplished experimentally.[47]

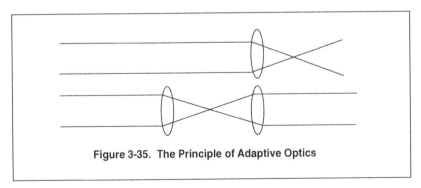

Figure 3-35. The Principle of Adaptive Optics

Figure 3–36 snows schematically how this has been done. The key to the technique is a *deformable mirror*—one in which small actuators move the surface up and down to distort the outgoing beam in such a way that turbulence will compensate for this distortion, resulting in a nearly diffraction-limited beam on target. The degree of distortion required is found by examining some of the light which is reflected back from the target. This light, indicated by the dashed line in Figure 3–36, is fed into a phase sensor, which compares the quality of the returning light with that in the outgoing beam. The difference between these is, of course, related directly to the turbulence along the beam path. A computer uses this information to provide instructions to the actuators which then deform the mirror appropriately.

There are, of course, practical considerations which may limit the ability to do this in realistic scenarios. First, the number of actuators required may be quite large. Since the beam is being broken up into segments of a size r_o, it follows that the mirror surface must be broken up into segments of area less than πr_o^2. As we have seen, propagation over large distances requires large mirror sizes—1–10 m. Since r_o is typically 5–10 cm, the mirror must be divided into something on the order of 10,000 segments, with a corresponding number of actuators. These actuators must be able to produce the necessary degree of distortion sufficiently fast to compensate for a continually shifting environment as well. Typically, this requires that any section on the mirror surface be able to move 1–10 μm in times on the order of 10^{-3} sec.[48]

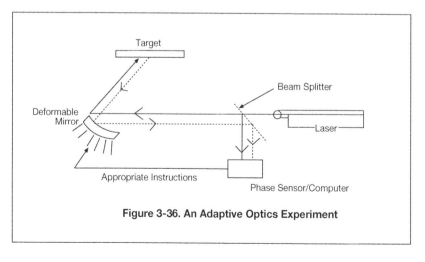

Figure 3-36. An Adaptive Optics Experiment

Additionally, the incoming and outgoing beams must pass through the same region of air and see the same turbulence. While the speed of light is fast, it is finite, and in tracking fast moving targets at large distances (as may be the case in ground-to-space propagation) it may be necessary to lead the target so that the light arrives at a given point when the target does. In this case, you can't rely on reflected light from the target for turbulence information. This is why it is generally envisioned that a space-based relay mirror for a ground based laser would have a beacon laser, ahead of the mirror, which would propagate down and provide turbulence information for the region of space the beam would traverse in going to the mirror. A useful parameter for use in evaluating the need for such a scheme is known as the *isoplanatic angle*. This is the maximum angle by which a beam can steer and still see essentially the same turbulent environment. If the angle by which a target must be led exceeds this angle, then the beam can no longer be used to provide its own reference, and a separate beacon is required. Typically, the isoplanatic angle is on the order of 1–10 μrad.[49]

Summary: Index of Refraction Variations.

1. Atmospheric turbulence has the effect of introducing small "lenses" into the volume of the beam as it propagates. The characteristic size of these lenses is known as the coherence length, r_o. This quantity depands upon the propagation length, path, time of day, and laser wavelength, and is typically 5–10 cm.

2. The effect of turbulence is to change the beam divergence angle from λ/D to λ/r_o. This reduces beam brightness by a factor of $(r_o/D)^2$. Figure 3–34 summarizes the effect of turbulence on brightness, and may be used together with Figure 3–20 to estimate the impact of turbulence on meeting damage criteria.

3. In many scenarios of interest, particularly those which may be characterized as strategic rather than tactical, turbulence-induced beam divergence is unacceptable, and adaptive optics is required to compensate for it.

4. Adaptive optics is a technique in which the beam is intentionally distorted so that the turbulence which is present restores it to a diffraction-limited configuration. This is done by evaluating

the turbulence present in real time, probing the beam path with a reference beam and using the resulting information to distort a deformable laser output mirror. If adaptive optics techniques are successfully employed, turbulence may essentially be ignored in assessing damage criteria.

Nonlinear Effects

To this point, everything we've considered has been independent of the laser's intensity. Absorption, for example, reduces the intensity at a given range z by a fraction, $S(z)/S(0) = e^{-Kz}$, which is independent of $S(0)$. This means that the transmitted intensity, $S(z)$, is directly proportional to the intensity out of the laser, $S(0)$. If we were to plot $S(z)$ as a function of the $S(0)$, the plot would be a straight line, as shown in Figure 3–37(a). For this reason, the propagation effects we've looked at so far are known as linear effects.

As intensity increases, it is usually found that at some point the relationship between $S(z)$ and $S(0)$ is no longer linear—there is a sudden shift in behavior, like that shown in Figure 3–37 (b). This typically occurs when $S(0)$ exceeds some threshold value, and beyond that threshold the relationship between $S(z)$ and $S(0)$ can be quite compex and not at all linear, so that *nonlinear* propagation effects are said to have occurred. The physical reason for nonlinear effects is that when intensities are strong enough, the beam actually modifies the environment through which it propagates in such a way that its physical characteristics are altered. For example, a very intense beam might vaporize the aerosols in its path,

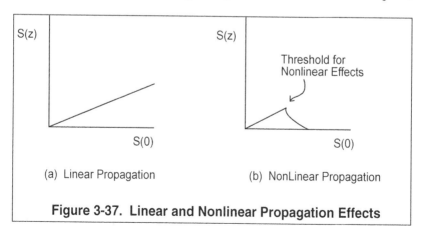

(a) Linear Propagation   (b) NonLinear Propagation

Figure 3-37. Linear and Nonlinear Propagation Effects

and suffer less degradation due to aerosol absorption and scattering than a lower intensity beam. Or it might ionize the atmosphere in its path, increasing absorption to the point where propagation ceases. Unfortunately, most nonlinear effects degrade, rather than enhance the intensity on target. In this section, we'll consider nonlinear effects which affect both propagation (thermal blooming and bending) and attenuation (stimulated scattering, breakdown, and absorption waves). Our emphasis will be on those effects which are of concern from the standpoint of beam propagation in weapon applications.[49]

Thermal Blooming. One of the first nonlinear phenomena recognized as likely to affect the propagation of a high power laser, thermal blooming results from the energy which a laser deposits in the air through which it propagates. The beam loses energy as a result of absorption. This energy is deposited within the beam path, where it causes a temperature rise in the air. This temperature rise modifies the air's density, alters its index of refraction, and can severely affect the beam's propagation. The sequence of events which results in thermal blooming is illustrated in Figure 3–38.

Figure 3–38 (A) shows the intensity profile of a typical laser beam viewed end-on: higher in the center than at the edges, where the intensity falls to zero. The temperature of the air through which the beam propagates will exhibit a similar profile, as suggested by Figure 3–38 (B). This is because absorption of energy by

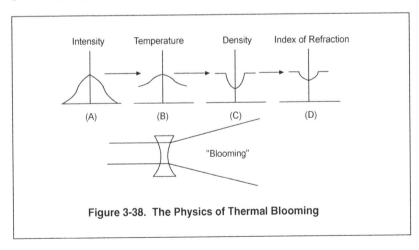

Figure 3-38. The Physics of Thermal Blooming

the air is a linear phenomenon—as intensity goes up, the amount of energy absorbed, being a constant fraction of the the incident intensity, goes up as well. The absorbed energy manifests itself as in increase in temperature. But hot air is less dense than cold air—at constant (atmospheric) pressure, an increase in temperature implies a decrease in density. Thus, the density profile in the air through which the beam propagates assumes a form inverse to the intensity profile, as shown in Figure 3–38 (C). The implication of this is that the index of refraction of the air through which the beam propagates, shown in Figure 3–38 (D), mirrors the density profile, since (n–1) is proportional to density (see Figure 3–30). This sequence of events has the effect of introducing within the volume of the beam what amounts to a diverging lens, with a greater optical density at the edges than at the center. As shown at the bottom of Figure 3–38, this causes the beam to *bloom*, or diverge, at a rate greater than would otherwise be expected.

In practical scenarios, wind sweeps across the beam—either a naturally occurring wind or one which results from the relative motion of beam and atmosphere as the beam slews to keep itself on target. Such a cross-wind causes the beam to *bend* as well as bloom. The physical reason for this is illustrated in Figure 3–39. In this figure, we begin with the temperature profile which produced thermal blooming. However, wind is blowing across the beam and introduces cold air. As a result, the upwind portion of the temperature profile becomes cooler and the downwind portion warmer. In effect, the wind tries to push the hot air downstream. As a result, the index of refraction profile assumes a shape like that shown, and

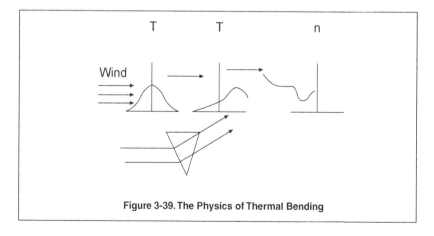

Figure 3-39. The Physics of Thermal Bending

the beam sees what looks like a wedge inserted into it. This wedge causes the beam to bend into the wind, as indicated. Another way of looking at it might be to think that the wind displaces the diverging lens of thermal blooming, so the the beam sees only one half of that lens, and bends in a single direction.

Looking at Figures 3–38 and 3–39, you can easily imagine that the analysis of thermal blooming and bending will be quite difficult, involving gas flow, laser heating, and the temperature and density dependence of the index of refraction of air. In any realistic scenario, wind velocity will vary along the beam path, and beam blooming and bending will occur simultaneously. The resulting distortions of the beam's intensity profile can be quite complex, as shown in Figure 3–40, which compares a beam's intensity on target in the presence of these effects with what it would have been in their absence. Our goal will be to determine the thresholds for thermal blooming, the magnitude of the effect, and the potential for dealing with it through techniques such as adaptive optics in those cases where target range and damage criteria prevent operation below threshold.

We must first recognize that there is a pulse width threshold for thermal blooming. Even though the atmosphere absorbs energy and its temperature begins to rise almost immediately, some finite time is required for the heated air to expand and move out of the beam, creating the density "hole" shown in Figure 3–38 (C). The characteristic velocity at which disturbances propagate in air is the

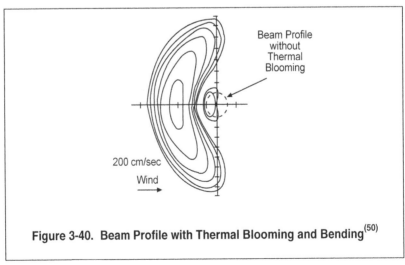

Beam Profile
without
Thermal
Blooming

200 cm/sec

Wind

Figure 3-40. Beam Profile with Thermal Blooming and Bending[50]

speed of sound, a (= 3 × 10⁴ cm/sec). Therefore, the time for air to move out of a beam of radius w and for blooming to begin is approximately w/a. Figure 3–41 is a plot of the time for thermal blooming to develop as a function of beam radius.

You can see from Figure 3–41 that thermal blooming is not likely for pulsed lasers, where the goal is to place all the energy on target in short time scales—10⁻⁵ seconds or less, for example. On the other hand, if seconds of interaction time with the target are required, there is a potential for thermal blooming to be a problem, even for strategic applications, where the beam radius may be relatively large. Therefore, we must consider next the magnitude of the effect, to see if thermal blooming will pose a serious threat to mission accomplishment should it occur.

The quantitative analysis of all nonlinear phenomena is quite complex and difficult, since it depends on a beam intensity which is itself changing in response as the interaction proceeds. Predicting how the spot size and intensity vary with time on target for a beam of arbitrary intensity distribution therefore requires a computer program in which all these effects are modeled.[51] Considerable insight can be gained, however, by looking at simplified examples for which exact solutions exist. One case which has been

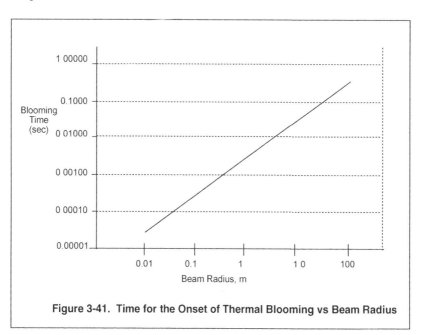

Figure 3-41. Time for the Onset of Thermal Blooming vs Beam Radius

extensively studied is that of a beam in a uniform crosswind of velocity v, having an intensity profile[52] which varies with radius as $S(r) = S_o \exp(-2r^2/w^2)$. Such a beam can be characterized through a *thermal distortion factor*, N_t, which is given by[53]

$$N_t = -\frac{(dn/dT)}{n\rho c_p} \times \frac{KSZ^2}{vw}$$

The first factor in the expression for N_t contains parameters related to the gas through which the laser is propagating, and the second contains parameters related to the laser and scenario in which it is employed. The individual terms have the following interpretation:

- (dn/dT) is the slope of a curve of index of refraction, n, as a function of temperature, T. The greater the dependence of n on T, the more pronounced will be the lens or wedge introduced as the beam heats the air.

- C_p is the heat capacity of the air (J/gm ^{0}K), and ρ its density (gm/cm^3). Their product, ρC_p, is the number of Joules of energy which must be absorbed to heat a cubic centimeter of air by one degree.

- K is the absorption coefficient of the air (cm^{-1}), and S the laser intensity (W/cm^2). Their product, KS, is the number of Joules being deposited in a cubic centimeter of air each second.

- z is the range to target, w the beam radius, and v the wind velocity. N_t increases as z goes up, because the thermal lens has a longer distance over which to act. It decreases as v and w increase. A stronger wind will cool the beam volume, perhaps even blowing the heated air out of it. Since the intensity changes the most near the edge of the beam, a larger w reduces the relative importance of these edge effects and the blooming or bending which results from them.

As N_t increases, the beam becomes more and more distorted, and its intensity falls off as shown in Figure 3–42. Since N_t is proportional to the beam intensity S, it's not possible at large distortion numbers to overcome the effect of thermal blooming by increasing S. For example, if N_t is 10, the intensity on target will be about 0.1 of what it would have been in the absence of blooming. If we try to compensate for this by increasing S by a factor of 10, we'll increase N_t to 100, since it's proportional to S. But at an N_t of

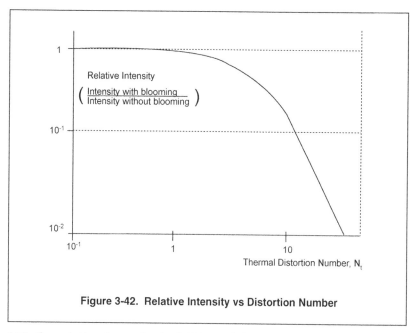

Figure 3-42. Relative Intensity vs Distortion Number

100, the relative intensity is 0.001, and the net effect of increasing S by a factor of 10 will have been to reduce the intensity on target! This illustrates one of the more unpleasant features of nonlinear effects. Actions taken to correct them can have an effect opposite to that intended, because of the many feedback loops which affect how the system responds to its inputs.

It is interesting to note as another example that an instability may occur when adaptive optics is employed in the presence of thermal blooming. The reason for this is sketched in Figure 3–43.

In the upper portion of the figure, we see what an adaptive optics system perceives as thermal blooming begins—that a diverging lens has been inserted into the beam path. As a response, the system, tries to do what is shown in the bottom portion of the figure—send a converging beam into the lens so that the diverging nature of the lens will only serve to straighten the beam out. Unfortunately, this serves to increase the intensity in the center of the beam, increase the temperature in this region, and aggravate the diverging lens effect, leading to further focusing, further divergence etc, etc. Thus the algorithm responsible for adaptive optics must be capable of adapting to and compensating for nonlinear phenomena such as thermal blooming, as well as linear phenom-

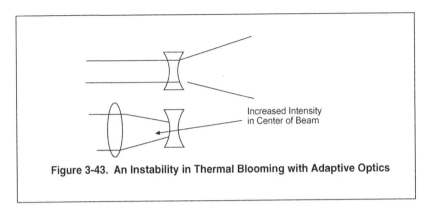

Figure 3-43. An Instability in Thermal Blooming with Adaptive Optics

ena such as turbulence. The spatial scale for thermal blooming is on the order of the beam width, and may be much greater than the coherence length which characterizes turbulence. This can create both hardware and software challenges in dealing with the two phenomena together. Developing adaptive optics schemes capable of handling both thermal blooming and turbulence is an ongoing area for research.[54]

If we want to avoid the complexities of dealing with thermal blooming, Figure 3–42 tells us that the distortion number must be of order unity or less. What are the implications from the standpoint of beam design? Figure 3–44 shows the relationships among intensity, range, velocity, and beam radius subject to the constraint that $N_t = 1$. The curve may be used in the following way. Suppose we wish to engage a target at a range of 10 km with a beam whose radius is 0.5 m (50 cm), and anticipate that the crosswind will be 5 mi/hr (about 200 cm/sec). Then the product vw is 10^4 cm²/sec. As the lines drawn on the figure show, the product KS must therefore be less than or equal to about 3×10^{-6} W/cm³ if the distortion number is to be kept less than one. If we know that the beam intensity needs to be 10^4 W/cm² in order to meet our damage criteria, this implies that the absorption coefficient K must be less than 3×10^{-10} cm⁻¹ (3×10^{-5} km⁻¹) for no thermal blooming or bending to occur. Since absorption coefficients within propagation "windows" are more like $10^{-3} – 10^{-2}$ km⁻¹, you can see that it's very unlikely that we can accomplish this mission without thermal blooming.[55] On the other hand, if the target is an aircraft moving at 500 mi/hr, vw will be increased to 10^6 cm²/sec and KS to 3×10^{-4} W/cm³. Under these circumstances, a 10^4

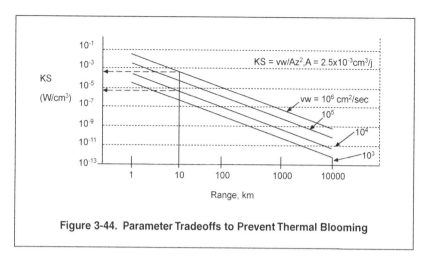

Figure 3-44. Parameter Tradeoffs to Prevent Thermal Blooming

W/cm² laser can do the job if K is less than 3×10^{-3} km^{-1}, a more reasonable value.

You can play with Figure 3–44 and look at the likelihood of avoiding thermal blooming under a variety of scenarios.[56] Such an examination will convince you that there are far more circumstances where thermal blooming needs to be considered, than where it does not. The only sure-fire way around the problem is to shorten the interaction time to the point where blooming can't develop (Figure 3–41). This solution can bring problems of its own with it, however, since at short pulse widths the intensity necessary for damage can become quite high, and may exceed the threshold for other nonlinear effects, such as stimulated scattering and air breakdown.

Stimulated Scattering. Thermal blooming is a nonlinear propagation effect, which causes the beam to diverge more rapidly and follow a different path than it would in a vacuum. *Stimulated scattering* is a nonlinear form of scattering. Normal scattering events are independent of one another. When we derived the absorption equation, the probability of a photon scattering when it encountered a molecule depended only on the molecule's scattering cross section, σ, and had nothing to do with what other molecules were present, or how many other photons had scattered. As a result, the attenuation coefficient K was simply a sum of contributions from the different molecules present, and was independent of the intensity, S. By contrast, stimulated scattering occurs when one photon is induced (or *stimulated*) to scatter because other photons have done so. In a sense, it's as though the photons exert peer pressure on one another, and when the number which have scattered reaches some critical number, suddenly everybody wants to get into the game, and the amount of scattering increases dramatically.

Mathematically, the increase in the intensity of the stimulated scattered light, S_s, with distance obeys the relationship $dS_s/dz = g S_s S$, where S is the intensity of the laser light, and g is a constant of proportionality, known as the gain, having units of cm/W. The fact that dS_s/dz is proportional to S_s reflects the stimulation provided by photons which have already scattered. The solution to this equation is an exponential growth in the scattered light: $S_s(z) = S_s(0) \exp(gSz)$. By contrast, the normal scattering of light obeys the relationship $dS_s/dz = \sigma_s NS$, where σ_s is the cross section for scattering. The solution to this equation is a linear growth in S_s: $S_s(z) = \sigma_s NS z$. Under normal circumstances, the intensity of scattered light, S_s, is small, and stimulated scattering is not important. However, over a sufficiently long range and at a sufficiently high intensity of laser light S, S_s can build up to the point where stimulated scattering exceeds normal scattering, and due to its exponential growth, the laser light is rapidly depleted. The contrast between normal and stimulated scattering is illustrated in Figure 3–45.

In Figure 3–45, you can see that as long as the scattering is normal and exceeds the stimulated scattering, there is relatively little decline in the laser intensity. However, the stimulated scattering grows exponentially with distance, and at some critical distance, z_c, exceeds normal scattering, rapidly depleting the laser beam. Therefore, the analysis of stimulated scattering involves determining z_c as a function of laser parameters, so that these may be chosen to avoid the problem over the range to target.

There can be different types of stimulated scattering, according to the nature of the scattering mechanism. The general theory of stimulated scattering relies on quantum mechanics and is quite complex. The theory is discussed in detail in many sources.[57] For our purpose, it will be sufficient to focus in on the form of scattering which is considered to be most limiting from the standpoint of high power propagation in the atmosphere. This is known as *stim-*

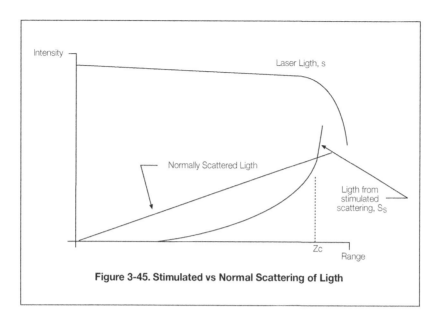

Figure 3-45. Stimulated vs Normal Scattering of Ligth

ulated Raman Scattering, and is often referred to as SRS in the litera-ture.[58]

It is generally accepted that a good rule of thumb for SRS to grow to the point where it exceeds normal scattering is that the intensity of the SRS-scattered light must grow by 11 orders of magnitude. That is, the SRS scattered light, which is growing as $S_s(z) = S_s(0) \exp(gSz)$, must increase to the point where $\exp(gSz) = 10^{11}$, or $gSz = \ln(10^{11}) \approx 25$. We can use $gSz_c = 25$ as a criterion for SRS to prevent the propagation of a high power laser, and find the critical range, z_c, as a function of the laser intensity, S, and the gain, g. This requires that we have an understanding of g and how it varies with such parameters as altitude and wavelength. Figure 3–46 is a plot of the SRS gain for a 1.06 μm laser propagating in the atmosphere.[59]

As you can see from Figure 3–46, the gain for SRS declines rapidly above about 40 km, so that from a practical standpoint stimulated scattering is of concern only at lower altitudes. As a function of pulse width, there is a modest decline at higher altitudes. For short pulses; near sea level, there is essentially no dependence on pulse width. The gain for SRS may be shown on theoretical grounds to be proportional to the laser frequency, *v*. Therefore, Figure 3–46 can be scaled to different frequencies or

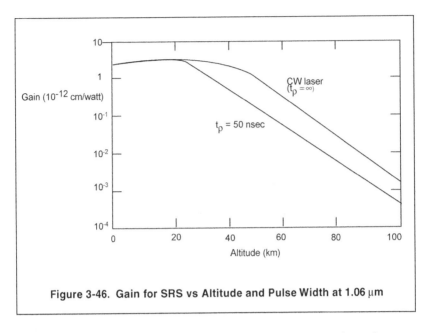

Figure 3-46. Gain for SRS vs Altitude and Pulse Width at 1.06 μm

wavelengths by multiplying by the ratio v/v_o, or λ_o/λ, where v_o and λ_o are the frequency and wavelength for 1.06 m radiation. For example, if the light were in the far infrared at 10.6m, the gain would be reduced by a factor of 0.1 from that shown in Figure 3–46.

Using the data in Figure 3–46, we can plot the range z_c to which a given intensity S can propagate before SRS becomes a concern, using as a criterion $gz_cS = 25$. This is done in Figure 3–47.

Figure 3–47 tells us that for tactical applications at ranges of 100 km or less, SRS limits us to intensities of about 10^7 W/cm² or less in the far infrared, and about 3×10^5 W/cm² or less in the visible. For strategic applications, the beam might be shooting up into the atmosphere with some elevation angle ϕ (see Figure 3–25). In this case, since the gain for SRS is significant only below 40 km, the effective range in the atmosphere is $z = 40$ km/sinϕ. For ϕ close to 90°, the limitations on intensity are roughly the same as at tactical ranges, and at very long slant paths, as ϕ approaches zero, intensity becomes ever more limited.

If damage criteria are such that we believe we'll need to operate above the threshold for stimulated scattering, there are various ways by which this limitation might be overcome. In strategic appli-

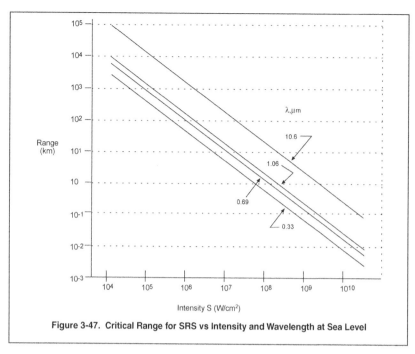

Figure 3-47. Critical Range for SRS vs Intensity and Wavelength at Sea Level

cations, we could increase the laser's aperture and focus the beam towards the target. In this way, the intensity could be below the threshold for SRS within the atmosphere, yet above the threshold for damage on target. This approach would not work, of course, for a beam in space fired at a target on the earth, where the highest intensities would be in the lower regions of the atmosphere.

It might also be possible to shorten the pulse width. As you can see from Figure 3–46, the altitude at which the gain for SRS begins to decline is lower at shorter pulse widths. Of course, the penalty for doing this is that the intensity will be higher if damage criteria require a constant energy in target, and it may be that the higher intensity will again exceed the threshold for excessive stimulated scattering.

Beyond the obvious remedies of playing with the diameter and pulse width of the laser, various more esoteric schemes at reducing SRS have been proposed.[60] These generally rely on quantum-mechanical techniques to suppress the stimulated scattering by injecting into the main beam other beams at the slightly shifted frequencies of the SRS scattered radiation, to "encourage" the scattered photons to propagate along with the main beam, not diverging from it. Whether any of these ideas will work in practice has yet to be demonstrated experimentally.

Air Breakdown. Stimulated scattering is a nonlinear scattering effect, and *air breakdown*, in which the neutral gases of the atmosphere are transformed into a highly absorbing plasma, is a nonlinear absorption effect. It is somewhat ironic that this dramatic and terminal effect in beam propagation begins with the absorption of laser light in something so small that it makes no discernable contribution to the absorption coefficient—free electrons in the air.

Free electrons (those not bound to atoms or molecules) interact strongly with laser light. They're electrically charged, and laser light, after all, is electromagnetic radiation. They have a small mass, only about 10^{-4} that of a molecule, and so they are easily accelerated by electromagnetic radiation. If there were a substantial number of free electrons in the air it would strongly absorb any electromagnetic radiation.[61] Fortunately for those who contemplate using lasers as directed energy weapons, there are very few free electrons in the air—the vast majority are bound into atoms or molecules. There are about 100 free electrons per cubic centimeter,[62] as compared with the 3×10^{19} molecules per cubic centimeter present in air at sea level. These few arise from relatively rare events, such as cosmic rays penetrating the atmosphere and knocking electrons free from their parent molecules.[63]

Air breakdown is in essence the runaway growth of electron density to the point where almost all of the molecules in the air have lost at least one of their electrons. At this point, the air is highly absorbing and no laser can propagate. Molecules or atoms which have lost an electron are said to have been *ionized,* and a gas of ions and electrons is known as a *plasma* (not to be confused with the blood plasma that medical people like to talk about, of course!).

How does this runaway growth of electrons occur? The fundamental process is known as an *electron cascade*, and proceeds by the following steps:

- The few electrons which are naturally present in the atmosphere heat up by absorbing laser light, and become very energetic.

- Eventually, they gain sufficient energy that when they collide with an atom or molecule they can ionize it. This requires that they have at least an amount of energy called the *ionization potential,* typically 10–20 eV.

• When an electron succeeds in ionizing an atom, the electron population has grown. The newly born electron joins its predecessors in gaining energy, and is eventually able to ionize an atom itself.

• This process repeats until almost all of the atoms have been ionized, and the laser light is totally absorbed.

From the description of air breakdown just outlined, you can see that it will depend on two things—the rate at which electrons can gain energy in the presence of electromagnetic radiation of intensity S, and the rate at which they may lose that energy to ionization and to other competing processes that can serve as energy sinks, limiting the amount available for ionization. We'll consider how electrons gain and lose energy in turn.

We'll call the energy of an individual electron ϵ, and denote the rate at which it gains energy from laser light as $d\epsilon/dt$. The electron heating rate $d\epsilon/dt$ may be related to the intensity and frequency of the laser light as well as appropriate parameters characterizing the gas through which it propagates. The appropriate expression is[64]

$$\frac{d\epsilon}{dt} = \frac{e^2 S \nu_c}{2m \epsilon_o (\omega^2 + \nu_c^2)}$$

This formidable expression has a reasonably simple physical interpretation. It is not surprising that $d\epsilon/dt$ should be proportional to the laser intensity S—we'd expect that the more intense the laser beam, the more rapidly it could heat the electrons within its volume. The quantity e is the charge on the electron, and m its mass. If electrons had a greater charge, we'd expect that they'd heat at a greater rate, and if they were heavier, they'd be harder to accelerate and would heat more slowly. Thus, the proportionality of $d\epsilon/dt$ to ϵ^2/m seems appropriate. The quantity ν_c is the rate at which electrons collide with atoms in the gas. This factor is important because as the electrons move up and down under the influence of the laser's electromagnetic fields, they are progressively accelerated and decelerated, gaining and losing energy. Periodically, however, they collide with an atom or molecule. When they do so, the energy of motion which they have at that time is converted into random energy, or heat. Thus, it is the friction between the electrons and the background gas which results in their heating, just as the electrons in a metal heat as a result of their collisions with the impurities, vibrations, and other things responsible for the metal's electrical resistance.

In the denominator of the expression for $d\epsilon/dt$ there appears a factor, $(\omega^2 + \nu_c^2)$, which merits some discussion. This term reflects the time scale over which the electrons gain kinetic energy from the applied electric field before they collide with an atom and convert that energy into heat. The quantity ω is known as the *radian frequency* of the laser light—$2\pi\nu$, where ν is the frequency in Hertz of the light.[65] Two limits are of interest in evaluating $d\epsilon/dt$—$\omega > \nu_c$, and $\omega < \nu_c$. When we're dealing with typical laser frequencies and gas densities characteristic of the atmosphere, $\omega > \nu_c$. In this case, $1/\omega$ is clearly the amount of time an electron has to gain energy before the laser field turns around, decelerates it, and gives it the same amount of energy in the opposite direction. Thus, the electron is accelerated for a time on the order of $1/\omega$. If we recall that kinetic energy is $mv^2/2$, and that v is proportional to the acceleration time, it stands to reason that the kinetic energy an electron gains would be proportional to $1/\omega^2$. If, on the other hand, $\omega < \nu_c$, then the acceleration process will be terminated by a collision with an atom before the field has a chance to turn the electron around, and the energy gain is proportional to $1/\nu_c^2$. This limit is the one which applies at microwave frequencies, and will receive considerable attention in Chapter 4. The factor $(\omega^2+\nu_c^2)$ in the expression for the electron heating rate captures both limits.

The other factors which appear in the expression for the electron heating rate are simply constants which arise as a result of our choice of metric units: c is the speed of light, 3×10^8 m/sec, and ϵ_0 a constant known as the *permittivity of free space*, 8.85 x10^{-12} farad/m. Figure 3–48 is a plot of the electron heating rate at sea level as a function of intensity and wavelength.

As you can see from Figure 3–48, electrons will gain energy very rapidly in the absence of any energy loss mechanisms, reaching energies on the order of 10 eV that are necessary to begin an electron cascade in times on the order of 10^{-9} seconds at intensities on the order of 10^9 W/cm^2 or greater. Since the electron collision frequency ν_c is proportional to the atmospheric density, Figure 3–48 may be

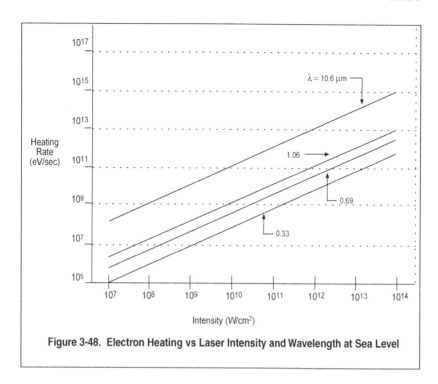

Figure 3-48. Electron Heating vs Laser Intensity and Wavelength at Sea Level

scaled to altitudes above sea level by multiplying the heating rate shown in the figure by the ratio of the density at the desired altitude to that at sea level. As we have already seen, this correction factor is to a first approximation $\exp(-h/h_o)$, where $h_o = 7$ km.

It is important to note that rapid electron heating does not imply strong absorption of energy from the laser beam. Figure 3–48 shows the heating rate per electron, and at the start of an electron cascade there are very few electrons around. The absorption coefficient due to electron absorption can be found from $KS = n(d\epsilon/dt)$, where n is the density of electrons. Initially, this is small compared to molecular or aerosol attenuation, but as breakdown proceeds, n increases and eventually dominates beam absorption.

With Figure 3–48, we know how free electrons in air will gain energy. Our next task is to examine how they may lose energy, since the balance between energy gain and loss will determine their average energy and the likelihood that they'll ionize molecules and grow in number. Energy loss is possible whenever an electron strikes a molecule with greater energy than is necessary to ionize it or to excite one of its degrees of freedom. You will recall from earlier in the chapter (see Figure 3–9) that molecules have ionization potentials on the order of 10 eV, electronic levels separated by energies on the order of 1eV, vibrational levels separated by about 0.1 eV, and rotational levels separated by about 0.01 eV. If an electron with 5 eV of energy strikes a molecule, it doesn't have the energy to ionize the molecule, but it may excite one of the electronic, vibrational, or rotational levels. If it does, it will lose the appropriate energy of excitation. For example, if the electron loses energy in exciting a vibrational level, it will lose energy on the order of 0.1 eV. Figure 3–49 is a plot of the average energy loss rate to various types of excitation as a function of average electron energy in a gas of molecules having thresholds of 0.1, 1, and 10 eV for vibrational, electronic, and ionization energy losses.[66] The actual atmosphere, with many species of molecules and many different levels to excite, is far more complex. Detailed analyses are available elsewhere; the simple model shown in Figure 3–49 is sufficient to illustrate the physics involved in breakdown, and is surprisingly accurate from a quantitative standpoint as well.[67]

As Figure 3–49 illustrates, electron energy losses become greater as their average energy increases, and they are able to excite more degrees of freedom in the gas molecules. At the lowest

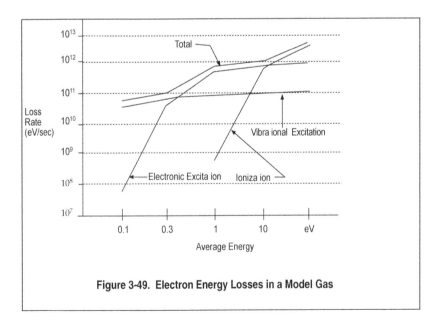

Figure 3-49. Electron Energy Losses in a Model Gas

energies, most of the electrons are exciting vibrational levels, and at the highest energies, they're primarily ionizing the molecules in the gas. Clearly, the threshold for breakdown lies between these two extremes.

Figure 3–49 may be used together with Figure 3–48 to estimate the minimum intensity at which electrons can cascade and the gas will break down. There will be no growth of electrons unless there can be some ionization. From Figure 3–49, almost all of the energy goes into vibrational excitation at average energies below about 0.1 eV, for which the energy loss rate is about 5×10^{10} eV/second. If the electrons are to gain energy to the point where breakdown can begin, the rate of energy gain from the laser must exceed this energy loss rate. From Figure 3–48, you can see that an energy gain of 5×10^{10} eV/sec requires an intensity of about 3×10^9 W/cm^2 at a wavelength of 10.6 μm. Therefore, about 3×10^9 W/cm^2 should be the threshold for gas breakdown with 10.6 μm radiation.

Figure 3–50 shows more detailed calculations of the breakdown threshold for air as a function of pulse width.[68] As you can see, our simple estimate closely approximates the result of much more elaborate analysis at longer pulse widths. More importantly, experimental data are also consistent with our analysis and that shown in Figure 3–50.[69] This gives us confidence that we understand the physics of the gas breakdown phenomenon.

The other features shown in Figure 3–50 may also be understood with the use of Figures 3–48 and 3–49. As the pulse width decreases, the breakdown threshold rises, and at the shortest pulses the intensity necessary for breakdown is inversely proportional to the pulse width. At very short pulse widths, we need very high ionization rates if the gas is to break down before the laser turns off. This means that almost all of the electron energy losses are to ionization. If all of the energy input from the laser is going into ionization, it must be true that $d\epsilon/dt \approx I R_i$ where I is the ionization potential, and R_i the rate at which electrons ionize neutral molecules. In other words, every collision is an ionizing one, and causes the colliding electron to lose an energy I.

If breakdown is to occur in a time t_p, the initial electrons must be able to ionize and multiply themselves g times, where g is the number of generations required for the electrons to cascade to breakdown, and ionize all the neutral molecules. About 56

147

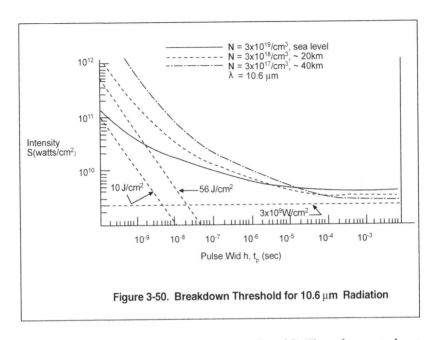

Figure 3-50. **Breakdown Threshold for 10.6 μm Radiation**

generations are required in air at sea level.[70] Therefore, at short pulses the ionization rate must be such that $R_i t_p = 56$, or $R_i = 56/t_p$. Thus, the short pulse criterion for breakdown becomes $d\epsilon/dt \approx I\, R_i = 56\, I/t_p$, which implies that the heating rate and intensity for breakdown must be inversely proportional to t_p, as seen in Figure 3–50. We can be more quantitative by observing from Figure 3–48 that at 10.6 μm the electron heating rate in eV/sec is about 10 times the intensity in W/cm². The criterion for breakdown at this wavelength can therefore be written as $10\, S = 56\, I/t_p$. For an ionization potential I of about 10 Joules, this implies $S t_p = 56$ J/cm². This estimate is shown on figure 3–50, and considering the simplicity of our analysis is amazingly close to the limit of 10 J/cm² obtained in more detailed work.

The altitude dependence exhibited by Figure 3–50 derives from the fact that the electron heating rate is proportional to the collision rate ν_c, and is therefore proportional to gas density. If the criterion for breakdown is $d\epsilon/dt \approx I\, Ri = 56\, I/tp$, and if ν_c is reduced by an order of magnitude, S must increase by an order of magnitude to keep $d\epsilon/dt$ constant. This behavior is observed in the short-pulse, high intensity limit of Figure 3–50. On the other hand, at long puses the threshold for breakdown is determined by a balance between $d\epsilon/dt$ and the energy losses shown in Figure 3–49. Since both of these are proportional to ν_c, there is effectively no density (altitude) dependence in this limit.

While Figure 3–50 has been sketched for laser radiation of wavelength 10.6 μm, it can be used to predict the air breakdown threshold at any other frequency simply by scaling as $1/\lambda^2$. Thus, at $\lambda = 1.06$ μm, the intensity at which breakdown will occur for a given pulse width will be 100 times greater than that shown in the figure.

Aerosol Induced Breakdown. To this point, we have treated breakdown as occuring in clean air—a mixture of oxygen, nitrogen, CO_2, H_2O, and smaller amounts of other gases. The real air which is encountered in weapon applications differs in having small solid particles suspended in it. Since these aerosols contribute to the absorption and scattering of laser light, it's probably not surprising that they can affect the breakdown threshold as well.

How Might Aerosols Affect Air Breakdown?

• Many aerosols are comprised of materials which are easier to ionize than the atmospheric gases. Salt, for example, is a common aerosol in a maritime environment, and sodium, one of the constituents of salt, has an ionization potential of only 5.1 eV, as compared with 14.6 eV for Nitrogen and 13.6 eV for Oxygen. Our expression for the breakdown threshold in the short pulse limit is directly proportional to I. Thus, this factor alone might lower the breakdown threshold by a factor of 2–3.

• Effects occurring at the surface of a solid aerosol, such as the boiling (thermionic emission) of electrons from the interior, can increase the local density of free electrons.[71] This increase in the initial electron density reduces the number of generations that the electrons have to go through to achieve breakdown, and may create a small mini-plasma that can grow to block and absorb the beam.

• As the aerosols absorb the laser light, they become hot. At higher intensities, they may even vaporize explosively, sending shock waves through the surrounding air. This will induce high temperatures in the region around an aerosol, and excite many of the vibrational and rotational degrees of freedom which limit electron energy growth at low intensities. In effect, in the hot region near an aerosol many of the energy loss mechanisms which would otherwise inhibit the growth of electron energy are bleached out, and no longer effective.

All of these factors would argue that in dirty, aerosol laden air, the breakdown threshold may be reduced from that which characterizes clean air. This is, in fact, observed experimentally. Indeed, early breakdown experiments were frequently difficult to interpret because the combined effects of gas and aerosol-induced breakdown contributed to the measured breakdown thresholds.[72] Figure 3–51 is illustrative of calculations performed to look at the effect of aerosols on the air breakdown threshold.[73] The fact that the impact of aerosols is size-dependent should not be surprising. The smaller an aerosol is, the more rapidly it vaporizes and dissipates when heated by a laser beam, and the less it can affect the breakdown threshold. An interesting corrolary to Figure 3–51 is that solid targets, representing aerosols of essentially infinite size, might be expected to lower the breakdown threshold to the greatest degree. We'll return to this point later in the chapter, when we discuss laser-target interaction.

Comparing the range of radii shown in Figure 3–51 with typical particle sizes seen in the atmosphere (Figure 3–27), it's apparent

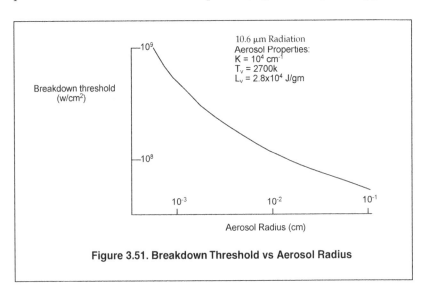

Figure 3.51. Breakdown Threshold vs Aerosol Radius

that only very large particles will lower the breakdown threshold to a significant extent. Nevertheless, when propagating beams of large diameter over long distances, there is a very large probability that at least one giant particle will be found within the volume of the beam to serve as an initiation site for breakdown. For example, Figure 3–27 shows that the density of particles having a size of about 10^{-3} cm is about 10^{-6}/cm^3. Thus, to be sure of finding a particle this big we'd need a beam volume in excess of 10^6 cm^3. For a beam of 1 m radius, this volume is exceeded in less than a meter of propagation distance. Since Figure 3–51 suggests that particles of this size might lower the breakdown threshold by two orders of magnitude, it seems clear that aerosols may dominate the initiation of breakdown in realistic scenarios.

Knowing the density of aerosols of a given size as a function of altitude (Figure 3–27), as well as the extent to which a given size aerosol will reduce the breakdown threshold (Figure 3–51), it's possible to estimate the extent to which aerosols will reduce the breakdown threshold as a function of altitude. Such an estimate has been made by the author, and is shown in Figure 3–52.

As common sense suggests and Figure 3–52 indicates, aerosols will have the greatest effect on the air breakdown threshold near the surface of the earth, where winds and other local phenomena can loft very large particles, over 10 μm in size, into the air. Particles this large rapidly settle through the force of gravity, how-

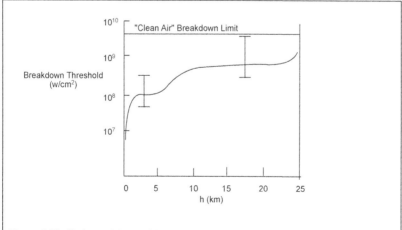

Figure 3-52. Estimated Aerosol-Induced Breakdown Threshold vs Altitude (10.6 μm)

ever, and aren't found above a few km altitude. The error bars shown in the figure are indicative of the range of breakdown thresholds which have been ascribed to particles of a size prevalent at that altitude, and indicate clearly the lack of precision in so dirty a business as determining the effect of lofted dirt on the air breakdown threshold.

Figures 3–51 and 3–52 show the effect of aerosols in lowering the breakdown threshold of 10.6 μm radiation. The next logical question to ask is how these results might scale with frequency or wavelength. To a first approximation, we might think that everything should scale as λ^2, since the electron heating rate is proportional to this factor, and it is the heating of electrons by the laser light which ultimately results in breakdown. The clean air limit to breakdown scales in this way, as we have already seen. However, when considering solid aerosols, we need to recognize that the interaction of light with solid matter has no simple dependence on wavelength. The absorption characteristics of a solid depend upon its energy gap (if an insulator) or its conductivity (if a conductor), as well as the wavelength of the light. Thus, a change in wavelength may take a given aerosol from being a major contributor to breakdown to being a non-player.

Experimental data on the frequency dependence of aerosol induced breakdown are sparse, but suggest the following: The number and variety of aerosols present in any naturally occurring environment is sufficiently great that there are likely to be aerosols which are strongly absorptive of any wavelength.These, then, will heat, vaporize, and serve as the source of small seed plasmas, which will either grow to encompass the beam or will die out. The first process—the initiation of small plasmas from the aerosols—will be essentially independent of wavelength, while the second—the growth or decay of the plasmas—will be wavelength dependent, as it results from a wavelength-dependent interaction between the light and the expanding plasma. This motivates us to examine the extent to which laser light will maintain a pre-existing plasma or allow it to cool, recombine, and cease to exist.

Plasma Maintenance and Propagation. Once a plasma has been created as a result of breakdown in the air, from aerosols, or at a target surface, it will continue to interact with and absorb the laser light. From the standpoint of propagation, this interaction is important because if a small plasma initiated from an aerosol grows to encompass the beam, it will prevent further propagation. The maintenance, growth, and propagation of a plasma is also important in target interaction. Plasmas created at a target's surface can greatly affect how (and if) any energy is deposited within it. As a nonlinear effect, plasma propagation is certainly the most dramatic, replacing the normally invisible propagation of light through the atmosphere with lightning-like balls and streaks of glowing plasma.

It requires less laser intensity to *maintain* a pre-existing plasma than to *create* one from a neutral gas. The reason is relatively simple. In a neutral gas, electrons can absorb energy from the laser when they collide with neutral gas molecules. In a plasma, the neutral molecules have become ions—electrically charged particles. Because of their electrical charge, ions have a much greater collision cross-section and collision frequency with electrons than neutral molecules. Typical electron-ion collision cross sections are on the order of 10^{-12} cm^2, while typical electron-neutral cross sections are on the order of 10^{-15} cm^2—about three orders of magnitude smaller.[74] The effect is to increase $d\epsilon/dt$, the electron heating rate, by about three orders of magnitude at a given laser intensity S. Once a gas has been ionized, a laser intensity three orders of magnitude below that required for breakdown of the neutral gas may be sufficient to maintain the plasma which has been created.

Since the transition from neutral gas to plasma is accompanied by a rapid increase in the power absorbed, it should not be surprising that once created, a plasma won't stand still, but will tend to grow and propagate. How this happens is illustrated in Figure 3–53.

Shown in Figure 3–53 is a small plasma, formed, for example, at the site of an aerosol in the volume of a laser beam. The plasma is by nature very hot, since to remain ionized a gas must have a temperature on the order of an electron volt (about 12,000° K!) or greater. The resulting temperature gradient between the hot plasma and the surrounding neutral gas causes heating in the region surrounding the plasma through thermal conduction, radiation, or other energy transfer mechanisms. As this region heats it, too, becomes ionized, transforms into plasma, and heats regions still further out. In this way, the plasma expands radially. This process can continue only as long as sufficient energy can be ab-

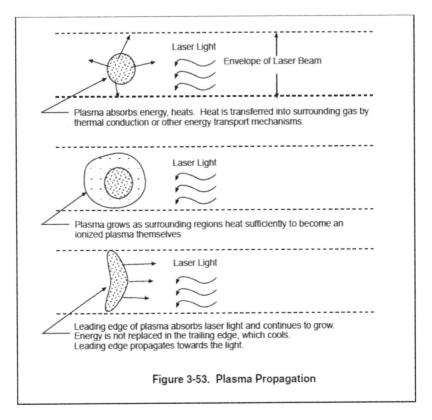

Plasma absorbs energy, heats. Heat is transferred into surrounding gas by thermal conduction or other energy transport mechanisms.

Plasma grows as surrounding regions heat sufficiently to become an ionized plasma themselves

Leading edge of plasma absorbs laser light and continues to grow. Energy is not replaced in the trailing edge, which cools. Leading edge propagates towards the light.

Figure 3-53. Plasma Propagation

sorbed from the laser to replace the energy used up in heating and ionizing additional layers of gas. If the plasma becomes too large its leading edge will absorb most of the laser light, shielding the rear end from any energy deposition. At this point, the plasma can no longer grow symmetrically. Instead, the front end can propagate towards the laser, while the rear end must cool and die. The plasma then propagates preferentially up the beam towards the source of light, as illustrated in Figure 3–53. The characteristic thickness of the propagating plasma will be 1/K, where K is the absorption coefficient (cm^{-1}) of the plasma for laser light.

In poetic terms, the plasma shown in Figure 3–53 has become a *wave of absorption*, moving towards the laser. Therefore, a plasma propagating in this way has come to be known as a *laser absorption wave*, or LAW. Understanding absorption waves requires a knowledge of the mechanisms by which energy is transferred from the hot plasma to the surrounding gas, how a neutral gas becomes a plasma as it heats, and how the absorption of laser light varies with the temperature, density, and degree of ionization in the gas through which it propagates. We'll look at each of these issues and develop criteria for the propagation of absorption waves.

The propagation of absorption waves is best understood by analogy with a common, everyday phenomenon—the burning, or combustion, of a fuel in an exothermic chemical reaction.[75] Paper, for example, would like to *burn*, or combine with the oxygen in the air to form carbon dioxide and other by-products which we perceive as smoke. It can't do this at room temperature, however, because there is a certain amount of energy, known as the *activation energy*, which the molecules of carbon in the paper must have in order to react with oxygen. The reaction rate for a combustible fuel is therefore a strong function of its temperature T, and is proportional to $e^{-A/\kappa T}$ where A is the activation energy. The reaction rate becomes significant, and combustion can begin, at a temperature known as the *flash point*, $kT \approx A/10$.

Once combustion begins it will continue, because the energy to sustain it is released in the combining of carbon with oxygen (the reaction is *exothermic*). We can burn a sheet of paper by touching a match only to one corner. The match serves to ignite the fuel, raising that corner to the flash point. As the corner reacts, it releases energy and heats adjacent regions of the paper to the flash point. These react in turn, and provide the energy to ignite regions of the paper still further from the corner. Thus, after igniting the corner of the paper with a match, we observe a wave of combustion, which propagates over the paper, consuming it.

In a similar manner, once a plasma is formed within the volume of a laser beam, it absorbs considerable energy. This energy heats adjacent regions of the gas, which themselves become ionized and absorbing when their temperature exceeds some critical level. The absorption of laser light in regions which have become ionized gives them the energy to heat still further portions of the gas which, in turn, ionize and become absorbing. In this way, a laser absorption wave (LAW) propagates through the gas. There is one significant difference between a LAW and a wave of combustion, however. The energy which serves to propagate a LAW does not come from within the gas itself, but is absorbed from the laser. Therefore, a LAW propagates towards the source of laser light. If we ignite a piece of paper in the middle, it will burn in all directions. By contrast, if we create a plasma in the middle of a laser beam its rear edge cannot receive enough energy to sustain its temperature. The rear regions cool and recombine into a neutral gas. The forward edge, which can absorb energy, heats regions ahead of it. In this way the LAW propagates up the beam, as illustrated in Figure 3–53.

Because of the strong analogy between the propagation of exothermic chemical reactions and LAWs, much of combustion theory has been of value in understanding LAW propagation. One of the most significant insights to emerge from this theory is that there are two mechanisms by which LAWs might propagate, just as there are two mechanisms by which exothermic chemical reactions can propagate—detonation and combustion.[76]

There are two ways in which a combustible fuel might react. In one of these, the reaction proceeds relatively slowly, such as burning a piece of paper. On the other hand, if we were to grind the paper up into fine dust, confine it in some type of enclosure, and then ignite it, something much more explosive would result. Similarly, various types of explosives can either burn more or less gently or, if properly ignited, burn much more rapidly and blow up. These two ways in which reactions proceed correspond to two physically different mechanisms of propagation, known as *combustion* (or more precisely, *deflagration*) and *detonation*, respectively.

The essential feature of absorption wave propagation in the combustion mode is that it occurs at atmospheric pressure, and the mechanism of propagation is thermal conduction or radiation. Figure 3–54 shows how the temperature (T, $^\circ$K), pressure (P, J/cm^3), and molecular density (N, cm^{-3}) of a gas vary as we move along the axis of a laser beam into a region of plasma propagating in the combustion mode. You may recall that the temperature pressure, and density of a gas are related by $P = N\,kT$.[77] Therefore, if P is held fixed at the pressure of the surrounding atmosphere, and T rises going into the plasma, the density, N, must be less on the interior of the plasma than in the surrounding gas. The length of the plasma will be on the order of the absorption length 1/K. Over greater distances the light is essentially all absorbed, and none is available for plasma maintenance.

As you can see in Figure 3–54, the temperature in the ambient gas actually begins to rise in the region ahead of the plasma—this is because energy is flowing into this region from the hot plasma core by thermal conduction or radiation. When the temperature becomes high enough for ionization to begin, a plasma forms, the laser light begins to be absorbed, and the temperature rises rapidly. The heated gas expands, and the density drops, as shown in the figure. An essential feature of this combustion mode of propagation is that the plasma moves subsonically, at a velocity less than the speed of sound in the surrounding gas. The reason for this is straightforward. As we discussed in the context of thermal blooming, the speed of sound is the characteristic velocity with which pressure disturbances can propagate in a gas. If the plasma were to move more rapidly than this, there would be no time for the pressure balance shown in Figure 3–54 to be established, the pressure would rise rapidly going into the plasma, and a transition would be made to the detonation mode of propagation, illustrated in Figure 3–55.

In Figure 3–55, a plasma is propagating *supersonically* as a detonation. A number of consequences are immediately apparent. Since the plasma advances more rapidly than gas can flow from its interior, density remains high and the pressure rises as we go into the absorbing plasma region. Because of the greater density within the plasma, its absorption coefficient K is greater, and the plasma's

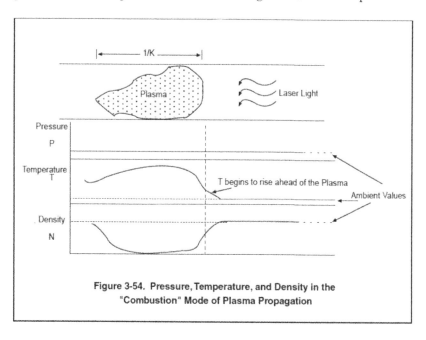

Figure 3-54. Pressure, Temperature, and Density in the "Combustion" Mode of Plasma Propagation

157

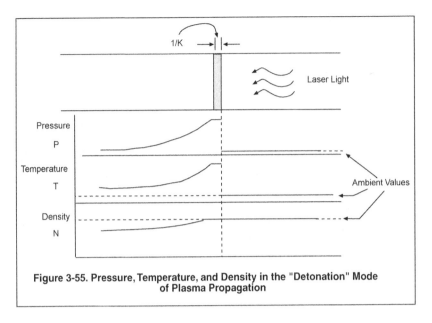

1/K

Laser Light

Pressure

P

Temperature

T

Ambient Values

Density

N

Figure 3-55. Pressure, Temperature, and Density in the "Detonation" Mode of Plasma Propagation

physical length is much reduced. Since there is no time for subsonic energy transfer processes like thermal conduction to propagate energy ahead of the wave, the temperature rises almost instantaneously at the point where the plasma meets the neutral gas.

If thermal conduction can't heat the region ahead of the plasma, how is it possible for the plasma to advance as an absorption wave? The mechanism of propagation is known as *shock heating*. It is a well known result in fluid mechanics that a rapid increase in pressure will propagate through a gas at supersonic speed as what is known as a *shock wave*.[78] Behind this wave, the temperature rises rapidly, since the pressure increases, the density doesn't have time to decline, and $P = N kT$. It is this rapid rise in pressure and temperature which enables the region behind the shock front to ionize, absorb energy from the laser, and continue to propagate. In a similar manner, if you ignite the detonator on an explosive, it causes a rapid rise in pressure which propagates supersonically through the explosive as a shock wave, raising the temperature at each point above the flash point so that the explosive is rapidly consumed.

Because of the analogy with detonation and combustion in chemical reactions, laser absorption waves have been classified as laser supported combustion (LSC) waves or as laser supported detonation (LSD) waves, depending on whether their propagation is sub- or supersonic. A quantitative analysis of the conditions under which LSC or LSD waves can exist and propagate depends upon the hydrodynamic equations for gas flow, coupled with an understanding of how the degree of ionization and absorption coefficient for laser light depends upon the density and temperature of a gas.[79]

Calculating the degree of ionization in a gas with a given temperature and density is a familiar problem in high temperature physics. As molecules heat, they move more rapidly, their average energy of motion (kinetic energy) being a measure of temperature. Periodically, the molecules collide with one another, and if they're hot enough, some of these collisions will result in ionization. The equilibrium level of ionization is that for which the probability of ionization equals the probability of recombination, the recapturing of an electron by an ion to create a neutral molecule.[80] Figure 3–56 is a plot of the fraction of atoms ionized in a gas of hydrogen of density N at temperature T.[81]

You can see from Figure 3–56 that as temperature rises, the transition from a gas being essentially neutral to almost fully ionized occurs rapidly, and is more abrupt at lower densities. In fact, the initial rise in degree of ionization with temperature is proportional to $e^{-I/kT}$, and the transition from a neutral gas to an ionized plasma occurs at a temperature which is on the order of one-tenth the ionization potential.[82] In a sense, the ionization potential I plays a role in plasma formation analogous to the role of the activation energy in chemical reactions.

Once we know the degree of ionization at a given temperature, it is straightforward to find the absorption coefficient for laser light in a gas with that level of ionization. You will recall that the absorption coefficient for light which is heating electrons at a rate $d\epsilon/dt$ is simply $K = n \, (d\epsilon/dt)/S \approx e^2 n v_c / 2mc\epsilon_0 \omega^2$, where n is the density of electrons, v_c is the frequency with which electrons collide with heavy particles (neutral atoms or ions), and ω is 2π times the frequency of the light in Hertz. In a neutral gas, v_c is simply $\sigma_c N$, where σ_c is the collision cross section for electrons with gas molecules of density N. In a partially ionized gas, v_c becomes $\sigma_c N \, (1-f) + \sigma_i Nf$, where σ_i is the collision cross section with ions, and f the fraction of molecules which have been ionized. Since σ_i is much greater than σ_c, the second term will domi-

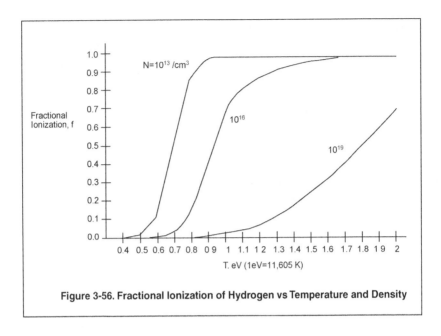

Figure 3-56. Fractional Ionization of Hydrogen vs Temperature and Density

nate the absorption coefficient whenever the fractional ionization, f, is greater than about 10^{-3}.

Figure 3–57 shows the absorption coefficient for nitrogen gas as a function of temperature and density for 10.6 μm wavelength radiation.[83] You can see that in an ionized gas whose density is that of air at sea level, almost all the laser light will be absorbed within a very short distance. At lower densities, of course, the absorption length becomes progressively longer. Knowing the absorption characteristics of a propagating plasma, it becomes possible to see how it propagates as a function of the energy absorbed, and make quantitative assessments of propagation velocities and thresholds as a function of laser intensity and wavelength. While detailed analysis is beyond the scope of this book, we'll provide the highlights of analyses which provide good insight into plasma propagation as detonation or combustion waves.

The detonation mode of LAW propagation is easiest to treat mathematically, because the transition from "non-plasma" to "plasma" is made so rapidly that its details are not important. Instead, the shock front can be treated as a discontinuity, with ambient values for T,P, and N ahead of the front, and plasma values for these quantities behind the front. The flow of the gas may also

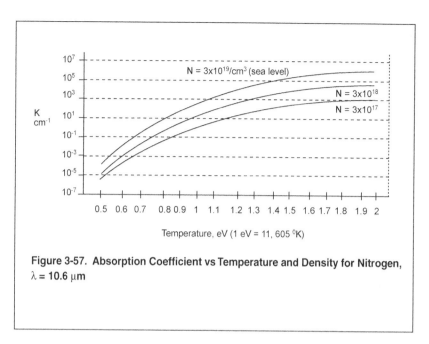

Figure 3-57. Absorption Coefficient vs Temperature and Density for Nitrogen, $\lambda = 10.6\ \mu m$

be treated as one-dimensional, since the absorption length for the laser light, 1/K, is typically much less than the radius of the laser beam. This means that any radial flow of hot gases occurs behind the region in the shock front where the deposition of laser light occurs, and cannot affect wave propagation. The results of such a one dimensional LSD analysis[84] show that the velocity of wave propagation, u, and the temperature behind the wave front are given by $u = 2[(\gamma^{2-1})S/\rho]^{1/3}$ and $kT = Mu^2/(\gamma+1)^2$. In these expressions, γ is a constant with a value of about 1.2,[85] M is the mass of a gas molecule, and ρ is the mass density of the ambient gas ($\rho = MN$, gm/cm³). It is interesting to note that the velocity and temperature of the LSD do not depend upon the absorption coefficient of the plasma, K. That's because of an assumption that K is so large that all the laser light is absorbed within the shock front, and serves to propagate the plasma. Figure 3–58 is a plot of the predicted LSD propagation velocity as a function of laser intensity and gas density, and Figure 3–59 is a plot of the predicted temperature within the plasma.

In Figure 3–58, you can see that LSD velocities are predicted to be quite high. At an intensity of 3×10^7 W/cm², for example, the velocity is about 6×10^5 cm/sec. Since the speed of sound is only

3×10^4 cm/sec, the velocities in Figure 3–58 are highly supersonic—about Mach 20 or greater. Note, too, that as the gas density ρ goes down, the propagation velocity, which varies as the one-third power of S/ρ, goes up. LSD waves are predicted to propagate more rapidly at higher altitudes.

Superimposed on Figure 3–58 are experimental data on LSD velocity as a function of intensity at sea level.[86] The data are in pretty good agreement with the theoretical curve, except that below about 10^7 W/cm² the velocity appears to be dropping off more rapidly than theory would predict. The reason for this is apparent from Figure 3–59.

You will recall from Figure 3–57 that the absorption coefficient of a gas begins to decline below temperatures of about 1 eV. From Figure 3–59, you can see that the data on Figure 3–58 begin to deviate from the theoretical curve in precisely the region where at sea level the temperature of an LSD is predicted to fall below 1 eV. In other words, we are seeing the beginnings of a threshold for LSD maintenance—an intensity below which high levels of ionization can't be maintained, and the theoretical assumption that all of the laser's intensity is absorbed in and helps to propagate the wave is no longer valid.

An LSD maintenance threshold may be estimated by assuming that a supersonic wave will no longer propagate when the absorption length within the plasma, $1/K$, becomes comparable to the beam radius.[87] The reasoning is that when laser energy is absorbed

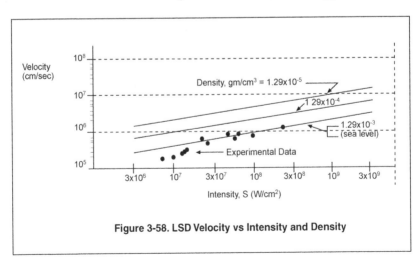

Figure 3-58. LSD Velocity vs Intensity and Density

over distances greater than a beam radius, some of the absorbed energy will be carried away as heated gases expand in a radial direction, and will not help to move the beam forward. Figure 3–60 is a plot of the LSD maintenance threshold, determined in this way, as a function of ambient gas density (altitude), laser frequency, and beam radius.[88] The dependence on ω^2/R as a scaling factor reflects the fact that the absorption coefficient, K, is proportional to $1/\omega^2$.

Figure 3–60 may be used in the following way to estimate LSD maintenance thresholds. The bottom curve is appropriate for a beam radius of 10 cm and a wavelength of 10.6 μm. The scaling parameter is ω^2/R, so that if the wavelength were 1.06 μm and the radius remained at 10 cm, ω^2/R would increase by a factor 100. At sea level, the threshold would rise from about 6×10^6 W/cm^2 to about 3×10^7. If the radius were 1 m and the frequency 1.06 μm, ω^2/R would be back to its original value, and the threshold under these conditions would be the same as for a 10 cm, 10.6 μm beam. As density decreases, a point is reached where the absorption coefficient is so low that an LSD can't be maintained even at full single ionization. This point is indicated by the thick cut-off bars, and occurs at a density of about 3×10^{-5} g/cm^3 for $\omega^2/R = 1$. The thresholds indicated on Figure 3–60 are in good agreement with those suggested by the data shown in Figure 3–58.

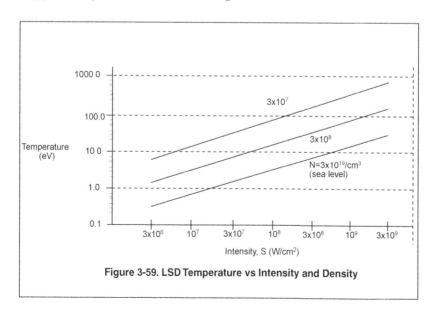

Figure 3-59. LSD Temperature vs Intensity and Density

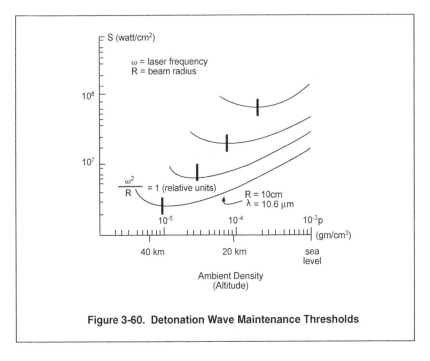

Figure 3-60. Detonation Wave Maintenance Thresholds

If a laser's intensity falls below the LSD maintenance threshold, the shock front will empty out, and the plasma might continue to propagate in the combustion mode, as an LSC. The analysis of LSC propagation is much more complex than that of the LSD, since gas flow in the radial direction, thermal conduction, and the transport of radiation emitted from the plasma, all of which can be ignored for an LSD, must now be considered. Additionally, these factors can all contribute in roughly equal measure to the energy balance in a combustion wave. Therefore, an LSC's characteristics are the net result of competing terms of comparable magnitude and differing signs. This means that a simple analysis, accurate to within factors of two or so, cannot hope to be quantitatively correct. Nevertheless, simple analyses have been used to provide valuable insights into the LSC mode of absorption wave propagation.[89]

There are two mechanisms by which subsonic plasma propagation can occur—thermal conduction and reradiation, or the absorption of photons emitted from the plasma core. Both of these energy transport mechanisms were discussed in Chapter 1, but reradiation is particularly complex for an LSC, and deserves a little more discussion here. Plasmas are very hot and energetic—

within them ionization and recombination are continually occurring, and with each recombination a photon is emitted with an energy corresponding to the energy difference between the free electron which existed prior to recombination and the bound electron which resulted from the process. Photons are also emitted as a result of transitions from higher to lower electronic, vibrational, or rotational states among the atoms and molecules in the gas. As a result of all this turmoil, photons are emitted from a plasma over a broad range of wavelengths.[90] Some of the photons emitted by a laser supported plasma will be at wavelengths which are strongly absorbed in the cold gas ahead of the wave, and will serve to heat this region. In a sense, the plasma acts as a "photon converter," absorbing light at the laser frequency and reemitting it at wavelengths which can be absorbed in the atmosphere. This process can also be important from the standpoint of target interaction.

Thermal conduction is inherently a surface phenomenon—energy is transported across the surface which separates a hot region from a cold one. By contrast, photon emission from a plasma is a volumetric phenomenon—the more volume a plasma has, the more space there is from which photons can be emitted. Therefore, thermal conduction will dominate the propagation of beams of small radius, which have a large surface to volume ratio. Radiation transport (photon emission and absorption) will dominate the propagation of beams of large radius. As a result, thermal conduction has been important in understanding the LSCs seen in laboratory scale experiments, while radiation transport will likely be of greater importance in any LSCs propagating within the large radius beams necessary for the long ranges required in weapon applications.

Simple theory predicts that the velocity of an LSC propagating through thermal conduction should be on the order of $u \approx (KSD/C_p \rho T)^{1/2}$, where K is the plasma's absorption coefficient, D is the thermal diffusivity of the ambient air, about 1 cm^2/sec, C_p is its heat capacity at constant pressure, ρ its density, and T the temperature, about 1 eV, at which the air becomes a plasma. If LSC propagation is dominated by radiation transport, theory suggests that its velocity should be on the order of $u = S/\rho \, C_p T$.[91] These velocities are plotted as a function of intensity at sea level in Figure 3–61.

165

The most striking feature to be seen in Figure 3–61 is that the velocities are quite low. Not only are they low compared to LSD velocities ($\approx 10^6$ cm/sec), they are also low compared to naturally-occurring wind velocities (10 mi/hr = 447 cm/sec). This suggests a strong possibility that for LSCs propagating in a natural environment, either local winds or those which result from slewing the beam will introduce cool air into the LSC faster than it can be heated, resulting in the LSC being blown out. This is completely analogous to blowing out a chemical flame, as on a match, by introducing cool air so fast that the flame temperature cannot be maintained, and cools below the flash point.

Detailed analyses of LSC propagation are in general agreement with these ideas and with experimental data. However, the comparison between theory and experiment is not as precise as in the LSD case, since theoretical predictions are strongly dependent upon the assumptions made, and experimental data are often difficult to interpret. An observed LSC velocity is that of the relative motion between laboratory air and the LSC, and may be substantially different from a theoretical calculation, which assumes propagation into still air.[92]

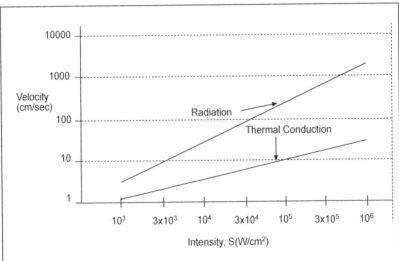

Figure 3-61. Velocities of Combustion Waves Propagating by Thermal Conduction and Radiation

Summary: Nonlinear Propagation Effects.

1. *Nonlinear effects* are those in which the beam modifies the environment through which it propagates, and this in turn affects its propagation characteristics.

2. *Thermal blooming* results when the absorption of laser energy causes the air density to change in a way which mimics a diverging lens. This causes the beam to spread as it propagates, and to bend into a wind flowing perpendicular to the beam's direction. Thermal blooming may be characterized in terms of a *thermal distortion number,* which relates to a decrease in the beam's on-axis intensity as shown in Figure 3–42. It will only occur if air has time to flow from the beam volume, a time roughly equal to the beam radius divided by the speed of sound (Figure 3–41).

3. *Stimulated Scattering* occurs when the intensity of scattered light is so great as to influence more photons to scatter in the same manner. If stimulated scattering becomes too great over the propagation path of the laser, significant energy will be lost from the beam. The critical range for this to occur is given as a function of wavelength and intensity in Figure 3–47.

4. *Air Breakdown* occurs when free electrons gain sufficient energy from the beam to ionize neutral molecules and multiply themselves. When this happens, electrons will multiply until the air is ionized, absorbs the beam, and propagation ceases. Figure 3–50 shows the air breakdown threshold as a function of density and pulse width for a 10.6 μm wavelength laser. The thresholds shown in that figure may be scaled to other wavelengths as $1/\lambda^2$.

5. *Aerosols* can reduce the breakdown threshold by up to two orders of magnitude. This effect is dependent upon the radius of the aerosols, and is particularly severe near the surface of the earth, where the largest aerosols are to be found.

6. *Absorption Waves* occur because an ionized plasma is highly absorbing, and can propagate towards the source of laser light at intensities below those necessary for plasma production through breakdown. There are two modes of plasma propagation: supersonic (detonation), driven by shock heating, and subsonic (combustion), driven by thermal conduction and radiation transport. Figure 3–60 shows the threshold for detonation waves as a function of ambient density, frequency, and beam

	Linear Effects			Nonlinear Effects				
	Absorption/ Scattering -molecules	Absorption/ Scattering -aerosols	Turbulence/ Adaptive Optics	Thermal Blooming	Stimulated Scattering	Gas Breakdown	Aerosol Breakdown	Plasma Propagation
Wavelength	Pick λ in a "window," and not on a molecular line	longer λ preferable- $2\pi a/\lambda$ less	longer λ preferable- reduces r_0	Same as absorption	longer λ reduces gain	shorter λ lowers $d\varepsilon/dt$	---	shorter λ lowers $d\varepsilon/dt$
Radius/Aperture	---	---	---	larger- lowers N_D	---	---	---	smaller- higher threshold
Pulse Width	---	---	---	Shorter- reduce w/a	Shorter lowers gain	---	---	Shorter
Power	---	---	---	Lower	---	---	---	---
Intensity	---	---	---	Lower	Lower	Lower	Lower	Lower

Table 3-3. Implications of Propagation Effects in the Atmosphere

radius. Figure 3–61 shows the velocities at which combustion waves are predicted to propagate as a function of laser intensity. If naturally occurring winds exceed these velocities, they will blow out the combustion wave, and it will cease to exist.

7. The dynamic nature of nonlinear effects makes them difficult to predict and account for in advance. Therefore, one must either compensate for them in real time, as in using adaptive optics to handle thermal blooming, or operate at intensities below their threshold for occurrence, as with air breakdown. In either event, it is important to recognize the limitations which these effects have on the laser parameters which may be available for use in achieving damage criteria and target effects.

Implications

If there is a single conclusion to be drawn from this section on propagation in the atmosphere, it's that there are many more variables that enter into placing energy on target than the D/λ which was the key ingredient in vacuum propagation. Additionally, the different effects that are possible can drive beam design in different directions. For example, the gain for stimulated scattering is less at longer wavelengths, but the air breakdown threshold is less at higher wavelengths. It is therefore not obvious without more detailed analysis what general wavelength region may be desired in a given application, let alone the specific wavelength to be chosen within a region. The same is true of other parameters, such as the beam's radius, pulse width, power, and intensity. They are all interrelated, and one effect can't be dealt with in isolation from the others. Table 3–3 is suggestive of the way in which the different effects considered in this section drive beam design. Any such summary is of necessity less than complete, but it is hoped that it can at least help you to keep in mind potential interactions among effects, rather than dealing with single effects in isolation. Finally, of course, all of these things must be judged by the constraints they place on damaging targets, which is the subject of the next section.

Laser-Target Interaction and Effects

To this point, our only consideration of target effects has been to assume that something on the order of 10,000 J/cm², delivered in a sufficiently short time, would be adequate to damage most targets. We must now be more quantitative, and consider in greater detail the types of effects which can occur and the criteria for their occurrence. We'll begin with a brief survey of the effects considered in this section. Broadly speaking, target effects may be classified as thermal—resulting from the heating of the target, or mechanical—resulting from pressure and impulse delivered to the target through the reaction forces of laser-produced vapor. Many of these effects occur above the intensity at which plasmas may form and propagate as laser-supported combustion or detonation waves. Therefore, we'll need to consider the effect of plasma formation and propagation on laser effects, both in vacuum and in the atmosphere.

Types of Effects

The simplest effect is heating. Some fraction of the laser light incident upon a target will be absorbed in a thin layer ($1/K \approx 10^{-4} - 10^{-8}$ cm) near its surface. The absorbed energy will appear as heat. Since heating begins as soon as a laser engages a target, there is no threshold for this effect. However, heating will by itself be insufficient to damage a target of military interest unless it is very soft. There are, however, industrial applications where heating is the desired effect, such as annealing semiconductor materials into which ions have been implanted by bombardment.[93]

As a laser's intensity on target rises, it can begin to melt a hole. There is a threshold for this effect, since energy must be delivered to the target more rapidly than thermal conduction or radiation can carry it away. Once melting begins, it is possible to melt through the target's surface, drilling a hole. There is a threshold for this as well. The laser must engage the target for a pulse width or dwell time greater than the target thickness divided by the rate of hole growth.

At still greater intensities, vaporization becomes possible. Above the threshold for vaporization, the reaction force which the jet of emerging vapor exerts on the surface delivers a mechanical impulse. This impulse may deform or damage the target, and may work together with target heating to produce levels of damage that either heating or impulse could not have achieved alone.

Effects in the Absence of Plasma

Melting. When the surface of a target is heated, the energy deposited will propagate into the surface a distance of about $\sqrt{Dt}$ in time t, where D is the thermal diffusivity of the target material (see Figure 1–5). We can use this result to estimate the threshold for melting. A laser of intensity S and radius w will deposit an amount of energy $E = \pi w^2 \alpha St$ into the target in time t, where α is the *thermal coupling coefficient*—the fraction of the incident laser energy that is absorbed.[94] During this same time, the energy absorbed will have propagated a distance $\sqrt{Dt}$ into the target, as shown in Figure 3–62. Thus, the mass of target material which has been heated is $M = \rho \pi w^2 \sqrt{Dt}$, where ρ is the density (g/cm³) of the target material. We can use the target's heat capacity C to find the degree of temperature rise ΔT above the target's initial temperature T_o which results from the energy deposited in a time t:

$$E = MC\ \Delta T, \text{ or } \pi\ w^2\ \alpha\ St = \rho\ \pi w^2\ \sqrt{DT}\ C\ \Delta T.$$

The target surface can begin to melt when $\Delta T = T_m - T_o$, and the heated region reaches T_m, the melting point of the target material. This must happen in a time less than the duration of the laser pulse, t_p. Therefore, the threshold for melting is $S_m = \rho C(T_m - T_o)(D/t_p)^{1/2}/\alpha$. Figure 3–63 shows this threshold as a function of pulse width and thermal coupling coefficient.

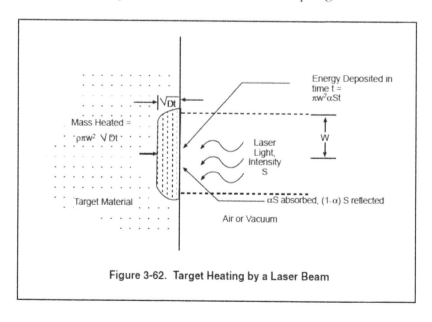

Mass Heated =
$\rho\pi w^2 \sqrt{Dt}$

Target Material

$\sqrt{Dt}$

Energy Deposited in time t = $\pi w^2 \alpha St$

Laser Light, Intensity S

W

αS absorbed, $(1-\alpha) S$ reflected

Air or Vacuum

Figure 3-62. Target Heating by a Laser Beam

A number of features are apparent in Figure 3–63. First, you can see that the thermal coupling coefficient α plays a big role in melting (and, indeed, in all target effects). Typically, α ranges from a few percent in the infrared to a few tens of percent at visible wavelengths. Second, as the pulse width gets longer, the melting threshold decreases, falling by one order of magnitude if t_p increases by two orders of magnitude. This would imply that for a CW (continuous wave) laser with an essentially infinite pulse width, the melting threshold could be made arbitrarily small. There are both practical and physical reasons why this can't be done. In military applications, few targets are likely to be in view or to sit idly by as they are irradiated for times in excess of, say, ten seconds. More fundamentally, as the intensity on target gets smaller and the heating becomes more gentle there are other energy loss mechanisms, such as convection and the reradiation of energy, that come into play. These are discussed in Chapter 1, and will typically limit interaction times to seconds or less. Therefore, Figure 3–63 implies that if the damage criterion is to initiate melting on a target's surface, intensities in excess of 1 kW/cm² will be required.[95]

The threshold for melting shown in Figure 3–63 is the intensity at which the target just begins to melt. In military applications, this is usually not sufficient for damage—we'd like to drill a hole through the target. Therefore, we need to determine how rapidly a

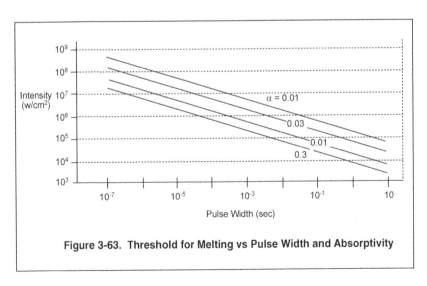

Figure 3-63. Threshold for Melting vs Pulse Width and Absorptivity

hole will grow, once we've exceeded the threshold for melting. The rate at which a hole increases in depth is known as the target's *erosion rate* (cm/sec).

There are two assumptions we could make in calculating a target's erosion rate. If we assume that all molten material is somehow flushed from the hole, then fresh material will be exposed to the laser light, melt, and in turn be flushed out, so that the depth of the hole increases in time. If we assume that molten material remains in the hole, it must continue to heat to the point where it is vaporized if it is to be removed. This requires much more energy. Therefore, these two assumptions will result in upper and lower bounds to the erosion rate. In practical engagements, it's likely that some of the molten material will be removed, and some vaporized.

Molten material might be removed from a hole through the force of gravity or, if the hole is shallow enough, through the flushing effect of a wind across the target's surface. A relatively simple argument, based on conservation of energy, is sufficient to estimate the erosion rate.[96] Figure 3–64 illustrates a hole of depth $\times$ (cm), growing at a velocity V_m (cm/sec).

In a small time dt, an amount of mass $dM = \rho \pi w^2 V_m\, dt$ is removed from the hole, where ρ is the density of the target material, and w the beam radius. The amount of energy which must be supplied to melt this material is $dE = [L_m + C(T_m-T_o)]dM$, where L_m is the heat of fusion, C the target's heat capacity, and T_m its melting temperature (see Chapter 1). The amount of energy absorbed from the laser during this same time period is $dE = \pi w^2 \alpha S\, dt$. At a constant rate of erosion, energy is supplied from the laser at the same rate that it is carried off by the molten material,

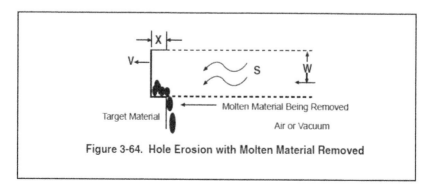

Figure 3-64. Hole Erosion with Molten Material Removed

and these two energies are equal. Equating them and solving for V_m, we can easily see that the rate at which a laser of intensity S will erode a surface whose thermal coupling coefficient is α will be $V_m = \alpha S/\rho[L_m + C(T_m - T_o)]$. Figure 3–65 is a plot of this erosion rate as a function of intensity and absorptivity.[97]

As you can see, both from the expression for the erosion rate and from Figure 3–65, the hole grows at a rate proportional to the absorbed laser intensity. Figure 3–65 can be used to estimate the intensities necessary to penetrate a target of a given thickness in a given time. Suppose, for example, that our goal is to penetrate a target of thickness 0.1 cm in less than 0.1 seconds. As shown by the lines on the figure, this requires an erosion rate greater than 1 cm/sec, and an intensity greater than 3×10^4 W/cm^2 if the target's absorptivity is 0.1.

Vaporization. If molten material is not removed from the hole, we have no choice but to vaporize it. This requires that the intensity exceed the threshold S_v for vaporization. This threshold is $S_v = [\rho C(T_v - T_o) + \rho L_m] (D/t_p)^{1/2}/\alpha$, and the rate V_v with which a vaporizing surface erodes is $V_v = \alpha S/\rho(L_m + L_v + C(T_v - T_o)] \approx \alpha S/\rho L_v$. This threshold and erosion rate are shown in Figures 3–66 and 3–67.[98] You can see from these figures that required intensities are about an order of magnitude greater, and the

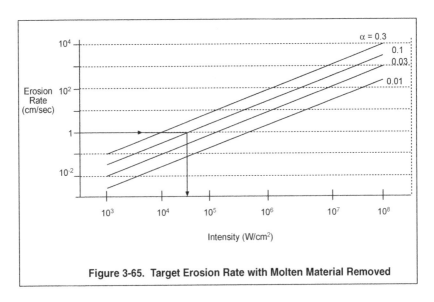

Figure 3-65. Target Erosion Rate with Molten Material Removed

erosion rates about an order of magnitude slower, if target material must be vaporized. This reflects the fact that heats of vaporization are about an order of magnitude greater than heats of fusion (see Table 1–1).

In using Figures 3–64 through 3–67 to estimate requirements for target damage in realistic scenarios, you should keep in mind that realistic erosion rates will probably lie between the extremes of Figures 3–65 and 3–67, and that the intensities given in these figures are the intensities at the target surface. In general, propagation losses will require that the laser fire with much greater intensities, in order to hit the target with the intensity necessary for damage.

Mechanical Effects. Mechanical effects result when momentum is transferred to a target by vapor shooting from it. In effect, the vapor serves as a small jet, and exerts a reaction force back on the target. If sufficiently intense, this force can deform the target, or punch a hole through it without the necessity of physically vaporizing and removing the bulk of the material. Thus, mechanical effects may require less energy to damage a target than thermal effects. That's the good news. The bad news is that higher intensities are required, and may take the beam above the threshold for nonlinear propagation effects. The threshold for mechanical effects is the threshold for vaporization. If we are to go further and quantify the magnitude of effect to be anticipated at a given level of

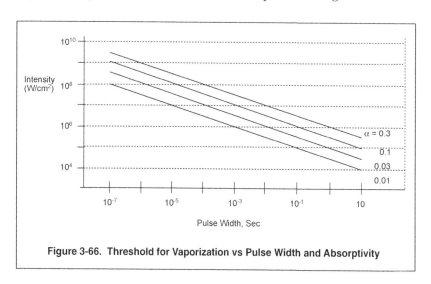

Figure 3-66. Threshold for Vaporization vs Pulse Width and Absorptivity

175

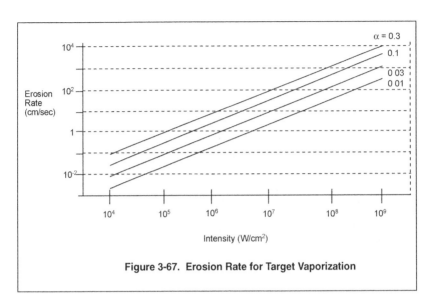

Figure 3-67. Erosion Rate for Target Vaporization

intensity, we must first ask what pressure the surface feels at a given vaporization rate. Then we can consider the effect of that pressure in terms of the target's response.

It is relatively straightforward to show[99] that the pressure exerted by the vapor streaming from a target as a result of its irradiation by a laser of intensity S is approximately

$$P = (kT_v/M)^{1/2}(\alpha S/L_v),$$

where T_v and L_v are the target's vaporization temperature and heat of vaporization, M is the mass of a vapor molecule, and α is the target's thermal coupling coefficient. The ratio $P/S = (kT_v/M)^{1/2}(\alpha/L_v)$ depends only on parameters for a given target, and is known as the *specific impulse*, I^*, for the target material. The parameter I^* derives its name from the fact that it's also the ratio of the impulse delivered to the target ($I = \pi w^2 Pt_p$) to the total energy in the laser pulse ($E = \pi w^2 St_p$). You may recall from Chapter 2 that impulse and pressure are two parameters related to target damage by kinetic energy weapons, which also rely on mechanical effects for damage. The specific impulse is on the order of 1–10 dyne sec/J for most materials.[100] Figure 3–68 shows the pressure on a target surface as a function of intensity and specific impulse.[101] Intuitively, pressures in excess of 10 atm will be needed to damage a target with any reasonable degree of strength. Therefore, Figure 3–68 indicates that intensities in excess of $10^7 - 10^8$

176

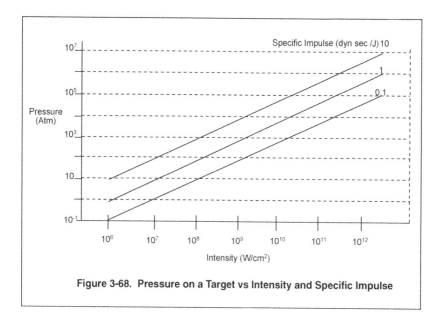

Figure 3-68. Pressure on a Target vs Intensity and Specific Impulse

W/cm² will be needed to achieve damage through mechanical effects. Our next task is to be more quantitative in estimating the intensities and pulse widths necessary for mechanical damage.

How much pressure and impulse are required to damage a target? The answer to this question revolves around the definition of damage. In some applications, it may be adequate to deform the target. In others, it may be necessary to punch a hole through it. What will happen when a given pressure is applied to a target over a given area for a given amount of time is highly dependent upon the nature of the target and its construction. Results may be quite different, for example, if there is a structural support below the irradiated area than if there is not. Quantitative analysis for specific targets is beyond the scope of this book. We can only treat the target in a generic sense as a slab of material with some given thickness. However, just as in Chapter 2, we can outline some of the main features of target damage by mechanical means, and examine how damage might scale with intensity and pulse width. Figure 3–69 shows the physical situation when a laser beam of intensity S engages a target of thickness d.

After a brief time delay vaporization begins, and the emerging vapor exerts a pressure $P = I^* S$ and an impulse $I = \pi w^2 I^* St_p$ to the irradiated area, where I^* is the specific impulse for the target material. The impulse delivered transfers momentum Mv to a portion of the target whose mass is M = $\rho \pi w^2 d$, where ρ is the density (g/cm³) of the target material. This momentum drives it down with a velocity v = I/M. The target therefore receives a blow of energy $Mv^2/2 = I^2/2M$. However, the irradiated portion of the target can't just fly away. It's connected to the rest of the target, and there are internal forces which seek to hold it together. Damage will be achieved when the energy in the blow from the laser exceeds the strength of the bonds which maintain the target's shape, and it deforms or ruptures.[102]

How much energy will be required for a damaging blow? In a solid, the forces that seek to deform it are known as *stresses*, and the stretching or compression that results from these stresses are known as *strains*. You will recall from Chapter 2 that stress has the same units (J/cm³ or Nt/cm²) as pressure, and is analogous to pressure in a gas. Strain is the fractional change in volume, e = $\Delta V/V$, which results from an applied stress. Just as the work done when a pressure P causes a gas to expand from a volume V to V + ΔV is P ΔV, the work done when a stress P causes a strain e is VPe, where V is the volume of material which has been stressed.[103] The energy necessary to strain the solid to the point where it damages is VP*e*, where e* is the amount of strain necessary for damage, and P* is the stress needed to exceed that strain.[104]

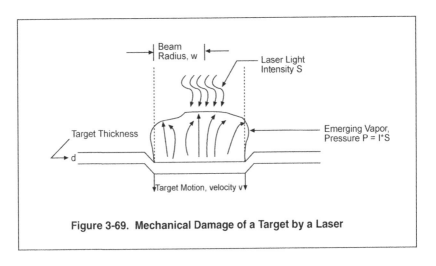

Figure 3-69. Mechanical Damage of a Target by a Laser

The criterion for damage is that the energy in the laser's impulsive blow, $I^2/2M$, equal or exceed the energy needed to strain the target to damage, VP^*e^*. Using $I = \pi w^2 I^* St_p$, $M = [\rho\pi w^2 d]$, and $V = \pi w^2 d$, it's easy to show that a laser of intensity S and duration t_p will damage a target if $St_p > (2\rho P^*e^*)^{1/2} d/I^*$. Figure 3–70 is a plot of the intensity, S, necessary to damage a target as a function of pulse width and target thickness for $I^* = 3$ dyn sec/J.[105] You can see from the figure that intensities of at least 10^7 W/cm^2 and fluences on the order of $10^3 - 10^4$ J/cm^2 are required to damage targets of reasonable thickness.

Energy Requirements for Damage. It's interesting to compare the fluences shown in Figure 3–70 with those necessary to melt or vaporize a hole through targets of similar thickness. The rate of erosion for a target is between $V_m = \alpha S/\rho[L_m + C(T_m - T_o)]$, and $V_v \approx \alpha S/\rho L_v$. These erosion rates can be divided into a target's thickness d to determine the time required for penetration. This time can be multiplied by the intensity to find the fluence necessary for penetration. These fluences are $F_m = d\rho[L_m + C(T_m - T_o)]/\alpha$

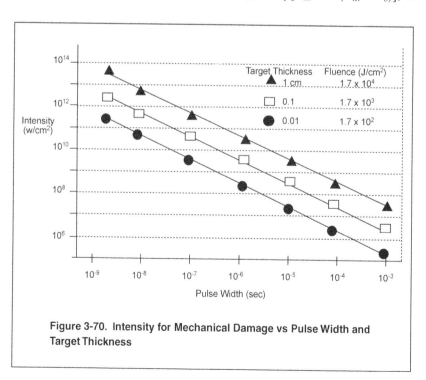

Figure 3-70. Intensity for Mechanical Damage vs Pulse Width and Target Thickness

and $F_v = d\rho L_v/\alpha$ for target melting and vaporization, respectively. Figure 3–71 is a comparison of these fluences for a coupling coefficient α of 0.1 with the fluence necessary for mechanical damage, $F_d = (2\rho P^* e^*)^{1/2} d/I^*$. You can see that it may be more energy–efficient to damage a target of a given thickness by mechanical means, rather than by chewing all the way through it. The reason is simple—in mechanical damage. Target material is not physically removed, it's just the target's structure that's deformed or ruptured. Of course, the relative positions of the lines shown in Figure 3–71 may change in any specific case, depending on the coupling coefficients, target construction, and degree of thermal or mechanical damage required.

If it's energetically more efficient to damage targets mechanically, why is there any interest in thermal damage? One reason is that thermal damage is a relatively sure thing, depending only on the thermal properties of the target material. By contrast, mechanical damage thresholds can be greatly affected by details of the target's construction. These may not be known with any precision. Another reason is because of the time scales and intensities involved. If we are to damage a target as shown in Figure 3–69, the impulse must be delivered in a time shorter than the stresses can relax in a radial direction and be spread out over the target. This time is on the order of the sound speed in the target material divided into the beam radius. Sound speeds in solids

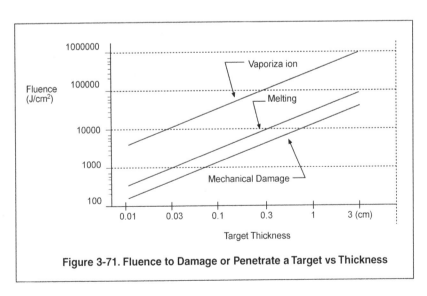

Figure 3-71. Fluence to Damage or Penetrate a Target vs Thickness

are fairly high, on the order of 10^6 cm/sec. For a one meter beam radius, this implies a pulse width of less than 10^{-4} seconds, and intensities of about 10^8 W/cm^2 (see Figure 3–70). By contrast, you can melt through targets with pulse widths on the order of seconds, and intensities on the order of 10^4 W/cm^2 (see Figure 3–63). At the higher intensities associated with mechanical damage, plasma effects are much more likely to occur. These can drastically affect the interaction, and are discussed next.

Summary.

1. The effects that can occur when a laser engages a solid target include heating, melting, vaporization, and momentum transfer. Heating begins as soon as laser light is absorbed at a target's surface. The other effects begin at progressively higher intensity thresholds.

2. The threshold for melting and the resulting erosion rates are shown in Figures 3–63 and 3–65. As the pulse width t_p is increased, the threshold drops. Radiation, convection, and other energy loss processes limit the pulse width to times on the order of seconds or less.

3. If molten material can't be flushed from the irradiated region on a target, it must be vaporized. The threshold for vaporization and the resulting erosion rate are shown in Figures 3–66 and 3–67.

4. The reaction force imparted to a surface by the vapor as it blows off produces a pressure, shown in Figure 3–68. This pressure can serve to damage the target, provided the impulse is great enough to rupture the target's surface. The threshold for this type of "mechanical" damage is shown in Figure 3–70.

5. The advantage of target erosion (melting or vaporization) as a damage mechanism is that the effects are well understood and require lower intensities (W/cm^2). Mechanical damage through impulse delivery requires less fluence (J/cm^2), but is more difficult to characterize, and requires higher intensities and shorter pulse widths. Plasmas are more likely to occur and influence the interaction at these higher intensities.

Effects of Plasmas on Target Interaction

At short enough pulse widths, the intensities required for any of the effects discussed in the previous section may lie above the threshold for plasma production, particularly from aerosols. Indeed, the target may be considered an aerosol with a very large (effectively infinite) radius, having a correspondingly low threshold for plasma initiation (Figure 3–51). It's possible to imagine ways in which plasmas might either help or hinder laser-target effects, as suggested in Figure 3–72.

In Figure 3–72(a), a plasma exists in close contact with a target surface. Since plasmas are very hot and absorb the laser light well, the absorption of energy in this plasma and its transfer to the target by thermal conduction or radiation could deposit a greater fraction of the laser's energy in the target than if there were no plasma. The heavy black lines in the figure suggest such a transfer of energy.

On the other hand, if a plasma propagates away from the target, it will continue to absorb almost all of the laser light, but very little energy will find its way into the target. This is shown in Figure 3–72(b). Clearly, plasmas may be good or bad from the standpoint of laser effects. Whether they are good or bad will depend upon the laser intensity, which determines the type of plasma and its mode of propagation, and the pulse width, which determines how far a plasma can travel as the beam engages the target. In this sec-

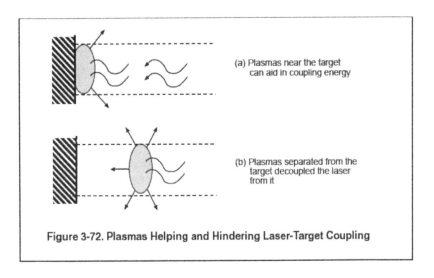

(a) Plasmas near the target can aid in coupling energy

(b) Plasmas separated from the target decoupled the laser from it

Figure 3-72. Plasmas Helping and Hindering Laser-Target Coupling

tion, we'll consider the effect of laser-supported detonation and combustion waves on both thermal and mechanical effects in air and vacuum.

Plasma Effects in a Vacuum. At first glance, you might question the need for this topic, since a vacuum contains no molecules to ionize into a plasma. Nevertheless, even in a vacuum, plasmas can occur if vapor emerging from the target becomes ionized. Of course, a plasma formed in this way can't completely shield the target from the laser. If it did, vaporization would cease and the plasma would disperse. The analysis of target coupling in the presence of a vapor plasma in vacuum requires a self-consistent theory that accounts for energy reaching the target either as laser light which has penetrated the plasma, or as reradiation or thermal conduction from within the plasma. Figure 3–73 summarizes the results of such a calculation.[106]

In the calculation represented in Figure 3–73, it was assumed that a fraction α_p of the radiation absorbed in ionized vapor was coupled back into the surface, aiding its erosion and augmenting the fraction α_c of the laser radiation absorbed at the target surface. The effective coupling coefficient is $\alpha = \alpha_p\, f + \alpha_c\, (1–f)$, where f is the fraction of the laser light absorbed within the vapor plasma. If α_p is small compared to α_c, the effective coupling coefficient behaves like the lowest curve in Figure 3–73. It is always less than or equal to α_c, and as the intensity rises and the rate of erosion in-

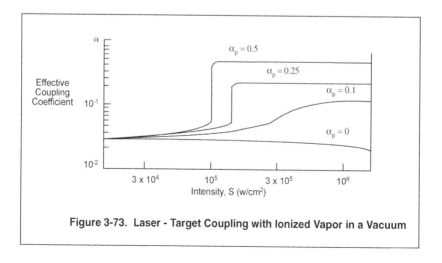

Figure 3-73. Laser - Target Coupling with Ionized Vapor in a Vacuum

creases, there is a gradual decline in α, roughly as $S^{-2/3}$. By contrast, if α_p is large compared to α_c, the effective coupling coefficient rises with intensity to a value approximately equal to α_p.

This behavior can be related to two self-consistent ways in which targets can vaporize in the presence of a plasma. If reradiation from the plasma contributes little to target erosion, then as S increases the additional energy accelerates the vapor, leaving its density unchanged. This is because if the vapor density were to increase, the plasma would become more absorbing, target erosion would decrease, and the increase in density could not be maintained. On the other hand, if reradiation from the plasma is most important in target vaporization, an increase in S will increase the vapor density. That's because in this case an increase in density is beneficial, serving to increase the rate of erosion. Therefore, the effective coupling of a laser to a target at intensities where ionization can occur in the evolving vapor will depend critically on the degree of coupling to the bare metal and how this compares with the absorption of radiation emitted from the ionized vapor. As a general rule, it's clear from Figure 3–73 that if a plasma is created in the vapor emerging from a target in a vacuum there is a strong potential for enhanced coupling, and in the worst case there will be at most a small decline in the effective coupling coefficient. From Figure 3–16, you can see that the coupling of laser light to metals is least for long wavelength infrared radiation. Therefore, the potential for enhanced coupling through plasma ignition is greatest at long wavelengths. Experimentally, increases in α by factors of 3–10 have been seen upon plasma ignition with infrared lasers.[107]

Since plasma ignition can affect the thermal coupling coefficient α, it will affect the rate of erosion and the specific impulse I^* as well. The momentum transferred to the target by the vapor is on the order of ρv^2, where ρ is the vapor density and v its velocity: the energy it carries away is on the order of ρv^2. Thus, the ratio of momentum to energy is proportional to $1/v$. Therefore, in the case where α_p is small compared to α_c, and increased intensity increases the vapor's velocity, plasma ignition results in a gradual decline in I^* as $S^{-1/3}$.[108] In the case where α_p is large and there is enhanced coupling, the fact that an increased intensity primarily increases the vapor's density means that it should be enhanced along with the effective coupling coefficient, and be roughly independent of intensity.

In summary, when plasmas are produced over a target surface in vacuum, the result is on average beneficial for laser effects. Both the thermal coupling coefficient and specific impulse may increase, and in any case they won't decline precipitously. The logical next step is to ask what can happen when plasmas are produced within the atmosphere.

Plasma Effects on Coupling in the Atmosphere. In the atmosphere, any plasmas which are created at the target surface may propagate away from the target as an absorption wave, decoupling the radiation from the target. Thus, plasmas could have a much more profound effect on α and I^* in the air than in a vacuum. Quantitative analysis is quite involved, and must include the effect of light transmitted through the plasma, light reradiated from the plasma to the target, and the propagation characteristics of the plasma as a function of laser intensity. Figure 3–74 is a good example of the type of calculations that have been performed, and illustrates many of the features exhibited by analyses of this type.[109]

The graphs shown in Figure 3–74 show the evolution in time of three quantities—the intensity of radiation being deposited in the target (Q) the integral of Q over time, and the instantaneous thermal coupling coefficient, α.[110] The intensity Q includes both laser light and plasma radiation which reach the surface and are absorbed there. The two graphs correspond to two different laser intensities, S. The first of these, 10^6 W/cm^2, supports plasma propagation as a laser supported combustion (LSC), while the second, 10^7 W/cm^2, supports propagation as a laser-supported detonation (LSD). In the upper graph on Figure 3–74, we see that when an LSC is ignited α is initially very high. This reflects the close proximity of the plasma to the target and its effectiveness in absorbing laser energy and reradiating it to the target. As the LSC moves away from the target, α decreases and remains relatively constant at about 10% for a fairly long time. This is because the LSC plasma is moving slowly, and does not begin to decouple the radiation from the target until about 15 μsec. The point at which decoupling begins is evident as Q begins to fall off and the integral of Q over time becomes constant.

In the lower half of the figure, you can see how differently things behave when an LSD is ignited. The plasma propagates rapidly away from the target surface, Q falls to zero, and α drops

185

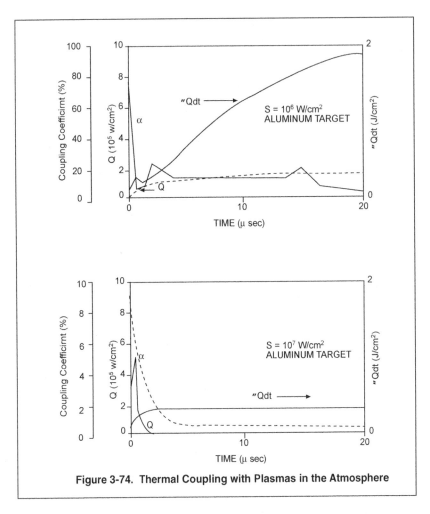

Figure 3-74. Thermal Coupling with Plasmas in the Atmosphere

to a very low value—less than 1%. (Note that the scale for α in the lower graph is an order of magnitude less than that in the upper graph.) From these and similar calculations, it can be concluded that plasma ignition in the atmosphere will only serve to enhance thermal coupling if the laser intensity lies below the threshold for LSD propagation, and then only if the laser pulse width is sufficiently short that LSC propagation can't ultimately decouple the beam from the target as well.

Next let's turn our attention to the influence of plasmas on mechanical coupling in the atmosphere. You will recall that the pressure in an LSD can be quite high, on the order of 10–100 atmos-

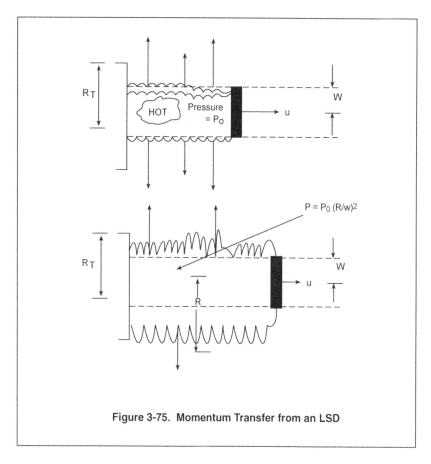

Figure 3-75. Momentum Transfer from an LSD

pheres. This high pressure, as it relaxes towards equilibrium with its surroundings, will transfer some momentum and impulse to a target over and above that which the target receives as a result of vaporization. Theory and experiment are consistent in demonstrating such an effect.

A relatively simple model, illustrated in Figure 3–75, can be used to capture the physics of momentum transfer in the presence of detonation waves.

Figure 3–75 shows an LSD propagating away from a target. As the thin, absorbing shock front moves forward, it leaves behind hot, high-pressure gases. These gases are initially at the high pressure P_0 associated with an LSD wave. Since the LSD propagates at a supersonic velocity, u, the hot gases form what is effectively a long cylinder, and expand radially to pressure balance as a cylindrical wavefront. As the gases expand from their initial radius, w (the beam radius), to some greater radius, R, their pressure is reduced by a factor of $(w/R)^2$. This is entirely analogous to the expansion of the high pressure gases resulting from the detonation of a bomb (Chapter 1), where the pressure falls off as $1/R^3$ due to its three-dimensional (spherical) expansion. In this case, the pressure falls off as $1/R^2$ because the expansion is two dimensional (cylindrical).[111]

The expanding gases exert a pressure on the target surface. The force exerted on the target is a constant, even though the pressure is decreasing as the gases expand. This is because force = pressure × area, and while the pressure is decreasing as $1/R^2$, the area over which it is applied is increasing as R^2, so that the product of these two quantities is constant. Therefore, the impulse delivered to the target, which is the integral of force over time, increases linearly with time, until the expanding gases either reach the edge of the target at a radius R_T and relax around it, or the pressure in them decreases to the point where it equals the surrounding atmospheric pressure, and expansion ceases. An interesting consequence of this is that for small targets, the impulse delivered should scale with the *target* area, rather than the beam area.[112] On the other hand, for large targets we'd expect the impulse delivered to be independent of target size.

What are the implications of these results from the standpoint of target damage? Both pressure and impulse are important in establishing damage thresholds. In the presence of detonation waves, a large measured impulse may reflect a low pressure applied over a large area, as opposed to a large pressure being applied over the irradiated area. Because the energy transferred to a target area of mass M by an impulse I is $I^2/2M$ you can see that as the area and mass over which the pressure is applied increase, the energy and stress delivered to the target decrease. Accordingly, measured data on the specific impulse I* in the presence of detonation waves must be carefully interpreted before drawing conclusions from them relative to the likelihood of exceeding damage thresholds.

Summary.

1. There are mechanisms through which plasmas can both help and hinder either thermal or mechanical effects. The help arises from the fact that plasmas are generally more strongly absorb-

ing than the bare target surface, and can serve as an efficient means of energy transfer to the surface. The hindrance arises from the fact that plasmas may propagate away from the target surface, decoupling the absorbed energy from it.

2. In a vacuum, plasma ignition within the evolving target vapor generally serves to enhance thermal coupling, particularly when the intrinsic absorptivity at the target surface is low.

3. In a vacuum, plasma ignition will enhance momentum transfer to the extent that increased thermal coupling enhances the target ablation rate.

4. In the atmosphere, plasma ignition will enhance thermal coupling at intensities below the threshold for detonation wave propagation and pulse widths too short to permit combustion wives to propagate substantial distances.

5. In the atmosphere, plasma ignition below the threshold for LSD propagation will enhance momentum transfer to the extent that thermal coupling and target ablation are enhanced. Above the threshold for LSD propagation, target erosion ceases but momentum is transferred as high pressure gases left behind the advancing LSD wave front relax to pressure balance. Substantial impulse may be delivered in this way, but it is qualitatively different from that delivered in a vacuum and results from lower pressures applied over larger areas.

Summary of Main Concepts. We have covered considerable territory in this chapter. Let's summarize the main ideas we have presented.

1. Lasers are intense sources of electromagnetic radiation, with wavelengths from about 10 to 0.4 μm and frequencies from about 3×10^{13} to 8×10^{14} Hz.

2. The materials with which lasers might interact are characterized by an index of refraction, n, and an attenuation coefficient, K. When light passes regions of different n, it is bent according to the law of refraction. This can occur either deliberately, in lenses, or inadvertently, since density fluctuations in the atmosphere are accompanied by fluctuations in n. When light propagates a distance z through a region whose attenuation coefficient is K, its intensity is decreased by a factor exp(–Kz).

3. A laser of wavelength λ emerging from an aperture of diameter D can propagate a distance on the order of D^2/λ as a collimated beam. Beyond this distance, it will diverge at an angle $\theta \approx \lambda/D$ through diffraction.

4. Decreases in intensity resulting both from diffraction and attenuation will reduce the fraction of a beam's energy which can be brought to bear on a target. Beam parameters which may be adjusted to compensate for these effects and enable the delivery of damaging intensities to a target include the energy, pulse width, wavelength, and diameter of the beam.

5. In the atmosphere, K is highly wavelength dependent, containing contributions from absorption and scattering from both molecules and particles (aerosols). If a beam becomes too intense, free electrons in the atmosphere will multiply and the air will break down, forming an ionized plasma which will absorb the beam. Following breakdown, plasmas can propagate towards the source of laser light as combustion or detonation waves.

6. In the atmosphere, n can vary through turbulence or through expansion induced by the absorption of laser light. The second effect results in beam expansion (thermal blooming) or bending. These effects must generally be compensated for in real time through adaptive optics.

7. When laser light encounters a target, a fraction of the light is absorbed in the target surface, and appears as heat. Thresholds for melting and vaporization are established by the criterion that energy be deposited so rapidly that it cannot be carried away within the pulse width of the laser. Targets can be damaged either through the erosion which results from melting or vaporization (thermal damage), or through the momentum transferred to the target surface by an evolving vapor jet (mechanical damage).

8. The ignition of plasmas at a target surface, and their subsequent propagation as detonation or combustion waves, can greatly affect the thermal and mechanical coupling of a laser to a target, either in air or vacuum. In a vacuum, coupling will most likely be enhanced, while in the air it will most likely be degraded.

Implications

Having seen how lasers interact with targets, what can we conclude regarding the optimal intensity and pulse width for target damage? Any such optimum needs to consider propagation as well as interaction effects, since these work together to constrain the operating parameters which are available. Figure 3–76 is an attempt to draw together and plot on a single graph some of the main effects considered in the last two sections.

Shown on Figure 3–76 are the thresholds for melting, vaporization, and mechanical damage which we developed in this section, together with approximate thresholds for thermal blooming, stimulated Raman scattering (SRS), and plasma production. All of the lines on the figure should be considered only approximate, of course, because they will shift up or down with different assumptions regarding range, frequency, coupling coefficients, and so on. However, you can see that those shown are reasonably representative by comparing the lines in the figure with the more detailed figures presented earlier for each effect.

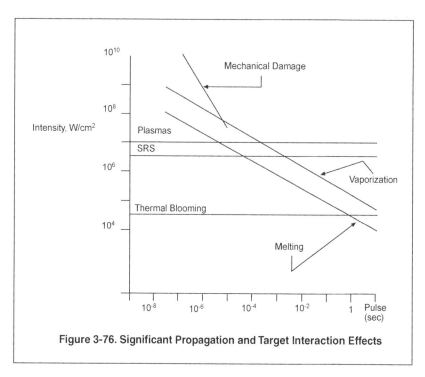

Figure 3-76. Significant Propagation and Target Interaction Effects

You can see from Figure 3–76 that there is very little opportunity to damage targets in the atmosphere without operating at intensities where potentially deleterious propagation effects must be dealt with. Even melting through targets in times less than seconds will likely require dealing with thermal blooming, and if mechanical damage is contemplated the full range of propagation effects could constrain the interaction between a laser and its target. Because of these potential constraints, it is not yet clear which approach is best for damaging targets—longer pulses of lower intensity or shorter pulses of higher intensity. Lower intensity phenomena are easier to understand and model, and are often favored for this reason alone. However, the interaction times can become so long that it may not be possible to deal with multiple targets in stressing scenarios. Higher intensities and shorter pulses permit the rapid engagement of targets, and may even be more energy efficient, but are more difficult to model in a reliable way, and are possibly more challenging from the standpoint of device construction.

Throughout this chapter, the analysis has been kept simple by assuming that the laser is a pure device, putting out a single intensity S for a given time period t_p. While this is useful from the standpoint of understanding interaction and propagation phenomena, there is no reason why this needs to be so. It might be possible, for example, to obtain enhanced coupling with a pulse that starts off with a high intensity to insure plasma ignition, and then drops down to a lower intensity where the plasma can be maintained in close proximity to the target. Thermal blooming might be used to advantage, with a long duration, low intensity pulse used to develop an underdense channel with an elevated air breakdown threshold, followed by a short, high intensity pulse which damages the target. Combination of low and high intensity pulses could alternately melt target material and flush it away with mechanical pressure. In short, there is almost no limit to combinations of effects that might be considered as an aid in achieving target damage, and the material presented here needs to be viewed with an eye toward the possibilities, as well as the limitations that it represents.

In realistic engagements, it must also be recognized that true damage means more than drilling holes or buckling plates. There are many cars on the road that attest to the fact that holes and dents do not necessarily prevent a target from functioning. And a sailboat will continue to function if someone shoots a small hole in the sail, but will be dead in the water if a wind of much lower pressure rips the sail or snaps the mast. Therefore, a serious trade-off among different damage mechanisms needs to account for the specific vulnerabilities of the intended target. The material we have presented can only serve as a general guide in contemplating different damage mechanisms.

It is also possible to trade the constraints of physics for the constraints of engineering. Because of the many constraints that the atmosphere places on laser propagation and target interaction, interest has arisen in space-based lasers as weapons. In the vacuum of space, the only potential effect would be the ignition of plasmas at a target's surface, and this could actually improve the coupling of energy to it. Another possibility for attacking targets in space would be to use ground based lasers with very large apertures, actually focusing the beam so that its greatest intensity is not achieved until it has exited the densest portion of the atmosphere. Solutions like these trade physics problems for engineering problems, which may be more amenable to ingenuity and capital investment.

Notes and References

1. A good general discussion of the principles of laser operation and of some of the more common types of lasers can be found in Bela A. Lengyel, *Lasers,*2nd ed. (New York: Wiley Interscience, 1971. Jeff Hecht, The Laser Guidebook (New York: McGraw-Hill, 1986) is a simpler book, aimed at more general audiences. More detailed discussion of specific laser types can be found in more specialized texts, such as J. D. Anderson, Jr., *Gas Dynamic Lasers* (New York: Academic Press, 1976), or T.C. Marshall, *Free Electron Lasers* (New York: Macmillan, 1985). Unfortunately, the state of the art in laser technology is advancing so rapidly that published textbooks are generally inadequate for the purpose of obtaining current performance capabilities and limitations. Information of this sort must usually be found in conference proceedings and journal articles, though occasionally a good summary appears in the literature. The most up-to-date summary available in 1988 was Chapter 3 of the "Report to the American Physical Society of the Study Group on Science and Technology of Directed Energy Weapons," published in *Reviews of Modern Physics* vol. 59, pt II (July 1987).

2. John D. Jackson, *Classical Electrodynamics* (New York: John Wiley and Sons, 1962) is a good text on electromagnetic theory at the graduate level.

3. Wave phenomena are discussed in great detail and with minimal mathematical complexities in John R. Pierce, *Almost All About Waves* (Cambridge, MA: MIT Press, 1974).

4. The speed of light, c, is a very important parameter in physics. Einstein's theory of relativity asserts that the measured value of c in a vacuum will always be the same, regardless of any relative motion between the source of radiation and the observer. In addition, no physical object can exceed the speed of light, so that electromagnetic radiation is the fastest bullet possible for weapon use.

5. The *Hertz* is named for Heinrich Hertz (1857-1894). Hertz was the first to broadcast and receive radio waves, and to demonstrate that these waves could be reflected and refracted like light.

6. Figure 3–3 has been adapted from Figure 3.13 in Eugene Hecht and Alfred Zajac, *Optics* (Reading, MA: Addison-Wesley, 1976).

7. The theory of lenses is discussed in any text on optics, such as Chapter 5 of Hecht and Zajac (note 6).

8. The divergence angle, θ, of light from a circular aperture is 1.22 λ/D. For other types of apertures, θ is less well defined, since the dimension of a square aperture, for example, is different along a diagonal than along a side. In every case, however, θ is approximately λ/D. See Hecht and Zajac (note 6), Chapter 10.

9. The fact that a converging lens can't focus light to an infinitely small point is another manifestation of the wave nature of light and its diffraction.

10. See section 3.4 in Joseph T. Verdeyen, *Laser Electronics* (Englewood Cliffs, NJ: Prentice-Hall, 1981) for a discussion of laser beam expansion and the concept of a beam's "spot size."

11. Propagation within the Rayleigh Range is known as "near field" propagation, and at greater distances as "far field" propagation.

12. The word *quantum* comes from the Latin for "how much," and refers to the fact that when seen on a fine scale no physical processes are continuous, but occur in small steps, or quanta. Quantum mechanics is the mathematical theory that describes such phenomena. The dual wave and particle nature of light is discussed in any text on modern physics, such as Paul L.Copeland and William E. Bennett, *Elements of Modern Physics* (New York, Oxford University Press, 1961).

13. Interestingly enough, the allowed orbits are those for which an integral number of particle "wavelengths" will fit around the path. Just as waves exhibit some of the properties of particles in quantum mechanics, so also particles exhibit some wavelike properties. See section 4.7 in Arthur Beiser, *Concepts of Modern Physics*, 3rd ed (New York: McGraw-Hill, 1981).

14. Figure 3–9 is adapted from Figure 4–20 in Beiser (note 13).

15. If the hydrogen atom is not in its ground state, with its electron in the lowest level, then the photon energies which can be absorbed are those which will promote the electron from the level where it resides to some other. For example, an electron in the 10.2 eV level can be excited to the 12.1 eV level by absorbing a 1.9 eV photon. Thus, the absorption properties of a hot, excited gas will be different from those of a cold gas, and the absorption and

emission of light from a gas can be used as a measure of its temperature, or degree of excitation.

16. Figure 3–10 is based on Figure 9.28 of Lengyel (note l).

17. Figure 3–11 is based on Figure 3–23 in Robert J. Pressley (ed), *CRC Handbook of Lasers* (Cleveland, OH: Chemical Rubber Co, 1971).

18. The band structure of solids and how it relates to their electrical and optical properties is discussed in any text on solid state physics, such as Chapter 9 of Charles Kittel, *Introduction to Solid State Physics*, 3rd ed. (New York: John Wiley and Sons, 1966).

19. Figure 3–13 has been adapted from Figure 3b, p 540, of Kittel (note 18).

20. The data in Table 3–1 were taken from Table 1, p 302, of Kittel (note 18).

21. The fact that the electric field must vanish on the interior of a conductor is a consequence of Maxwell's equations in the limit where nothing varies with time, and is discussed in almost any undergraduate physics text, such as Chapter 28 of David Halliday and Robert Resnick, *Physics, Part II* (New York: John Wiley and Sons, 1967).

22. Shielding electronic components with metal boxes is especially important as a countermeasure against microwave weapons. See Chapter 4.

23. The plasma frequency is discussed in detail in any text on plasma physics, and its implication from the standpoint of light penetrating a conductor is developed in books on electromagnetic theory. See Jackson (note 2), Chapter 7.

24. This expression for the reflectivity assumes that the skin depth is small compared to the wavelength of the radiation, which is the case at all frequencies of interest here and in Chapter 4. See Chapter 6 of Jerry B. Marion, *Classical Electromagnetic Radiation* (New York: Academic Press, 1968).

25. More precisely, the definitions "near" and "far" field relate to approximations which can be made in diffraction calculations. Diffraction in the far field is known as Fraunhofer diffraction, and in the near field as Fresnel diffraction. See Hecht and Zajac (note 6) Chapter 10.

26. This definition of solid angle is analogous to the mathematical definition of a plane angle. Let two lines diverge from a point, and draw a circle about that point. The constant of proportionality between the arc of the circle the lines cut off and the radius of the circle is the angle between the lines in radians.

27. The utility of the brightness concept is attested to by the fact that similar concepts have emerged for almost every form of beamed energy. See Chapters 4 and 5.

28. The treatment of binary (one-on-one) interactions in terms of cross sections is common in physics, and will be used throughout this book. A good discussion of the cross section concept can be found in Chapter II of M. Mitchner and Charles H. Kruger, Jr., *Partially Ionized Gases* (New York: Wiley Interscience, 1973).

29. Pierre Bouguer (1698–1758) made some of the earliest measurements of the absorption of light in the atmosphere. Many scientists have corrupted Bouguer's name to the point where the ansorption law is sometimes referred to as "Beer's Law." Johann Lambert (1728–1777) also studied heat and light, but (1728–1777) was at heart more of a mathematician. He was the first to prove that the number π is not a rational number.

30. A good summary of absorption as a function of frequency, adequate for zero-order analysis, can be found in Section 14, "Optical Properties of the Atmosphere," in Waiter G. Driscoll, ed., *Handbook of Optics*, (New York: McGraw-Hill, 1978).

31. The upper portion of Figure 3–24 is based on a figure on p.115 of R. D. Hudson, Jr., *Infrared Systems Engineering* (New York: John Wiley and Sons, 1969). The lower, expanded portion of the figure is based on Figure 2 in Frederic G. Gebhardt, "High Power Laser Propagation, " *Applied Optics* 15, 1484 (1976). Gebhardt's paper is a good summary of many of the phenomena discussed in this chapter, at a somewhat higher level of technical detail.

32. This example is from Gebhardt (note 31).

33. This result is seen experimentally and may be derived using statistical mechanics. It assumes that temperature is roughly independent of altitude, and that the acceleration due to gravity is a constant. Therefore, it is most accurate near the surface of the earth. Since this is where absorption is the greatest, the "exponential atmosphere" is often adequate for "zero-order" analysis. See

Section 6.3 in F. Reif, *Fundamentals of Statistical and Thermal Physics* (New York: McGraw-Hill, 1965).

34. Since different atmospheric constituents have different molecular weights, they each fall off differently with altitude. The "7 km" value for h_o is an average over all constituents. Species whose weight is lighter than the average will fall off less rapidly, and those whose weight is heavier than the average will fall off more rapidly. Since absorption may depend on a single species at a given wavelength, the exact scale length for absorption may differ from the nominal value in a specific application.

35. Figure 3–26 is a plot of the expression $_0\int^z K(z)dz = [K(0)h_o/\sin\phi][1-\exp(-z\sin\phi/h_o)]$.

36. Figure 3–27 is adapted from figures found in C. E. Junge, *Air Chemistry and Radioactivity* (New York: Academic Press, 1963) and in J. E. Manson's article in S.L. Valley (ed), *Handbook of Geophysics and Space Environments* (Hanscom AFB: Air Force Cambridge Research Laboratories, 1965).

37. A commonly used mathematical expression for the density of particles of size r is $n(r) = ar^\alpha \exp(-br^\gamma)$. The constants a, b, α, and γ will vary depending on climate and other conditions. Representative values may be found in Section 3.14 of V. E. Zuev, *Laser Beams in the Atmosphere* (New York: Consultant's Bureau, 1982).

38. All of the gory details of Mie's theory can be found in Max Born and Emil Wolf, *Principles of Optics*, 5th ed. (Oxford: Pergamon Press, 1975).

39. Figure 3–28 is based on Figure 13.14 in Born and Wolf (note 38).

40. A number of representative curves, along with references to the original literature, can be found in Born and Wolf (note 38).

41. Figure 3-30 is based on data from p. E-373 in Robert C. Weast (ed) *CRC Handbook of Chemistry and Physics*, 67th ed. (Boca Raton, FL: CRC Press, 1987).

42. A good description of the two quantities which affect propagation and its correction through adaptive optics, the coherence length and isoplanatic angle, can be found in Section 5.4.4 of the *APS Report on Directed Energy Weapons* (note 1).

43. A good discussion of the refractive index structure coefficient and its variation with altitude and time of day can be found in S.F.

Clifford, "The Classical Theory of Wave Propagation in a Turbulent Medium," Chapter 2 in J. W. Strohbehn (ed), *Laser Beam Propagation in the Atmosphere* (Berlin: Springer-Verlag, 1978).

44. Figure 3–33 Is based on Figures 2.1 and 2.4 in Clifford's article (note 43).

45. See Table 4.1 in Zuev (note 37) for the fluctuations about its average value which C_N undergoes during various times of day.

46. APS Report on Directed Energy Weapons (note 1), section 5.4.4.

47. J. E. Pearson, "Atmospheric Turbulence Compensation Using Coherent Optical Adaptive Techniques," *Applied Optics 15, 622* (1976.)

48. The time scale for mirror motion is related to the frequency with which the turbulent environment shifts from one configuration to another, and the degree of motion is related to the wavelength of the light. See Pearson (note 47).

49. There are many nonlinear effects not considered here which may be important at the intensities and powers appropriate to other applications, such as laser fusion, or which are of interest from a scientific standpoint for insight into the structure of matter.

50. Figure 3–40 has been adapted from Gebhardt's paper (note 31). This figure has become a classic, and can be seen in almost any discussion of thermal blooming.

51. See P. B. Ulrich, "Numerical Methods in High Power Laser Propagation," AGARD Conference Proceedings No. 183, *Optical Propagation in the Atmosphere*, Paper No. 31 (27–31 October, 1975).

52. A beam having this intensity profile is known as a *gaussian* beam. Many lasers, especially lower-power "research" devices, have an intensity profile of this shape. See H. Kogelnick and T. Li, "Laser Beams and Resonators," *Applied Optics 5, 1550* (1966).

53. See Gebhardt (note 31). Figure 3–42 is based on Gebhardt's Figure 7.

54. See Section 5.4.8 of the *APS Report on Directed Energy Weapons* (note 1).

55. See, for example, Figure 3 in Gebhardt (note 31).

56. In realistic scenarios, of course, the wind is unlikely to be constant over the whole path, and the beam profile may not be gaussian. An effective distortion number can nevertheless be

calculated by integrating over factors which change along the beam path and over the beam front, much as we did in integrating K(z) dz to obtain the optical depth when K was not a constant. The procedure is described in Gebhardt (note 31). The relative intensity varies with distortion number as in Figure 3–42 for a surprisingly broad range of experimental conditions.

57. Zuev (note 37) discusses some of the types of stimulated scattering that can occur in Section 5.8.

58. APS Report on Directed Energy Weapons (note l), section 5.8.

59. Figure 3–46 is based on Figure 5.23 in the *APS Report on Directed Energy Weapons* (note l).

60. Some of the potential cures for SRS are discussed in Section 5.4.9.4 of the *APS Report on Directed Energy Weapons* (note 1).

61. Of course, if the electron density were so great that it exceeded the plasma frequency at the wavelength of the light, the laser would primarily be reflected, and not absorbed. However, as you can see from Figure 3–14, laser light at infrared and shorter wavelengths will exceed the plasma frequency of singly-ionized air at sea level. This is not, however, the case for microwaves (see Chapter 4).

62. For large beams propagating in the atmosphere, there will be no problem in finding some free electrons to start a breakdown cascade. Early breakdown experiments, however, were often difficult to interpret because the low powers of the available lasers required that the beam be focused to a very small spot. The probability of finding an initial electron in these small focal volumes was small, and breakdown was often very statistical in nature.

63. A more extensive discussion of the ionization of atmospheric molecules by energetic particles can be found in Chapter 5.

64. See Section 5.1 in Zuev (note 37).

65. The "radian frequency" derives its name from the fact that going around a circle once (one cycle) encompasses an angle of $360°$ (2π radians).

66. Figure 3–49 assumes that the rate for electrons of average energy ϵ to ionize a molecular degree of freedom whose threshold is X is $v_c \exp(-X/\epsilon)$. The implicit assumption is that the distribution of energies among the electrons is roughly that of particles in thermal equilibrium. In actuality, the distribution of energies in a gas

of electrons having an average energy ϵ can be quite different from that assumed, though this simple model is more than adequate to illustrate the general features of the interactions between the electrons and the neutral gas.

67. The general theory of gas breakdown is described in P. E. Nielsen and G.H. Canavan, "Electron Cascade Theory in Laser Induced Breakdown of Preionized Gases," *Journal of Applied Physics* 44, 4224 (September 1973). Cross sections for the excitation of various degrees of freedom in many of the species present in the atmosphere are presented as a function of energy in L. J. Kieffer, "A Compilation of Electron Collision Cross Section Data for Modeling Gas Discharge Lasers," *JILA Information Center Rept 13*, Joint Institute for Laboratory Astrophysics, Boulder CO (September, 1973). Data such as these are a prerequisite for detailed breakdown calculations.

68. Figure 3–50 is based on calculations for air which are analogous to those described for helium in Nielsen and Canavan (note 67).

69. For example, see D. E. Lencioni, "Laser-Induced Air Breakdown for 1.06 μm Radiation," *Applied Physics Letters* 25, 15 (1 July, 1974). The data in this paper must be scaled by a factor of 100 to compare with the 10.6 μm calculations shown in Figure 3–50.

70. If n_0 is the initial number of electrons and N the density of the neutral gas, the number of generations required for breakdown is found from $2gn_0 \approx N$, or $g = \log_2(N/n_0)$.

71. Thermionic emission, field emission, and other mechanisms by which electrons may be drawn out from a solid are discussed in Chapter V of James D. Cobine, *Gaseous Conductors,* (New York: Dover, 1958).

72. David C. Smith and Robert T. Brown, "Aerosol-Induced Air Breakdown with CO_2 Laser Radiation," *Journal of Applied Physics* 46, 1146 (3 March 1975).

73. Figure 3–51 is based on Figure 2 in 6. H. Canavan and P. E. Nielsen, "Focal Spot Size Dependence of Gas Breakdown Induced by Particulate Ionization," *Applied Physics Letters* 22, 409 (15 April 1973).

74. See Mitchner and Kruger (note 28).

75. A thorough technical discussion of combustion can be found in Irvin Glassman, *Combustion* (New York: Academic Press, 1977).

76. See Glassman (note 75). In addition, a very readable account of the detonation mode of exothermic chemical reaction is in William C. Davis, "The Detonation of Explosives," *Scientific American 256,* 106 (May, 1987).

77. The relationship P = N kT is known as the *equation of state* for the gas. This is only an approximate form, reasonably accurate at intermediate temperatures. The actual equation of state differs at low temperatures, where intermolecular forces become important, and at high temperatures, where molecules may dissociate and more internal degrees of freedom may be excited.

78. See Chapter I, Section 2 in Ya. B. Zel'dovich and Yu. P. Raizer, *Physics of Shock Waves and-High Temperature Hydrodynamic Phenomena,* Vol I (New York: Academic Press, 1966).

79. A good review of the theory for LAW propagation, along with comparisons with early experimental data, can be found in Yu. P. Raizer, "Propagation of Discharges and Maintenance of a Dense Plasma by Electromagnetic Fields, *Soviet Physics—Uspekhi* 16, 688 (May-June, 1973). A review aimed more at atmospheric propagation is in P. E. Nielsen and G. H. Canavan, "Laser Absorption Waves in the Atmosphere," *Laser Interactions and Related Plasma Phenomena,* Vol 3, p 177 (New York: Plenum, 1974).

80. A detailed discussion of ionization as a function of temperature can be found in Chapter III of Zel'dovich and Raizer (note 78).

81. Figure 3–56 is a plot of Equation 3–46 in Zel'dovich and Raizer (note 78).

82. See Chapter V in Zel'dovich and Raizer (note 78).

83. Figure 3–57 was developed from Equations 3.46 and 5.21 in Zel'dovich and Raizer (note 78).

84. Yu. P. Raizer, "Heating of a Gas by a Powerful Light Pulse," *Soviet Physics—JETP* 21, 1009 (November, 1965).

85. The constant γ is the ratio of the heat capacity at constant pressure to that at constant volume. It is not a true constant, but varies with temperature, so that a value must be chosen which is appropriate in the temperature range of interest. See Table 3.2 in Zel'dovich and Raizer (note 78).

86. The data on Figure 3–58 were taken from R. B. Hall, W. E. Maher, and P. S. P. Wei, "An Investigation of Laser-Supported

Detonation Waves," *Air Force Weapons Laboratory Technical Rept.* No AFWL-TR–73–28 (Kirtland AFB, NM: Air Force Weapons Laboratory, June, 1973).

87. This approach was originally suggested by Raizer (note 84).

88. Figure 3–60 has been adapted from Figure 2 in Nielsen and Canavan (note 79).

89. Yu. P. Raizer, "Subsonic Propagation of a Light Spark and Threshold Conditions for the Maintenance of Plasma by Radiation, *"Soviet Physics—JETP* 31, 1148 (December, 1970).

90. An everyday example is the light emitted from the sun, which is a high temperature plasma. This light is emitted over a broad range of frequencies from the infrared to the ultraviolet.

91. J. P. Jackson and P. E. Nielsen, "Role of Radiative Transport in the Propagation of Laser Supported Combustion Waves," *AIAA Journal 12*, 1498 (November, 1974).

92. The effect of the relative motion between laboratory air and a propagating LSC can make orders of magnitude differences in the observed velocity. This is especially true when the initial breakdown event that forms the plasma sets the surrounding air into motion. See Raizer (note 79) and Jackson and Nielsen (note 91).

93. The advantage of lasers in annealing semiconductors is that energy is deposited in a thin layer near the surface, where it removes imperfections caused by the implantation of dopants, but doesn't heat the bulk of the material to the point where the distribution of implanted ions will change through thermal diffusion. Heating alone can also be of value in some military applications, such as the blinding of heat-sensitive infrared sensors.

94. The thermal coupling coefficient, α, is approximately 1–R, where R is the reflectivity shown in Figure 3–16. In general, however, α is a function of temperature, and may undergo abrupt changes as a surface melts or vaporizes. The value that should be used in analysis is an average value, approximately correct for the duration of the laser pulse. Representative values are provided for different materials and wavelengths in Appendix B.

95. Figure 3–63 was calculated under the assumption that $\rho = 3g/cm^3$, $T_m - T_o = 700$ °K, $C = 1 J/g$ °K, and $D = 1 cm^2/sec$. The curves in the figure may be scaled as $\rho C(T_m - T_o) \sqrt{D}$ for different values of these parameters.

96. This argument assumes that the time required to heat the surface to the vaporization point is small compared to the total pulse width. See J. F. Ready, "Effects Due to Absorption of Laser Radiation," *Journal of Applied Physics 36*, 462 (February, 1965). Ready's book, *Effects of High Power Laser Radiation* (New York: Academic Press, 1971) is a good source of general information on laser effects.

97. The parameters assumed in Figure 3–65 are the same as those in Figure 3–63, along with $L_m = 350$ J/g. The erosion rates shown in the figure may be scaled as $1/\rho(L_m + C(T_m - T_o))$.

98. The threshold for vaporization and the erosion rate when target material is vaporized may be derived in a manner analogous to the approach used in deriving the threshold and erosion rate for melting. The threshold for vaporization may be scaled as

$\rho(L_m + C)((T_m - T_o))\sqrt{D}$, and the erosion rate as

$1/\rho(L_m + L_v + C (T_v - T_o))$.

The parameters assumed in Figures 3–66 and 3–67 are the same as those assumed in Figure 3–65, along with $L_v = 8 \times 10^3$ J/g.

99. S.I. Anisimov, "Vaporization of a Metal Absorbing Laser Radiation," *Soviet Physics—JETP 27*, 182 (July, 1968).

100. Representative values for I* are provided in Appendix B. See also the *APS Report on Directed Energy Weapons* (Note 1), Figures 6.11–6.14.

101. The specific impulse I* should scale as $(kT_v/M)^{1/2}(\alpha/L_v)$ in going from a material where I* is known to another where it must be estimated.

102. A good qualitative discussion of impulsive damage can be found in Michael S. Feld, Ronald E. McNair, and Stephen R. Wilk, "The Physics of Karate," *Scientific American 240*, 150 (April, 1979).

103. See Kittel (note 18), Chapter 4. In reality, the expression is somewhat more complex, since a solid may strain differently in different directions.

104. The stress P* necessary to damage the plate is known as the *modulus of rupture*. Representative values are provided in Appendix B.

105. The derivation of the threshold for mechanical damage presented here is attributed to G.H. Canavan in the *APS Report on Directed Energy Weapons* (note 1), section 6.3.5.

106. P.E. Nielsen, "High-Intensity Laser-Matter Coupling in a Vacuum," *Journal of Applied Physics* 50, 3938 (June, 1979).

107. J.A. McKay et al, "Pulsed CO_2 Laser Interaction with Aluminum in Air: Thermal Response and Plasma Characteristics," *Journal of Applied Physics* 50, 3231 (May, 1979). Note especially Figures 3 and 4.

108. The classic example of I* decreasing as $S^{-1/3}$ is D.W. Gregg and S.J. Thomas, "Momentum Transfer Produced by Focused Laser Giant Pulses," *Journal of Applied Physics* 37, 2787 (1966).

109. Michael R. Stamm, "The Formation, Propagation, and Structure of Laser Supported Detonation Waves and their Effect on Laser-Target Interactions," PhD Dissertation, University of Nebraska, 1977 (unpublished).

110. The instantaneous coupling coefficient is defined as $\alpha = \int Q\, dt / \int S\, dt$.

111. P.E. Nielsen, "Hydrodynamic Calculations of Surface Response in the Presence of Laser-Supported Detonation Waves," *Journal of Applied Physics* 46, 4501 (October, 1975).

112. The dependence of impulse on target area is reported in S.A. Metz, et al "Effect of Beam Intensity on Target Response to High Intensity Pulsed CO_2 Laser Radiation," *Journal of Applied Physics* 46, 1634 (April, 1975).

4: MICROWAVES

You may recall from Chapter 3 that the light from lasers is a special case of *electromagnetic radiation*—waves traveling through space, carrying energy, and characterized by a specific frequency and wavelength. Microwaves are another type of electromagnetic radiation, having a much longer wavelength and much lower frequency than light. For example, red light has a wavelength of about 0.7 μm and a frequency, c/λ, of about 4×10^{14} Hertz. By contrast, microwaves have wavelengths of about 1 cm, and frequencies on the order of 10^{10} Hertz, or 10 Gigahertz (GHz).

Since microwaves and lasers are both electromagnetic radiation, most of the results developed in Chapter 3 will apply here as well. Therefore, many topics in this chapter are treated by reference to those in Chapter 3. A more detailed discussion of the physics behind many phenomena in this chapter can be found in the equivalent section of Chapter 3.

Microwaves have been around much longer than lasers, and are used in many devices. Figure 4–1 shows the microwave portion of the electromagnetic energy spectrum, along with some of the

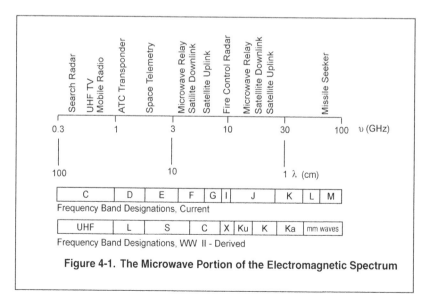

Figure 4-1. The Microwave Portion of the Electromagnetic Spectrum

applications that are common at different frequencies.[1] From Figure 4–1, you can see that many devices of military significance operate with microwaves. Typical applications include radars, communication links, and missile seekers.

Also shown in Figure 4–1 are some of the letter designations which are used to define different regions ("bands") of the microwave spectrum.[2] Letter designations are a shorthand way of specifying frequency ranges, but there is ambiguity in them since some letters have referred to different frequencies over the years. To avoid any ambiguity, we'll state frequency or wavelength explicitly.

Most microwave devices are designed to detect and amplify a weak microwave signal. A radar, for example, sends out microwaves which bounce off a target and return with much less intensity, since they diverge and are attenuated as they propagate from the radar, to the target, and back. The radar receiver must detect this signal, amplify, and analyze it. A very powerful microwave source can overwhelm the radar's signal, jamming it. At high enough intensities, it may even permanently damage the radar. This is analogous to the human eye, which detects and amplifies weak light signals, and can be temporarily or permanently blinded by an intense light source. It should not be surprising, then, that intense microwaves have been suggested as weapons against military systems which have built in vulnerabilities to them. Unfortunately, target vulnerability to microwaves is more difficult to quantify than vulnerability to other weapons.

Whether the potential of microwaves as weapons can be exploited depends, of course, on bringing the energy produced by a weapon to bear on a target. Accordingly, we'll follow the pattern established in previous chapters. After discussing the fundamental features of microwaves, we'll look at how they propagate in vacuum and air, and use this information to see how much intensity a microwave weapon must develop to engage targets of different vulnerability at different ranges.

Fundamentals of Microwaves

Microwaves differ from lasers only in their wavelength and frequency. This difference can, however, have profound implications.

For example, the window on a microwave oven is lined with a metallic screen. Visible light can penetrate this screen because its wavelength is much smaller than the size of the screen's mesh. Microwaves, on the other hand, cannot penetrate. Their wavelength is larger than the mesh, and it appears to them to be a solid sheet of metal. In this way, you can see what is cooking in the oven, without danger of being roasted by microwaves escaping through the window. We'll look in this section at some of the fundamental features of microwave propagation and interaction with matter.

Fundamentals of Propagation

Like all electromagnetic radiation, microwaves travel at the speed of light, c, (= 3 × 10⁸ m/sec) in vacuum. They have a frequency, v, and wavelength, λ related through the expression $v = c/\lambda$. As you can see from Figure 4–1, microwave frequencies lie in the range 0.1–100 GHz, and the associated wavelengths lie in the range 100–0.1 cm. Microwaves are unique in that their wavelengths are similar to the size of the physical objects with which they interact. This means that their "wavy" nature can be important in analyzing how they propagate around or interact with objects. Microwaves are therefore more difficult to analyze than either light waves, whose wavelength is much smaller than most objects, or radio waves, whose wavelength is much larger.

You will recall from Chapter 3 that when collimated electromagnetic radiation of wavelength λ emerges from an aperture of diameter D, the resulting beam has an angular divergence $\theta \approx \lambda/D$. For lasers, with wavelengths on the order of 10⁻⁵ cm, a 10 cm aperture produces a beam of divergence 10⁻⁶ radian, or 1 μrad. For microwaves, with wavelengths on the order of 1 cm, a 10 km aperture would be required to achieve the same divergence! Such large apertures are clearly impractical, especially for military systems, which often must be mobile and capable of deployment. Therefore, microwaves diverge much more than laser light, so that their energy spreads and their intensity drops much more rapidly with distance.

For light, the aperture through which the radiation emerges is obvious—it's the last lens or optical element in the system. For microwaves, the transmitting antenna is the "window" or aperture through which they are sent into the world. The divergence

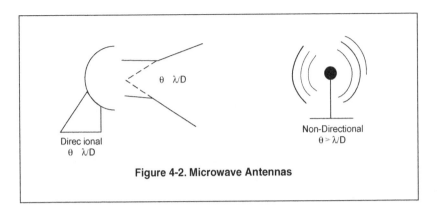

θ ≈ λ/D

Direc ional
θ ≈ λ/D

Non-Directional
θ > λ/D

Figure 4-2. Microwave Antennas

$\theta \approx \lambda/D$ is applicable to directional antennas, such as the parabolic dish illustrated in Figure 4–2. Other types of antennas, such as the "whip" on a police car, are designed to send radiation in all directions, so that communication is possible between transmitter and receiver regardless of their relative orientation. Antennas of this sort have a much greater divergence than λ/D. Since our emphasis is on directed energy weapons, we'll assume that the intent of the weapon designer is to be energy efficient, making divergence as low as possible. The divergence $\theta \approx \lambda/D$ is the best that can be done, corresponding to the diffraction-limited optical system discussed in Chapter 3.

When propagating in a medium such as air, microwaves travel at a velocity less than that in a vacuum, and the ratio of the velocity in vacuum to that in the medium is known as the *index of refraction*, n. As with lasers, microwaves traveling from a region characterized by one index of refraction to another will be bent in accordance with the law of refraction, $n_1 \sin\theta_1 = n_2 \sin\theta_2$. As illustrated in Figure 4–3, the direction of travel is bent towards the "normal" (a line perpendicular to the surface) when going into a region where n is greater, and away from the normal when going into a region where n is less.

With lasers, refraction finds application in lenses, where the change in n going from air to glass can be used to expand or focus the beam (see Figure 3–5). This is not very practical for microwaves, since the radius of the beam is very large, and expands rapidly with distance. Nevertheless, lensing effects can occur as a beam of microwaves travels through the atmosphere, since the index of refraction of air depends on both density and water

210

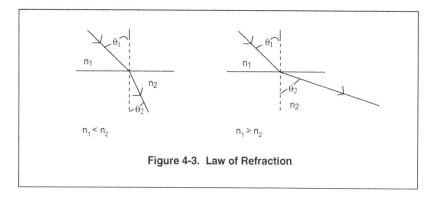

Figure 4-3. Law of Refraction

vapor content, and these can change over distances comparable to the beam size. We will see that this can result in some unusual behavior from the standpoint of beam propagation.

Fundamentals of Interaction with Matter

Electromagnetic radiation can be absorbed when the energy associated with a unit or *photon* of electromagnetic energy is equal to the difference in energy between two allowed energy levels in the absorbing material. A photon has energy $h\nu$, where h is Planck's constant, 6.63×10^{-34} Joule sec, and ν is the frequency of the radiation in Hz. Microwave photon energies lie in the range 10^{-25} to 10^{-22} Joules, or 10^{-6} to 10^{-3} eV (1 eV $= 1.6 \times 10^{-19}$ J). Since the rotational, vibrational, and electronic energy levels in atmospheric gases are separated by energies on the order of 10^{-2}, 10^{-1}, and 1 eV respectively, microwaves are unlikely to be absorbed by most of the gases in the atmosphere. Indeed, this lack of attenuation makes microwaves useful as radars and communication devices. However, there are some important exceptions to this general rule. Both oxygen and water vapor can absorb radiation in the microwave region of the electromagnetic spectrum, and even liquid water interacts well with microwaves.[3] Therefore, humidity and rain can be important factors in microwave propagation. The interaction between microwaves and water is employed in microwave ovens. Since water is a major constituent of organic matter, microwaves are absorbed in, and heat, foods placed in the oven. Yet they are not absorbed in ceramic dishes, which don't contain water. In this way, the food in a dish is heated while the dish itself remains cool.

When they encounter solid targets, microwaves will to a first approximation pass through insulators and be reflected from metals. This is because, as you may recall from Chapter 3, electromagnetic radiation is not absorbed in dielectric (insulating) solids unless the photon energy is greater than the band gap in the material, and is primarily reflected from metallic solids unless its frequency exceeds the *plasma frequency*. The frequency of microwaves is far below the plasma frequency of metals, and their photon energy is far below the band gap of most insulators. In this way the *window* or *radome* through which a radar beam passes is an insulating solid that is opaque to visible light, and sensitive electronic components can be shielded from microwaves by enclosing them in metal containers.

Summary: Microwave Fundamentals

1. Microwaves are electromagnetic radiation with a wavelength of 0.1–100 cm. This wavelength is comparable to the size of the physical objects with which they might interact, so that the wavy nature of microwaves is important in their analysis.

2. Like all electromagnetic radiation, microwaves emitted from a directional antenna of diameter D spread with a divergence angle of about λ/D. Due to the large wavelength (λ) of microwaves, they spread much more than light for realistic aperture sizes.

3. When crossing regions with different indices of refraction, microwave beams are bent just as laser beams are. Because of the large size of microwave beams, only large scale fluctuations in the index of refraction have an effect on propagation. Typically, these effects occur between different layers within the atmosphere.

4. Microwave photon energies are quite small, less than 10^{-3} eV. As a result, they pass through most insulating materials. And their frequency is quite low, less than 100 GHz. As a result, most metals reflect them.

Microwave Propagation in a Vacuum

Propagation Tradeoffs

A beam of electromagnetic radiation of wavelength λ emitted from an aperture of diameter D will remain collimated for a distance $z_r \approx \pi D^2/\lambda$, before diverging at an angle $\theta \approx \lambda/D$ The distance z_r is known as the *Rayleigh Range,* and is illustrated in Figure 4–4. Figure 4–5 is a plot of the Rayleigh Range as a function of aperture (that is, antenna) size for wavelengths in the microwave region.[4] You can see from this figure that for microwaves to be beamed over substantial distances, large apertures or short wavelengths must be employed.

For microwaves with a nominal 1 cm wavelength, apertures in excess of 10 m are required for a beam to travel distances in   excess of 10 km without spreading. Apertures this large are practical only for fixed installations, rather than mobile systems. Even for fixed installations, a large antenna is a very vulnerable element for a weapon system. Consequently, microwave propagation will probably be in the *far field,* with a divergence of λ/D, even over tactical ranges. As a result, if we need to place a given Intensity (W/cm²) on target, it will be necessary that a greater intensity be emitted by a microwave weapon. In Chapter 3, we used the concept of *brightness* to examine tradeoffs among energy, wavelength, and aperture in an electromagnetic radiation weapon.[5]

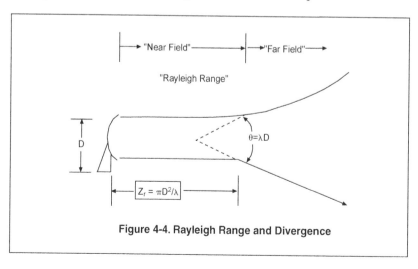

Figure 4-4. Rayleigh Range and Divergence

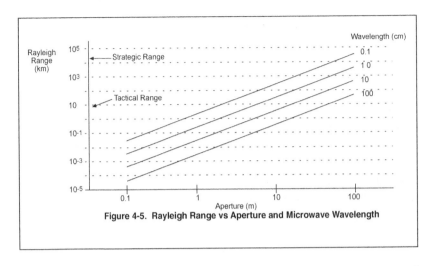

Figure 4-5. Rayleigh Range vs Aperture and Microwave Wavelength

The brightness of an electromagnetic beam having power P and wavelength λ, emitted from an aperture of diameter D, is B = $PD^2/\pi \lambda^2$. Physically, brightness (Watts per steradian, W/sr) is the power in the beam, divided by the *solid angle* into which the beam is spreading.[6] If B is divided by the square of the range to target, z, the result is the intensity of the beam (W/cm²) at the target's surface. If that intensity is in turn multiplied by the time the beam illuminates the target, Δt, the result is the total energy density, or fluence (Joules/cm²), delivered to the target. Damage criteria are typically expressed in terms of the fluence or intensity required on target, along with time constraints to insure that the target doesn't dissipate energy faster than it is absorbed (see Chapter 1).[7]

Figure 4-6 shows the range to which microwave beams can deliver various intensities (W/cm²) as a function of brightness. This figure is the same as Figure 3–21, since the range to a given intensity for a given brightness is independent of the type of radiation. Of course, since microwaves have a much greater wavelength than lasers, much greater apertures are required to provide the same brightness and intensity on target.

Figure 4–6 can be used to examine the tradeoffs associated with placing a given intensity on a target at a given range. Suppose, for example, that we need to place 10 W/cm² on a target at a range of 100 km. As the arrows on Figure 4–6 indicate, brightness must be at least 10^{15} W/sr to meet these criteria. Since B = $PD^2/\pi \lambda^2$, we can go further and investigate tradeoffs in the

214

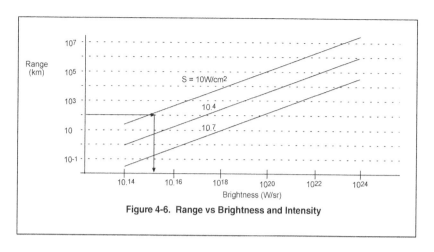

Figure 4-6. Range vs Brightness and Intensity

design of a microwave weapon. For example, suppose $\lambda = 1$cm ($\nu = 30$ GHz). Then achieving a brightness of 10^{15} W/sr requires that $PD^2 = \pi \lambda^2 B \approx 3 \times 10^{15}$ cm^2 W. If we are constrained to a 1 meter aperture, then $D^2 = 10^4$ cm^2, and our weapon must transmit 10^{11} Watts. If we didn't feel that this power level was an achievable goal, we could reduce power requirements by increasing the aperture or reducing the wavelength.

Figure 4–6 summarizes all we need to know about propagation of microwaves along a clear path in a vacuum. From it, we can find the brightness necessary to damage a target at a given range, and then investigate the implications of that brightness from the standpoint of the power, wavelength, and aperture required in a microwave weapon.

Diffraction and Interference Around Objects

Imagine that a beam of microwaves or other electromagnetic radiation encounters a physical object on its way to a target. A simple example might be a screen such as that illustrated in Figure 4–7, which reflects or absorbs the radiation incident upon it. We would expect a screen to cast a shadow, so that regions behind it would be shielded from the radiation. This is approximately true, but a detailed investigation would show that some radiation *does* get into the shadowed or shielded region, and that the intensity near the border of the geometrical shadow undergoes a series of fluctuations, also illustrated in Figure 4–7. This spreading of radiation into regions which would appear shielded is referred to as *diffraction*, and is another manifestation of the diffraction responsible for the spreading of radiation which passes through or is emitted from an aperture.

The scale of the fluctuations in intensity, and the distance radiation penetrates into the region of geometrical shadow, is on the order of $(\lambda z)^{1/2}$, where λ is the wavelength of the radiation and z the distance from the shield to the point of observation.[8] For infrared or visible light from a laser, this is of little importance. In this case, the wavelength is 10^{-4} cm or less, and at a point 1 m from a shield, fluctuations in intensity would occur over a distance of 1 mm or less. For microwaves, on the other hand, a wavelength of 1 cm produces fluctuations on the order of 10 cm at a 1 m range. This means that microwave energy can reach objects which to a first approximation are shielded from a microwave transmitter by natural barriers.

The situation becomes more complex when microwaves pass through a slit or series of barriers. This results in a variety of fluctuations in intensity, whose pattern is difficult to predict except in a few

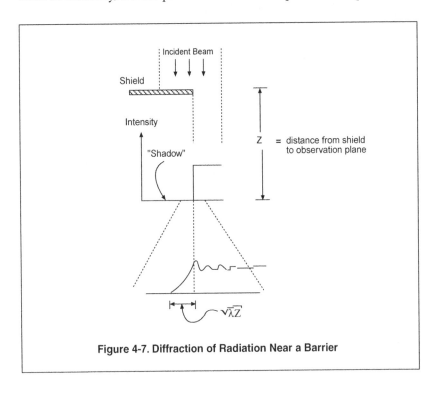

Figure 4-7. Diffraction of Radiation Near a Barrier

216

simple cases.[9] From the standpoint of target interaction, this means that predicting the actual intensity on a target and the vulnerability of that target can be quite difficult. Microwave energy will enter a target through gaps and slits in the plates or other shields which surround it.[10] Diffraction of the beam as it passes these points will lead to fluctuations in intensity on the interior of the target which occur on space scales similar to the separation of elements within the target. Thus, a vulnerable element might be damaged in one interaction and undamaged in another whose gross features (range, etc.) are essentially identical. Similarly, target vulnerability will be highly dependent upon the details of the target's construction, which will determine where target elements lie relative to various shields and entry points for radiation into the interior.

Summary: Microwave Propagation in a Vacuum

1. Like all electromagnetic radiation, microwaves of wavelength λ emerging from an aperture or antenna of diameter D diverge with an angle on the order of λ/D in the far field—distances greater than about $\pi D^2/\lambda$. Because of the size ($\approx$1cm) of wavelengths in the microwave region, almost all propagation is in the far field, and divergence is much greater than for laser light from an aperture of similar size.

2. The brightness of a beam of radiation in Watts per steradian, along with its dwell time on target, will determine the intensity and fluence on a target at a given range. Figure 4–6 can be used to determine the range at which beams of different brightness can place different intensities on target. This information can then be used to perform tradeoffs among power, wavelength, and aperture for specific applications.

3. When microwaves pass around objects, diffraction spreads the radiation by a substantial amount into regions which on the basis of geometry would be shielded. Therefore the actual intensity within a target is in practice difficult to quantify.

Implications

The theory of microwaves is in essence no different than that for lasers—only the wavelengths are different. Since beam divergence is on the order of λ/D, why would anyone be interested in microwaves as weapons? Lasers, with their much shorter wavelength, have a much smaller divergence, and are therefore more directed in their energy. There are several reasons why microwaves are seen to have potential as weapons.

Lasers are a relatively new invention, the first having been constructed in 1960. By contrast, the microwaves have been used for radar and communication since the 1940s. The long ranges needed for these microwave applications, together with the large divergence angles, required the development of high power sources. As a result, the technology for high power microwaves is more advanced than that for high power lasers.[11] Indeed, some high power lasers, such as the free electron laser, are themselves powered by microwave energy. Thus, it is possible that in a given application the higher available power in a microwave device could compensate for a larger divergence to place more energy on target.

Many interesting military targets are themselves microwave receivers. They are sensitive to the weak signals they have to receive and interpret, and are vulnerable to microwaves of much greater intensity than they were designed to encounter. With a few exceptions (such as the human eye or an optical detector), most military targets are not as vulnerable to light. Therefore, a microwave weapon may achieve damage at a lower intensity than a laser.

Diffraction is much greater for microwaves than for laser light. This means that if microwave energy penetrates a target at any small point, such as an opening where a wire emerges from a black box, the energy will spread within the box, possibly finding vulnerabilities which neither the designer nor the attacker contemplated. Laser light, on the other hand, is largely confined to straight line propagation beyond the point of entry, and is much less likely to find targets of opportunity on the interior of a target.

In short, lasers damage targets through a frontal assault—melting their way through the surface and on into the interior of a target. Microwaves damage targets by more subtle means, going on through an already prepared entry point and wandering around on the interior. The entryway may be obvious such as an antenna, or it may be some gap or slit in the target's surface. Damage when entry is through an antenna is known as *front door* damage, if entry is through some less obvious point it's known as *back door* damage. Front door damage is more strongly wavelength dependent, since antennas and receivers are tuned to accept radiation in specific wavelength ranges. Because of the way in which they damage targets, microwaves may be more effective as weapons than they would appear on the basis of propagation alone.

Microwave Propagation in the Atmosphere

In Chapter 3, we saw that an atmosphere had many effects on laser propagation. Molecules or aerosols could absorb or scatter the light. Self-induced index of refraction fluctuations (thermal blooming) could cause the beam to bend and wander. And at sufficiently high intensities, air breakdown could prevent propagation entirely. Analogous phenomena occur for microwaves, and we'll consider these here, contrasting our results with those in Chapter 3.

Losses due to Absorption and Scattering

You may recall from Chapter 3 that the intensity, (W/cm^2), of electromagnetic radiation propagating a distance z in an absorbing medium decays as $S(z) = S(0) \exp(-Kz)$, where K is known as the attenuation coefficient. The attenuation coefficient can in turn be written as a sum of coefficients arising from absorption or scattering from the various molecules or small particles (aerosols) present in the atmosphere. For microwaves, the most important contributions to K come from oxygen, water vapor, and liquid water (rain or other precipitation).[12] We'll consider the effect of molecules first, and then look at liquid water and other aerosols.

Molecular Absorption and Scattering. Figure 4–8 shows the attenuation coefficients due to oxygen and water vapor for radiation at microwave frequencies.

Figure 4–8 assumes that the density of oxygen is that at sea level, and that there are 7.5 gm/m^3 of water vapor. At higher altitudes and different levels of humidity, the attenuation coefficient Scales with the density of molecules. Thus, at an altitude where the density of oxygen is half that at sea level, the attenuation coefficient due to oxygen will be half that shown in Figure 4–8. Figure

4–9 gives the concentration of water vapor at 100% humidity as a function of temperature.[14] Figure 4–9 may be used to scale the contribution of water vapor from that assumed in Figure 4–8. For example, at 0 °C and 50% humidity, the concentration of water vapor is half that shown in Figure 4–9, or about 2.5 gm/m³. Since this is one third of the vapor density assumed in Figure 4–8, the attenuation coefficient for water vapor under these conditions will be one third of that shown in Figure 4–8.

In scaling Figure 4–8 to altitudes above sea level, you can use the fact that at lower altitudes, atmospheric density scales as $\rho = \rho_o\,e^{-h/h_o}$, where ρ is the density at altitude h, ρ_o the density at sea level, and h_o is approximately 7 km.[15] This relationship is plotted in Figure 4–10. You can use figures 4–8, 4–9, and 4–10 to estimate the atmospheric attenuation coefficient for microwaves due to oxygen and water vapor at any temperature, altitude, and humidity.

In many cases, a microwave beam propagates up into the atmosphere, and the attenuation coefficient is not constant along the beam path. As we saw in Chapter 3, the intensity at a range z in this case is no longer S(z) = S(0) exp(–Kz), but rather S(0) exp[$-_o\int^z$ K(z) dz].[16] In order to solve this equation, we need to know the attenuation coefficient, K(z), at all points z along the beam's path. In general, this isn't possible without making sim-

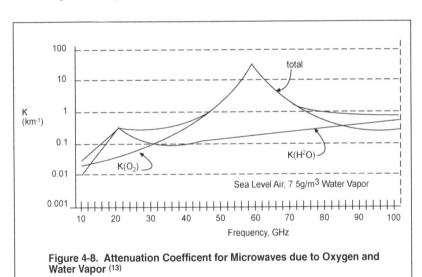

Figure 4-8. Attenuation Coefficent for Microwaves due to Oxygen and Water Vapor [13]

plifying assumptions. For example, we might assume that a beam of microwaves is fired into the air at some angle ϕ, and that both oxygen and water vapor fall off with altitude as shown in Figure 4–10.

This case is illustrated in Figure 4–11, and the solution for the relative attenuation factor or optical depth is shown in Figure 4–12. You will recognize that Figures 4–11 and 4–12 are essentially the same as Figures 3–25 and 3–26. The physics is the same as that discussed in Chapter 3; only the sea level attenuation coefficient, K(0), is different. However, the assumptions involved in this analysis are not as valid for microwaves as they are for lasers. This is because water vapor is a major contributor to microwave attenuation, and humidity can vary with altitude. In addition, we shall

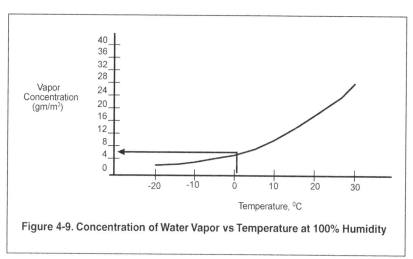

Figure 4-9. Concentration of Water Vapor vs Temperature at 100% Humidity

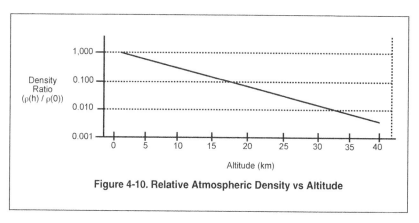

Figure 4-10. Relative Atmospheric Density vs Altitude

see later in this chapter that refractive effects in the atmosphere can cause a microwave beam to travel in paths which are not nearly as straight as that illustrated in Figure 4–11.

Because the assumptions used in deriving it are not fully realistic, Figure 4–12 is probably not suitable for quantitative analysis. Nevertheless, there are useful qualitative conclusions to be drawn from the figure. First, optical depth and attenuation are virtually independent of elevation angle for ranges less than the distance over which atmospheric properties vary significantly. This distance is 7 km in the example, but variations in humidity and water vapor concentration may shorten it. Over short ranges, then, attenuation is simply $S(z) = S(0) \exp(-Kz)$. Second, at larger elevation angles, attenuation virtually ceases as the beam emerges from the lower, high density regions of the atmosphere. Thus, only these lower levels of atmosphere are significant in beam attenuation. This suggests that given information regarding the extent in altitude of significant water vapor, it would be possible to add the appropriate attenuation coefficient for water vapor over that lower altitude range only. Some authors suggest that absorption due to water vapor will occur primarily at altitudes below 2 km.[17]

A final point should be made regarding microwave absorption from oxygen and water vapor. Looking at Figure 4–8, and recalling that 1/K is the distance over which a beam's intensity will fall by a factor of 1/e (approximately 1/3), you can see that depending on the wavelength, microwaves in the atmosphere will travel between

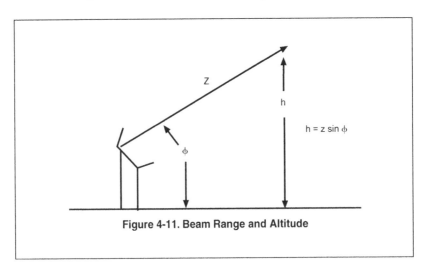

Figure 4-11. Beam Range and Altitude

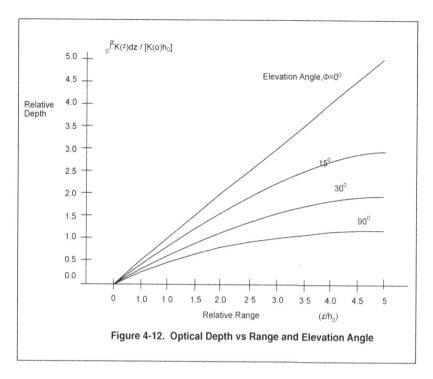

$\int_0^z K(z)dz / [K(o)h_0]$

Relative Depth

5.0
4.5
4.0
3.5
3.0
2.5
2.0
1.5
1.0
0.5
0.0

Elevation Angle, $\Phi=0^0$

15^0

30^0

90^0

0   1.0   1 0   1.5   2.0   2 5   3.0   3 5   4.0   4.5   5

Relative Range (z/h_0)

Figure 4-12. Optical Depth vs Range and Elevation Angle

100 and 0.1 km without significant attenuation. There is an interesting tradeoff between absorption and beam divergence. Lower frequency beams are absorbed less, but have a longer wavelength and therefore diverge more rapidly than higher frequency beams. Therefore, it is not immediately obvious which frequency will enable the greatest energy to be placed on target at a given range. Of course, target vulnerabilities may also be frequency dependent, further complicating the choice of frequency for a given application.

Effect of Liquid Water and Atmospheric Aerosols. Water molecules interact strongly with microwaves, and water vapor contributes to their attenuation in the atmosphere. Therefore, it's logical to expect that when water is concentrated into a liquid as rain it will have a severe effect on propagation. The effect of rain on microwave propagation depends upon the scattering and absorption from a drop of water of a given radius, together with the number of drops of various radius that are likely to be encountered. This last information is related to the type of rain storm—a mist or fog has many drops of small radius, while an afternoon thundershower has fewer drops of much larger radius. Let's first consider the attenuation from a given rain drop, and then the distribution of rain drops.

In Chapter 3, we discussed the fact that when electromagnetic radiation of wavelength λ encounters a small particle (aerosol) of radius a, there is an effective *cross section* or size which the particle presents to the radiation from the standpoint of absorption and scattering. The attenuation coefficient, K, is given by Nσ, where N is the concentration of particles (cm^{-3}), and σ the cross section (cm^2). When the particle size, a, is much greater than the wavelength of the radiation, the cross section is roughly $2\pi a^2$. This is the case for laser light encountering most atmospheric aerosols. On the other hand, when the particle is smaller than the wavelength of the radiation, the cross section deviates from this general rule, and is highly wavelength dependent (see Figure 3–28).

When the particle size is much less than the wavelength of the radiation, the cross section goes to zero. For this reason, solid particles in the atmosphere, whose size is 10 μm or less, have negligible effect upon microwaves, whose wavelengths are millimeters or greater. Water droplets come in sizes that approach microwave wavelengths, however, and can be an important source of attenuation. Since microwaves have wavelengths on the order of 1 cm, and raindrops rarely exceed 2 mm in radius, quantitative analysis from first principles is quite difficult. You can't assume that the wavelength is much larger than the particle size, so that σ goes to zero, or that the wavelength is much smaller than the particle size, so that $\sigma = 2\pi a^2$. Therefore, research has focused on developing empirical attenuation formulas or curves by measuring attenuation as a function of wavelength and rain conditions. Figure 4–13 is a typical plot of the attenuation coefficient of rain as a function of microwave frequency and rate of rainfall.[18] Comparing this figure with Figure 4–8, you can see that at higher rates of precipitation, rain can be more important than atmospheric molecules in attenuating microwaves. Table 4–1 provides the rain rates associated with different types of precipitation, so that you can relate to Figure 4–13 on more familiar terms.[19]

You need to be careful in using Figure 4–13 and Table 4–1 to estimate microwave attenuation under a given set of conditions.

The figure is based on average conditions, and as Table 4–1 points out, there is a range of drop sizes and precipitation rates associated with a given type of rain. Since attenuation is a strong function of the ratio of drop size to wavelength, there could be large variations from the average given in the figure in any particular case. Additionally, it is unlikely that the rate of precipitation will be constant over the entire path from microwave source to target. Therefore, even if the estimates shown in Figure 4–13 were known to be accurate, it would be necessary to measure the rain rate all along the propagation path, integrating the attenuation coefficient to find the total attenuation along the path. This procedure might be possible for experiments over a well-instrumented range, but is impractical for use in the real world. Therefore, the most you can hope to have in realistic situations are general guidelines based on an accumulation of experimental data. In weapon design, then, the available energy needs to be sufficient to insure that damage criteria are met even if climactic conditions are near the extreme end of their range of probability.

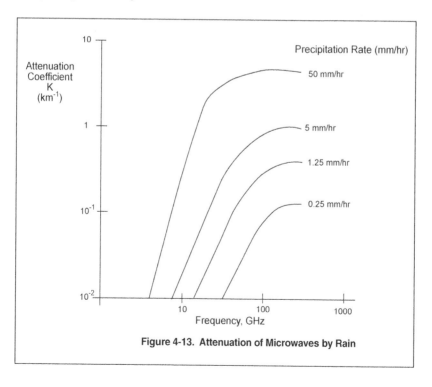

Figure 4-13. Attenuation of Microwaves by Rain

Condition	Precipitation Rate (mm/hr)	Drop Size (mm)
Drizzle	0.2 - 0.5	<0 5
Light Rain	< 2	1 - 2
Moderate Rain	2 - 6	1 - 2
Heavy Rain	>7	1 - 2

Table 4-1. Rain Rates vs Meteorological Conditions

Summary: Absorption and Scattering.

1. Like all electromagnetic radiation, microwaves are removed from a beam through absorption and scattering from molecules and aerosols in the atmosphere. For microwaves, the most important molecules are O_2 and H_2O, and the most important aerosols are those of precipitation—solid ice or liquid water.

2. Energy loss from the beam follows the attenuation law $S(z) = S(0) \exp(-Kz)$, where K, the attenuation coefficient, is the sum of individual coefficients for each contributor to attenuation. Figure 4–8 provides attenuation coefficients for oxygen and water molecules, and Figure 4–13 provides them for liquid water aerosols as a function of precipitation rate.

3. Attenuation from atmospheric molecules scales with their density. Figure 4–12 is an estimate of the effective Kz, or optical depth, to be used in the attenuation law when a beam is aimed into the atmosphere at some elevation angle. Most attenuation occurs below 7 km in the atmosphere.

4. Attenuation from water vapor scales with relative humidity and temperature. Figure 4–9 provides data on water vapor concentration as a function of temperature which may be used to scale Figure 4–8 to different conditions.

5. Attenuation due to rain scales with the rain rate and drop size. Table 4–1 may be used to estimate these from observed precipitation conditions, and the appropriate attenuation coefficient can be estimated from Figure 4–13.

6. Estimates made using the tables and figures in this section should be considered order of magnitude only. Physical conditions can vary greatly along a beam's propagation path, and

data are typically available at only a limited number of points along the path. Microwave weapons must therefore be designed to be capable of placing damaging energy on target even at the extreme end of conditions considered operationally realistic.

Losses Due to Index of Refraction Variations

In Chapter 3, we saw that the index of refraction of air depends upon its density and temperature, as well as the wavelength of the radiation (see Figure 3–30). At optical frequencies, small fluctuations in density and temperature resulting from atmospheric turbulence act as mini-lenses, breaking up the coherence of the beam front, and causing it to diverge at a rate much greater than would be expected from its aperture. This requires that active measures (adaptive optics) be taken to insure that a laser beam will propagate over long ranges in the atmosphere without substantial loss of intensity. At microwave frequencies, the situation is considerably different. The wavelength is long compared to the size of turbulent density fluctuations in the atmosphere, so that they do not affect a beam's propagation to the same extent. Thus, adaptive optics and other techniques which are needed to enable long range laser propagation in the atmosphere are not required for microwaves. This is fortunate, since otherwise microwaves would not have found so many applications as a means of communication, where accurate phase and amplitude information are required if a coherent signal is to be received.

We cannot conclude from this, however, that density fluctuations within the atmosphere do not affect the propagation of microwaves from source to target. While this is true for the small-scale fluctuations resulting from turbulence, there is another density variation which can affect microwave propagation—the large scale variations in density that occur as a beam passes between different atmospheric layers.

At microwave frequencies, the index of refraction of air is insensitive to wavelength, and is a function of pressure, temperature, and the amount of water vapor present, as shown in Figures 4–14 and 4–15. Figure 4–14 shows the index of refraction as a function of temperature for dry air (no water vapor present), and Figure 4–15 shows correction factors which can be added to the curves in Figure 4–14 to account for the amount of water vapor present.[20]

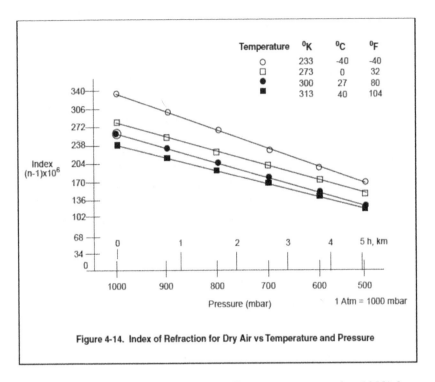

Temperature	^{0}K	^{0}C	^{0}F
O	233	-40	-40
□	273	0	32
●	300	27	80
■	313	40	104

Figure 4-14. Index of Refraction for Dry Air vs Temperature and Pressure

The correction factor in Figure 4–15 is appropriate for 100% humidity at any pressure. This factor scales with humidity, so that at 50% humidity, for example, the appropriate correction factor is simply half that shown in Figure 4–15.

From Figure 4–14, you can see that normally the index of refraction of air for microwaves decreases with altitude, and its deviation from 1 changes substantially over altitude ranges on the order of a kilometer. What is the implication from the standpoint of propagation in the atmosphere? Basically, this variation results in a beam of microwaves following a curved, rather than a straight path, as illustrated in Figure 4–16.

Shown in Figure 4–16 is a simplified example in which a microwave beam travels between two regions of the atmosphere—the lower one having index of refraction n_1, and the upper one having index of refraction n_2, with n_1 greater than n_2. A ray of electromagnetic radiation passing from one region into another where the index of refraction is less is bent away from the normal to the surface at the point where the ray crosses between the regions (see Figure 4–2). You can see in the blow up of the point where the

228

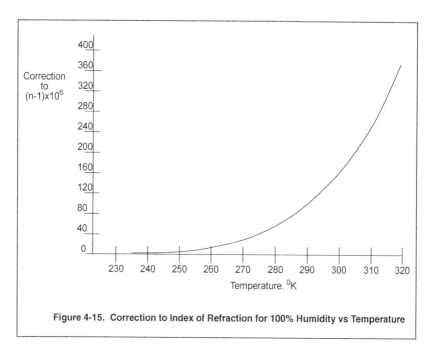

Figure 4-15. Correction to Index of Refraction for 100% Humidity vs Temperature

beam crosses regions in Figure 4–16 that this results in the beam being bent back towards the surf ace of the earth. The tall antenna, which would otherwise not be in line of sight from the microwave transmitter, can now receive its signals. In other words, the range of the microwave beam over the surface of the earth has been extended by refraction.

In a real situation, the index of refraction decreases continuously, rather than in discrete regions as shown in Figure 4–16. As a result, a beam will follow a curved path rather than one composed of discrete line segments, but the net result will be the same, the beam's range will be extended. As you can see from this example, the exact path a microwave beam will travel in the atmosphere will depend on how the index of refraction varies with altitude in the region between a microwave source and receiver. A variety of attempts have been made to capture this effect in a simple formula to approximate beam propagation in practical circumstances. One such approach is known as the *effective earth radius* transformation.

Because microwaves for the most part travel from source to receiver by line of sight, it is the horizon, or curvature of the earth, which limits propagation between stations located on the earth's

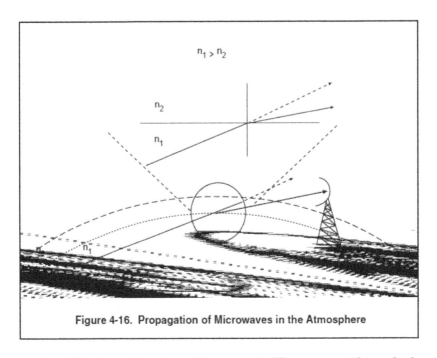

Figure 4-16. Propagation of Microwaves in the Atmosphere

surface. This is evident from Figure 4–16. The range within which line of sight communication can be maintained is limited by the radius of the earth R_e; if R_e were greater, the range would be longer. As we have seen, index of refraction changes in the atmosphere have the effect of bending a microwave beam, giving it a longer range along the surface than it otherwise would have. The effective earth radius transformation is one in which this effect is modeled as an increase in the radius of the earth—R_e is changed to a new, effective value R_e^*, such that if R_e^* is substituted into an expression for the range of a beam in the absence of refraction, the true range in its presence results.[21] If dn/dh is the slope of the curve of index of refraction as a function of altitude, the effective earth radius is given by $R_e^* = R_e/[1 + R_e(dn/dh)]$, where R_e is the true radius of the earth (6370 km), and dn/dh is the rate of change of n—the amount by which n changes for each kilometer increase in altitude.[22]

Looking at Figure 4–14, you can see that in going from sea level to 1 km altitude, the quantity $(n–1) \times 10^6$ changes from about 240 to 200. Thus, dn/dh is about $–40 \times 10^{-6}$/km, and the ratio R_e^*/R_e can be found from the expression above to be about 4/3. In other words, under normal circumstances microwaves travel line of sight

230

between points on the earth as though the earth had a radius 4/3 times its true radius, or about 8500 km. Figure 4–17 is a plot of R_e^*/R_e as a function of $-dn/dh$. As the magnitude of the index of refraction gradient increases, R_e^* becomes greater and greater, and is infinite for $dn/dh \approx -160 \times 10^{-6}/km$. When the magnitude of dn/dh exceeds 160×10^{-6}, R_e^* actually becomes negative! The physical meaning of these results are shown on the figure. At a rate of change of n of $-160 \times 10^{-6}/km$, the curvature of the beam equals that of the earth, so that the earth is essentially "flat" from the standpoint of microwave propagation. When the index gradient exceeds this critical value the beam actually bends back towards the earth, and its range is less than it would be in a vacuum.

You can see from Figure 4–17 that a variety of interesting effects can occur as a result of the change or gradient in refractive index with altitude. These can be particularly dramatic if the index of refraction gradient is very large, and this can actually occur under certain conditions. The nominal value for the index of refraction gradient is about $-40 \times 10^{-6}/km$, and the resulting effective earth radius is about $4R_e/3$, but there can be considerable variation in dn/dh, both over time at a given point and at different points at the same time. One of the biggest factors affecting n and dn/dh is humidity. At high temperature and humidity, the "correction" to (n–1) from Figure 4–15 can be as large as the value for dry air in Figure 4–14. Worldwide values of dn/dh vary from -30×10^{-6} in dry climates to over -100×10^{-6} in hot, humid climates. Greater extremes, even exceeding the critical value of about -160×10^{-6}, can be found, for example, when dry inland air blows over damp, humid air in a coastal region. Because of the importance of dn/dh to microwave propagation, there are actually published tables of this parameter for different regions of the earth and different times of the year.[23] Of course, such values are averages and only an indication of what might occur. There can be considerable variation from the value in a table at any given time and place.

The mere bending of microwaves is not all that can occur. Under appropriate conditions, variation in n can lead to *ducting,* or the channeling of microwaves along a given direction in the atmosphere. This can happen, for example, when dn/dh exceeds -160×10^{-6} per km over the ocean. Salt water is a fairly good conductor of electricity, and reflects microwaves as a metallic surface would do. Beams which have been bent back to earth may therefore reflect off

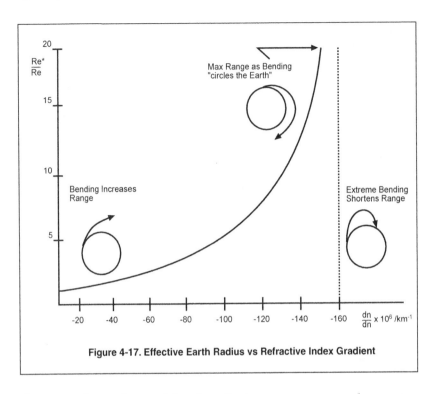

Figure 4-17. Effective Earth Radius vs Refractive Index Gradient

the ocean's surface, skipping their way over much greater distances that would be predicted on the basis of simple theory, as illustrated in Figure 4–18.

Ducting can also occur above the surface of the earth, if a region for which dn/dh exceeds -160×10^{-6}/km lies above a region in which dn/dh has a more normal value. Whether or not a particular beam or portion of a beam will be trapped in a duct depends upon the angle with which it enters the ducting region. Obviously, beams directed more vertically than horizontally are less likely to be trapped in this way, since at normal incidence the degree of bending due to refraction goes to zero (see Figure 4–3). These effects are somewhat analogous to the internal reflection which is evident to swimmers underwater. As viewed from below, the surface of the water appears silvery. Many of the light rays striking the surface from below are reflected back, since n decreases in going from water to air. Nevertheless, some rays do escape, and someone in a boat can see swimmers below the surface (assuming, of course, that the water is clean enough!).

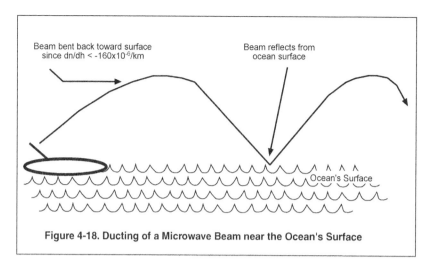

Figure 4-18. Ducting of a Microwave Beam near the Ocean's Surface

Summary: Index of Refraction Variations.

1. At microwave frequencies, the index of refraction of air (n) depends strongly on temperature, pressure, and water vapor content. All of these can vary with altitude, resulting in large-scale fluctuations in n that act as huge lenses to bend microwave beams from the straight line path which they would otherwise follow in a vacuum. As a result, the intensity at a given point distant from a transmitter can vary greatly from what would have been predicted from vacuum propagation theory.

2. A key factor in microwave propagation is dn/dh, the rate at which n changes with altitude. Figure 4–17 shows how the effective earth radius varies with dn/dh. The effective radius obtained from this figure can be used to estimate the range over which microwaves can reach targets via line of sight propagation.[21]

Nonlinear Effects

In nonlinear propagation, a beam's intensity is so great that it modifies the environment through which it propagates, altering its propagation characteristics. In chapter 3, we saw that there were many nonlinear effects in the propagation of laser light. Among these were thermal blooming, stimulated scattering, and air breakdown. There are similar nonlinear effects in the propagation of microwaves. However, they are different in character or magnitude from those affecting lasers, due to the different frequencies and spatial scales involved.

Air Breakdown. The ultimate limit to atmospheric propagation is air breakdown, in which a beam's intensity is sufficient to heat free electrons within its volume to the point where they can ionize neutral atoms, multiplying their number in an electron cascade. The electron density grows until the air has been transformed into an absorbing plasma and propagation is no longer possible.[24]

The electron cascade which leads to breakdown occurs in the following way:

- Free electrons which are naturally present within the beam volume heat up by absorbing electromagnetic radiation from the beam. These initial electrons (about $100/cm^3$) arise through cosmic rays and other natural sources.

- As the electrons heat, they may gain sufficient energy to ionize a neutral atom or molecule when they collide with it. To do so, an electron's energy must exceed the ionization potential of a molecule in the air. Ionization potentials are on the order of 10^{-20} eV. (1 eV, or electron volt, $= 1.6 \times 10^{-19}$ Joules.)

- The electron density grows as ionization occurs and the newly born electrons also heat and ionize molecules. Eventually, almost all the neutral molecules are ionized, and the gas becomes a conducting plasma which absorbs the incident radiation, making propagation impossible.

The key to a quantitative analysis of breakdown lies in knowing the rate at which electrons will heat by absorbing electromagnetic radiation, the rate at which they may lose energy through collisions with atmospheric particles, and their probability of ionizing molecules as their average energy increases. Of these factors, only the heating rate depends upon the type of electromagnetic radiation. The rate at which electrons heat in the presence of electromagnetic radiation of intensity S (W/cm²) is[25]

$$\frac{d\epsilon}{dt} = \frac{e^2 S \nu_c}{2mc\epsilon_o (\omega^2 + \nu_c^2)}$$

where ϵ is the electron energy (Joules), e and m are the electron charge (Coulombs) and mass (kg), ν_c is the frequency with which electrons collide with neutral molecules (sec^{-1}, or Hz), c is the speed of light (m/sec), ω is 2π times the frequency in Hertz of the radiation, and ϵ_0 is a constant known as the *permittivity of free space* (8.85×10^{-12} fd/m). The factors which appear in this expression for the electron heating rate are discussed in detail in Chapter 3, and make sense on physical grounds. We certainly expect $d\epsilon/dt$ to be proportional to the intensity of radiation, S. The factor ν_c in the numerator is the frequency with which an electron collides with a heavy molecule, and reflects the fact that it is the friction between the electrons and the background gas which results in their heating.

The factor $(\omega^2 + \nu_c^2)$ in the denominator of the electron heating rate expression is particularly interesting and significant from the standpoint of the difference between electron heating at optical and microwave frequencies. This factor is related to the average gain in energy which an electron achieves every time it collides with a neutral molecule. If an electron is simply bobbing up and down at the radiation frequency ω between collisions, the longest time it will gain energy is about $1/\omega$—the time an electron moves in one direction before the field reverses direction and begins decelerating the electron, reducing its energy. Thus, if ω is very large, the electron simply quivers in place, gaining very little energy between collisions. On the other hand, if the collision frequency ν_c is greater than ω, the electron cannot gain energy for a full cycle of the radiation frequency—its energy gain will be interrupted by the collision. Thus, the factor $(\omega^2 + \nu_c^2)$ in the denominator of the heating rate expression reduces the energy gain appropriately in the limits of high radiation frequency or high collision frequency.

The difference between lasers and microwaves from the standpoint of air breakdown lies in the factor $(\omega^2 + \nu_c^2)$. A typical value for ν_c at sea level is about 4×10^{12} Hz.[26] By way of comparison, the frequency of infrared laser light is about 10^{14} Hz, and that of microwaves is about 10^7 Hz. Thus, laser-induced breakdown occurs in the limit where the radiation frequency exceeds the collision frequency, and microwave-induced breakdown occurs in the limit where the radiation frequency is less than the collision frequency.

What are the implications of these two limits from the standpoint of breakdown thresholds and how they scale with frequency and atmospheric density (altitude)? Looking at the expression for the electron heating rate, you can see that If $\omega > \nu_c$, the heating rate is approximately $d\epsilon/dt = e^2 S\nu_c/2mc\epsilon_0\omega^2$; if $\omega < \nu_c$, it is approximately $d\epsilon/dt = e^2 S /2mc\epsilon_0\nu_c$. These two limits behave quite differently as frequency or altitude are varied. In the laser limit, there is a strong frequency dependence, and $d\epsilon/dt$ decreases as the square of the light frequency. Since the collision frequency is proportional to the gas density, you can also see that in this limit the heating rate will decline as altitude increases and density decreases. By contrast, in the microwave limit $d\epsilon/dt$ is independent of the radiation frequency, and is inversely proportional to the gas density. The ratio of the laser to the microwave heating rates is $(\nu_c/\omega)^2$. Table 4–2 compares these two limits to electron heating by electromagnetic radiation in a background gas.

Once we're comfortable with the electron heating rate for microwaves, we're prepared to deal with air breakdown. The other factors which determine the breakdown threshold, such as ionization rates and electron energy loss mechanisms, do not depend on the frequency of the applied radiation. Indeed, all of the results that were developed in Chapter 3 can be used here, as long as we use the proper electron heating rate for microwave frequencies.

In Chapter 3, we identified two limits to the breakdown problem: a high energy limit, in which almost all of the energy absorbed by the electrons was effective in ionizing molecules; and a low energy limit, in which the input of energy to the electrons was just equal to the rate at which energy was lost in collisions that excited vibrational or electronic energy levels of the gas molecules, leaving none of it available to further the cause of breakdown. For 10.6 μm laser radiation at sea level, the first of these limits was about 10 J/cm^2, and the second was

	Microwaves	Lasers
Electron Heating rate, $d\epsilon/dt$	$e^2 S/2mc\epsilon_0\nu_c$	$e^2 S\nu_c/2mc\epsilon_0\omega^2$
Frequency Scaling	Independent of ω	Proportional to $1/\omega^2$
Density Scaling	Proportional to 1/N	Proportional to N
Intensity Scaling	Proportional to S	Proportional to S

Table 4-2. Electron Heating in Microwave and Laser Frequency Limits

about 3×10^9 W/cm², with the transition occurring at a pulse width of about 10^{-8} sec. Figure 4–19 is a summary of these results (see also Figure 3–50).

We can modify Figure 4–19 to make it appropriate for microwaves simply by scaling the electron heating rate appropriately. Since the ratio of laser to microwave heating rates is just $(v_c/\omega)^2$, it follows that a lower microwave intensity, $S_m = (v_c/\omega)^2 S_l$, will heat electrons to the same degree as a laser of intensity S_l. Figure 4–19 is for sea level air ($v_c = 4 \times 10^{12}$ Hz), with a 10.6 µm laser ($\omega = 1.8 \times 10^{14}$ sec^{-1}). In this case, $S_m = 5 \times 10^{-4} S_l$. This means that a microwave beam with an intensity (W/cm²) almost 4 orders of magnitude less than a 10.6µm laser beam will heat electrons to the same extent. Using this scaling, it follows that at short pulses the microwave breakdown threshold should be about $(5 \times 10^{-4}) 10$ J/cm² $= 5 \times 10^{-3}$ J/cm², and that for long pulses, it should be about $(5 \times 10^{-4}) 3 \times 10^9 = 1.5 \times 10^6$ W/cm².

You can see from these results that microwaves will induce air breakdown at very low intensities compared to lasers. Moreover, the microwave breakdown threshold scales differently with altitude. As you can see from Figure 3–50, the high intensity limit to optical breakdown is inversely proportional to the gas density N, while the low intensity limit is virtually independent of N. The ratio of laser to microwave heating rates, (v_c^2/ω^2), is proportional to N^2, since v_c is proportional to N. Therefore, the high intensity limit to microwave breakdown is proportional to N, and the low intensity limit is proportional to N^2. These results are summarized in Figure 4–20, a curve for microwaves which is analogous to Figure 3–50 for lasers.

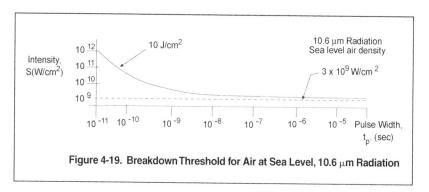

Figure 4-19. Breakdown Threshold for Air at Sea Level, 10.6 µm Radiation

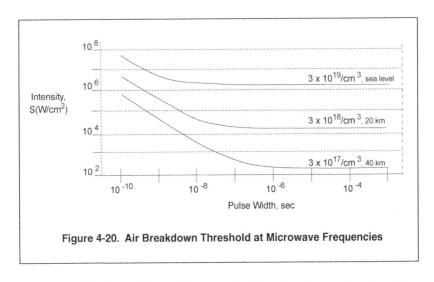

Figure 4-20. Air Breakdown Threshold at Microwave Frequencies

Aerosol-Induced Breakdown. In Chapter 3, much attention was paid to the effect of dirty air on breakdown. There, we saw that small, micrometer sized particles in the atmosphere could absorb energy from a laser beam, vaporize, and lower the breakdown threshold from that expected for clean air. Is this effect important in microwave induced breakdown? You may recall that the cross section for attenuation of radiation of wavelength λ by particles of radius a falls rapidly to zero if $2\pi a/\lambda \ll 1$ (see Figure 3–28). Atmospheric particles are 10μm or less in size (see Figure 3–27), while microwaves have wavelengths of about cm. Therefore, $2\pi a/\lambda$ is about 10^{-2} or less, and very little microwave energy is absorbed in these aerosols. Accordingly, they do not heat as much as they would in the presence of laser light, and are less likely to serve as a source for the initiation of breakdown. Additionally, the microwave breakdown threshold is quite low even in pure air—on the order of 10^6 W/cm^2 or less, as compared to 10^9W/cm^2 or more at laser frequencies. Thus, initiation of breakdown from aerosols, which is roughly wavelength independent, is unlikely to be an important effect at microwave wavelengths, where the pure gas breakdown threshold lies below the threshold associated with the impurities in a dirty gas.

Plasma Maintenance and Propagation. Once breakdown has taken place, how does the resulting plasma interact with the radiation? In Chapter 3, we saw that plasmas could be maintained at intensities below the breakdown threshold, and could propagate towards the source of radiation as supersonic detonation or subsonic combustion waves. Do similar phenomena occur when microwaves interact with a breakdown plasma?

A plasma will propagate if sufficient microwave energy can be absorbed to replace energy it loses through radiation, thermal conduction, and heating up the cold, ambient air which it entrains as it propagates. Thus, as with breakdown, the key factor in plasma maintenance and propagation is the absorption coefficient of a plasma with a given electron density for microwave radiation of a given frequency. Let us consider, then, how a plasma interacts with microwaves.

The interaction of microwaves and plasmas has been studied for some time, and indeed microwaves have long been used as diagnostic tools to probe and measure plasma properties.[27] If air at sea level is fully ionized, the electron density will be about $10^{19}/cm^3$. At this density, the plasma frequency, v_p, is about 10^{13} Hz (see Figure 3–14). You will recall that if the frequency of radiation incident on a plasma lies below the plasma frequency, electrons within the plasma can shield its interior from the incident radiation. The radiation will primarily be reflected, and absorption will occur only within a short distance of the plasma's surface (the *skin depth*). Lasers, having frequencies of 10^{14} Hz and greater, are able to penetrate to the interior of a breakdown plasma, where they are efficiently absorbed. Microwaves, with frequencies of 10^{11} Hz and less, are largely reflected from a plasma whose electron density equals that of air at sea level. This means that microwaves cannot support plasma propagation as a detonation wave. This type of wave propagates supersonically, with a density roughly equal to that of the surrounding atmosphere (see Figure 3–55). The threshold intensity for such a wave, even assuming that all the incident radiation is absorbed in the shock front and serves to propagate it, is about 10^7 W/cm^2. This is well below the threshold for laser-induced breakdown, but well above the threshold for microwave induced breakdown. This means that microwave-supported detonation waves are not a real problem from the standpoint of microwave propagation. Provided the intensity of the beam has been kept below the air breakdown threshold, these waves will not occur.

Microwaves can, however, support plasma propagation as a subsonic combustion wave. This type of wave is in pressure balance with its surroundings, so that at the high temperature associated with a plasma, its density is much less than that in a detonation wave (see figure 3–54). Combustion waves are a common phenomenon in waveguides for high power microwaves, where an impurity within the waveguide, such as a flake of metal, can ignite a plasma which absorbs or reflects most of the radiation, preventing further propagation through the guide.[28] These waves can be maintained at intensities below that for breakdown, and have been seen at intensities of a few hundreds W/cm². By contrast, the microwave breakdown threshold in air is on the order of 10^6 W/cm² (see Figure 4–20). Typical wave velocities are on the order of 100 cm/sec, similar to laser-supported combustion waves (see Figure 3–61).

The quantitative analysis of microwave-supported combustion waves can be performed in a manner analogous to that which we outlined in Chapter 3 for laser-supported combustion waves. The major difference lies in the fact that since the plasma frequency may exceed the microwave frequency, a substantial portion of the incident radiation will be reflected, rather than absorbed. You may recall from Chapter 3 that simple solutions for wave thresholds and velocities are not possible except under simplifying and largely unrealistic assumptions. The same situation applies in the microwave case.

Fortunately, combustion waves are unlikely to have an effect on propagation for two reasons. First, there are no sources for the ignition of these waves other than at the surface of a target. While laser-supported combustion waves could be ignited in dirty air breakdown from aerosols, we have seen that these aerosols do not interact with microwaves to any appreciable extent. Second, even if they should be created near a target surface, they are unlikely to propagate away from the surface, decoupling the radiation from it. This is because the velocity of a combustion wave is so slow that either naturally occurring winds or those generated by the motion of the target are likely to blow it out as it tries to propagate towards the microwave transmitter. Therefore, microwave supported plasmas are more of an issue from the standpoint of target interaction than beam propagation.

Thermal Blooming. In thermal blooming, heating of the air through which the beam travels leads to density and index of refraction gradients that cause the beam to expand at a greater rate than it would in a vacuum (see Figure 3–40). Is this likely to be a significant effect for microwaves? The answer is no, due to the much larger spatial scale of a microwave beam. You may recall from Chapter 3 that there are two ways to prevent thermal blooming from affecting beam propagation. The first is to use a beam whose pulse width is shorter than the time necessary for blooming to develop (Figure 3–41), and the second is to choose beam parameters such that the thermal distortion number is less than unity (Figures 3–42 and 3–44). Both of these approaches are easier as the beam radius increases, and a microwave beam will have a radius at least 10^4 greater than a laser beam with the same divergence. Moreover, the intensity of a microwave beam is likely to be less than that of a laser beam, since the air breakdown threshold is less for microwaves, and microwaves are more likely to be employed for soft damage that can be accomplished at lower intensities. All of these things combine to remove thermal blooming as an issue from the standpoint of microwave propagation.

Summary: Nonlinear Effects.

1. Air breakdown is the most significant nonlinear effect for microwaves. Its threshold is many orders of magnitude less for microwaves than for lasers, and it scales differently with altitude and frequency as well, (see Figure 4–20)

2. Once breakdown has occurred, plasma evolution is more complex for microwaves than for lasers, since the plasma frequency in breakdown plasmas may exceed the frequency of the radiation. In this case, much of the radiation is reflected rather than absorbed in the plasma. A strongly-absorbing detonation wave plasma cannot be maintained by microwaves, though a low density combustion wave can.

3. Other non-linear effects which are important in the propagation of lasers are not significant for the propagation of microwaves, either because the spatial scales are too large (e.g. thermal blooming), or because their thresholds lie above the

threshold for microwave-induced air breakdown (e.g. dirty air breakdown).

Summary: Propagation in the Atmosphere

For microwaves as for all weapon types, propagation in the atmosphere is considerably more complex than propagation in a vacuum. A microwave beam will lose energy through absorption, with water, both liquid and vapor, contributing significantly to the attenuation coefficient. The natural variation of the atmospheric index of refraction with altitude will make a microwave beam bend, extending its range along the surface of the earth beyond that achievable in a vacuum. Proper atmospheric conditions can even cause the radiation to proceed over great distances along "channels" in the atmosphere. And if a beam's intensity becomes too great, the atmosphere will break down, propagation ceasing. None of these effects are truly new; they affect lasers as well, and were introduced in Chapter 3. However, the relative importance and scaling of these effects differs from lasers to microwaves. Table 4–3 is a summary of those things which affect both laser and microwave propagation, highlighting their similarities and differences.

Implications

Microwaves are qualitatively different from lasers as directed energy weapons. In the popular mind, lasers are seen as bullets—flashes of light which proceed in a straight line toward targets which are destroyed by the holes drilled in them. While not strictly correct, this view is close enough to reality that it's not terribly misleading. If a laser beam is like a bullet shot from a rifle, a microwave beam is more like the shot from a shotgun. Through divergence, the energy spreads with distance, and the effective range is less. Moreover, the unusual paths which a beam may take in the atmosphere, together with the intensity limitations imposed by breakdown, suggest that microwaves are unsuited for the precision destruction of threatening targets. Rather, they're more likely to be fired at an array of targets, hoping that most will receive a dose of energy sufficient to exploit internal vulnerabilities and result in target negation even at intensities below that required for physical destruction. Therefore, a crucial and difficult to quantify problem in microwave weaponry is to understand the mechanisms by which they might damage targets.

	Microwaves λ= 0.1-100cm	Lasers λ= 0.4-10μm
Attenuation (absorption/scattering)		
Main causes	Atmospheric molecules liquid water drops (<1mm)	Atmospheric molecules dust particles (<10μm)
Main cures	Increase intensity	Increase intensity choose λ in a propagation "window"
Index of Refraction Changes/gradients		
Main effect	Bending and ducting	Increased divergence
Main cures	None	Adaptive Optics
Self-induced Refractive effects		
Main effect	None	Thermal Blooming
Main cures	None	Adaptive Optics
Atmospheric Breakdown		
Main causes	electron cascade	electron cascade dust (aerosol) initiation
Main cures	Operate below threshold	Operate below threshold
Breakdown Plasma maintenance	Combustion Waves	Combustion Waves Detonation Waves

Table 4-3. Issues Affecting Microwave and Laser Propagation in the Atmosphere

Microwave Interaction with Targets

Microwaves have an inherent divergence, rather unpredictable propagation in the atmosphere, and a low threshold for atmospheric breakdown. These things make them unsuitable for *hard* kill of a target through the deposition of sufficient energy to melt or vaporize it. Therefore, the thought of microwaves as directed energy weapons usually begins with the assumption that the target is *soft*, having a built-in vulnerabilities which microwaves can exploit.

Unfortunately, any vulnerabilities a target may have to microwaves will depend on its construction—the frequencies it is designed for, the arrangement of its components, their shielding by the black boxes which encase them, and so forth. Therefore, the

243

data needed to assess a target's vulnerability are not generally available. If we want to drill a hole in a target with a laser, the thermal properties that we need to know to calculate a damage threshold are available. But if we want to damage the logic circuit in the guidance section of an anti-aircraft missile, we will have little information to use in predicting its damage threshold. Therefore, this discussion of microwave interaction with targets must be general and qualitative. Detailed analysis of microwave-target interaction cannot be done on a zero-order basis as it can for the other directed energy weapons discussed in this book.

Mechanisms of Soft Kill

Since we anticipate that we can't use microwaves to blow targets out of the sky, it's logical to ask what we can accomplish. How can targets be damaged or negated below the intensity necessary for physical destruction? There are two ways in which microwave radiation can get into and damage a target. The easiest way is if the target is itself a microwave receiver, such as a radar or communication link. In this case, the target is designed to detect, amplify, and process microwaves at some specific frequency. If the attacking microwaves have the same frequency and a much greater intensity than those which were anticipated, you can easily imagine that the target's circuitry might be damaged. This is known as *in band* damage, since the microwave weapon operates in the same frequency band as the target. The opposite case, in which the attacking microwaves are at a frequency unrelated to the nature of the target, is known as *out-of-band* damage. Both modes of damage have advantages and disadvantages.

In-Band Damage. In an in-band attack, the idea is to exploit the circuitry within the target. Consider, for example, the situation illustrated in Figure 4–21, where a radar illuminates a target at some range z, and the target returns fire with microwaves of the same frequency. Of necessity, the radar receiver must detect and process low intensity radiation, since only a small fraction of the power that it transmits is received in the return signal. If the radar beam has a brightness B, the intensity of its radiation at a range z is B/z^2. Only a small fraction of the radiation received at the target

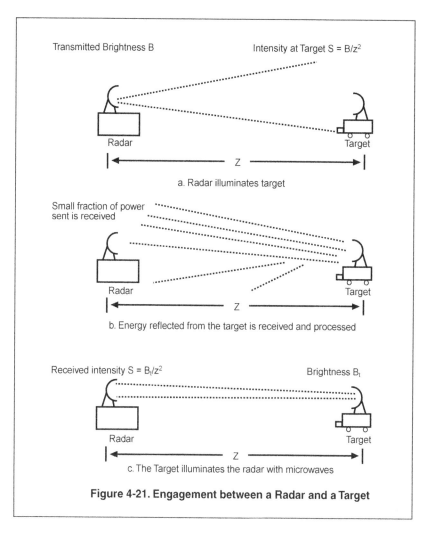

Figure 4-21. **Engagement between a Radar and a Target**

is reflected back towards the radar. This fraction is quantified by defining the target's effective brightness as seen by the radar as $B' = B\sigma/4\pi z^2$, where σ is the radar cross section of the target.[29] The intensity of the radiation returned to the radar is then $S = B'/z^2 = B\sigma/4\pi z^4$. The important point to note is that the intensity of the received signal decreases as the fourth power of the range. This makes physical sense, since the intensity falls off by a factor of $1/z^2$ in propagating to the target, and the reflected radiation again falls off by a factor of $1/z^2$ in returning to the radar. If it is to be useful, the radar must detect targets at long range, so that the received intensity could be quite low.

Now suppose that the target, recognizing that it has been "painted" by the radar, returns fire with a beam of microwaves of brightness B_t. When it arrives at the radar, this beam will have an intensity $S_t = B_t/z^2$. The ratio of the signal sent by the target to the signal returned from the target is simply $S_t/S = B_t\, 4\pi\, z^2/\sigma B$. This ratio will be greater than one, and the radar will be "jammed" and incapable of discerning its signal from the noise it receives, as long as $B_t/B > \sigma/4\pi\, z^2$. Typical radar cross sections are quite low (square meters or less) compared to typical ranges, which are kilometers or greater.[30] Thus, the jammer can be effective even if its brightness is much less than that of the radar, an advantage which becomes greater as the target and radar move farther apart. The situation is analogous to looking for someone in the dark with a flashlight. If the person sought has a flashlight of his own and shines it in your eyes, you will be unable to identify or locate him with the reflected light from yours.

In-band attack is not limited to jamming. If the power of the attacking microwaves is great enough, it can damage the radar's circuitry. This is because the receiver must detect and amplify very weak signals. If the received signals are too great, currents can be induced which are so great that they will burn out ele-

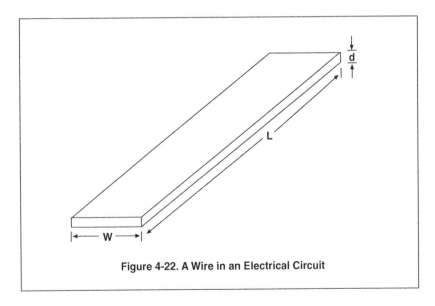

Figure 4-22. A Wire in an Electrical Circuit

ments in the radar's circuit boards. Modern equipment is particularly sensitive to this type of damage, since the wires and other circuit elements are thin strips of metal or semiconductor etched on a board. It does not take too much current before they can heat to the point of self destruction. Consider, for example, the wire illustrated in Figure 4–22. The electrical resistance of such a wire is $R = L/wd\Sigma$ where Σ is the conductivity (mho/m) of the wire's material and L, w, d are its length, width, and thickness. The resistance of the wire goes up as its cross sectional area, wd, goes down, and in modern circuits there is motivation to make these dimensions as small as possible.

If a current I flows through the wire, the power dissipated within it is simply $P = I^2R$.[31] This means that in time t an energy $E = Pt = I^2Rt$ will have been deposited in the wire by the flowing current. In any circuit design, allowances must be made for cooling or heat sinks to get rid of this energy before wires and components are damaged by the associated rise in temperature. The design is made based on assumptions regarding the maximum power to be dissipated, and if that maximum is exceeded, temperature can rise to the point where damage will occur. If the wire shown in Figure 4–22 were thermally insulated and could not get rid of any energy, it would begin to melt when the energy deposited was sufficient to raise its temperature to the melting point, or when $I^2Rt = I^2Lt/wd\Sigma = \rho wdLC(T_m - T_o)$, where C is the heat capacity of the wire's material, ρ its density, T_m its melting point, and T_o its initial temperature (see Chapter 1). This expression may be solved to find the current I necessary to melt the wire in time t: $I = wd [C\Sigma\rho(T_m - T_o)/t]1/2$. This expression is plotted in Figure 4–23.

On a printed circuit board, a wire might be less than a micrometer in thickness, and about a micrometer in width, for a cross sectional area of less than 10^{-8} cm^2. Less than a milliamp of current could be sufficient to melt conducting paths on a circuit board with wires of this size.

The solid state devices that these wires connect can be even more sensitive to transient currents and voltages. Unlike metals, whose resistance increases with temperature, semiconductors have a resistance which decreases with temperature if the temperature exceeds some critical value, as illustrated in Figure 4–24. You may recall from Chapter 3 that a semiconductor is a

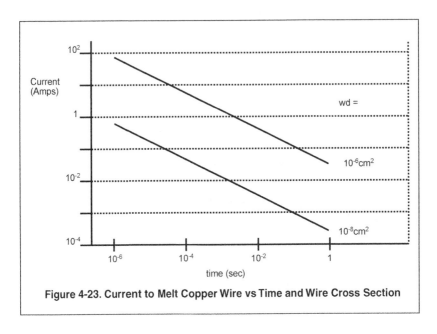

Figure 4-23. Current to Melt Copper Wire vs Time and Wire Cross Section

insulator with a relatively narrow band gap, so that at higher temperatures electrons can be thermally excited from the valence band into the conduction band. Once this happens, the current flow increases, since there are more current carriers, and the rate of energy deposition $P = I^2R$ increases, since it is proportional to the square of the current. Thus, an instability can develop in a semiconductor at elevated temperatures, in which a temperature rise leads to increased current flow and an even greater heating rate and more rapid temperature rise. This process is known as *thermal runaway*, and has been the subject of considerable research as a mechanism for semiconductor failure.

Clearly, excessive transient currents have the potential to produce a destructive rise in temperature. Circuit designers try to anticipate such events, and include in their design circuitry to shunt off into harmless channels current and voltage signals which exceed some threshold. But neither the attacker nor the defender knows how effective these measures might be in the face of pulse forms and intensities which are unknown in advance. And the present trend towards ultra miniaturization and large scale integrated circuits means that space on a circuit board is at a premium, leaving less room for such luxuries as protective circuitry and wider, more robust current paths.

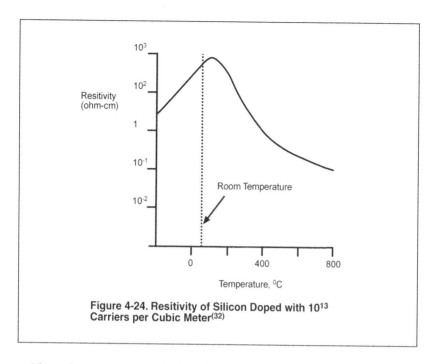

Figure 4-24. Resitivity of Silicon Doped with 10^{13} Carriers per Cubic Meter[(32)]

The advantage to an in-band attack on a microwave device is that weapon power is most efficiently used. It enters the target via the front door, an antenna which is designed to receive microwaves, and the target's internal circuits may amplify the received signal to even greater and more destructive power levels. The disadvantage to such an attack is that you need to know in advance the frequency at which your untended target is operating, or you need to obtain that information in real time and adjust the weapon's output appropriately. The target may not sit idly by while this done. A common countermeasure to in-band attack is *frequency hopping,* in which a radar, for example, changes frequency with each pulse, and thus is not jammed by a return signal at a frequency it is no longer looking for. The counter to this countermeasure is to attack over a broad band of frequencies, but this carries with it the disadvantage of spreading the weapon's available energy over a broad band, so that only a fraction of the total output power will be received by the target. In the end, if the desire is to be able to attack generic targets, it may be more appropriate to consider an out-of-band attack.

Out-of-Band Damage. In an attack on a target with radiation not in its frequency band, the damage mechanism is simply raw power absorbed by the target's circuits. It might seem as though this would be difficult to do, but there are many examples of random electromagnetic radiation damaging electronic circuits. Lightning storms, for example, can induce fluctuations in the line voltage supplied to houses, so that computers, microwave ovens, and similar devices are frequently damaged if not protected by surge suppressors. Even the small electrical discharge associated with someone walking across a carpet in dry weather has been associated with loss of data or damage in computer systems, so that in the workplace computer stations are frequently located on grounded surfaces, and operators are asked to touch such a grounded surface before touching the equipment. And the military has invested considerable time and effort in protecting its systems against *EMP*—the electromagnetic pulse of radiation which accompanies the detonation of a nuclear weapon, and which can damage electronic equipment at great ranges from the location of the detonation.[33]

How does microwave energy get into a target, and what does it do when it gets there? Energy cannot enter through metallic surfaces, which are highly reflective of microwaves, and typically enters through windows or gaps in the target's surface. Due to their long wavelength, microwaves are strongly diffracted as they pass through small apertures, and can irradiate areas which would seem to be well shielded by the target's external surface. A target designer seeks to keep potential entry points to a minimum, but will never know without extensive testing how successful he has been. An elaborate program of shielding and testing against microwave attack may be practical for a small number of extremely important targets, such as strategic bombers or missiles, but is impractical for a large number of military systems such as trucks, small radios, and so forth. All such items contain solid state circuitry and may be vulnerable to attack, though the level of vulnerability is virtually impossible for either the attacker or defender to quantify.

Once microwaves enter a target, they can be absorbed in electronic circuit elements and damage them. Since the microwave radiation is a time-varying electromagnetic field, it can induce currents in the target's circuits, resulting in heating and thermal damage. Even metallic strips will be subject to absorption and damage. Their thickness is typically comparable to the skin depth to which microwaves can penetrate metal, and they are laid down on a dielectric surface which may be a thermal insulator. This inhibits the efficient transport of energy away from them. Table 4–4 shows the skin depth and absorptivity of copper as a function of microwave frequency.[34]

From the table, you can see why metals are considered effective shields against microwaves—they don't penetrate very far, and only a small fraction of the incident intensity, on the order of 10^{-4}, will be absorbed. Nevertheless, this small amount of penetration and absorption can damage the thin conducting paths on a circuit board, which are only 1–10 μm in thickness, and are frequently thermally isolated, so that their temperature can build up rapidly.

As an example, consider the conducting wire of Figure 4–22. If a fluence F is incident on the wire, and it has absorptivity α, the energy absorbed will be αFwL. The mass of the wire is $wLd\rho$, and so the energy required to bring it to the melting point is $wLd\rho C(T_m - T_o)$, where T_m is the melting temperature and T_o is the initial temperature of the wire. Equating the energy absorbed to the energy necessary to bring the wire to the threshold of melting and solving for F, we find $F = d\rho C(T_m - T_o)/\alpha$. If we assume as typical values that the thickness d is 0.5 μm and that $\alpha = 10^{-4}$, we find that for copper[35] the necessary fluence is 1800 J/cm². This value is an order of magnitude less than the all purpose damage criterion of Chapter 1, even though only a small fraction of the incident energy is absorbed. The wire is so thin and tenuous that there is little mass to melt, and it doesn't take much absorbed energy to melt it.

Frequency (GHz)	Skin Depth, δ (μm)	Absorptivity, α
0.1	6.6	2.8×10^{-5}
1.0	2.1	8.8×10^{-5}
10	0.66	2.8×10^{-4}
100	0.21	8.8×10^{-4}

Table 4-4. Skin Depth and Absorptivity of Copper at Microwave Frequencies

The fluence just derived would be much reduced if the absorptivity were greater. In Chapter 3, we saw that the coupling of radiation to a target could be enhanced if plasmas were ignited at the target surface (see Figure 3–74). The criteria for this enhanced coupling were that the plasma not propagate away from the surface, and that the bare target surface couple poorly to the incident radiation (see Figure 3–73). Since microwaves have a very low absorptivity at metal surfaces, and since they will only support slow moving combustion waves, these criteria are likely to be satisfied in microwave-target interaction. It would be necessary, of course, for the microwave intensity to exceed the threshold for the ignition of such plasmas at the target surface. This threshold lies in the range 10^2–10^3 W/cm^2.[36]

Estimates of Damage Thresholds

Damaging targets with microwaves is quite different from damaging them with the other directed energy weapons discussed in this book. If we were after hard kill, it would be a straightforward exercise to calculate damage thresholds and then incorporate propagation constraints to design a weapon for a particular application. But when dealing with soft kill, specific details of the target's construction come into play. For microwaves, the problem is exacerbated since their long wavelength means that diffraction and interference effects within the target make the specific environment that it sees difficult to predict, and difficult to duplicate under operational conditions even if it has been measured in laboratory experiments.

In view of these uncertainties, we cannot develop definitive damage criteria for microwave weapons. About the most we can do is review some published estimates for the levels of energy or power necessary to achieve damage, either in or out-of-band. A single number for the damage threshold for a target is not of much value, unless we know the conditions under which that number was obtained. Published damage thresholds are most useful if presented along with the mechanism of damage and the limits on pulse width for which that mechanism is likely to determine the threshold. Typically, however, this is not the case. At least in the more popular literature, it is more likely that a single damage estimate will be published. In this circumstance, it should be assumed in the absence of other data that a quoted fluence level is appropriate for short pulses, and a quoted intensity level is appropriate for long pulses, with the definition of short and long being undefined. About the most that can be said is that times less than 10^{-8} sec are almost certainly short, and times greater than 10^{-3} sec are almost certainly long (see Chapter 1).[37]

Type of Damage	Fluence Threshold (J/cm^2)	Intensity Threshold (W/cm^2)
In-Band		10^{-8} - 10^{-6}
Out-of-Band	10^{-5} - 10^{-2}	10 - 100
Thermal (target melting, vaporization)		10^3 - 10^4

Table 4-5. Damage Estimates for Microwaves(38)

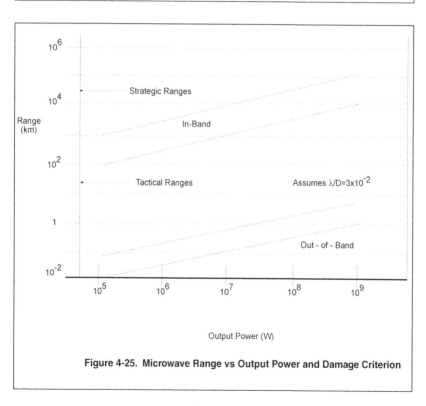

Figure 4-25. Microwave Range vs Output Power and Damage Criterion

Keeping the uncertainties associated with published damage levels in mind, Table 4–5 provides a summary of some damage threshold estimates for microwaves which have appeared in the literature.

As you can see from the table, there is considerable uncertainty in the energy and power levels at which microwaves might damage targets. Bearing this in mind, Figure 4–25 provides a graphical summary of some of the damage criteria in Table 4–5, showing the range to which targets might be damaged to different levels with microwave devices of different wavelength and output power.

Figure 4–25 has been drawn for $\lambda/D = 3 \times 10^{-2}$—the value appropriate for 3 cm microwaves emitted from a 1 m aperture. The ranges in the figure scale inversely as λ/D, so that if the aperture were 10 m (or the wavelength 3 mm), the curves would all move up by an order of magnitude. Clearly, the greatest potential for microwave devices of modest output power is in achieving in-band damage of electrical equipment. Only for such soft damage can damage levels be exceeded over ranges of interest. There is a large region of uncertainty, where powers exceed those necessary for in-band damage, yet fall below those necessary for out-of-band damage. Within this region, it is likely that in some engagements targets would be damaged, and in others not, depending on the nature of the target and its vulnerabilities.

Summary: Target Interaction

1. Microwaves are likely to damage targets through soft kill mechanisms—those which exploit inherent target vulnerabilities. There are two types of soft kill: in-band and out-of-band.

2. With in-band damage, microwaves enter a target through its own antenna. This requires that the attacking microwaves be of the same frequency as those the target is tuned to receive. Damage occurs when the target's circuits are loaded beyond their design capacity.

3. In out-of-band damage, microwaves enter the target through the back door—apertures which were not designed for their entry. Damage occurs as the microwaves are absorbed in thin, sensitive electronic components, heating them to the point of damage.

4. Because of uncertainty in knowing by what paths microwaves will enter the target, and in predicting the intensity that components will see on the interior, it is difficult to develop definitive damage criteria for microwaves. Table 4–5 and Figure 4–31 provide a summary of some limited data, and suggest that microwaves can certainly be used for in-band damage, can occasionally be used for out-of-band damage, and are unlikely to be used for hard or thermal damage of target structural components.

Implications

Anecdotal evidence has always suggested that microwaves have great potential as weapons. Radiation at microwave frequencies from radars, lightning, and microwave ovens has been associated with the damage of various types of equipment. Unfortunately, the difficulty in quantifying these effects and in knowing the vulnerabilities and shielding in potential targets makes microwaves difficult to rely on from a military standpoint. The major exception is in the area if in-band attack, where jammers are an established element in the arsenal of electronic warfare. If microwaves find broader uses as weapons, it will be because devices developed as jammers are found through experience to have broader application in achieving out-of-band damage. As technology makes greater powers available, it will be possible to exploit targets of opportunity and see what happens. The uncertainty in performing *a priori* calculations of damage makes it unlikely that a microwave weapon will be developed from first principles for the attack and damage of a specific target.

Notes and References

1. Figure 4–1 was adapted from Stephen Cheung and Frederic H. Levien, *Microwaves Made Simple: Principles and Applications*. (Dedham, MA: Artech House, 1985). This book is a good introductory reference on the principles of microwave generation and engineering.

2. The older frequency band designations originated during WW II as a means of keeping the frequency of radars classified. From this beginning, they developed acceptance as a convenient form of shorthand. However, it's easy to become confused when comparing articles in which band designations are used, since some of the letters have changed meaning over the years, and some engineers persist in using the older designations. A "C band" device operates at about 6 GHz using the WW II-derived band designations, and at about 0.5 GHz using the newer designations. Authors are not always clear on the convention they're using. The older designations are common in radar engineering, and the newer ones in other applications.

3. One reason why water interacts strongly with microwaves is that it has a *permanent electric dipole moment*. This means that the centers of positive and negative charge are separated in a water molecule, so that it interacts with an applied electric field just as a permanent magnet interacts with an applied magnetic field.

4. Because of their larger wavelength, there are diffraction effects with microwaves that make the pattern of radiation from an antenna less than the ideal illustrated in Figure 4–4. The main portion of the beam (or main lobe) behaves as illustrated in the figure, but some fraction of the energy goes out to the side just as diffraction carries energy into regions of geometric shadow. This diffracted energy is called *side lobe* radiation.

5. Brightness, as we use the term here, refers to main lobe radiation. In microwave engineering, the concept of "antenna gain" is usually used instead of brightness. The gain, G, of a directional antenna is the ratio of the intensity along its preferred direction to what the intensity would be if the antenna radiated uniformally in all directions (isotropically). In terms of G, the intensity at a range z is $S = PG/4 \pi z^2$. Thus, brightness may be expressed in terms of antenna gain as $B = PG/4\pi$, and the gain of a directional antenna having aperture D is $G = 4\pi B/P \approx 4D^2/\lambda^2$. A good discussion of antennas and their radiation patterns can be found in Chapter 16 of Cheung and Levien (note 1).

6. If you imagine a spreading beam passing through a sphere that surrounds the beam's source, the solid angle that the beam encompasses is the constant of proportionality between the area through which it passes and the square of the sphere's radius. Therefore, an isotropic source, spreading equally in all directions, is spreading into a solid angle of 4π sr. This definition is analogous to that of plane angles, for which the angle in radians between two diverging lines is the ratio of the arc of a circle they cut off to the radius of the circle.

7. There are a variety of different measures of beam strength to be found in the literature. Our definitions of fluence (energy/area), intensity (power/area) and brightness (power/solid angle) are common in directed energy work. Other terms may be used for these quantities, so it's useful to check on the units of any quantity used in the literature as a measure of beam strength. See Table C in Chapter 17 (Optics) of Herbert L. Anderson (ed.), *Physics Vade Mecum.* (New York: American Institute of Physics, 1981).

8. A good quantitative discussion of diffraction from a straight edge can be found in section 18.11 of Francis A. Jenkins and Harvey E. White, *Fundamentals of Optics,* 3rd ed. (New York: McGraw-Hill, 1957).

9. Some nice pictures of different diffraction patterns can be found in Chapter 10 of Eugene Hecht and Alfred Zajac, *Optics* (Reading, MA: Addison-Wesley, 1976).

10. The gaps or slits through which microwaves enter targets need not be physical holes. Most non-metallic materials are trans-

parent to microwaves, so they can penetrate through windows, rubber grommets, weather stripping, and so on.

11. Microwave tubes are commercially available with average powers at 3 GHz of about 1MW and peak powers of about 10 MW (see Figure 10.2 of Cheung and Levien, note 1). By contrast, the "Report to the American Physical Society of the Study Group on Science and Technology of Directed Energy Weapons" *Rev. Mod Phys* 59, pt II (July 1987), reports that only recently has MW-class pulsed power become available from lasers that stress the state of the art. Of course, since laser technology is more in its infancy, it may be that there is more potential for growth and breakthroughs in laser power output.

12. A good summary of issues affecting microwave propagation can be found in S. Parl and A. Malaga "Theoretical Analysis of Microwave Propagation," *Rome Air Development Center Technical Report no. RADC–TR–84–74* (April, 1984). [AD–A143–762].

13. Figure 4–8 has been adapted from Figure 2–9 of Parl and Malaga (note 12). In reviewing this and other sources of data on microwave attenuation, you'll note that data are often presented in terms of dB/km rather than km^{-1}. A "dB" (decibel) is one tenth of an order of magnitude. Thus, a one dB drop in intensity means that $\log(I_o/I) = 0.1$, or $I_o/I = 1.26$. This notation is common in radio and radar engineering. The absorption length, $1/K$, is the distance over which intensity falls by a factor of $1/e$, or $I_o/I = 2.72$. This notation is more common in optical engineering. The appropriate conversion factor is $1\ km^{-1} = 4.3\ dB/km$. The use of decibels as a way of treating quantities which can vary by many orders of magnitude is discussed in Chapter 2 of Cheung and Levien (note 1).

14. Figure 4–9 is based on data from a table on p E–23 of Robert C. Weast (ed), *Handbook of Chemistry and Physics*, 45th ed (Cleveland, OH: Chemical Rubber Co, 1964).

15. The exponential decay of density with altitude is a common approximation for the lower atmosphere. See Chapter 4 in the *APS Report on Directed Energy Weapons* (note 11). This type of behavior may also be derived theoretically. See Section 6.3 in F. Reif, *Fundamentals of Statistical and Thermal Physics* (New York: McGraw Hill, 1965).

16. The physical meaning of this integral is that the propagation path is broken up into many small segments. Along each of these, the attenuation coefficient is roughly constant. The total attenuation is the product of the attenuations along each segment, and the effective "Kz" is the integral $_0\int^z K(z)\,dz$.

17. See Section 2 of Parl and Malaga (note 12).

18. Figure 4–13 has been adapted from Figure 2–10 of Parl and Malaga (note 12).

19. Table 4–1 was developed from data in the *Encyclopedia Britannica*, 15th ed. (Chicago: Encyclopedia Brittanica, Inc, 1978). See "Rain" (Micropedia, vol VIII, p. 390), and "Precipitation" (Macropedia, vol 14, p. 960). There can, of course, be considerable variation in the characteristics of any given rainfall.

20. Figure 4–14 is based on Eq. 2.2, Parl and Malaga (note 12). Figure 4–15 is based on a table of vapor pressure of water found on p. D–92 of the *Handbook of Chemistry and Physics* (note 14).

21. The maximum line or sight range between a transmitter of height h_t and a receiver of height h_r is $Z \approx (2R_e)^{1/2}[h_t^{1/2} + h_r^{1/2}]$, where R_e is the radius of the earth.

22. See Parl and Malaga (note 12), Eq. 2–6.

23. For example, see C.A. Sampson, "Refractivity Gradients in the Northern Hemisphere," *ITS Report* no. OTR–75–59 (1975) [AD–A009 503]

24. Almost everything you ever wanted to know about breakdown with microwaves can be found in A.D. MacDonald, *Microwave Breakdown in Gases* (New York: John Wiley and Sons, 1966).

25. See Equation 5.3 in V. E. Zuev, *Laser Beams in the Atmosphere* (New York: Consultant's Bureau, 1982).

26. See Figure 43 in M. Mitchner and Charles H. Kruger, Jr., *Partially Ionized Gases* (New York: John Wiley and Sons, 1973). The collision rate is $\nu = N\sigma v$, where σ is the collision cross section and N the density of molecules.

27. A brief description of plasma diagnostics with microwaves can be found in section 4.6 of Nicholas A. Krall and Alvin W. Trivelpiece, *Principles of Plasma Physics* (New York: McGraw Hill, 1973).

28. See Section 7 in Yu. P. Raizer, "Propagation of Discharges and Maintenance of a Dense Plasma by Electromagnetic Fields," *Soviet Physics-Upsekhi* 15, 688 (May-June, 1973).

29. The idea of a *radar cross section* comes from the idea that if the intensity on target is B/z^2 (W/cm^2), then the power reflected back at the radar will be some area, σ, multiplied by that intensity. The radar cross section is a measured quantity, and need not be the same as the physical cross section of the target. Indeed, the idea behind *stealth* technology is to make σ as small as possible by absorbing radar waves or reflecting them in directions away from the radar. In general σ will depend on the frequency of the radar, the nature of the target, and the orientation between radar and target.

30. For example, fighter aircraft have radar cross sections on the order of 2 m², and missiles on the order of 0.5 m². See Chapter 14 in Cheung and Levien (note 1).

31. This expression for the power dissipated on a wire can be found in any discussion of elementary circuit theory, such as Chapter 32 of David Halliday and Robert Resnick, *Physics, Part II* (New York: John Wiley and Sons, 1967).

32. Figure 4–24 has been adapted from Figure 3 in D.C. Wunsch, "The Application of Electrical Overstress Models to Gate Protective Networks," in the *Proceedings of the 16th Annual International Reliability Symposium,* San Diego, CA, 18–20 April, 1978. Published by the Electron Devices Society and the IEE Reliability Group, these annual proceedings are a good source of information on the failure modes of circuit elements and techniques which can be used to prevent failure from current or voltage transients.

33. EMP arises because a nuclear burst ionizes the air in its vicinity. The electrons which result from this ionization are lighter and move more rapidly than the ions from which they were separated. This results in a separation of charge which is asymmetrical, since the density of the ionized air decreases with altitude. The resulting currents generate strong electromagnetic fields. Malfunction and damage of electronic equipment as a result of EMP were first observed during atmospheric nuclear tests in the 1950's. See Chapter XI of Samuel Glasstone and Philip J. Dolan (eds.), *The Effects of Nuclear Weapons*, 3rd ed. (Washington, DC: US Government Printing Office, 1977).

34. See Figures 3–15 and 3–16 in Chapter 3. Expressions for skin depth and absorptivity may be found in any text on electromagnetic theory, such as Section 16–4 of John R. Reitz and Frederic J. Milford, *Foundations of Electromagnetic Theory* (Reading, MA: Addison-Wesley, 1960).

35. The thermal properties of copper can be found in Table 1–1, Chapter 1.

36. See Raizer (note 28).

37. These estimates of long and short time scales are of necessity soft, since in any given interaction between a weapon and a target the specific mechanisms of interaction and energy loss, and the time scales associated with them, must be taken into account.

38. Generic damage thresholds such as those in Table 4–5 are always suspect, but are provided here simply to give a feeling for the wide range of levels at which microwaves may damage targets. The intensity thresholds are from Chapter 8 of Jeff Hecht, *Beam Weapons: The Next Arms Race* (New York: Plenum Press, 1984). The Fluence threshold is from Theodore B. Taylor, "Third Generation Nuclear Weapons," *Scientific American 256*, 38 (April, 1987).

5: PARTICLE BEAMS

Particle beams are composed of large numbers of small particles moving at speeds approaching that of light. By "large numbers," we mean densities on the order of 10^{11} particles per cubic centimeter, and by "small" particles we mean the fundamental particles which comprise matter: electrons, protons, or perhaps neutral atoms, such as hydrogen. Particle beams are not easy to analyze and understand in detail. The atomic and sub-atomic scale of the particles in the beam means that their interactions with each other and with the target can be understood only on the basis of atomic and nuclear physics. The fact that the particles are traveling at velocities approaching that of light means that their propagation is governed by Einstein's theory of relativity. And the large number of particles in the beam means that their interactions with one another need to be taken into account—the behavior of an individual particle is affected by behavior of the other particles in the beam. Relativity, nuclear physics, and many of the other concepts needed to understand particle beams are outside the scope of everyday experience. Perhaps for this reason, particle beams have not attracted public attention to the same extent as lasers, whose description as intense beams of light involves concepts which are much more intuitive.

Therefore, we will devote a significant portion of this chapter to some of the fundamental physics which affects particle beams as they propagate and interact with matter. We cannot treat these fundamentals in detail, but we'll try to develop a physical feeling for the factors which determine the effectiveness and utility of particle beams as directed energy weapons. As always, we will emphasize the relative magnitude of important factors and how they scale with the parameters which characterize the beam, the atmosphere through which it propagates, and the target with which it interacts.

Fundamental Principles of Particle Beams

Electromagnetic Fields and Forces

There are two types of particle beams: charged and neutral. A charged-particle beam (CPB) is made up of particles such as electrons or protons which possess an electrical charge, and a neutral-particle beam (NPB) is made up of particles such as atomic hydrogen which are electrically neutral. Even an NPB begins its existence as a CPB, since only charged particles can be accelerated to high velocities and energies through electromagnetic forces in a particle accelerator.[1] Therefore, any discussion of particle beams must begin with a discussion of electromagnetic fields and the forces they produce on charged particles.

There exist in nature electrical fields, commonly denoted E, and magnetic fields, commonly denoted B. These fields are *vector* quantities, which means that they have associated with them at every point in space both a magnitude, or strength, and a direction in which they point.[2] Like the gravity field, electric and magnetic fields cannot be seen, but their presence can be inferred from their effect on matter. When a particle whose electrical charge is q encounters an electric field of strength E, the particle feels a force $F = qE$, pushing it in the same direction as E. When a particle whose charge is q, moving with velocity v, encounters a magnetic field of strength B, the particle feels a force $F = qvB \sin \theta$, where θ is the angle between the direction of motion of the particle and the direction of B. The direction of this magnetic force is perpendicular to the directions of both B and v, as shown in Figure 5–1.[3]

Where do these electrical and magnetic fields come from? Interestingly enough, they originate from charged particles. A particle of charge q (coulombs) produces an electric field which points radially outward, and whose magnitude a distance r from the particle is $E = q/4\pi\epsilon_0 r^2$ (Volts/m). A current (flow of charged particles) of magnitude I (Amperes) produces a magnetic field which encircles the direction of current flow, and whose magnitude at a distance r is $B = I/2\pi c^2 \epsilon_0 r$ (Webers/m^2). The constant ϵ_0 is known as the *permittivity of free space* (8.85×10^{-12} fd/m in MKS units), and c is the speed of light (3×10^8 m/sec). These relationships are also illustrated in Figure 5–1.

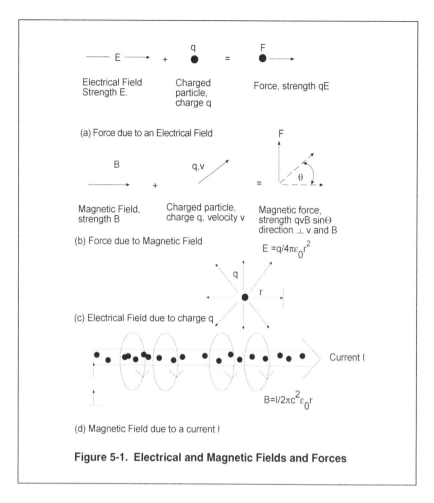

(a) Force due to an Electrical Field

(b) Force due to Magnetic Field

$$E = q/4\pi\varepsilon_0 r^2$$

(c) Electrical Field due to charge q

$$B = I/2\pi c^2 \varepsilon_0 r$$

(d) Magnetic Field due to a current I

Figure 5-1. Electrical and Magnetic Fields and Forces

The study of charged particles and their interaction with electric and magnetic fields can be quite complex: any fields which are present affect the particles, and particle motion, in turn, affects the fields which are present. The complex relationships between these fields and their forces were first fully described mathematically by James C. Maxwell in 1873. He developed four interrelated equations, appropriately known as Maxwell's Equations, which form the basis of electromagnetic theory even today. These equations quantify the experimental observation that charged particles produce electric fields, and that moving charged particles (currents) produce magnetic fields. In addition, Maxwell's equations predict that a time—varying electric field will produce a magnetic field, and that a time-varying magnetic field will produce an electric field. This last phenomenon results in the propagation of electric and magnetic fields coupled together as electromagnetic radiation (Chapter 3).

Relativistic Particle Dynamics

Since electromagnetic fields produce forces on charged particles, we'll need to understand how these particles respond to the forces they feel. In classical mechanics, the response of a particle of mass m to an applied force of strength F is given by Newton's Law: F = ma, where a = dv/dt is the acceleration, or rate of change of the velocity, v, of the particle. We see this law in action every day. A force accelerates a heavier, more massive, object to a lesser extent than a lighter one, and as long as a force is applied, the acceleration of an object continues, with its velocity becoming greater and greater. However, this common experience fails us as an object's velocity approaches the speed of light, c (3×10^8 m/sec). No force, however long applied, can induce a particle to exceed that speed. Einstein's theory of relativity explained this strange behavior and other contradictions to common experience that appear when distance, length, and time scales are such that the speed of light is an important parameter.[4]

Einstein's theory extended Newton's law to account for motion at speeds approaching that of light. This generalization is to write F = ma as F = dP/dt, expressing it in terms of the rate of change of a particle's momentum $P = \gamma mv$. The factor γ is defined as $\gamma = 1/(1 - v^2/c^2)^{1/2}$. If v << c, γ is essentially 1, and dP/dt becomes d(mv)/dt = m dv/dt = ma, since the mass m of the particle is a constant, and the acceleration, a, is the rate of change of velocity, dv/dt. Thus, at velocities characteristic of everyday life, Newton's law applies as it always has. On the other hand, as v approaches c, you can see that γ gets bigger and bigger, and the effective mass of a particle, γm, becomes greater and greater. As γm increases, a particle's resistance to further acceleration increases, so that an applied force can never push it over the edge into velocities exceeding c. The relativistic factor, γ, appears as a modifier in many formulas for relativistic particles, and is plotted in Figure 5–2.

From Figure 5–2, you can see that that we don't really need to concern ourselves with γ and its effect on particle dynamics until

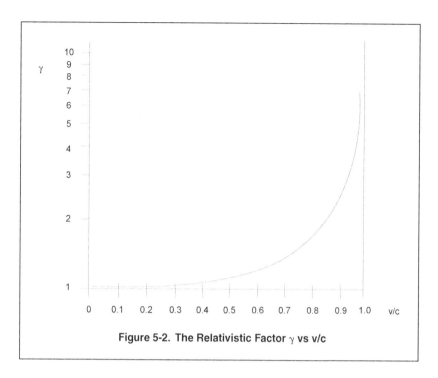

Figure 5-2. The Relativistic Factor γ vs v/c

velocities get very close to the speed of light. However, once we do approach that speed, γ becomes the dominant factor in shaping a particle's response to applied forces.

At this point, we need to introduce some common terminology that has evolved for use in discussing relativistic particles—those whose velocities approach the speed of light. The ratio v/c is frequently of interest, and by convention has come to be called β. Therefore, γ may be written as $1/(1 - \beta^2)^{1/2}$. The mass of a particle is often expressed in terms of an energy, using Einstein's most popular formula, $E = mc^2$. Using this relationship, the mass of an electron, 9.11×10^{-31} kg, corresponds to an energy of 8.2×10^{-14} Joules, and the mass of a proton, 1.67×10^{-27} kg, corresponds to 1.5×10^{-10} Joules.[5] The energies corresponding to the masses of electrons, protons, and other sub-atomic particles are very small, and it's common when dealing with small quantities to introduce new units which make them appear larger. The electron volt (1 eV = 1.6×10^{-19} Joules) is the traditional unit of energy in particle physics. Physically, it represents the amount of energy which a particle having the electrical charge of an electron (1.6×10^{-19} Joules) gains

267

when accelerated by an electrical potential of one volt. In terms of
this unit, the mass of an electron is 0.511 MeV, and that of a proton
is 938 MeV. (1 MeV = 10^6eV.) Therefore, a traditional rule of thumb
is that the mass of an electron is about half an MeV, and that of a
proton is about one GeV (1 GeV = 1000 MeV.)

In addition to its mass, a particle has some kinetic energy associated with its motion. You may recall from Chapter 2 that the kinetic
energy of a bullet with mass M and velocity v is K = $Mv^2/2$. The
kinetic energy of a relativistic particle is K = $(\gamma - 1) mc^2$. This definition may seem strange at first, but it can easily be shown[6] that for
v << c it reduces to the traditional expression, K = $mv^2/2$. The kinetic energy of a particle, $(\gamma - 1)mc^2$, is equal to its mass expressed
in energy units, mc^2, when γ = 2. A good rule of thumb is that particles must be treated relativistically when their kinetic energy is
comparable to their rest energy, or mass expressed in units of energy. This corresponds to a velocity of about 0.7c. The sum of the
kinetic energy and rest energy of a particle, γmc^2, is often referred
to as its total energy, though of course only the kinetic energy of a
particle may be deposited in a target, damaging it.

When particles are relativistic, some of the distinctions between
them tend to disappear. This is illustrated in Table 5–1, which
shows parameters for an electron and a proton, each having a kinetic energy of 2 GeV.

The mass of a proton is about 2,000 times greater than that of an
electron. If it were non-relativistic, the momentum of a proton
would be about 45 times greater than that of an electron at the
same kinetic energy. Yet at energies where both are relativistic,
there is hardly any distinction between the momentum of an electron and that of a proton. This is because the lighter electron has a

Particle	Kinetic Energy K (GeV)	$\gamma = 1 + K/mc^2$	$v/c = (1-1/\gamma^2)^{1/2}$	Momentum $P = \gamma mv$ (kg m/sec)
Electron	2	4000	0.999999938	1.1×10^{-18}
Proton	2	3	0.943	1.4×10^{-18}

Table 5-1. Relativistic Parameters for Energetic Electrons and Protons

much greater γ, making its effective mass, γm, much closer to that of the heavier proton. In this and other ways, we'll often encounter surprising results when dealing with the relativistic particles which comprise particle beams. These results may run counter to our experience, since velocities near the speed of light are not a part of that experience. This can make the interpretation of particle beam phenomena difficult.

Major Forces Affecting Charged-Particle Beams

We're now in a position to look at the major forces affecting a charged-particle beam (CPB) as it propagates. Let's consider the idealized CPB shown in Figure 5–3.

The CPB shown in the figure is an assembly of n particles per cubic centimeter, each having a charge q and a velocity v. This assembly is confined to what is effectively an infinitely long cylinder of radius w. What are the electric and magnetic fields resulting from these particles, and how do these fields affect their motion? Using Maxwell's equations, it can be shown that the electric field associated with these particles grows linearly with the distance, r, from the center of the beam, reaching a maximum value of $E = qnw/2\epsilon_o$ at the beam's surface. For r > w, E falls off from this maximum as $1/r$. The direction of this field is radially outward, and the resulting force pushes the particles apart, making the beam expand. This behavior is an example of the well known fact that like charges repel one another. The particles in the beam, having the same charge, exert repulsive forces on one another.

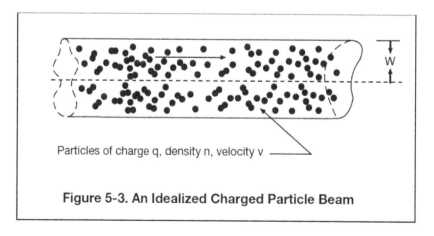

Particles of charge q, density n, velocity v

Figure 5-3. An Idealized Charged Particle Beam

Similarly, Maxwell's equations may be used to show that the magnetic field resulting from the current flow that these moving particles represent is proportional to r for r < w, and decays as $1/r$ for r > w, reaching a maximum value of $B = qnvw/2c^2\epsilon_0$ at r=w. The direction of the magnetic field is circular, surrounding the beam, and results in a force which is radially inward, tending to make the beam contract. This phenomenon represents the attraction of parallel currents that is commonly discussed in elementary physics texts. Figure 5–4 is a plot of these electric and magnetic fields, along with a sketch to indicate why they are repulsive and attractive, respectively.[7]

Because of the electric and magnetic fields shown in Figure 5–4, a particle at the surface of the beam feels a net force $F = nq^2w(1 - v^2/c^2)/2\epsilon_0 = nq^2w/2\epsilon_0\gamma^2$. As you can see, this force involves a factor of $1 - v^2/c^2$. The first term in this factor results from the repulsive electric force, and the second from the attractive, magnetic force. Since v is always less than c, the repulsive term will always dominate, and the beam will tend to spread. This is why neutral particle beams, whose particles are not charged and therefore do not repel one another, are favored for applications in the vacuum of space. We'll see later that other phenomena which arise when a charged particle beam (CPB) propagates in the atmosphere can serve to negate the repulsive force just discussed, making a CPB more suited to atmospheric applications.

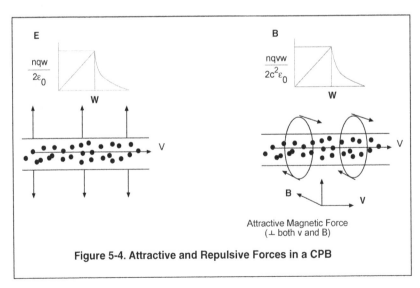

Figure 5-4. Attractive and Repulsive Forces in a CPB

What are the magnitudes of the electric and magnetic fields we've been discussing? Suppose that the CPB shown in Figure 5–3 has particles with a charge, q, equal to the electron charge: a density, n, of $10^{17}/m^3$ (8 orders of magnitude below the atmospheric density of $10^{25}/m^3$), a radius, w, of 1 cm, and a velocity, v, of 0.9c. These values result in an electric field at the surface of the beam of $E = qnw/2\epsilon_o = 9 \times 10^6$ V/m, and a magnetic field of $B = nqvw/2c^2\epsilon_o = 270$ Gauss. By contrast, naturally occurring electric and magnetic fields at the earth's surface are on the order of 100 V/m and 0.5 Gauss, respectively.[8] Electric fields on the order of 3 $\times$ 10^6 V/m are sufficient to induce the electrical breakdown of the earth's atmosphere and produce lightning. Clearly, the electric and magnetic fields of a particle beam will be important in determining its behavior.

Particle Beam Characteristics

So far, we've described particle beams in terms of particle mass, density, charge, velocity, and so on. These are the fundamental quantities which enter into Maxwell's equations for electric and magnetic fields, and into the force equation which tells us how the particles respond to these fields. But these aren't the quantities typically quoted by beam engineers, who prefer to speak in terms of the current their beams carry, the energy of their particles, and the brightness their beam possesses. We need to relate this traditional terminology to the more fundamental quantities we've been using, as well as to parameters which can be related to damage criteria, such as the number of Joules or Watts deposited by the beam on its target.

Current, as electricians use the term, is a measure of the flow of electricity. The unit of current is the *Ampere*. One Ampere is a Coulomb of charge passing through a wire in one second. Imagine that current is being carried through a wire of radius w by some charged particles, as shown in Figure 5–5. If there are n particles per cubic centimeter, and each has a charge of q Coulombs, then there are nq Coulombs per cubic centimeter. The quantity nq is known as the *charge density*, and is commonly denoted by ρ. If the particles in Figure 5–5 are moving at a velocity v, nqv Coulombs will pass through each square centimeter of the wire in one second. The quantity nqv is commonly called the *current*

271

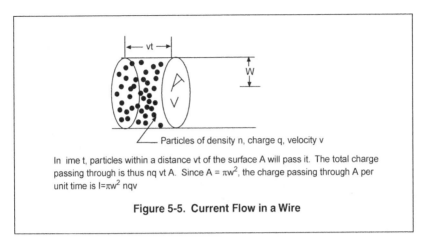

Particles of density n, charge q, velocity v

In ime t, particles within a distance vt of the surface A will pass it. The total charge passing through is thus nq vt A. Since A = πw^2, the charge passing through A per unit time is I=πw^2 nqv

Figure 5-5. Current Flow in a Wire

density, and denoted j. The current in the wire, or the total number of Coulombs passing through its cross-section each second, is I = $\pi w^2 j$ = π $w^2 nqv$.

Of course, the particles in a particle beam aren't confined to a wire, but nevertheless they are generally flowing in a straight line with a reasonably well defined radius. Therefore, the current in a particle beam can be defined as I = $\pi w^2 nqv$. The particle beam of radius 1 cm whose surface fields we calculated earlier had particles of density $10^{17}/m^3$, velocity 0.9c, and charge 1.6 × 10^{-19} Coul. This corresponds to a current of 1,360 Amp (1.36 kAmp).

It requires more than current to characterize a particle beam. Since I = $\pi w^2 nqv$, the same current can be achieved in a beam with particles of high density and low velocity, or of low density and high velocity. This ambiguity is resolved by providing the kinetic energy of the particles in electron Volts.[9] As we have seen, K can be related directly to the velocity of the particles, through the relationship K = $(\gamma - 1)mc^2$, where $\gamma = 1/(1 - v^2/c^2)^{1/2}$. In the beam used previously as an example, a velocity of 0.9c corresponds to a γ of 2.29 and a kinetic energy of about 0.7 MeV if the particles are electrons, for which mc^2 = 0.5 Mev.

How can the energy of individual particles and the beam's current be related to such macroscopic parameters as the total energy or power carried by the beam? If each particle has an energy K, then the energy density (J/cm^3) in the beam is nK, just as the charge density is nq when each particle carries a charge q. Just as the charge density, nq, becomes the current density, nqv, when multiplied by the particle velocity v, so also the energy density, nK, becomes the power density or beam intensity, Knv. If K is in Joules, n in cm^{-3}, and v in cm/sec, then Knv will be in $Joules/cm^2/sec$, or $Watts/cm^2$. So, the beam parameters we've been using for illustrative purposes (n = $10^{17}/m^3$, v = 0.9c, K = 0.7 MeV) correspond to an energy density of 1.1×10^4 J/m^3., and an intensity of S = 3×10^{12} W/m^2 (3×10^8 W/cm^2). If the beam has a total duration (pulse width) of t_p, the fluence (J/cm^2) it delivers is just F = St_p. Table 5–2 provides a translation guide which can be used for conversions among the quantities commonly employed in fundamental physics, beam engineering, and weaponeering.

The quantities in Table 5–2 characterize an ideal beam, in which there is no variation in K or v among the particles. In reality, no beam is perfect, and a beam will consist of particles having a distribution of energies and velocities about their nominal, or average, values. Therefore, the complete characterization of a particle beam requires some measure of its deviation from perfection to supplement the nominal beam parameters in Table 5–2. The most significant way in which a beam can deviate from the ideal is if the velocities of its particles have a significant component perpendicular to the direction of beam motion. In this case, the beam will diverge, or spread with distance, as illustrated in Figure 5–6.

In Figure 5–6 we see the contrast between a perfect beam, with each particle's velocity identical and oriented in the same direction, and a real beam, where each particle's velocity is slightly different, both in magnitude and direction. It's convenient to express any in-

Fundamental Physics	Beam Engineering	Weaponeering
Particle charge, q	Current, 1	Beam intensity, S
	$I = nqv\ \pi w^2$	$S = nKv$
Beam radius, w		
Particle density, n	Kinetic Energy, K	Beam Fluence, F
	$\gamma = 1/(1-v^2/c^2)^{1/2}$	$F = S\ t_p$
Particle velocity, v	$K = (\gamma - 1)mc^2$	
	Pulse Width, t_p	Pulse Width, t_p

Table 5-2. Quantities Used to Characterize Particle Beams

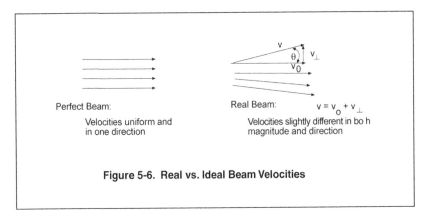

Perfect Beam:
Velocities uniform and in one direction

Real Beam: $v = v_0 + v_\perp$
Velocities slightly different in bo h magnitude and direction

Figure 5-6. Real vs. Ideal Beam Velocities

dividual particle velocity, v, as the sum of the velocity v_0 which an ideal particle would have, and an additional velocity, $v_\perp$ which represents the deviation of that particle's velocity from the ideal, as illustrated in the figure.[10] When the square of $v_\perp$ is taken and averaged over all the particles in the beam, we have a quantity, $< v_\perp{}^2>$, which represents in an average way the degree to which the particles deviate from ideal motion. From this quantity, an average *perpendicular temperature*, $T_\perp = \gamma m< v_\perp{}^2>/2k$ can be defined, where k ($=1.38 \times 10^{-23}$ Joules/°K) is Boltzmann's constant. This quantity has a simple physical interpretation as the temperature associated with the random motion of the beam particles in directions perpendicular to the direction of beam transport, just as the temperature of a gas is a measure of the average motion of the particles in the gas, a random energy divided by Boltzmann's constant. This concept of a random beam temperature is of considerable utility, and will allow us to discuss some aspects of beam motion and expansion by analogy with similar behavior in an ideal gas.

Other concepts of value in characterizing the deviation of a particle beam from perfection are the *divergence* and *brightness* of the beam. A beam's divergence is just the average[11] of the angle, $\theta = v_\perp/v_0$, by which the direction of motion of a particle deviates from the beam axis (Figure 5–6). As we saw in Chapter 1, a beam of divergence θ will expand to have a radius $w = z\theta$ after it has propagated a distance z. This is the case for a neutral particle beam. However, the repulsive and attractive forces that a charged particle beam feels as a result of the charges on its particles tend to dominate in determining how a charged beam's radius changes with distance. Therefore, divergence is not as useful a concept for a charged particle beam as for a neutral particle beam.

In Chapter 3, the *brightness* of a laser was defined as the beam's power (Watts) divided by a measure of the beam's divergence, the solid angle into which the beam was spreading (see Figure 3–20). Thus, a bright beam will send a lot of power into a narrow cone as it propagates. There is a related concept for particle beams. The brightness of a particle beam is defined as the beam current per unit cross-sectional area per unit solid angle, or $B = I/[\pi\, w^2\, (\pi\theta^2)]$, where I is the beam's current, w its radius, and θ its divergence. This parameter is different from the brightness defined for lasers, although it still relates to the fundamental idea of how much power is being sent into how small an angle. Current is a more natural parameter for beam engineers, and is equivalent to power, since power is energy per time and current is charge per time. Power is related to current by a factor of K/q, where K is the kinetic energy and q the charge carried by a beam particle. fn this way, you can convert the brightness quoted in the beam literature to that quoted in the laser literature, making appropriate connections between these quantities.[12]

Propagation in a Vacuum

Having discussed some of the fundamental concepts and terminology associated with particle beams, we can now consider how they propagate. The propagation characteristics of charged and neutral particle beams are different, both in space (a vacuum) and in the atmosphere. Therefore, we'll treat each of these cases separately, beginning with the simplest case of neutral particle beams propagating in a vacuum.

Neutral Particle Beams in a Vacuum

The concept of divergence is sufficient to understand neutral beam propagation in a vacuum. In propagating a distance z, a neutral beam's radius will grow to a size $w = w_0 + z\theta$, where θ is the beam's divergence and w_0 is the beam's radius as it emerges from the particle accelerator. Consequently, a beam's intensity will decrease by a factor of $[w_0/(w_0 + z\theta)]^2$ in propagating a distance z. This implies that a beam of a given output intensity

(W/cm²) can propagate only a limited distance before its intensity falls below that necessary to damage a target in the time available. Suppose, for example, that w_o is 1 cm, and that the beam can expand by no more than a factor of 10 before its intensity becomes unacceptably low. Then the criterion $z\theta = 10$ cm would define the maximum range, z, achievable with a beam of divergence θ. Figure 5–7 shows combinations of z and θ which will satisfy different criteria for $z\theta$. Since propagation in a vacuum implies that the beam and its target are in the vacuum of space, strategic ranges are clearly of interest in this section. These ranges might lie somewhere between low earth orbit, 200 km, and the altitude of a geosynchronous satellite, about 40,000 km. If we don't want the beam to waste energy by expanding to a size that exceeds a typical target, its radius needs to be kept below something on the order of 10 m. Figure 5–7 tells us that divergences on the order of microradians or better are required if the beam is not to expand beyond 10 m over strategic ranges.

We have seen that the divergence of a particle beam is given by $q = <v_\perp>/v_o$, where $<v_\perp>$ is the average particle's speed perpendicular to the direction of beam propagation, and v_o is the average velocity along the direction of beam propagation.[13] From

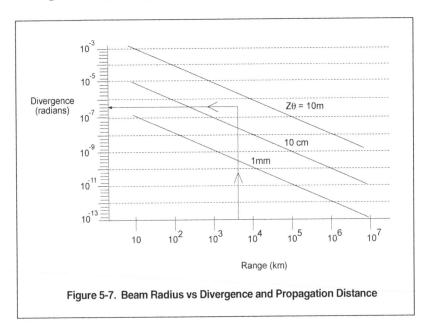

Figure 5-7. Beam Radius vs Divergence and Propagation Distance

this definition, you can see that there are two ways in which you can reduce a beam's divergence θ. You can decrease $<v_\perp>$, or you can increase v_0. The second approach is limited—the particle's speed cannot exceed the speed of light no matter how much energy is given to it. Therefore, a beam divergence of 1 μrad or less requires that $<v_\perp>$ be less than $10^{-6}c$, or 300 m/sec. As a point of comparison, this ratio is approximately that of the speed of sound to the speed of light. Clearly, propagation of a neutral particle beam without significant divergence requires that the beam quality be very good, with little deviation of any individual particle's velocity from that of the main beam. Current technology results in neutral particle beams with a divergence of just about a μrad, and there is clear research interest in reducing this value so as to increase useful beam ranges.

Charged Particle Beams in a Vacuum

Expansion from Electrostatic Repulsion. Divergence due to differences in the motion of individual particles is responsible for the spread of neutral particle beams. For charged particle beams, there is also the more important effect of the mutual repulsion that the particles in the beam feel. You will recall that the net force felt by particles at the surface of a charged particle beam is given by $F = nq^2w/2\epsilon_0(1 - v^2/c^2) = nq^2w/2\epsilon_0\gamma^2$, where n is the density of particles in the beam, v their velocity, w the beam radius, and ϵ_0 a constant (8.85×10^{-12} fd/m). This force is directed radially outward, and pushes the particles apart, so that w increases and n decreases. As with the neutral beam, w can't be allowed to increase too much, or the energy carried by the beam will disperse, and little of it will intersect the intended target.

The growth of a charged particle beam's radius, w, is not as easy to calculate as that of a neutral particle beam, since the forces which make it expand are themselves dependent on w. As w increases, n decreases as $1/w^2$, and the net force F decreases as well. The equation of motion for particles near the surface of the beam is $F = dP/dt = d(\gamma mv_\perp)/dt$, where $v_\perp$ is the velocity which these particles have in the direction perpendicular to the beam's motion. The beam's radius w grows at a rate $dw/dt = v_\perp$. The solution to these equations is shown in Figure 5–8. This figure shows the relative beam radius, w/w_o, as a function of time, measured in units of t_d, the "doubling time" that it takes for w to grow to $2w_o$.

Initially, the beam expands quadratically, with $w/w_o = (1 + t/t_d)^2$. Later in time, as repulsive electric forces decrease, the expansion becomes more linear, with the beam radius growing at a constant velocity. The doubling time, t_d, is given by $t_d^2 = 4m\epsilon_o\gamma^3/n_oq^2 = 4(mc^2)^2\ c\epsilon_o\gamma^3(\gamma-1)\beta^3/Sq^2$, where m and q are the particle mass and charge, and n_o is the initial density of particles in the beam. In the second form, the beam's density n_o has been written in terms of its intensity, $S = (\gamma-1)\ mc^2n_ov$ (W/cm²). This is a more useful form, since it's more straightforward to relate intensity to damage criteria than particle density. The expression for the doubling time agrees with what we would expect on an intuitive basis. The doubling time decreases, and a charged particle beam expands more rapidly, if the beam is comprised of light particles, which are easily accelerated, or is very dense which makes repulsive electrostatic forces greater. Conversely, the doubling time increases if the beam's particles are highly relativistic for two reasons. The greater relativistic mass, γm, increases a particle's resistance to acceleration, and attractive magnetic forces more nearly compensate for repulsive electric forces.

If we multiply the doubling time t_d by the speed of the particles in the beam, we get the range to which the beam can propagate in that time. It is clear from Figure 5–8 that within a few doubling times a beam will expand to the point where it is no longer useful as a directed energy weapon. Therefore, $z_d = vt_d$ can be taken as a

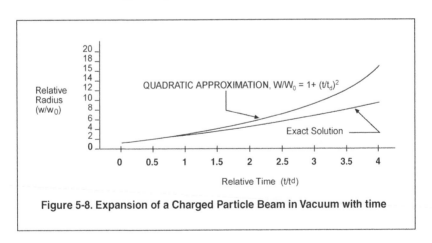

QUADRATIC APPROXIMATION, $W/W_0 = 1 + (t/t_d)^2$

Exact Solution

Relative Radius (w/w_0)

Relative Time (t/t_d)

Figure 5-8. Expansion of a Charged Particle Beam in Vacuum with time

measure of the useful range for a charged particle beam in vacuum. Figure 5–9 is a plot of z_d for electrons and protons as a function of kinetic energy for an intensity of S = 10^7 W/cm^2.

You can see from Figure 5–9 that electrostatic repulsion severely limits the range and utility of charged particle beams in a vacuum.[14] Only for energies in excess of a GeV do ranges even begin to approach the strategic ranges for which a space based particle beam would have some utility. And since z_d varies as $1/S^{1/2}$, it's a rather weak function of beam intensity. This means that we can't substantially improve the picture shown in Figure 5–9 by going to a less intense beam, and still hope to damage targets within reasonable time scales. Therefore, neutral particle beams are a more viable alternative for strategic applications in space.

Effects due to External Fields. Charged particles are affected not only by the electric and magnetic fields which they themselves generate, but also by any externally applied electric or magnetic fields. The most significant of these is the magnetic field of the earth. You will recall that a magnetic field produces a force which is perpendicular to both the magnetic field and the particle's direction of motion (see Figure 5–1). This causes charged particles to move in curved paths. Figure 5–10 illustrates the simple case

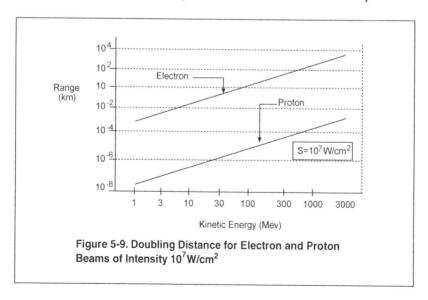

Figure 5-9. Doubling Distance for Electron and Proton Beams of Intensity 10^7W/cm^2

where the particle's motion and the direction of the magnetic field are perpendicular to one another.

Shown in Figure 5–10 is a particle of charge q, mass m, and velocity v. Throughout the region of space in which the particle travels there is a magnetic field of strength B, pointing into the plane of the paper. The force which a magnetic field produces on a charged particle is perpendicular to both v and B and has a magnitude qvB sin θ, where θ is the angle between v and B. In the situation sketched in Figure 5–10, the force is qvB, since B is perpendicular to v, and sin 90° = 1. This force will cause the particle to turn, and as it turns the force will turn as well, orienting itself so that it's always perpendicular to the particle's instantaneous velocity. As a result, the particle will travel in a circle. A good

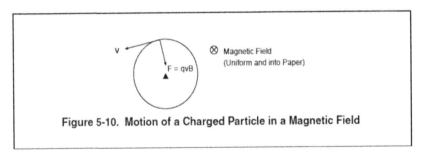

Figure 5-10. Motion of a Charged Particle in a Magnetic Field

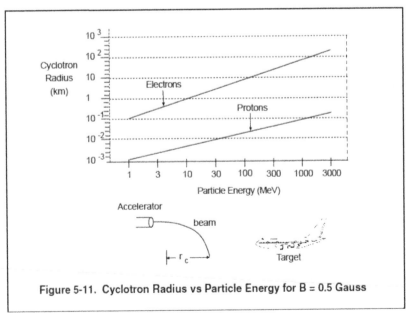

Figure 5-11. Cyclotron Radius vs Particle Energy for B = 0.5 Gauss

280

analogy is that of a stone swung in a circle on a string. The string exerts a force which is always inward and perpendicular to the direction the stone is moving, and the stone follows a circular path.

It's a straigntforward task to solve the equation of motion for a charged particle moving in a uniform magnetic field as illustrated in Figure 5–10. The radius of the circle traveled is $r_c = m\gamma v/qB$, where r_c is known as the *cyclotron radius*.[15] Figure 5–11 is a plot of r_c as a function of particle energy for electrons and protons in a magnetic field of strength 0.5 Gauss, a value roughly equal to the magnetic field of the earth. This figure gives a feeling for the type of deflections which a particle beam might experience while propagating. You can see clearly that except at very high energies r_c will actually be less than the ranges over which we might wish to employ a charged particle beam. This may prevent the beam from reaching its target, as indicated in the sketch shown in Figure 5–11. Clearly, the curvature of a charged particle beam propagating in the magnetic field of the earth must be taken into account in aiming the beam.

Of course, the magnetic field of the earth is far more compex than a uniform value of 0.5 Gauss, and in general a particle beam won't be propagating in a direction perpendicular to this field, whose orientation changes with latitude, longitude, and altitude. Indeed, the magnitude of the earth's magnetic field changes with time of day and season as well, since its affected by the *solar wind*—energetic particles emitted from the sun.[16] Since the precise nature of the earth's magnetic field can't be known or predicted in advance, charged particle beams in a vacuum would need to engage targets through a "shoot-look-shoot" technique, with a rough guess made of the beam's propagation, the beam path followed, and adjustments made to bring it toward the target. This process of iteration and adjustment would be analogous to the adaptive optics employed with lasers to deal with the bending and distortion of the beam resulting from thermal fluctuations in the atmosphere (see Chapter 3).

Summary: Propagation in a Vacuum

1. A neutral particle beam's radius, w, will grow with distance as $w = z\theta$, where θ is the beam's divergence. This divergence arises from the small, sideways components of velocity which

the particles in any real beam will have. If w becomes too great, the energy in a beam will no longer be efficiently directed at a target. Figure 5–7 shows the resulting limitations on beam range if w is to remain less than a specified value.

2. Charged particle beams will expand more rapidly than neutral particle beams because charged particles repel one another. The distance over which a charged particle beam will double in size is shown in Figure 5–9 for a beam of intensity 10^7 W/cm². The distances shown in this figure scale as $1/\sqrt{S}$ to other intensities.

3. Charged particle beams are also affected by external electric and magnetic fields. The most significant of these is the magnetic field of the earth, which makes the beam particles travel in a curved path. Figure 5–11 provides a rough estimate of the radius of curvature of this path as a function of particle energy. The specific path followed by a charged particle beam in the magnetic field of the earth will vary with latitude, longitude, altitude, time of day, time of year, and even sunspot activity, due to the sun's effect on the earth's magnetic field.

Implications

A charged particle beam is impractical for use in the vacuum of space. Even at energies well in excess of those produced by today's particle accelerators, a charged beam will expand by an unacceptable amount in a very short distance—kilometers or less. Therefore, only neutral particle beams are a viable option for space applications. Even these, as Figure 5–7 shows, will require a very good (< 1 μrad) beam divergence if they are to be useful over the long ranges associated with engagements in space.

Propagation in the Atmosphere

Neutral Particle Beams in the Atmosphere

Just as charged particle beams are impractical for applications in space, so neutral particle beams are impractical for applications in the atmosphere. This is because the neutral particles in the beam will collide with molecules of oxygen, nitrogen, and other substances in the atmosphere. As a result of these collisions the beam particles will become ionized, losing the electrons which make them electrically neutral. Thus, as it propagates through the air, a neutral particle beam becomes a charged particle beam. It is not a very good one, since the collisions which ionize the beam particles also impart momentum and velocity in the sideways direction, increasing the divergence of the beam. This process is shown in Figure 5–12. The probability of the event illustrated in Figure 5–12, and its threat to NPB propagation, depends upon the density of the atmosphere. Collisions are more likely if there are more molecules to collide with. Therefore, a key problem in neutral beam propagation is to find the greatest density, or lowest altitude, at which the beam will propagate.

The probability for the collision illustrated in Figure 5–12 is determined by the collision *cross section*, σ.[17] Imagine that the molecule shown in the figure has a cross section σ (m²), and that there are N molecules per cubic meter. If the neutral particle beam has a cross-sectional area A ($= \pi w^2$), and propagates through a thickness dz of atmosphere, it will encounter AN dz molecules. These will close out a fraction σ AN dz/A $= \sigma$ N dz of the beam's cross-sectional area. Therefore, the fraction of beam particles that will collide in propagating through a distance dz of the atmosphere is σN dz (see Chapter 3, Figures 3–22 and 3–23). Since the current and intensity of the beam are proportional to the density of particles in it, these quantities will be reduced by the same fraction. For example, the decrease in current I in propagating a distance dz must be dI $= -$I σN dz. This equation has the solution $I = I_0 e^{-\sigma Nz}$. This means that the beam's current decreases exponentially with propagation distance, and is reduced by a fraction 1/e (about 1/3) in propagating a distance 1/σN. Therefore, a good criterion for neutral beam propagation in the atmosphere is that the intended range of the beam be on the order of 1/σN or less.

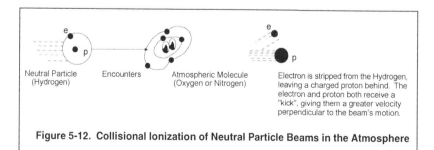

Neutral Particle   Encounters   Atmospheric Molecule
(Hydrogen)   (Oxygen or Nitrogen)

Electron is stripped from the Hydrogen, leaving a charged proton behind. The electron and proton both receive a "kick", giving them a greater velocity perpendicular to the beam's motion.

Figure 5-12. Collisional Ionization of Neutral Particle Beams in the Atmosphere

283

What is the cross section for a neutral particle such as hydrogen to be ionized as it collides with particles in the atmosphere? Since the atmosphere is primarily oxygen and nitrogen, the relevant cross sections will be those for ionizing collisions with these molecules. Figure 5–13 shows the ionization cross section for neutral hydrogen encountering O_2 and N_2 as a function of kinetic energy.[18] The cross section vanishes if the available kinetic energy is less than the ionization potential, or energy required to strip an electron from a hydrogen atom (13.6 eV). Above that energy, σ rises rapidly to a few times 10^{-16} cm^2 in the neighborhood of 100 keV, after which it gradually declines, and is about an order of magnitude less between 1–10 MeV. These cross sections lead to the general rule of thumb that the "size" of an atom or molecule is about 10^{-8} cm (1 Ångstrom).[19]

Let's use Figure 5–13 to estimate the minimum altitude at which a 1 MeV neutral particle beam might be used to engage a target 100 km away. This requires that $1/N\sigma$ be 100 km or greater. From the figure, σ is about 10^{-16} cm^2 for both N_2 and O_2 at 1 MeV kinetic energy. Therefore, in making an estimate, we can consider both oxygen and nitrogen the same, and treat the atmosphere as a homogeneous gas with a cross section of 10^{-16} cm^2 and density N. The requirement $1/N\sigma > 100$ km corresponds to the requirement that N be less than about 10^9 molecules per cubic centimeter. This corresponds to a density of about 10^{-10} that at sea level (3 $\times$ 10^{19}/cm^3), which is a pretty rarefied atmosphere, and a pretty high

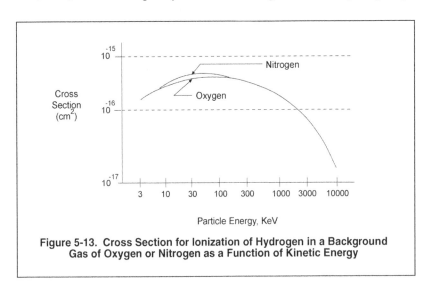

Figure 5-13. Cross Section for Ionization of Hydrogen in a Background Gas of Oxygen or Nitrogen as a Function of Kinetic Energy

altitude. Figure 5–14 is a plot of atmospheric density as a function of altitude.[20] From this plot, you can see that $10^9/cm^3$ is the density at an altitude of about 200 km. This is the altitude range (known as *low earth orbit*) at which the space shuttle operates. Clearly, neutral particle beams have little utility for applications in which significant penetration of the atmosphere is required.

The criterion $1/N\sigma > z$, where z is the intended range of a neutral particle beam, may be used together with data on the cross section for neutral beam ionization as a function of particle energy (Figure 5–13) and data on density as a function of altitude (Figure 5–14) to plot the minimum altitude for neutral beam employment as a function of range and particle energy. Such a plot is shown in Figure 5–15. This figure makes it clear that neutral particle beam employment is limited at reasonable particle energies and realistic ranges to altitudes on the order of 100 km or greater. Clearly, the neutral particle beam is a device suited to vacuum, as opposed to atmospheric, applications.

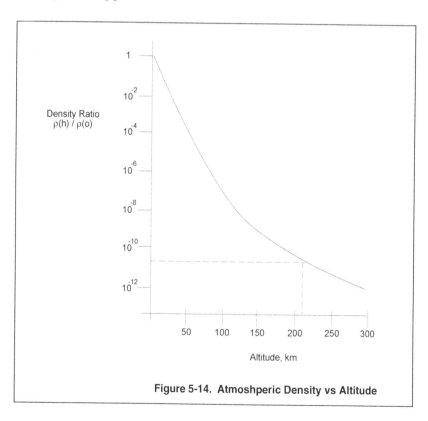

Figure 5-14. Atmoshperic Density vs Altitude

Charged Particle Beams in the Atmosphere

Charge Neutralization. From our earlier description of charged particle beam expansion (Figure 5–91) it might seem as though there would be no way in which a charged particle beam (CPB) could find application as a directed energy weapon. This is not the case, however, since a CBP in the atmosphere experiences a phenomenon known as *charge neutralization*. Charge neutralization has the effect of eliminating beam expansion through electrostatic repulsion. The sequence of events involved is illustrated in Figure 5–16.

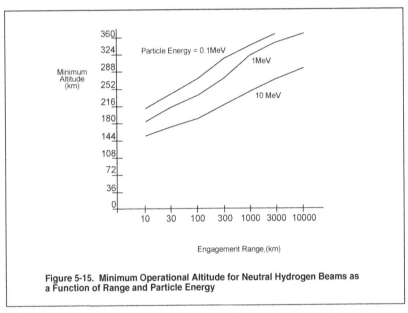

Figure 5-15. Minimum Operational Altitude for Neutral Hydrogen Beams as a Function of Range and Particle Energy

As a charged particle beam enters the atmosphere, it encounters atmospheric molecules (Figure 5–16a). Just as these molecules could ionize the particles in a neutral beam through collisions, so the particles in a CPB can ionize them through collision. (The opposite can't occur in this case since the particles comprising a CPB, electrons or protons, are already ionized, and have no further charges to be stripped off through collision.) As the beam passes through the air, the air becomes ionized, going from a neutral gas to an ionized plasma. The charged electrons and nuclei in the atmospheric plasma are free to carry electrical current (Figure 5–16b).

We saw earlier in the chapter that there is a strong electric field associated with the charge carried by the particles in the beam (see Figure 5–4). This field is responsible for the repulsive force that the particles in the beam feel, and it also exerts a force on the newly ionized atmospheric particles. Particles whose charge is the same as that of the particles in the beam are repelled from the beam volume, while those whose charge is opposite are attracted into it (Figure 5–16c). The net result of all this action is to move the charge imbalance to the surface of the beam, shorting out the electric field in the beam's interior. This is an illustration of the general principle that there can be no electrical fields on the interior of a conducting medium.[21]

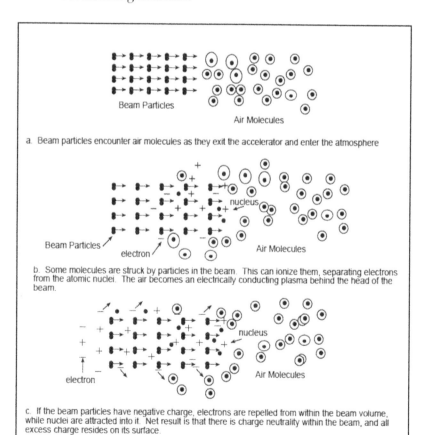

a. Beam particles encounter air molecules as they exit the accelerator and enter the atmosphere

b. Some molecules are struck by particles in the beam. This can ionize them, separating electrons from the atomic nuclei. The air becomes an electrically conducting plasma behind the head of the beam.

c. If the beam particles have negative charge, electrons are repelled from within the beam volume, while nuclei are attracted into it. Net result is that there is charge neutrality within the beam, and all excess charge resides on its surface.

Figure 5-16. Sequence of Events in Charge Neutralization

The configuration of electrical charges and the resulting radial electrical field in a *charge neutralized* CPB are illustrated in Figure 5–17.

If charge neutralization is to permit stable CPB propagation in the atmosphere, it must occur more rapidly than the beam can expand through the mutual repulsion of its particles. Therefore, we need to compare the time scale for charge neutralization with the beam doubling time illustrated in Figure 5–9, which is the time scale for beam expansion.

It is relatively straightforward to derive from Maxwell's equations that in a medium whose conductivity is Σ, any excess electrical charge density, ρ_o will decay in time exponentially as $\rho(t) = \rho_o e^{-\Sigma t/\epsilon_o}$. The electrical conductivity, Σ, is just the constant of proportionality between the electrical field at any point in space and the resulting current density, j: $j = \Sigma E$.[22] From this relationship, you can see that the charge density will decay by a factor of $1/e$ in a time $t_n = \epsilon_o/\Sigma$, where t_n may be considered a charge neutralization time.[23]

The conductivity of an ionized gas is given by $\Sigma = ne^2/mv$, where n is the density of current carriers (primarily electrons, since they're lighter and can respond more quickly to an applied electrical field), e and m the charge and mass of these carriers, and v the frequency of collisions between the current carriers and particles which retard their flow, such as ions or neutral molecules. The collision frequency v depends upon the density of the background gas and its degree of ionization. For singly-ionized air at sea level, it's approximately 10^{14}/sec. The resulting conductivity is

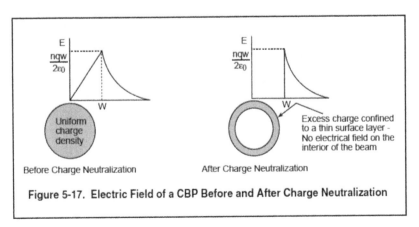

Figure 5-17. Electric Field of a CBP Before and After Charge Neutralization

about 8000 mho/m, and the corresponding neutralization time, ϵ_o/Σ, is about 10^{-15} sec.[24] By contrast, Figure 5–9 shows beam doubling times which are about 5 orders of magnitude longer. At sea level, therefore, charge neutralization will occur far more rapidly than beam expansion. This means that for CPB propagation in the atmosphere, there is a mechanism with the potential to negate the undesirable effects of beam expansion.[25]

What happens at altitudes above sea level? To a first approximation, the conductivity of the ionized atmosphere is unaffected, since $\Sigma = ne^2/mv$, and both n and v are proportional to the density of the atmosphere. As a practical matter, however, charge neutralization is not possible if the atmospheric density falls below that of the particles in the beam. In this case, ionizing the atmosphere cannot provide sufficient charge for neutralization. You'll recall that a beam's current, I, is related to its radius, w, and the density of its particles, n, through $I = nqv\pi w^2$. Therefore, the density of particles in a beam of current I and radius w is $n = I/qv\, w^2$. This density may be compared with a plot of atmospheric density as a function of altitude (Figure 5–14) to find the maximum altitude at which a beam of current I and radius w can propagate, as shown in Figure 5–18.

You can see from Figure 5–18 that charged particle beams with sufficient current to be of interest from the standpoint of weapon

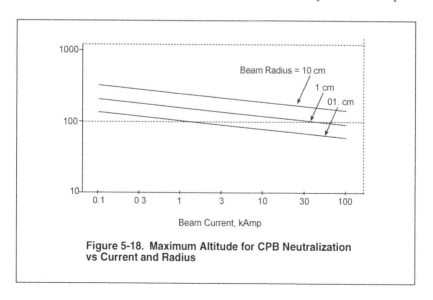

Figure 5-18. Maximum Altitude for CPB Neutralization vs Current and Radius

applications are limited to operation at altitudes below about 200 km. At altitudes above this, the air is too thin to permit charge neutralization, and beam expansion will limit propagation as in a vacuum. It is interesting to note (Figure 5–15) that neutral particle beams are for the most part constrained to operate at altitudes above 200 km, since at lower altitudes they are ionized, and lose their integrity. The utility of particle beams as weapons therefore falls into two distinct categories: neutral beams in space and charged beams within the atmosphere.

The Evolution of Beam Radius. A charged particle beam feels two forces: an electrical force which pushes it apart, and a magnetic force which squeezes it together. In space, the electrical force always dominates, and a CPB will expand. We have just seen that in the atmosphere, charge neutralization can eliminate the electrical force. However, charge neutralization won't eliminate the magnetic force, which depends upon the beam current. Even though the net charge on the interior of the beam is zero, the net current is not, since only the beam particles have a net motion downstream. The atmospheric electrons and ions which neutralize the charge are standing still, relatively speaking, as the particles in the beam stream through them. Therefore, a charge-neutralized beam will initially pinch down in radius under the influence of the magnetic force which remains.

Of course, the pinching and reduction of a beam's radius under the influence of its self-generated magnetic field can't go on forever. Something must arise to counteract that force and establish an equilibrium radius. That something is the small, random sideways components to the velocities of the particles in the beam. This sideways motion arises from fluctuations and inhomogeneities in the performance of the accelerator which creates the beam, as well as from collisions in which beam particles encounter air molecules. An equilibrium radius is established when the outward pressure resulting from motion perpendicular to the beam is sufficient to counteract the inward magnetic force, as illustrated in Figure 5–19.

The problem of determining the equilibrium beam radius, w, when an inward "magnetic pressure" opposes an outward kinetic "temperature" is a standard one in plasma physics. It arises not only in particle beam propagation, but also when charged parti-

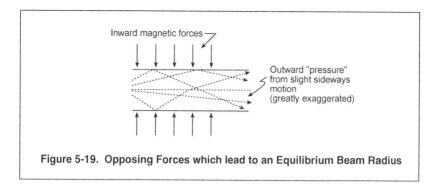

Inward magnetic forces

Outward "pressure"
from slight sideways
motion
(greatly exaggerated)

Figure 5-19. Opposing Forces which lead to an Equilibrium Beam Radius

cles are to be contained by externally applied magnetic fields, as in plasma fusion reactors.[26] In the case of a charged particle beam propagating in the atmosphere, there is an additional complication due to the fact that the beam's temperature is not a constant, but grows with distance as the beam propagates. As a beam propagates through the atmosphere, its particles continually encounter atmospheric molecules. They interact with one another, as in the collisions which produce the ionization that permits charge neutralization. In each of these collisions, a beam particle receives some small, sideways deflection. The effect of these interactions is to increase the beam's temperature as it propagates downstream. In effect, there is friction between the propagating beam and the atmosphere through which it moves. As the beam's temperature rises, its internal pressure increases, and its radius grows as it expands against the compressive magnetic force. In order to analyze the evolution of beam radius following charge neutralization, we need to consider the rate at which random energy or "temperature" is added to the beam, and how this energy is expended in pushing out the beam's boundary.

A simple estimate can be made by equating the energy added to the beam to the work done in expanding against the pinching magnetic force. Consider the situation shown in Figure 5–19. The total pinching force F per unit beam length is the magnetic force per particle, $nq^2w\beta^2/2\epsilon_o$, multiplied by the number of particles per unit length, $\pi w^2 n$. Since the beam current is $I = \pi w^2 nqv$, this force may be written as $F = I^2/2\epsilon_o wc^2$. If the temperature of the beam rises, and its radius increases from w to w + dw, the small increment of work, dW, done through this expansion is just $dW = F\,dw = [I^2/2\epsilon_o \pi c^2](dw/w)$. This last expression is a useful form, since the total current, I, is unaffected by the beam radius. Thus, the only variable in the expression is the fractional change in the beam radius, dw/w.

The work done in beam expansion must equal the energy given to the beam through collisions between its particles and those in the atmosphere. Suppose each particle's "perpendicular energy," $T = \gamma m <v_\perp^2>/2$, increases at a rate dT/dz. Since there are $\pi w^2 n$ particles per unit length, the beam's energy per unit length will be enhanced by an amount $dE = \pi w^2 n \, (dT/dz) \, dz$ in propagating a distance dz. Using the fact that the beam current is $I = \pi w^2 nqv$, we can write $dE = (dT/dz)(I/qv) \, dz$. Equating the energy deposited, dE, to the work done in expansion, dW, yields an equation for the beam radius as a function of propagation distance, $(dT/dz) (I/qv) \, dz = [I^2/2\epsilon_o \, \pi \, c^2] \, (dw/w)$. This equation is of a form we've seen several times before, and is easily solved to find $w(z) = w(o) \, \exp[(2\epsilon_o \, \pi \, c^2/Iqv)(dT/dz)]z$. The beam radius will grow exponentially with distance, and will grow by a factor of e (roughly 3) in a distance $z_g = Iqv/[2\epsilon_o \, c^2(dT/dz)]$. The radial growth distance z_g increases linearly with I, since high-current beams have stronger magnetic fields to hold them together, and is inversely proportional to (dT/dz), since a greater heating rate results in a more rapid expansion.

All we need to do to complete our analysis is to estimate dT/dz, the rate of increase in the perpendicular energy of the beam particles. It is a straightforward but tedious exercise to arrive at the estimate $dT/dz = 4\pi \, NZ \, q^2 e^2 \, lnQ/[\gamma M \, (4\pi\epsilon_o)^2 \, v^2]$. The various terms which appear in this expression and their physical interpretation are as follows:

- N is the density of molecules in the atmosphere, and Z is the number of electrons associated with each of these molecules. Beam particles collide primarily with the orbital electrons of atmospheric molecules, so that the rate of these collisions is proportional to NZ.

- The quantity q is the charge on a beam particle, and e the charge on an electron. The factor q^2e^2 reflects the fact that beam particles of greater charge will interact more strongly with electrons orbiting the molecules in the atmosphere.

- γM is just the relativistic mass of the beam particles. More massive and relativistic particles will be less deflected in their encounters with atmospheric particles.

- v is the velocity of the beam particles. The rate of energy addition is proportional to $1/v^2$ because beam particles which are moving more rapidly spend less time in the vicinity of a given atmospheric particle, and thus have less time to be affected by it.

The other quantities appearing in the expression for dT/dz are simply constants or factors which vary so little that we need not concern ourselves with them. A thorough discussion of the physics which underlies dT/dz may be found in most texts on electromagnetic theory.[27]

Our expression for dT/dz may be substituted into our expression for the distance over which the beam radius will grow by a factor of e, $z_g = Iqv/[2\epsilon_o \pi c^2(dT/dz)]$, to obtain an estimate of a charged particle beam's useful range as a function of particle type, energy, and beam current: $z_g = [2\beta^3\epsilon_o/Zcqe^2 \ln Q] \times [\gamma Mc^2I/N]$. This range is proportional to the total energy of the particles in the beam and the beam current, and is inversely proportional to the atmospheric density. As a numerical example, $z_g = 0.42$ meters for a 1 kAmp beam of MeV electrons at sea level, for which $\gamma = 3$, $Mc^2 = 0.5$ MeV, and $N = 3 \times 10^{25}/m^3$. It is a straightforward exercise to scale this result to other cases; Figure 5–20 is a plot of z_g as a function of beam current for different particles and energies.

You can see from Figure 5–20 that for a charged particle beam to achieve substantial range in the atmosphere requires high currents and either heavy or very relativistic particles. For example, $\gamma mc^2 = 1$ GeV corresponds either to protons of 1 MeV kinetic energy ($\gamma \approx 1$) or to electrons of 1 GeV kinetic energy ($\gamma \approx 2,000$). Currents of a few kiloamps are required as a minimum for engagements even over tactical ranges. The curves in Figure 5–20 scale as $1/N$, where N is the atmospheric density, so that at an altitude where N is $1/10$ of its value at sea level, the beam expansion distance will be greater than that shown in the figure by a factor of ten.

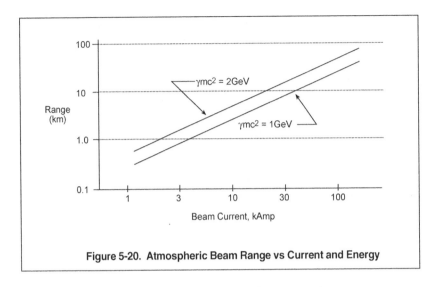

Figure 5-20. Atmospheric Beam Range vs Current and Energy

More generally, it may be that the atmospheric density varies significantly over the propagation path of a charged particle beam. In this case, dT/dz can no longer be considered a constant in integrating the expression for beam radius as a function of distance. The appropriate generalization is

$$w(z) = w(o) \exp[(2\epsilon_o \pi \, c^2/Iqv) \int_o^z (dT/dz)dz],$$

where the integral is taken over the propagation path. You may recall that a very similar situation was encountered in Chapter 3, when variations in atmospheric density along a laser beam's path had to be accounted for in evaluating the attenuation in beam intensity in propagating over that path. The simple model for the variation of atmospheric density with altitude which was used there may also be used in this case.

Within the lower atmosphere (0 – 120 km), atmospheric density varies exponentially with altitude.[28] That is, the density of molecules N(h) at altitude h is related to the density N(o) at sea level by the relationship N(h) = N(o) exp(–h/h_o), where the constant h_o is about 7 km. Since dT/dz is also proportional to N, we can say that dT/dz at some altitude h is equal to dT/dz at sea level multiplied by exp(–h/h_o).[29] Suppose a charged particle beam is fired into the air at some elevation angle $\emptyset$, as illustrated in Figure 5–21.

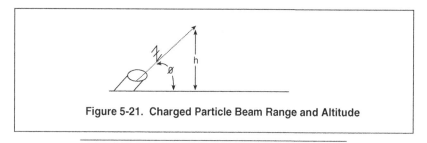

Figure 5-21. Charged Particle Beam Range and Altitude

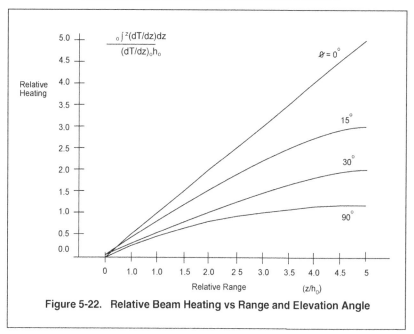

Figure 5-22. Relative Beam Heating vs Range and Elevation Angle

The altitude h is related to the beam range z and the elevation angle $\emptyset$ through the simple geometrical relationship h = z sin $\emptyset$. Using this relationship between h and z, we can evaluate $\int_0^z$ (dT/dz)dz to any range z. The result is shown in Figure 5–22.[30]

Figure 5–22 shows that the degree of heating and expansion experienced by a charged particle beam is not strongly affected by elevation angle as long as the range is less than h_o, the distance over which atmospheric density varies significantly. Beyond that, elevation angle makes a considerable difference. At $\emptyset$ = 0°, the beam propagates horizontally, density is constant, and the amount of heating increases linearly with distance. At $\emptyset$ = 90°, the beam propagates straight up and rapidly emerges from the atmosphere,

295

after which no further expansion due to heating should be expected.[31] At intermediate angles, the beam has greater and greater lengths of atmosphere to traverse, the total heating is greater, and it approaches a limiting value later.

You can use Figure 5–22 together with the.equation for beam expansion, $w(z) = w(0)\exp[(2\epsilon_0\pi c^2/Iqv)(dT/dz)]z$ to estimate a beam's growth at any range and elevation angle. All you need to do is evaluate $(dT/dz)z$ for propagation over a range h_0 in a constant density atmosphere at sea level, and then modify this result with the appropriate factor from Figure 5–22, substituting the result into the expansion equation. Suppose, for example, that the range to a target is $z = 21$ km, at an elevation angle of 30°. The relative range is $z/h_0 = 3$. From Figure 5–22, the relative heating at this range and elevation angle is about 1.5. This means that the beam radius at this range is $w(o)\exp[(2\epsilon_0\pi c^2/Iqv)(dT/dz)]z$, where dT/dz is evaluated at sea level and $z = 1.5\,h_0 = 10.5$ km. The sea level value of dT/dz is about 8.2×10^4 eV/m for MeV electrons in sea level air. This value scales as $1/\gamma mc^2\beta^2$ to other particles and energies.

Summary: Beam Radius vs Distance. The initial radius for a charged particle beam undergoes considerable modification as it propagates. Following a brief initial period of expansion through electrostatic repulsion, charge neutralization occurs and the beam begins to pinch down in radius. As the beam continues to propagate, its random energy rises as a result of collisions with atmospheric molecules, and its radius grows exponentially with distance. Figure 5–23 provides a summary of this behavior. The figure is not to scale, since neutralization and any initial contraction occur very rapidly relative to the prolonged period of continued beam expansion.

Energy Losses. We have seen that as a charged particle beam propagates through the atmosphere, encounters with atmospheric particles give it some random motion and cause it to expand. In each of these encounters, a beam particle gives up some of its directed energy as well. Therefore, particle energy decreases with distance. Both of these effects lower the intensity of the beam, and limit its useful range for weapon applications.

There are two primary mechanisms through which particles propagating in the atmosphere lose energy. One is ionization, in

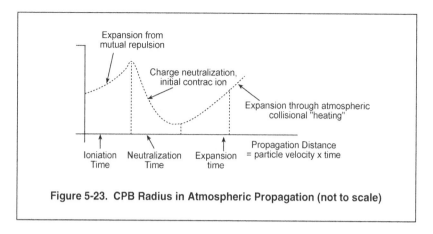

Figure 5-23. CPB Radius in Atmospheric Propagation (not to scale)

which beam particles give up energy to strip electrons off of atmospheric molecules. The other is radiation, in which the deflection of beam particles causes them to lose energy as electromagnetic radiation. Therefore, there is both good news and bad news associated with the interaction between charged particle beams and the atmosphere. Ionization causes the atmosphere to become a plasma. Without it, charge neutralization could not occur and there would be no propagation. At the same time, however, it causes a loss of energy from the beam. The scattering of beam particles gives them a "perpendicular temperature," and prevents the beam from pinching down to so small a radius as to be unstable. At the same time, however, it leads to energy losses in the form of radiation. We'll consider each of these energy loss mechanisms in turn.

Ionization—Figure 5–24 shows how ionization occurs. A beam particle passes within some distance b of an electron orbiting the nucleus of an atom in the atmosphere. In ionization, the beam particle gives the electron a sufficient kick to rip it free of its parent atom. With every ionization, a beam particle loses an amount of energy at least equal to the ionization potential, the degree of energy by which an electron is bound to an atom. Ionization potentials are typically on the order of 10–20 eV.

The analysis of energy losses through ionization may be found in many advanced texts on electromagnetic theory.[32] The details are mathematically complex, but the physics is straightforward. The goal of the analysis is to calculate dK/dz, the rate at which the kinetic energy of the beam particles decreases as they propagate

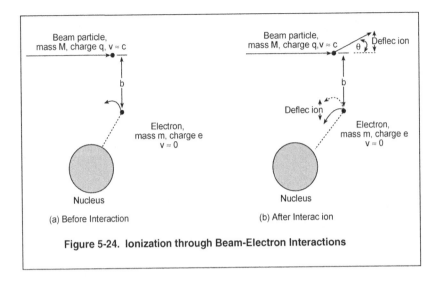

Figure 5-24. Ionization through Beam-Electron Interactions

and lose energy in ionizing atoms. This is done in two steps. First, the energy loss $\Delta K(b)$ associated with a single encounter between a beam particle and an electron at a distance b is calculated. It should not be surprising that $\Delta K(b)$ is proportional to $(qe/vb)^2$—particles with a large charge q will interact more strongly with an electron of charge e, particles moving more rapidly (greater v) will spend less time in the vicinity of the electron and be less affected, and particles approaching more closely to an electron (smaller b) will interact more strongly.

After $\Delta K(b)$ has been calculated, it must be averaged over all values of b, weighted by how many electrons are likely to be encountered at each value of b. This result depends, of course, upon the density N of particles in the atmosphere, and leads to an energy loss rate, dK/dz, which is proportional to $N(qe/v)^2$. It is apparent from this expression that dK/dz will be minimized at relativistic energies, where v approaches its maximum value—the speed of light, c. Figure 5–25 is a plot of dK/dz as a function of $(\gamma-1)$, which is proportional to particle kinetic energy.[33]

For air at sea level, $\gamma = 2$, and $q = e$, dK/dz is about 7×10^5 eV/m. At this rate of energy loss, a 1 MeV particle can propagate about 1.5 m, and a 1 GeV particle about 1.5 km. From the figure, you can see that it is adequate to use this estimate at all relativistic energies ($\gamma > 2$), scaling it as $1/v^2$ at non relativistic energies. Since dK/dz is proportional to $N(qe/v)^2$, it can be scaled for different at-

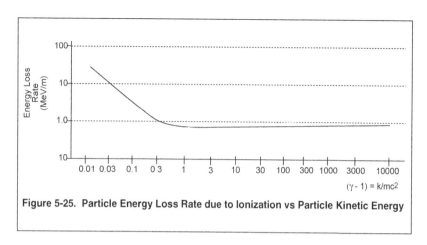

Figure 5-25. Particle Energy Loss Rate due to Ionization vs Particle Kinetic Energy

mospheric densities and charged particle species as well. It is interesting to note that dK/dz due to ionization does not depend upon the mass M of the beam particles—electrons and protons of the same γ will lose energy at the same rate. Of course electrons, being less massive, will have a much larger γ at a given K than will protons. The fact that dK/dz is minimized at relativistic energies is another reason why relativistic particle beams are envisioned for weapon applications.

Radiation—When charged particles are accelerated or decelerated, they lose energy as electromagnetic radiation.[34] This fact is employed in radio transmitters, which drive electrons up and down in an antenna, so that they radiate the radio signal. When charged particles in a CPB encounter particles in the atmosphere and are deflected or accelerated to the side, they will radiate some of their energy away. Because the particles lose energy and are slowed down, this radiation is referred to as *bremsstrahlung*, the German word for "braking radiation."

As with ionization, detailed treatments may be found in any standard text.[35] The qualitative treatment which follows will give you a feeling for what happens. If a particle of mass M and charge q is accelerated in a direction perpendicular to its direction of motion, energy is radiated at a rate proportional to the square of its acceleration. The acceleration can be obtained as a function of the particle's distance of approach, b, to an electron or nucleus in an atom. It is proportional to qe/vbM since particles which approach one another closely feel a greater force, those which are moving more quickly feel the force for a shorter time, and heavier particles are accelerated less. Using these results, the energy radiated can be calculated as a function of b, and averaged over all b. The bremsstrahlung energy loss rate derived in this way is shown and contrasted with the ionization energy loss rate in Figure 5–26.

From Figure 5–26, you can see that at non-relativistic energies, bremsstrahlung is less important than ionization as an energy loss mechanism. However, at relativistic energies, dK/dz due to bremsstrahlung is proportional to K, so that for higher energies (γ >300) it exceeds ionization in importance for electrons. At these higher energies, dK/dz due to bremsstrahlung is of the form dK/dz = $-K/z_0$ where z_0, the so-called "radiation length," is proportional to M^2/Nq^4. This equation has the solution $K(z) = K(0)\exp(-z/z_0)$. Particle energy decays exponentially with distance, and falls by a factor of 1/e in a distance equal to the radiation length, z_0. The radiation length scales inversely with atmospheric density, N, and is proportional to the square of the particle mass. Electrons, being very light, will suffer much more energy loss due to bremsstrahlung than other particles. For electrons propagating in air at sea level, the radiation length is approximately 300 m, while for protons it is approximately 10^6 km. Thus, bremsstrahlung is an important energy loss mechanism only for electrons.

Table 5–3 contrasts ionization and bremsstrahlung as energy loss mechanisms for charged particle beams. Ionization must be considered for both electrons and heavy particles, while bremsstrahlung need only be considered for electrons.

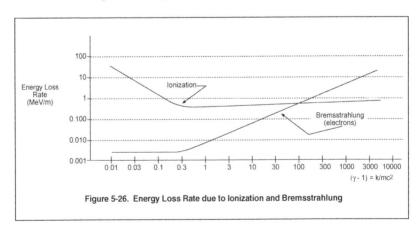

Figure 5-26. Energy Loss Rate due to Ionization and Bremsstrahlung

	Energy Dependence	Particle Mass Dependence
Ionization	Roughly independent of γ for $\gamma > 2$	Mass Independent
Bremsstrahlung	Proportional to γ $\gamma > 2$	Proportional to $1/M^2$

Table 5-3. Scaling of Energy Loss Mechanisms

Current Losses. Ionization and bremsstrahlung cause the particles in a beam to lose energy. But as long as the particles are relativistic, with a velocity close to the speed of light, the current in the beam, nqv, is unaffected. By contrast, collisions between beam particles and the nuclei of molecules in the atmosphere decrease a beam's current while leaving the energy per particle relatively unaffected.

In a nuclear interaction, a particle in the beam approaches close enough to an atomic nucleus to interact with it through the short range strong nuclear force.[36] These collisions therefore occur only for heavy particles, since electrons do not possess this force. Nuclear interactions are relatively rare, because the nucleus occupies a small fraction (about 10^{-12}) of an atom's volume. On the other hand, when they occur, nuclear interactions are quite catastrophic. Since the nucleus contains almost all the mass in an atom, it is a much more efficient scatterer than the very light orbital electrons. Interactions with electrons merely reduce the energy in a beam particle slightly, leaving it still within the beam, while collisions with nuclei actually send particles out of the beam, as illustrated in Figure 5–27.

With each ionizing collision, a particle loses energy on the order of the ionization potential—10–20 eV. Since particle energies are in the MeV to GeV range, many collisions are required before a particle loses sufficient energy to drop out of the beam. This type of interaction is relatively frequent, so that all particles in the beam lose energy at the same rate, dK/dz. By contrast, nuclear collisions are less frequent, but when they occur, the affected particle is lost from the beam. Nuclear collisions are the sort of atom smashing interactions used by physicists to probe the inner structure of nuclear matter. Frequently, the target nucleus is shattered by the

301

A. In Ionization and Bremsstrahlung, beam particles lose a small amount of energy with each interaction, but are generally not lost from the beam. Beam current, therefore, is relatively unaffected as energy per particle decreases.

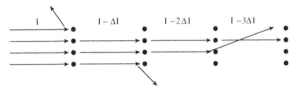

B. Nuclear interactions deflect particles from the beam, reducing its current. The energy per particle is unchanged in those particles which remain in the beam.

Figure 5-27. Nuclear Collisions vs Ionization and Bremsstrahlung

collision, and various collision products, characteristic of both the beam and target particles, are produced.[37]

The effect of nuclear collisions on a beam's current may be determined from the nuclear collision cross-section. A zero-order estimate for the cross section for a collision between a relativistic proton and a nucleus of atomic number A is $\sigma = 4 \times 10^{-30}$ m² $\times$ $A^{2/3}$.[38] For nitrogen, whose atomic number is 14, this is about 2.3×10^{-29} m². By contrast, we saw earlier that the cross section for neutral beam particles to be ionized in the atmosphere is about 10^{-20} m². Clearly, nuclear encounters are much less likely than atomic encounters. You'll recall that in an atmosphere of molecules whose collision cross section is σ and whose density is N, beam intensity or current falls off exponentially with distance as $I = I_o\, e^{-\sigma N z}$. Therefore, nuclear collisions will cause the current to fall to 1/e of its initial value in a distance $z_N = 1/N\sigma$. For air at sea level, $N = 3 \times 10^{25}/m^3$, and z_N is about 1.45 km. You Can see from this that the effect of nuclear interactions on particle beam propagation is not trivial, and must be considered in calculating the intensity of the beam as it propagates. At higher altitudes, of course, the effect of these collisions becomes progressively less, since z_N scales as $1/N$.

Hole-Boring. A particle beam's intensity (W/cm²) is given by S $= IK/\pi qw^2$, where I is the beam current, K the particle kinetic energy, q the particle charge, and w the beam radius. We have seen that there are phenomena which will affect each of the variables in this expression for intensity. These are summarized in Table 5–4, along with the characteristic length over which each variable is likely to be severely affected at sea level. When all the phenomena we have considered act together, charged particle beams are unlikely to have useful ranges in the atmosphere at sea level, even for tactical applications.

All of the phenomena listed in Table 5–4 are reduced at higher altitudes, since z_g, z_o, and z_N are proportional to $1/N$, and dK/dz is proportional to N. Therefore, propagation over useful ranges might be possible if the density of the air along the beam path could somehow be reduced. This has led to the concept of hole-boring. In hole boring, a particle beam initially serves to heat a channel of air. The hot air in the channel is then allowed to expand to a lower density, permitting propagation over a greater distance.[39] This process is analogous to the rarification of the atmosphere that produces thermal blooming in a high power laser (Chapter 3). However, the degree of heating and density decrease is much greater for a particle beam, which interacts strongly with the atmosphere, than for a laser, whose frequency is chosen to have as little interaction as possible with the air. The sequence of events that occurs in hole-boring is illustrated in Figure 5–28.

As particles propagate through the atmosphere, they lose energy to ionization and bremsstrahlung. Much of this energy appears along the beam path as a rise in the temperature of the atmosphere. Since the pressure of a gas is proportional to its temperature, there is a corresponding rise in pressure. This pressure

Beam Attribute	Affected by	Relationship	Characteristic Length (Sea Level Air)
Radius, w	Expansion	$w(z) = w(o) \exp(z/z_g)$	$z_g \approx 3km$ (Fig 5-20)
Kinetic Energy, K	Ionization	$K(z) = K(o) - (dK/dZ) Z$	$K/(dK/dz) \approx 1.5km$ ($K \approx GeV$)
	Bremsstrahlung (electrons only)	$K(z) \approx K(o) \exp(-z/z_0)$	$z_0 \approx 0.3km$
Current, I	Nuclear Collisions (heavy particles only)	$I(z) = I(o) \exp(-z/z_N)$	$z_N \approx 1.5km$

Table 5-4. Factors Affecting Beam Intensity

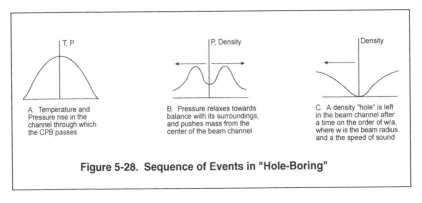

A. Temperature and Pressure rise in the channel through which the CPB passes

B. Pressure relaxes towards balance with its surroundings, and pushes mass from the center of the beam channel

C. A density "hole" is left in the beam channel after a time on the order of w/a, where w is the beam radius and a the speed of sound

Figure 5-28. Sequence of Events in "Hole-Boring"

pushes gas out of the beam center, reducing the density there. Eventually, a quasi-equilibrium is established, in which the underdense beam channel is at pressure balance with its surroundings. Since pressure disturbances travel at a velocity on the order of the speed of sound, a (= 3×10^4 cm/sec), the time required for hole boring is about w/a, where w is the beam radius. For a beam whose radius is 1 cm, this time is about 30 μsec.

If hole boring is to be used for propagation over long ranges, particle beams may require complex pulse structures. There are two time scales involved: the time necessary to heat the beam channel to a point where it will expand to the desired lower density, and the time necessary for the heated air to expand out of the beam volume. These two time scales are illustrated in Figure 5–29.

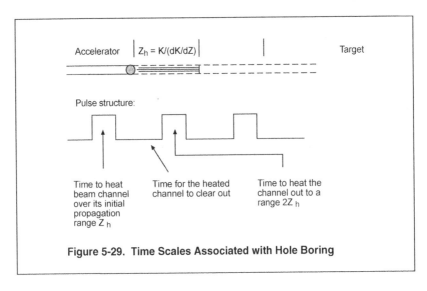

Accelerator | $Z_h = K/(dK/dZ)$ | | Target

Pulse structure:

Time to heat beam channel over its initial propagation range Z_h

Time for the heated channel to clear out

Time to heat the channel out to a range $2Z_h$

Figure 5-29. Time Scales Associated with Hole Boring

When the particle beam initially penetrates into the atmosphere, it is limited by energy losses in atmospheric density air to a range z_h on the order of $K/(dK/dz)$, where K is the kinetic energy of the beam particles, and dK/dz the total energy loss rate per unit path length due to ionization and bremsstrahlung. Therefore, we can only heat a segment of the beam path of length z_h. If the goal is to reduce the density in the beam channel by a factor of 10, the beam must be on for a time period sufficient to increase the temperature in this channel by a factor of 10. After that, the beam should be off for a time w/a, to allow the heated zone to expand, lowering its density.[40] The beam can then be turned on again, and as a result of the reduced density over its initial range it will now propagate further, to a distance of about $2z_h$. The newly encountered air must in turn be heated and allowed to expand, and the process repeated until the beam has been able to chew its way, segment by segment, to its target. If the total range to the target is Z, then there are Z/z_h channel segments which must in turn be heated and allowed to expand before the target can be engaged. The total time necessary to bore a hole to the target at range Z is therefore $(t_e + t_h)Z/z_h$, where t_e is the time for each heated segment to expand, and t_h is the time to heat it to the desired temperature.

We know that the channel expansion time t_e is on the order of w/a, where w is the beam radius and a the speed of sound. What is the time span t_h for each segment to be heated to a given temperature? The approach to use in calculating t_h is shown in Figure 5–30.

Figure 5–30 shows a portion of the beam channel of thickness Δz. Particles enter this region with kinetic energy K, and leave with energy $K - (dK/dz)$, Δz. The flow of particles into the region is just nv (particles per unit area per unit time), so that the total energy deposited in the region per second is $nv(dK/dz) \Delta z \pi w^2$, and the energy deposited per unit volume per second is just $nv(dK/dz)$. But energy per unit volume is just pressure, so if we want to raise the pressure in the region by a factor of 10, we must leave the beam on for a time t_h such that $nv(dK/dz)t_h = 10p_o$ where P_o is the initial (atmospheric) pressure. Therefore, the necessary heating time is $t_h = 10p_o/[nv(dK/dz)]$. For a relativistic beam ($v \approx c$) of density $n = 10^{17}/m^3$ in air at sea level, the energy loss rate is $dK/dz \approx 7 \times 10^5$ eV/m, and t_h is about 0.3 μsec. Scaling this value to different temperature rises and energy loss rates is straightforward. Since

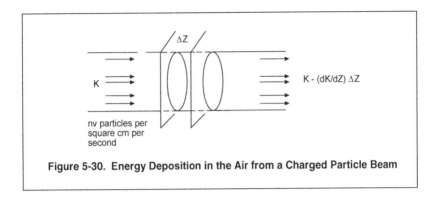

Figure 5-30. Energy Deposition in the Air from a Charged Particle Beam

dK/dz and the pressure in the atmosphere are both proportional to the atmospheric density N, t_h is independent of altitude.

In reality, of course, the dynamics of the atmosphere as it interacts with a charged particle beam is more complex than that sketched above. Some expansion of the air occurs as it is being heated, and over the range $z_h = K/(dK/dz)$ the beam energy and atmospheric heating rate are decreasing. Nevertheless, since the heating time is generally small compared to the expansion time (0.3 μsec vs 30 μsec for a 1 cm radius beam), it is usually adequate to think of the interaction and subsequent expansion as occurring in discrete phases as discussed here.

Non-uniform Atmospheric Effects. When we discussed beam expansion, we used the simple model of an atmosphere whose density decreases exponentially with altitude to examine the effect of a nonuniform atmosphere (Figure 5–22). This same approach may be used to model the effect of a nonuniform atmosphere on ionization, bremsstrahlung, and nuclear collisions. The mathematics is straightforward and completely analogous to our treatment of beam expansion; the results are summarized in Table 5–5 and Figure 5–31.

Energy and current losses in a nonuniform atmosphere may be treated just as in a uniform atmosphere, except that the total range, z, is replaced by a relative depth, D, which depends upon the elevation angle and ratio of Z to the atmospheric decay height h_o as shown in Figure 5–31. The ionization loss rate, dK/dz, the radiation length, z_r, and the atmospheric density, N, are all to be evaluated at the beam's initial propagation altitude (normally sea level), as implied by the "o" subscripts in the equations appearing in the table.

	At Sea Level	In an Nonuniform, Exponential Atmosphere
Ionization	$K(z) = K(o) - (dK/dz)_o z$	$K(z) = K(o)-(dK/dz)_o D$ (D = relative depth from Fig 5-31)
Bremsstrahlung	$K(z) = K(o) \exp(-z/z_r)$	$K(z) = K(o) \exp(-D/z_r)$
Nuclear Collisions	$I(z) = I(o) \exp(-N_o \sigma z)$	$I(z) = I(o) \exp(-N_o \sigma D)$

Table 5-5. Effect of a Nonuniform Athmosphere on Energy and Current Losses. The relative depth, D, may be obtained from Figure 5-31.

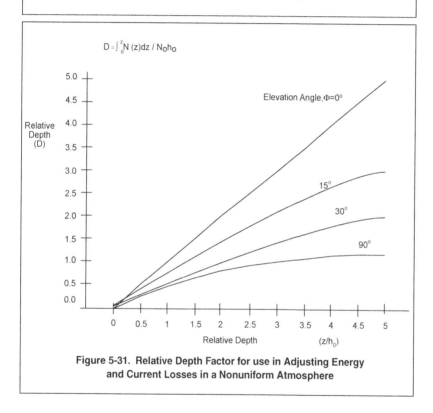

$$D = \int_0^z N(z)dz \ / \ N_o h_o$$

Relative Depth (D)

Elevation Angle, $\Phi = 0°$

$15°$

$30°$

$90°$

Relative Depth (z/h_o)

Figure 5-31. Relative Depth Factor for use in Adjusting Energy and Current Losses in a Nonuniform Atmosphere

Summary: Energy and Current Losses. As a charged particle beam propagates from an accelerator through the air, many factors will affect the intensity that ultimately strikes a target. The beam radius changes as a result of increases in the beam's perpendicular temperature, and particles in the beam lose energy through ionization of atmospheric particles and possibly bremsstrahlung. Ionization is important both for electrons and heavy particles. It causes particles to lose energy at a rate which at relativistic energies is roughly independent of their energy. Bremsstrahlung is important only for electrons, causing them to lose energy at a rate proportional to their energy. Heavy particles may collide with the nuclei of atmospheric atoms, an event so catastrophic that they are removed from the beam entirely.

All of these effects are proportional in their severity to the atmospheric density. Therefore, the heating of a beam's path, and its subsequent expansion to a lower density (hole boring), can result in longer propagation ranges. The price to be paid is having to wait to engage a target until a channel can be cleared over the beam's entire range. In evaluating all these propagation phenomena, the effect of the decline in atmospheric density with altitude is easily accounted for, at least at the lower altitudes where density decays exponentially, by using the relative depth provided in Figure 5–31 in place of the actual range.

Nonlinear Effects (Instabilities). There is a final type of phenomenon which can affect the propagation of a charged particle beam in the atmosphere—beam instabilities. Ionization, bremsstrahlung, and nuclear collisions are all one-on-one effects, arising from interactions between single particles in the beam and single particles in the atmosphere. By contrast, instabilities arise through *collective* effects, in which the total assembly of particles in the beam, acting in concert, leads to its breakup and destruction. An instability occurs when small perturbations in the beam's parameters grow without bound as a result of nonlinear interactions between the beam and its environment. Ultimately, instabilities destroy a beam's integrity, and propagation is no longer possible. A good analogy might be found in a school bus. A bus rocks at a natural frequency, determined by its mass and suspension system. As it propagates, it jostles to and fro, both from bumps in the road and the motions of its occupants. However, these motions occur randomly and are not in phase with the bus' natural frequency, so that the perturbations decay and do not affect its motion. However, if school children in the bus conspire to rock together in phase with the bus's natural frequency, their perturbations will add to the displacement of the bus with each cycle. Ultimately, the bus will tip over, its propagation ceasing. Under appropriate circumstances, perturbations to a particle beam can in a similar way provide feedback which is in phase with a natural frequency of the beam, causing those perturbations to grow to the point where propagation ceases.

Any survey of the literature on particle beams and their propagation in the atmosphere will reveal that instabilities seem far more likely than unlikely. It is probably more meaningful to ask what beam configurations can propagate in a stable manner, than to ask under what circumstances instabilities can occur.[41] Stable propagation of a charged particle beam over a substantial range in the atmosphere has yet to be demonstrated, and the area of instabilities, their growth rates, and how beams can be configured to avoid them is one of active research. Accordingly, we cannot provide a detailed compendium of instabilities that might occur and of known techniques for avoiding them. Rather, we'll provide a qualitative description of two instabilities currently thought to limit propagation in the atmosphere, along with some indication of how these instabilities might be avoided.

The *resistive hose instability* results from an interaction between the beam particles and the magnetic field that they generate. It can occur when the beam receives a small, sideways perturbation from its original direction as a result, for example, of jitter in the device which aims the beam at a target. This instability can be understood by analogy with a fire hose directing a stream of water, as illustrated in Figure 5–32. Suppose a small kink occurs somewhere in the hose. The flowing water will exert forces which tend to straighten the hose out again. ff these forces over-react, an even

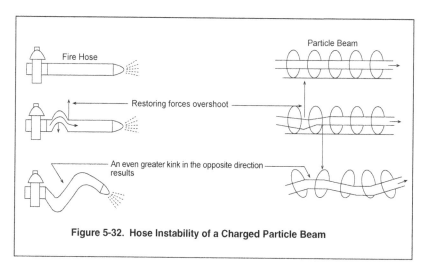

Figure 5-32. Hose Instability of a Charged Particle Beam

greater kink in the opposite direction will result. After several cycles of this destructive action and reaction, the hose will be so twisted that its effectiveness in directing the stream of water will be limited. This is one reason why fire hoses require a team of firemen to keep them pointed in the proper direction.

For a charged particle beam, the encircling magnetic field plays a role analogous to that of the fire hose for a stream of water. It confines the beam, pinches its particles into a narrow channel, and opposes their tendency to expand due to random, sideways motions (perpendicular temperature). If the beam wanders from its original path, restoring forces will be set up that tend to drive the beam back to where it was.

However, these can overshoot and induce an even greater kink in the opposite direction. Under the proper conditions, small kinks will grow in time until the beam loses its integrity.

Having seen qualitatively how a hose instability could occur in a propagating particle beam, let's look more closely at the mechanism for its growth. In this way, we can gain insight into how a beam can be structured to avoid the instability. The hose for a particle beam is the magnetic field which surrounds it and confines its particles. Maxwell's equations predict that a magnetic field will be "frozen" into a background plasma. That is, if a magnetic field exists inside of a plasma, it will continue to exist and remain fixed in the plasma, even if the original source of the magnetic field should move or decay. Physically, this occurs because if a plasma moves relative to a magnetic field within it, the resulting forces on the charged particles in the plasma induce currents that in turn generate a magnetic field which mimics the initial field. From the perspective of an outside observer, the magnetic field has remained unaltered, frozen into the plasma. Of course, this situation cannot be maintained indefinitely. Eventually, the induced currents that are responsible for freezing the magnetic field into the plasma will decay due to the electrical resistance which is present in any plasma. As these currents decay, the magnetic field will thaw, returning to the value and location dictated by currents external to the plasma.[42] In Chapter 3, this effect is responsible in another form for the fact that light, as electromagnetic radiation, cannot penetrate into the interior of a metallic conductor. Since there is no magnetic field in the conductor before the light impinges, there can be none afterward—the light is frozen out by the flow of electrons on the interior of the conductor.

What does all of this have to do with the resistive hose instability? A charged particle beam in the atmosphere is propagating in a background plasma of ionized air. When a kink develops in the particle beam, or if the beam tries to move sideways, the encircling magnetic field will not immediately move along with it, but will remain fixed in this background plasma. This disparity between what *is* and what *should be* regarding the relationship between the beam and its magnetic field leads to restoring forces that try to return the beam to its original direction.

There would be no problem if a particle beam developed a kink and its magnetic field were permanently frozen into the surrounding plasma. Restoring forces would drive the beam back to its original position. The beam might oscillate about its initial position like a pendulum, but no instability would occur. But the magnetic field is not permanently frozen. In time, it begins to thaw, and rejoin the particle beam which created it. But by this time, the kink has moved downstream, and the field lines are moving down on a previously "unkinked" portion of the beam, perturbing it and initiating another kink. The delay between the perturbation of the beam and the response of the encircling magnetic field causes the feedback between the beam and its field to be out of phase, so that an instability develops. That's why this instability is known as the *resistive hose* instability. The resistance of the background plasma is responsible for the delayed response that can lead to an instability.[43]

This insight into the origin of the resistive hose instability can suggest ways in which it might be prevented. Since the instability arises because of feedback between one portion of the beam and another, it might be avoided by chopping the beam into segments, where the length of these segments is shorter than the distance over which the instability grows, and the time between them is great enough for any frozen magnetic field lines to thaw, so that each beam segment enters an environment with no memory of what has happened to previous beam segments. This approach is illustrated in Figure 5–33. In order to carry out this scheme, we need to quantify the necessary length of the segments and separation between them in terms of appropriate beam and atmospheric parameters.

How can we quantify the pulse width, t_p, and pulse separation, t_s, shown in Figure 5–33? The necessary separation time is straight-

311

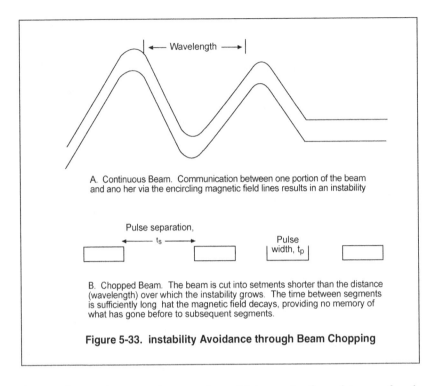

A. Continuous Beam. Communication between one portion of the beam and ano her via the encircling magnetic field lines results in an instability

B. Chopped Beam. The beam is cut into setments shorter than the distance (wavelength) over which the instability grows. The time between segments is sufficiently long hat the magnetic field decays, providing no memory of what has gone before to subsequent segments.

Figure 5-33. instability Avoidance through Beam Chopping

forward to estimate, using results which can be found in any book on plasma physics. If a magnetic field whose characteristic size is w is frozen into a background plasma of conductivity Σ, and if the current responsible for the magnetic field goes away, then the field will decay in time as $B = B_o \exp(-t/t_d)$, where $t_d = \Sigma w^2/c^2\epsilon_o$ is known as the *magnetic diffusion time*.[44] The expression for the magnetic diffusion time t_d makes sense on physical grounds. In plasmas of little resistance (high conductivity), B will take longer to thaw, and a physically larger magnetic field (w large) will persist for a longer time. For a beam of radius 1 cm and a conductivity characteristic of singly-ionized air at sea level

$$(\Sigma = 8.4 \times 10^3 \text{ mho/m}), t_d = 1 \text{ } \mu\text{sec}.$$

Thus, for these conditions, the pulse separation time shown in Figure 5–33 should be several microseconds. This will enable the magnetic field associated with the beam to decay to zero between pulses. This criterion scales to other altitudes with the atmospheric density, N, since Σ is proportional to N.

What should be the pulse width, t_p, shown in Figure 5–33? There is a characteristic wavelength at which the instability grows. This wavelength is the distance between the perturbation of the magnetic field and the associated response of the propagating beam. Clearly, the pulse width should be chosen so that the length of a beam segment, vt_p, is less than this wavelength. In this way, each individual beam segment is shorter than the distance over which the instability can grow. The determination of the wavelength or range of wavelengths at which an instability will grow is a tedious exercise, in which the beam is assumed to be perturbed at a given wavelength, and the equations for the response of the beam and its magnetic field under this assumption are studied to see if the perturbation grows or decays. It can be shown from such an analysis that the wavelength for growth of the hose instability is proportional to $(vE/I)^{1/2}w$, where v is a beam particle's velocity, E its total energy (γMc^2), I is the beam current, and w the beam radius.[45] This length is about 4 meters at $v = 0.9c$, $E = 2$ GeV, $w = 1$ cm, and $I = 1$ kAmp. This means that for a beam with these parameters, the pulse width must be less than 4 m$/0.9c$, or about 1.5×10^{-9} sec. Therefore, the hose instability can be avoided in a kAmp beam of GeV particles by chopping the beam into segments about a nanosecond in length, and separating these segments by several microseconds. Scaling these criteria to other beam sizes, currents, and energies is straightforward, using the scaling relationships provided above.

Another instability of some concern from the standpoint of charged particle beam propagation in the atmosphere is the *sausage instability*.[46] While the resistive hose instability results from perturbations in the beam's position perpendicular to its direction of motion, the sausage instability results from longitudinal perturbations in the beam's density. You will recall that the equilibrium beam radius results from a balance between the pinching magnetic field which the beam generates and the outward pressure of its perpendicular temperature. Both the outward pressure and the inward magnetic field depend on the density, n, of particles in the beam. Should this density increase somewhere within the beam, the outward pressure will increase, while the magnetic pinching, being frozen into the background plasma, cannot respond immediately. Therefore, the beam radius in this region will begin to grow. At a later time (on the order of the magnetic diffusion time, t$_d$), the magnetic field will increase to reflect the increased density. But by this time the density increase has moved downstream, and at the point on the beam where the magnetic field finally responds, the density has not increased. At this point, the magnetic compression exceeds the outward pressure, and the radius tends to decrease. Under these circumstances, the beam will alternately grow and pinch, attaining the appearance of a string of sausages, as illustrated in Figure 5–34.

As with the hose instability, avoiding the sausage instability involves chopping the beam into pulses separated by several magnetic diffusion times, and restricting each pulse to a length shorter than that over which the instability can develop. In general, the sausage instability places limitations on pulse width and separa-

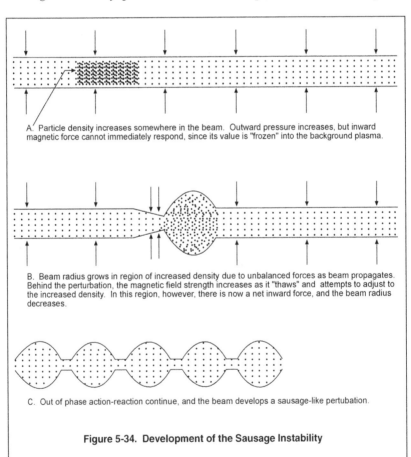

A. Particle density increases somewhere in the beam. Outward pressure increases, but inward magnetic force cannot immediately respond, since its value is "frozen" into the background plasma.

B. Beam radius grows in region of increased density due to unbalanced forces as beam propagates. Behind the perturbation, the magnetic field strength increases as it "thaws" and attempts to adjust to the increased density. In this region, however, there is now a net inward force, and the beam radius decreases.

C. Out of phase action-reaction continue, and the beam develops a sausage-like pertubation.

Figure 5-34. Development of the Sausage Instability

tion that are not as severe as those resulting from the hose instability. Therefore, choosing beam parameters to avoid the hose instability should prevent the sausage instability as well. However, the theoretical analysis of instabilities, the criteria for their growth, and techniques to avoid them can be quite complex. Existing treatments invariably involve numerous simplifying assumptions. Accordingly, theoretical predictions of beam structures that can propagate without instabilities must be validated and extended through a careful experimental program. To date, technology limitations to available accelerators have not permitted a comprehensive investigation of beam propagation or a complete validation of theoretical analysis. Indeed, the greatest problem in the design of high-current, high-energy accelerators is the development of instabilities within the accelerators themselves.[47]

Summary: Propagation in the Atmosphere

1. Neutral particle beams can't propagate in the atmosphere because collisions with atmospheric particles ionize the particles in the beam, converting it into a charged particle beam of poor quality. Figure 5–15 shows how the minimum altitude at which a neutral beam can be employed varies with particle energy and beam range. Practically speaking, neutral beams are limited to altitudes above 100 km.

2. As charged particle beams (CPBs) propagate through the atmosphere, they will ionize atmospheric gases. This permits charge neutralization, a flow of charge which shorts out the internal electric fields which would otherwise prevent CPB propagation. Figure 5–18 shows the maximum altitude at which charge neutralization can occur as a function of beam radius and current. Practically speaking, charged particle beams are limited to altitudes below about 200 km.

3. Following charge neutralization, a CPB contracts to a radius at which the self-generated magnetic field, which tends to pinch it, is balanced by internal pressure from the small, sideways motions (perpendicular temperature) of its particles. This radius then grows as $w(z) = w(o) \exp(z/z_g)$ because collisions with atmospheric particles increase the beam's internal pressure as it propagates. Figure 5–20 shows the beam expansion range

315

z_g as a function of beam current and particle energy. In air at sea level, this range is on the order of 10 km.

4. As a charged particle beam propagates, its particles lose energy through ionization and bremsstrahlung, and its current declines through nuclear collisions. Energy losses to ionization are independent of energy for relativistic particles, so that a particle's energy decreases in proportion to its range. Ionization losses limit the range of a 1 MeV particle at sea level to about 1.5 m. The energy loss to bremsstrahlung is proportional to a particle's energy, so that its energy decreases exponentially with distance by this mechanism. The range for a 1/e decrease in an electron's energy through bremsstrahlung at sea level is about 300 m. This range scales inversely with atmospheric density and as the square of a particle's mass. Accordingly, bremsstrahlung is not an important energy loss mechanism for particles other than electrons. Nuclear collisions occur only for heavy particles, not electrons, and cause a beam's current to decline exponentially with distance. For protons in air at sea level, the 1/e distance is about 1.45 km, scaling inversely with atmospheric density.

5. All the factors which affect the intensity of a charged particle beam in the atmosphere become less severe as the atmospheric density decreases. Therefore, hole boring may increase a charged particle beam's range in the air. This involves heating a channel of air as far as a beam will go, then turning off the beam as the heated air expands to a lower density. Following this expansion, the beam can then propagate through the heated channel, heating another region of air further downstream. Thus, the beam must be chopped into segments whose width is long enough to heat the air to the desired degree and whose separation is great enough for the heated air to expand out of the beam channel. Heating times are typically on the order of 1 μsec, and channel expansion times in excess of 10 μsec.

6. Over long ranges, the decrease in atmospheric density with altitude must be accounted for in evaluating the effect of expansion, energy losses, and current losses on a beam's intensity. Figures 5–22 and 5–31 provide correction factors to apply to sea level analysis for a beam aimed into the air at a given range and elevation angle. The bottom line is that most beam losses occur in the lowest 7 km of the atmosphere.

7. Particle beams have no rigid structure, and may wiggle, both along and perpendicular to their axis. Because of the interaction between a beam's magnetic field and the ionized air plasma through which it propagates, these wiggles may be magnified, with the beam becoming unstable. Prevention of instabilities in a propagating beam requires that the beam be chopped into segments whose length is less than the distance over which an instability can grow, and whose separation is sufficiently great that each segment is independent of its predecessor. This requires pulse widths on the order of nsec, and pulse separations on the order of μsec.

Implications

Propagation in the atmosphere places severe constraints upon the energy, current, and pulse structure of a charged particle beam. If energy losses are to be minimized, the particles must be relativistic. If expansion is to be minimized, high currents are required. If hole boring is to be attempted and instabilities avoided, extremely complex pulse structures may result, as illustrated in Figure 5–35.

The division of the beam into "macropulses" and "micropulses" as shown in Figure 5–35 can be a challenge in designing a particle accelerator to create the beam. Moreover, much of the theory of instability growth and suppression has yet to be tested experimentally. While there can be no doubt that the broad outlines of our discussion are valid, specific details and operating constraints cannot be validated until weapons grade particle accelerators are built.

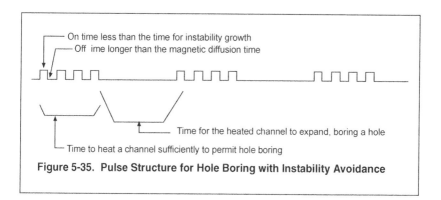

Figure 5-35. Pulse Structure for Hole Boring with Instability Avoidance

317

The complexities of propagation in the atmosphere have in recent years caused interest in particle beams to shift to applications in space, where the more straightforward problems of propagation in a vacuum must be dealt with. Here, of course, it is neutral particle beams that find application, and the primary technical challenge is to reduce beam divergence to the point where targets can be damaged over the ranges anticipated. It is unfortunate that in space the distances involved are of necessity great, so that this challenge is not trivial. Nevertheless, the primary challenges in space are technical and engineering—reducing divergence, orbiting and maintaining particle accelerators and associated equipment, and so forth. By contrast, the primary challenges in the atmosphere are physical. You can't repeal Maxwell's equations or Einstein's theories, and so the constraints these place on beam design must be accounted for. It is not yet clear which applications in the atmosphere have a solution consistent with these constraints.

Interaction with Targets

Energy Deposition and Flow

Knowing how neutral and charged particle beams propagate, we can turn our attention to their interaction with targets. All the physics we need is already in place, since the deposition of beam energy in targets occurs by the same mechanisms that cause a loss of beam intensity in air: ionization, bremsstrahlung, and nuclear interactions. The only difference is that target material is denser than atmospheric gases. Since all the energy loss mechanisms are proportional to the density of molecules the beam encounters, we'll need to scale our atmospheric results appropriately. In essence, then, beam-target interaction is simply beam-atmospheric interaction, scaled with density. The interaction of beams with targets is not qualitatively different from their interaction with the atmosphere.[48]

From the standpoint of target interaction, it makes no difference whether the particle beam is charged or neutral. The two types of beams propagate in different environments: air for a charged particle beam and vacuum for a neutral particle beam. In interacting with targets, however, they're both alike, since a neutral beam is collisionally ionized immediately upon encountering a target

($1/N\sigma \approx 3$ μm), and the small amount of energy required (≈ 10 eV) is insignificant relative to the total particle energy.

Despite the fact that solid targets are denser than atmospheric air, it is nevertheless true that from the standpoint of energy loss from the beam, the air is thicker than the target. This is because the range to the target is much greater than the target thickness, so that a beam propagating in the atmosphere sees more molecules on its way to the target than it sees within the target itself. Consider, for example, a particle beam firing over a range of only 1 km to a target which is 10 cm thick.[49] Since the density of air is about 10^{-3} gm/cm^3, and solid densities are on the order of 1 gm/cm^3, there are about 1,000 times as many molecules encountered per unit path length in a solid than in the atmosphere. But the range to the target is 10,000 times greater than the target thickness, even at this short range. This means that the beam encounters ten times as many molecules on the way to the target than within the target itself, and ten times as much energy will be lost in propagation than in target interaction. The implication of this result is that target interaction is of much less concern for particle beams than for other types of directed energy weapons. For particle beams in the atmosphere, if you have sufficient energy to propagate to the target, you'll have enough energy to damage it. For particle beams in space, there are no propagation losses other than through beam divergence, and damage requirements can play a greater role in establishing beam parameters.

We have seen that relativistic particles lose about 7×10^5 eV/m to ionization in traveling through the atmosphere. There are additional energy losses to bremsstrahlung if the particles are electrons, and losses from the beam's current through nuclear collisions if they are heavy particles. While all of these effects would need to be considered in a detailed treatment of energy deposition from a specific type of beam in a specific target, it is adequate to look at the generic features of beam-target interaction using ionization losses alone. Solid matter is about 1,000 times more dense that air at sea level, and the energy loss rate is proportional to density, so that the energy loss rate of relativistic particles in solids should be about 7×10^8 eV/m, or 7 MeV/cm. Figure 5–36 is a plot of particle range as a function of energy at this energy loss rate.

You can see from Figure 5–36 that the ranges shown exceed the thickness of most targets. This means that a particle beam will

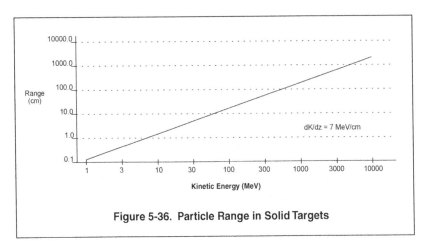

Figure 5-36. Particle Range in Solid Targets

penetrate deeply into a target; some particles will even pass through it. This is in contrast to a laser beam (Chapter 3), which deposits its energy in a very thin layer on the target surface. From the standpoint of damaging targets, this means that a particle beam will do serious damage sooner, reaching and engaging vital parts rapidly. A laser must heat, vaporize, and penetrate a target's outer surface before it can reach these vital parts.

Now let's consider the resulting differences in energy flow within a target. With a laser, energy flow is mostly from the surface of the target towards the interior. With a particle beam, it's mostly radially outward from the deposition region, which penetrates well into the target. This contrast is illustrated in Figure 5–37.

Heat flows downhill along a temperature gradient. With a laser, the greatest gradient is in the direction into the target, since all the laser's energy is deposited within a thin layer on the surface. A particle beam, on the other hand, penetrates into the depth of the target, and the greatest gradient is in the radial direction. What limitation will the flow of energy out of the heated region place on damage to targets with particle beams? Figure 5–38 illustrates the mechanisms of energy deposition and loss when a particle beam engages a target. You will recall that the intensity (W/cm^2) in a particle beam is just $S = nKv$, where n is the density of particles in the beam (cm^{-3}), v their velocity, and K their kinetic energy. In passing through a target of thickness d, each particle loses energy $(dK/dz)d$, so that the beam's intensity declines to $nv[K-(dK/dz)\,d]$. This means that the rate of energy deposition within the solid (W/cm^3) is

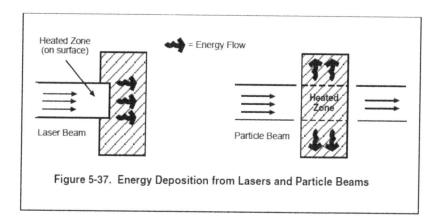

Figure 5-37. Energy Deposition from Lasers and Particle Beams

just dS/dz = nv(dK/dz). And since the volume of target through which the beam passes is πw²d, the total rate of energy deposition in that region is πw²d nv(dK/dz) (Watts).

Now let's consider how energy is carried out of the irradiated region either by thermal conduction or radiation. The flow of energy (Watts/cm²) across a surface due to thermal conduction is given by u = –k(dT/dx), where k is the thermal conductivity and dT/dx is the slope of a curve of temperature vs distance. Suppose we were to look end-on at the target shown on the left hand side of Figure 5–38. A radial temperature profile will look like that shown on the right hand side of figure 5–38. The temperature slope in the radial direction, dT/dr, is on the order of T/w, where T is the temperature within the beam volume and w is the radius of the beam. The resulting flow of energy through the surface of the energy deposition region and into the surrounding target material is about kT/w (Watts/cm²). Since the total surface area of that region is 2πwd, energy flows out of the irradiated volume at a rate of about 2πwd(kT/w) (Watts).[50]

As we saw in Chapter 1, energy can also be lost from the front and back surfaces of the target by radiation. If we assume that the target radiates as a black body, the intensity of radiation (W/cm²) emitted will be σT⁴, and the total energy loss rate by radiation will be 2πw² σT⁴ (Watts), where σ is the Stefan-Boltzmann constant (5.67 × 10⁻¹² W/cm² K⁴).

We have argued that the particle beam deposits energy in a target at a rate πw²dnv(dK/dz), that thermal conduction carries energy away at a rate 2πwd(kT/w), and that radiation carries it away at a

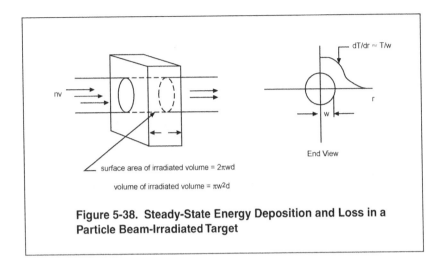

surface area of irradiated volume = $2\pi wd$

volume of irradiated volume = $\pi w^2 d$

Figure 5-38. Steady-State Energy Deposition and Loss in a Particle Beam-Irradiated Target

rate $2\pi w^2$ σT^4, where T is the temperature in the irradiated region. We can set the rates of energy deposition and loss equal to one another to find the temperature at which energy is carried away as fast as it is deposited. For thermal conduction, that temperature is T $= \pi w^2 nv$ (dK/dz)/$2\pi k$ = I (dK/dz)/$2\pi kq$, where I $= \pi w^2$ nqv is the beam current (Amperes). For radiation, it's [d I(dK/dz)/$2\pi w^2 \sigma$ q] $^{1/4}$. Figure 5–39 is a plot of these temperatures as a function of beam current for q = 1.6 × 10^{-19} coul, (dK/dz) = 7 MeV/cm, w = 1 cm, and k = 2.4 W/cm K (the thermal conductivity of aluminum).

As a particle beam engages a target, the temperature will rise until the target is vaporized or energy is carried away as fast as it is deposited, whichever occurs first. Most materials vaporize at temperatures on the order of 3000 °K (see Table 1–1). And from Figure 5–39, you can see that for almost any reasonable beam current, the vaporization point will be reached well before thermal conduction or radiation can limit the temperature rise in a beam-irradiated target. This means that we need not be concerned about the radial flow of energy from the heated zone or radiation from the target surface limiting the target's temperature. Particle beams with high currents and energies deposit energy too rapidly for energy loss mechanisms to affect the interaction. For all practical purposes, the irradiated region of the target may be assumed vaporized as soon as sufficient energy has been deposited. Our next task is to determine how long a time that is.

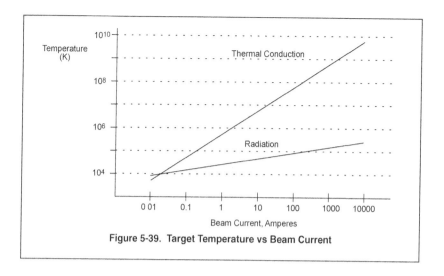

Figure 5-39. Target Temperature vs Beam Current

Damage and Interaction Times

There are two times of interest from the standpoint of damaging targets with particle beams—the damage time, or the time the beam must engage the target to damage it, and the interaction time, the actual time the beam must deposit energy within the target. In general, these two times will not be the same for charged particle beams. Atmospheric propagation constraints, such as the times the beam must be off to permit hole boring or to prevent instability growth must be considered in the total time to damage the target. Even for neutral particle beams, constraints in accelerator design may prevent pulse widths from being arbitrarily long, so that multiple pulses on target may be required. If the off time is too long relative to the on time, thermal conduction or radiation could begin to affect the energy density within the irradiated area, and the interaction time may increase.

How long will typical interaction times be? We know the rate of energy deposition (W/cm³)—$dS/dz = nv(dK/dz) = I(dK/dz)/\pi w^2 q$, where (dK/dz) is the particle energy loss rate, I is the beam current, q the particle charge, and w the beam radius. From Chapter 1, we also know the energy density (J/cm³) needed to vaporize the target material—$\rho(CT_v+L_m+L_v) \approx 10^4$ J/cm³. The time t to heat the target to the point where it vaporizes is simply the ratio of the energy required to the energy deposition rate, or $t = \pi w^2 q \, \rho(CT_v+L_m+L_v)/I(dK/dz)$. Figure 5–40 is a plot of this time as a function of beam current and radius.

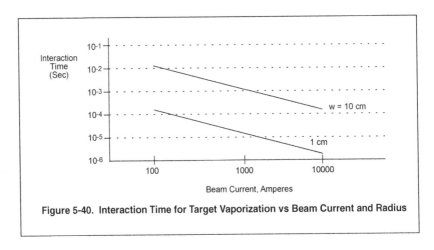

Figure 5-40. Interaction Time for Target Vaporization vs Beam Current and Radius

As you can see from Figure 5–40, interaction times are quite short. A 10 kAmp, 1 cm beam can vaporize a target in about 1 μsec. But even over short ranges, the total engagement time will be greater. You will recall, for example, that to avoid the hose instability the beam must be split up into segments about a nanosecond (10^{-9} sec) in length, separated by periods of several microseconds. It takes 1,000 pulses of 10^{-9} seconds each to add up to a microsecond of interaction time. If each of these pulses is separated by a microsecond, the total time the beam must engage the target will be at least $1000 \times 10^{-6} = 10^{-3}$ seconds. In this simple example, the total time to damage the target is about three orders of magnitude greater than the actual time the beam interacts with the target. More generally, if a particle beam of current I is composed of pulses of width t_p separated by a separation time t_s, the effective average current on target will be I $t_p/(t_p+t_s)$, and the actual engagement time can be found by using Figure 5–40 with this effective current. Should the effective current fail below the level where Figure 5–39 shows thermal conduction or radiation to be important, these loss mechanisms will increase the energy necessary for damage, and must be accounted for as well. In general, then, the current per pulse should be kept large enough that the effective current doesn't fall below about $10^{-2} - 10^{-1}$ Amperes.

Summary: Interaction with Targets

1. Particle beams interact with solid matter through one-on-one interactions, where individual particles in the beam lose energy through encounters with individual particles in the target. Since this is the same way in which particle beams interact with the atmosphere, energy deposition in targets may be estimated by scaling atmospheric energy losses with density.

2. Since the distance to a target is much greater than the thickness of a target, more energy is generally lost in propagation through the atmosphere than is deposited within the target itself. Therefore, beams with sufficient energy to propagate through the atmosphere will have sufficient energy to damage their target. As a result, target interaction is an important factor in beam design only for neutral particle beams propagating in a vacuum.

3. Relativistic particles have ranges in solids comparable to a typical target thickness. Therefore, a beam deposits energy throughout a target's volume, and not on its surface. This results in lower temperature gradients, and neither thermal conduction nor radiation are effective as mechanisms to limit target damage.

4. Relativistic beams of high current deposit energy in a target rapidly, and the time to achieve damage is short, on the order of microseconds. However, various factors affecting propagation, such as the need to avoid instabilities or bore through the atmosphere, can require that energy be delivered to a target in short bursts over a longer period. This decreases the average rate of energy delivery and increases the time necessary for the beam to engage its target.

Implications

Because of the way in which particle beams interact with targets, shielding by applying extra layers of material to a target's surface is not a practical way of limiting target damage. Relativistic particles penetrate so deeply that an inordinate weight and volume of material would be required for shielding. Consider, for example, a target whose nominal size is 1 meter. Such a target has a total surface area on the order of 12 m². To shield this target from particles of energy 10 MeV would require about a 1 cm layer of material over the entire surface of the target, for a total volume of 0.12 cubic meters of shielding material. At a density of 3 grams per cubic centimeter, this shielding would add about 360 kg (780 lb) to the weight of the target. This would be an unacceptable weight penalty for most targets, and it could easily be countered by increasing the energy in the beam to 20 MeV, which would necessitate doubling the amount of shielding. Thus, countermeasures against particle beams are much less practical than against lasers, where energy deposition is a surface effect, and a small amount of shielding can have a much greater protective effect.

Summary of Main Concepts

In looking at the propagation and interaction of charged and neutral particle beams, we've introduced numerous physical concepts. We'll summarize the main concepts here to give you a final glimpse of the forest after having wandered among the trees for so many pages.

1. Particle beams are large numbers of atomic or sub-atomic particles moving at relativistic velocities (velocities approaching that of light). Because of the large number or density of particles in these beams, their interactions among themselves can be as important as their interactions with the atmosphere and with targets.

2. There are two types of particle beams: charged and neutral. Charged particle beams consist of particles such as electrons and protons which have an electrical charge. These beams tend to spread because of the mutual repulsion of their particles. Neutral particle beams consist of electrically neutral particles, such as hydrogen atoms.

3. A particle beam is characterized by the current it carries, the energy of its particles, and its radius. These quantities may be related to more weapon related parameters such as intensity, through the relationships shown in Table 5–2.

4. Real particle beams deviate from perfection, in which all the particles propagate in the same direction with the same velocity. This lack of perfection may be expressed in many ways, such as the beam's *brightness* (current per area per solid angle), *divergence* (the angle which the beam's envelope makes as it

expands), or *temperature* (small, random fluctuations in energy about the average value).

5. Neutral particle beams can propagate only in a vacuum (altitudes greater than about 100 km). In the atmosphere, their particles will ionize through collision with atmospheric particles. Propagation over reasonable distances requires that a neutral beam's divergence be on the order of microradians or less.

6. Charged particle beams can propagate only in the atmosphere (altitudes less than about 200 km), since in a vacuum they rapidly diverge through electrical repulsion. In the atmosphere, charged beams ionize the gas through which they propagate, which enables charge to flow in such a way that electrical repulsion is neutralized.

7. Charged particle beams which have been charge neutralized pinch down to a smaller radius through magnetic forces, then expand again because of the random motion their particles receive in colliding with atmospheric particles. The resulting expansion is unacceptable except at currents in excess of a kiloamp. Figure 5–20 shows the distance over which the beam radius grows as a function of beam current and particle energy.

8. In propagating through the atmosphere, particles in a beam lose energy by ionizing the background gas, as well as through radiation (bremsstrahlung) induced by the acceleration they suffer in collisions. The rate of energy loss to ionization is independent of particle type, and at relativistic energies is roughly energy-independent. The rate of energy loss to bremsstrahlung is roughly proportional to energy, and inversely proportional to the square of the particle mass. Therefore, bremsstrahlung is of concern only for light particles (electrons).

9. In propagating through the atmosphere, a beam of heavy particles (protons or atomic nuclei) loses current from collisions with the nuclei of particles in the atmosphere.

10. All the adverse effects associated with atmospheric propagation (expansion, ionizaton, bremsstrahlung, and nuclear collisions) are reduced in magnitude as the atmospheric density is reduced. Losses are therefore greatest within the lowest 7 km of the atmosphere, and may be reduced by hole boring, in which the beam is initially used to heat the channel of air through

which it passes, and this channel then expands, becoming less dense and allowing propagation to greater distances.

11. Particle beams in the atmosphere can become unstable and cease to propagate when feedback from one portion of the beam to another enables small perturbations to grow catastrophically. These instabilities can be eliminated by chopping the beam into segments whose duration is less than the time it takes the instability to grow, and whose separation is sufficient for each beam segment to be an independent event.

12. Particle beams interact with targets just as they do with the atmosphere—through ionization, bremsstrahlung, and nuclear interactions. The energy deposited within the target may therefore be calculated by scaling with density. Typically, energy losses from a particle beam propagating through the atmosphere to a target are less than those within the target itself, so that target interaction is not of as much concern as propagation in this case.

13. The range of relativistic particles in solid matter is typically centimeters or greater, so that these particles deposit their energy in depth through the target, rather than on its surface. This reduces temperature gradients, and the resulting transfer of energy by thermal conductivity, to the point where it generally need not be considered in developing damage criteria.

14. For particle beams in the atmosphere, the total time it takes to destroy a target may be greater than the time required for a constant beam to deposit sufficient energy on it, since time must be allowed for hole boring, the suppression of instabilities, and so forth.

Overall Implications

In principle, particle beams should be ideal as directed energy weapons. Unlike lasers or microwaves, their propagation in unaffected by clouds, rain, or other meteorological effects, which add very little to the mass a particle beam might encounter on the way to its target. Therefore, they are in effect all-weather devices, capable of engaging targets under almost any circumstances. Once they encounter a target, the long penetration range of relativistic particles ensures that critical components on the interior of the target will be rapidly engaged. Time need not be wasted in eroding away protective layers of matter on the target's surface in order to reach them. Shielding targets as a defensive countermeasure is not a practical alternative.

In practice, the apparent difficulties in achieving stable propagation through the atmosphere have caused interest to focus on space-based neutral particle beams, where the physical problems of atmospheric propagation are replaced with the engineering problems associated with deploying and maintaining large constellations of particle accelerators in space. Both charged and neutral particle beam research has been hampered by the lack of weapon grade accelerators which might test our largely theoretical understanding of propagation and interaction issues. The theoretical potential of particle beams as directed energy weapons is clear, but the experimental demonstration of that potential awaits advances in the state of the art for particle accelerators.

Notes and References

1. A good summary of the different techniques used to accelerate particles can be found in Waldemar Scharf, *Particle Accelerators and their Uses* (New York: Harwood Academic Publishers, 1986).

2. Electric and magnetic fields, and the forces which they exert on charged particles, are discussed in any introductory physics text. See, for example, David Halliday and Robert Resnick, *Physics* (New York: John Wiley and Sons, 1967).

3. The way in which the vector quantities v and B are combined to yield the resultant force on a charged particle is known mathematically as the *vector product*, or *cross product*. Detailed treatments of vectors and the ways in which they are combined can be found in junior- or senior-level texts on electromagnetism or mechanics, such as Jerry B. Marion, *Classical Electromagnetic Radiation* (New York: Academic Press, 1968).

4. A very readable introduction to Einstein's theory of relativity and to the seemingly contradictory experimental data which that theory served to clarify can be found in Chapter VI of G. Gamow, *Biography of Physics* (New York: Harper and Row, 1964). A more technical treatment is in Robert Resnick, *Introduction to Special Relativity* (New York: John Wiley and Sons, 1968).

5. The physical meaning of the energy $E = mc^2$ is that this is the energy that would be liberated if a particle of mass m were totally annihilated. This is observed experimentally when particles and their antiparticles are brought together. See Chapter VII in Gamow (note 4).

6. The equivalence of the relativistic and traditional definitions of kinetic energy in the limit where $v \ll c$ can be demonstrated by making use of the definition of γ, together with the approximation $1/(1-x)^{1/2} \approx 1 + x/2$ for $x \ll 1$.

7. The electric and magnetic fields shown in Figure 5–4 are special cases of the more general situation where the particle beam propagates parallel to an external, guiding magnetic field, or has some fraction of its charge neutralized due to the presence of stationary background particles with a charge of the opposite sign. A detailed treatment of these fields can be found in R.C. Davidson, *Theory of Nonneutral Plasmas* (Reading, MA: W. A. Benjamin, 1974).

8. The earth's naturally occurring electric field results from a continual charging of the atmosphere through thunderstorms. See Chapter 9 in Volume II of Richard P. Feynman, Robert B. Leighton, and Matthew Sands, *The Feynman Lectures on Physics* (Reading, MA: Addison-Wesley, 1964). The earth's magnetic field arises from currents circulating in its molten core. The field strength of 0.5 Gauss is appropriate for the latitude of Washington, DC. See Halliday and Resnick (Note 2), Appendix B.

9. Electron volts are a convenient unit in particle physics because an electron of charge e = 1.6×10^{-19} coul gains 1 eV of energy if it is accelerated by a potential of 1 Volt. Thus, the energy of particles whose charge is ze gain an energy in electron volts numerically equal to zV when passed through an accelerator of potential V.

10. The subscript $\perp$ is meant to convey the fact that most deviation from ideal motion is in a direction perpendicular to the beam's main direction of motion. When particles are highly relativistic, their speed is so close to the speed of light that minor fluctuations in energy will make little difference in their speed of forward motion.

11. Strictly speaking, the average of θ is zero, since as many particles have deviations down as up. The divergence is really the average of the magnitude of θ.

12. Unfortunately,while the concept of brightness is relatively straightforward, there has been no movement towards a universally accepted definition. Various definitions, differing by factors of π or γ from one another, may be found in the literature. This can make it difficult to compare beam characteristics as reported by different laboratories. A detailed discussion of the brightness concept can be found. J. D. Lawson, *The Physics of Charged Particle Beams* (Oxford: Oxford University Press, 1978).

13. Just as the average of θ should be zero (note 11), the average perpendicular velocity, $<v_\perp>$, should be zero, since there are generally as many particles with $v_\perp$ going up (positive) as there are with $v_\perp$ going down (negative). What is really meant here by the symbol $<v_\perp>$ is the *root mean square* average of $v_\perp$, the square root of the average of $v_\perp^2$, or $[<v_\perp^2>]^{1/2}$.

14. It's interesting to note that electrons, the lighter particles, expand less rapidly than do protons at a given energy. This is because electrons have a much higher γ than protons at the same en-

ergy. For example, a I GeV electron has a γ of about 2000, while a GeV proton has a γ of about 2.

15. The cyclotron radius is discussed in almost any physics text, such as Halliday and Resnick (note 1). It receives its name from the fact that this type of circular motion in a magnetic field is employed in a particle accelerator called a "cyclotron."

16. An excellent review article on the earth's magnetic field and that of other planets in the solar system can be found in Louis J. Lanzerotti and Stamatios M. Krimigis, "Comparative Magnetospheres," *Physics Today* volume 38, 24 (November, 1985). When charged particles propagate in a direction which is not perpendicular to a magnetic field, their motion is helical, a combination of circular motion around the magnetic field lines and forward motion along the field lines.

17. The concept of a cross section is used throughout atomic, molecular, and nuclear physics to describe interactions between two particles (binary interactions). An introductory text in any of these areas will discuss the subject in detail. The probability for reactions to occur are typically presented in the literature in terms of cross sections. A good physical discussion of the cross section concept can be found in Feynman (note 8). See Volume I, section 32–5.

18. A good review of ionization cross section data can be found in H. Tawara and A. Russek, *Reviews of Modern Physics* volume 45, 178 (1973).

19. This rule of thumb can also be related to the fact that the distance at which electrons orbit nuclei is on the order of 10^{-8} cm. For example, the lowest orbit of electrons around the proton that is the nucleus of a hydrogen atom (the first Bohr orbit) is at a distance of 0.53×10^{-8} cm. Anders J. Ångstrom (1814–1874) was a Swedish spectroscopist who first discovered that the sun's atmosphere contained hydrogen.

20. Figure 5–14 is based on standard atmosphere data found in R. C. Weast (ed), *Handbook of Chemistry and Physics,* 45th ed. (Cleveland, OH: Chemical Rubber Co, 1964).

21. Halliday and Resnick (note 1), section 28–4.

22. Common notation is to use σ for conductivity. We've used the capital Σ to avoid confusion with the collision cross section, which is also commonly denoted by σ.

23. The expression for the decay of excess charge density is derived in Marion (note 2), section 4.2.

24. A discussion of the conductivity of an ionized gas can be found in Chapter II, Section 13 of M. Mitchner and C. H. Kruger, Jr., *Partially Ionized Gases*. (New York: John Wiley and Sons, 1973). Table 1 in Chapter IV provides typical conductivities for various plasmas.

25. The initial portion of a particle beam doesn't have the benefit of charge neutralization, since it is in the process of ionizing the air through which it passes. This leads to a phenomenon known as *beam head erosion*, in which the initial portions of the beam disperse as they make way for subsequent portions. It has been suggested that the beam channel can be pre-ionized with the use of a laser, so that the beam can have a path already prepared through which it can propagate. See Section 4.2.1 of the "Report to the APS of the Study Group on Science and Technology of Directed Energy Weapons," *Reviews of Modern Physics 59*. Part II (July, 1987).

26. See Davidson (note 7), section 2.5. A discussion of the dynamics by which the equilibrium radius is approached can be found in S. R. Seshadri, *Fundamentals of Plasma Physics*. (New York: American Elsevier, 1973), section 2.10.

27. A pretty comprehensive treatment may be found in chapter 13 of J. D. Jackson, *Classical Electrodynamics*. (New York: John Wiley and Sons, 1963). The quantity Q which appears in the expression for dT/dz is the ratio of the maximum to minimum values of the distance of approach of the beam particle to the atmospheric particle which scatters it. See Figure 5–24. The exact value of this parameter is not very important, since it only appears as a logarithm.

28. The exponential variation of density with altitude may be inferred from Figure 5–14, since an exponential function plots as a straight line on log-linear paper. The scale length can be found from the slope of this plot. The 7 km length used here is a common approximation for the lower atmosphere. See Chapter 4 of the *APS Report on Directed Energy Weapons* (note 25). This type of behavior may also be derived theoretically. See Section 6.3 in F. Reif, *Fundamentals of Statistical and Thermal Physics* (New York: McGraw-Hill, 1965).

29. This relationship for dT/dz is not exact, since the different atmospheric constituents fall off differently with altitude. However, it is sufficiently accurate for our purposes here.

30. Figure 5–22 is a plot of $\int_0^z (dT/dz)dz/[dT/dz(o)h_0] = [1- \exp(-z \sin\phi/h_0)]/\sin\phi$.

31. Of course, as the beam gets too high in the atmosphere, expansion will begin again as a result of electrostatic repulsion. See Figure 5–18.

32. See Jackson (note 27), Section 13.3.

33. Figure 5–25 is a plot of Equation 13.44 in Jackson (note 27).

34. A good discussion of radiation from accelerated charges can be found in Marion (note 3), Chapter 7.

35. See Jackson (note 27), Chapter 15. Figure 5–26 is based on Jackson's equations 15.26 and 15.45.

36. Particles interact through four forces: gravitational, electromagnetic, strong, and weak. Only the first two have a range sufficiently great to be a part of our everyday experience. The second two, however, are responsible for such fundamental things as how nuclei are formed and decay. In recent years, unified theories of these forces have emerged, in which the last three are seen as different manifestations of a single theory. These theories have implications both for the small-scale structure of matter and the large-scale structure of the universe. See A. Linde, "Particle Physics and Inflationary Cosmology," *Physics Today 40*, 61 (September, 1987).

37. Any text on nuclear physics will discuss nuclear collisions. for example, see Chapter 16 of I. Kaplan, *Nuclear Physics* (Reading, MA: Addison-Wesley, 1963).

38. Ibid Chapter 3.

39. While hole boring where the beam produces its own channel has not yet been observed experimentally, electron beams have been guided through an ionized channel created by a laser in low pressure gas. See S.L. Shope, et alt "Laser Generation and Transport of a Relativistic Electron Beam, *Transactions on Nuclear Science NS–32*, 3092 (October, 1985), and Theresa M. Foley, "Sandia Researchers Report Progress on Delphi Beam Weapon Technology," *Aviation Week and Space Technology*, 129, 79 (August 22, 1988).

40. It is, of course, possible to leave the beam on for the whole time that it's boring through the air to the target. However, this wastes energy compared to the pulsed approach discussed in the

text. The actual approach used would depend on energy, accelerator, and other constraints.

41. A good survey of instabilities can be found in Chapter 4 of R. B. Miller, *An Introduction to the Physics of intense Charged Particle Beams.* (New York: Plenum Press, 1982).

42. A derivation of the fact that magnetic field lines are frozen into a perfectly conducting plasma can be found in Seshadri (note 26), Section 2.9.

43. The hose instability is discussed in Miller (note 41), section 4.4.1. Figure 4.4 in that section is a nice picture of a hose instability in a relativistic electron beam.

44. A derivation of the time scale for magnetic field lines to thaw, or diffuse to their final position in a resistive plasma, can be found in Section 3.9 of N. A. Krall and A. W. Trivelpiece, *Principles of Plasma Physics.* (New York: McGraw Hill, 1973).

45. Miller (note 41), Section 4.4.1.

46. The sausage instability is discussed both in Seshadri (note 26), Section 2.11, and in Miller (note 41), Section 4.4.2.

47. See Chapter 7 in Scharf (note 1).

48. This is in contrast to lasers, whose interaction with targets is quite different from that with the air (Chapter 3). That's because collective effects among the molecules in a target dominate the target's response to laser light. The energies which bind molecules together into solids are so small compared to relativistic particle energies that they play no role in beam-target interaction.

49. Ten centimeters is a very large target thickness. You can see in Chapter 1 (Figure 1–10) that the amount of matter which must be penetrated to damage most targets is on the order of centimeters or less. Therefore, the conclusion that energy losses in propagating to a target are greater than those in propagating through a target is a fairly robust one.

50. If the target is in the atmosphere, there could be some loss of energy by thermal conduction from the surface of the target into the air. However, the thermal conductivity of air is so low compared to that of metals that this contribution to the energy loss may safely be neglected.

Appendix A

Units

   Hopefully, the concepts in the text have been developed with sufficient clarity to give you a good physical feeling for the issues associated with the propagation of directed energy weapons and their interaction with targets. The many graphs and figures should also enable you to make quantitative estimates of important parameters, such as the distance a particle beam can be expected to propagate in the atmosphere, or the time it will take a laser to melt a hole through a target of a given thickness. You may, however, want to evaluate some of the formulas in the text for yourself, either to extend our results beyond what is covered in the charts or to compare our results with those in other references or reports. If you do, you'll come up against the problem of units. Scientists and engineers in any specialized area like to express things in units which are easy to remember or which make their formulas easy to write. This is great for the initiated, but can cause confusion when one reference is compared with another. For example, in Chapter 5 the electric field a distance r from a particle of charge q is given as $E = q/4\pi\epsilon_o r^2$. But if you consult many of the references at the end of Chapter 5, you'll see that the same field is given as $E = q/r^2$. Both are correct, but the units of q and E in the two forms are different. And if quantities are not substituted into equations with the correct units, the answers obtained will be numerically incorrect. This could cause problems, if you calculated a weapon to have an effective range of 10 km, and the true answer was 10 cm!
   There are two ways around this problem. The first, and easiest, is scaling. Both $E = q/4\pi\epsilon_o r^2$ and $E = q/r^2$ scale as q/r^2. This means that if q doubles, E doubles, and if r doubles, E decreases by a factor of 4. Therefore, if you have an answer you trust, say from one of the charts or examples in the text, you can scale it by using ratios of parameters, and ratios are independent of the choice of units. For example, in Chapter 3 we estimate the rate at which a laser can melt through a target as $V_m = \alpha S/\rho[L_m + C(T_m - T_o)]$. Figure 3–65 is a plot of this relationship for four specific values of α. If you need to evaluate the erosion rate for a different value of α, you need only multiply one of the curves in Figure 3–65 by the ratio of the absorptivities for the new case and the one on the chosen curve.

If it's not possible to scale from a known answer, self consistency is the key to numerical accuracy. In this book, our preference is for "MKS" or "SI" units, where lengths are in meters, masses in kilograms, time in seconds, and electrical charge in Coulombs. In these units, energy will be in Joules, power in Watts, and current in Amperes—the familiar units of everyday experience. Formulas in the text will work out correctly as long as input quantities are in these units. For example, the rate at which electrons heat when interacting with microwaves is $d\epsilon/dt = e^2S/2mc\epsilon_0\nu_c$. This expression will come out correctly in Joules/sec, provided e is in Coulombs, S in Watts/m^2, m in kg, c in m/sec, and ν_c in sec^{-1}. Typically, of course, we express S in W/cm^2, since beam sizes for lasers and particle beams are more likely to be on the order of a centimeter, and particle beam people will express m in electron volts. But to evaluate the expression, you need to convert these to the self consistent set of meters, kilograms, seconds, and Coulombs. Having obtained the answer in J/sec, you can then convert it to some other more convenient unit, such as eV/sec, if you choose.

Almost any science or engineering text will have as an appendix tables of conversion factors for different units.[1] The following tables should be adequate for converting to the units we have used in the text. In keeping with our zero order approach, no attempt has been made to provide highly accurate conversion factors, which are available elsewhere.[2] If the general concept of constructing self-consistent sets of units is of interest, books on the subject are also available.[3] The official SI units for evaluating formulas are in the right hand column.

Power of 10 Prefixes

(e.g. 10^9 Watt = 1 Gigawatt (GW), 10^{-3} m = 1mm)

Power	Prefix	Abbreviation
12	Tera	T
9	Giga	G
6	Mega	M
3	Kilo	k
-2	Centi	c
-3	Milli	m
-6	Micro	μ
-9	Nano	n
-12	Pico	p

Dimensionless Units

1 degree (°)	=	1.745×10^{-2} radians (rad)
1 circle	=	2π rad
1 sphere	=	4π steradians (sr)

Units of Length

1 Ångstrom	=	10^{-10} m
1 micron	=	10^{-6} m (1 μm)
1 inch (in)	=	0.0254 m
1 foot (ft)	=	0.3048 m
1 mile (mi)	=	1609.3 m
1 nautical mile	=	1852 m

Units of Velocity

1 ft/sec	=	0.305 m/sec
1 km/hr	=	0.278 m/sec
1 mi/hr	=	0.447 m/sec
1 knot	=	0.514 m/sec

Units of Area

1 cm^2	=	10^{-4} m^2
1 in^2	=	6.45×10^{-4} m^2
1 ft^2	=	0.093 m^2
1 mi^2	=	2.59×10^6 m^2

Units of Volume

1 cm^3	=	10^{-6} m^3
1 in^3	=	1.64×10^{-5} m^3

Units of Mass

1 gm	=	10^{-3} kg
1 MeV	=	1.78×10^{-30} kg*
1 GeV	=	1.78×10^{-27} kg*
1 lb	=	0.454 kg**

*The eV is not really a unit of mass, but of energy. This is the mass equivalent using m = E/c^2.
**The pound is a unit of force. This is the mass that exerts a 1 lb force on the earth's surface.

Units of Density

1 gm/cm^3	=	10^3 kg/m^3
1 lb/ft^3	=	16 kg/m^3
1 lb/in^3	=	2.77×10^4 kg/m^3

Units of Energy

1 BTU	=	1055 J
1 kw hr	=	3.6×10^6 J
1 calorie	=	4.19 J
1 eV	=	1.6×10^{-19} J
1 erg	=	10^{-7} J

Units of Power

1 erg/sec	=	10^{-7} W
1 horsepower	=	746 W
1 BTU/hr	=	0.293 W

Units of Fluence and Intensity

1 J/cm^2	=	10^4 J/m^2
1 W/cm^2	=	10^4 W/m^2

Units of Pressure (Stress)

1 Atmosphere	=	10^5 Pascal (1 Pa = 1 Nt/m^2)
1 bar	=	10^5 Pascal
1 torr	=	133 Pa
1 dyn/cm^2	=	0.1 Pa
1 psi	=	6895 Pa

Units of Electromagnetic Theory

1 Gauss	=	10^{-4} Tesla (1 T = 1 Weber/m^2)
1 Statvolt	=	300 Volt
1 Statcoul	=	3.33×10^{-10} Coul
1 Abcoul	=	10 Coul
1 Statamp	=	3.33×10^{-10} Amp
1 Abamp	=	10 Amp
1 Amp hr	=	3600 Coul
1 ohm–cm	=	10^{-2} ohm–m
1 mho	=	1 Siemens (1 S = 1 ohm^{-1})

References

1. One of the most convenient and comprehensive sets of tables is in Appendix G of David Halliday and Robert Resnick, *Physics for Students of Science and Engineering*, 2nd ed. (New York: John Wiley and Sons, 1967).

2. Comprehensive, up-to-date, and accurate conversion factors may be found in Section 1.02 of Herbert L. Anderson (ed), *Physics Vade Mecum* (New York: American Institute of Physics, 1987).

3. The general theory of units and their dimensions is discussed in the "Appendix on Units and Dimensions" to John D. Jackson, *Classical Electrodynamics* (New York: John Wiley and Sons, 1963). For a more popular account, see William D. Johnstone, *For Good Measure* (New York: Holt, Rinehart, and Winston, 1975). Every obscure unit you could ever be interested in is contained in Stephen Dresner, *Units of Measurement* (Aylesburg; Harvey Miller and Medcalf, 1971).

Appendix B

Some Useful Data

Much of the data needed to calculate weapon effects, such as the thermal conductivities and heat capacities of different materials, are readily available in handbooks of science and engineering data. But other information, such as the energy loss rate for charged particles penetrating different materials, can be found only be searching through a variety of sources. Some of these less available data have been gathered here for your convenience in evaluating or extending results presented in the text. As with all data in this book, these are presented to give you a feeling for orders of magnitude and to enable you to make simple estimates. They should not be considered definitive numbers, since many of the details and assumptions involved in their derivation have been glossed over.

Characteristics of Common Kinetic Energy Rounds

Weapon Type	Bullet Type (Caliber)	Mass (g)	Velocity (m/sec)	Kinetic Energy (J)	Reference
Handgun	.38 Special	6.16	361	400	1
Handgun	.45 Automatic	11.99	272	444	1
Handgun	9 mm	7.45	363	491	1
Rifle	7.62×51 mm	9.33	838	3276	2
Rifle	7.62×39 mm	7.97	715	2037	2
Machine gun	9×19 mm	7.45	390	567	2
Machine gun	11.4×23 mm	15.16	280	594	2

Specific Impulse of Rocket Fuels

Fuel/Oxidizer	Isp (sec)	Reference
Hydrogen/Oxygen	391	3
UDMH*/Oxygen	310	3
Ammonia/N_2O_4	269	3

*Unsymmetrical dimethylhydrazine

Failure Data for Common Materials

Material	Modulus of Rupture (J/m³)	Strain at Rupture	Reference
Aluminum	3.0×10^8	0.15	4
Wood	3.6×10^6	0.03	5
Concrete	4.5×10^6	0.002	5

Thermal Coupling Coefficients for Lasers*

Material	Wavelength(μm)	α	Comments	Reference
Titanium (6 A1–4V)	3.8	0.23		6
	10.6	0.14		6
	2.8	0.24		8
Stainless Steel (604)	3.8	0.17		6
	10.6	0.10		6
	2.8	0.25		8
Aluminum (abraded)	10.6	0.09	without plasma ignition	7
	10.6	0.18	with plasma ignition	7
Aluminum	2.8	0.06		8
	10.6	0.03		
Nickel	2.8	0.13		8

*Thermal coupling coefficients can vary with sample, surface preparation, and laser intensity, especially if plasmas are ignited. Theoretically, the coupling coefficient should scale the square root of frequency. See Chapter 3.

Specific Impulse Coupling Coefficients for Lasers*

Material	Wavelength (μm)	I* (dyn sec/J)	Comments	Reference
Aluminum				
	10.6	0.3	without plasma ignition	9
	10.6	7.5	with plasma ignition	9
	1.06	1.0		10
	0.248	3.0		10
	0.53	1.0		10
Titanium				
	10.6	0.2		9
	0.248	3.0		10
Stainless Steel				
	10.6	0.2		9

*Specific impulses can show considerable variability shot-to shot, and are strongly affected by the ignition of plasmas.

Relativistic Particle Ionization Energy Loss Rates*

Material	dK/dz (MeV/cm)
Aluminum	4.05
Copper	13.44
Iron	11.85
Magnesium	2.61
Titanium	6.74

*Calculated values, based on Eq 6.40 in Reference 10. Assumes $\gamma > 2$.

Electron Radiation Lengths*

Material	Radiation Length (cm)
Aluminum	8.25
Copper	1.82
Lead	0.39
Magnesium	18.50
Iron	1.49
Titanium	3.08

*Calculated values, scaled from the value for lead by Equation 15.48 in Reference 11. Assumes $\gamma > 2$.

References

1. Mason Williams, *Practical Handgun Ballistics* (Springfield, IL: Charles C. Thomas, 1980).

2. C. J. Marchant-Smith and P. R. Hulsom, *Small Arms and Cannons* (Oxford: Brassey's Publishers, 1982).

3. Charles H. MacGregor and Lee H. Livingston (eds) *Space Handbook*, AU–18 (Maxwell AFB, AL: Air University, 1977).

4. "Report to the APS of the Study Group on Science and Technology of Directed Energy Weapons," *Reviews of Modern Physics 59*, Part II (July, 1987).

5. Michael S. Feld, Ronald E. McNair, and Stephen R. Wilk, "The Physics of Karate" *Scientific American 240*, 150 (April, 1979).

6. T.J. Wieting and J. T. Schriempf, "Infrared Absorptances of Partially Ordered Alloys at Elevated Temperatures, "*Journal of Applied Physics 47*, 4009 (September, 1976).

7. J.A. McKay, et al., "Pulsed CO_2 Laser Interaction with Aluminum in Air: Thermal Response and Plasma Characteristics," *Journal of Applied Physics 50*, 3231 (May, 1979).

8. R.B. Hall, W. E. Maher, D. J. Nelson, and D. B. Nichols, "High Power Laser Coupling," Air Force Weapons Laboratory, Kirtland AFB, NM, *Report no AFWL–TR–77–34* (June, 1977).

9. S.A. Metz, L. R. Hettche, R. L. Stegman, and J.T. Schriempf, "Effect of Beam Intensity on Target Response to High-Intensity Pulsed CO_2 Laser Radiation," *Journal of Applied Physics 46*, 1634 (April, 1975).

10. "Report to the APS of the Study Group on Science and Technology of Directed Energy Weapons," *Reviews of Modern Physics 59*, Part II (July, 1987).

11. John D. Jackson, *Classical Electrodynamics* (New York, John Wiley and Sons, 1963).

About the Author

Philip E. Nielsen is a director and senior technical advisor for MacAulay-Brown, Incorporated, a defense engineering services firm headquartered in Dayton, Ohio. Prior to joining MacAulay-Brown, Dr. Nielsen served on active duty with the U.S. Air Force (USAF) for 26 years, retiring as colonel. During this period, he served in a variety of positions related to the research, development, and acquisition of advanced weapon systems. He received the USAF Research and Development Award for contribution to high energy laser physics in 1975.

Made in the USA
Coppell, TX
23 January 2020